GW00506249

Queensland
See pages 181 - 215

ralia
235

Brisbane

New South Wales
See pages 31 - 175

Adelaide

Sydney

ACT - Canberra

ACT - Canberra
See pages 19 - 30

Melbourne Victoria
See pages 245 - 297

Tasmania
See pages 236 - 244

Hobart

The Australian
Bed & Breakfast
Book

"The difference between a hotel and a B&B is that you don't hug the hotel staff when you leave."

Mudgee Homestead, Mudgee NSW

Published
October 2005

The Australian Bed & Breakfast Book 2006
Accommodation with Character
18th Edition Fully Revised

Editor Carl Southern

Published by
Inn Australia
PO Box 8003, Coffs Harbour, NSW 2450
info@bbbook.com.au

Tel: 02 6658 5701 International: +612 6658 5701
Fax: 02 6658 5702 International: +612 6658 5702
www.bbbook.com.au

Copyright 2005 ©The Australian Bed & Breakfast Book
Printed in China by Book Builders
Includes Index.
ISBN 0-9758040-0-6

We welcome your comments or suggestions

Cover image;
From the mountains to the sea   by Meredith Brice Copland MacMasters Beach
NSW 2251   ©2005

Contents

Preface

Introduction

Accommodation

Index

The Noble Grape Bed & Breakfast, Cowaramup WA

The Australian Bed & Breakfast Book - 2006

Accommodation with Character

Australia was once popularly known as the 'Lucky Country' and the airports and seaports were full with migrants travelling 'down under' to start a new life. Now the ports are filled with cruise liners and the airports with travellers wanting to experience the country as a visitor. Perhaps because of the size of our country Australian's are great travellers too. We can still travel thousands of kilometres without a passport; spend one weekend in the snowfields, the next in the tropics, a few days in the wide open spaces of rural Australia and then live it up in one of our major cities. Flying has never been cheaper and petrol, though more expensive than before, is still cheaper than most other comparable countries.

More visitors than ever before are requesting alternative accommodation to hotels and motels. Travellers want to meet Australians as much as they want to see Australia and where better than in Bed & Breakfast's and similarly styled accommodation. More and more guests are trying B&Bs for the first time. After a short stay of one or two nights they leave converted forever to this unique style of accommodation.

Each and every B&B offers uniquely different characteristics – some and cosy and intimate, others are grand and luxurious. The uniqueness of Bed & Breakfasts is the distinctive quality of their hosts. They offer a commitment beyond normal customer service to ensure your stay is exceptional and enjoyable. Your breakfast will be generous - you may be tempted into a menu of many courses in the intimacy of your own suite or share a traditional hot cooked breakfast with your hosts.

Bed and Breakfast accommodation is *Accommodation with Character* offering great hospitality, wonderful breakfasts and terrific value - *A Commitment to Generous Hospitality.*

"We received the greatest hospitality, slept in the most wonderful bed and enjoyed the best breakfast in a long, long time. We will return!"

From one of our guests.

Perhaps we are still living in The Lucky Country!

Carl Southern © 2005

Australian Accommodation - Better than ever!

The Australian Bed & Breakfast Book 2006 - Still listing the largest selection of B&Bs in Australia.

Each listing in the guide has been written by the hosts themselves and you will discover special characteristics of the accommodation through the eyes, their warmth and personality through their writing. The Australian Bed & Breakfast Book is an introduction to a unique Australian experience.

New for 2006

The Australian Bed & Breakfast Book has been successfully published each year since 1989. Each year we invite our readers – both guests and hosts alike - for suggestions to improve the new edition. Thanks to all who wrote and called with their ideas and comments. This year we have re-established the 'signature' style of The Bed & Breakfast Book but other changes have been few and subtle. What is new are over 80 new accommodation listings included for the first time. We welcome these new properties, some are in familiar locations many are in places not visited before by The B&B Book. We commend these to our readers and guests as well as the familiar favourites for your travels in 2006 and beyond.

Website
Up to the minute information at www.bbbook.com.au

The Australian Bed & Breakfast Book
PO Box 8003, Coffs Harbour, NSW 2450, Australia
Tel: 02 6658 5701
International: +612 6658 5701
info@bbbook.com.au

The New Zealand Bed & Breakfast Book
PO Box 6843, Wellington, New Zealand
+64 4 385 2615
info@bnb.co.nz
www.bnb.co.nz

Bishopsgate Bed & Breakfast, Melbourne Vic

A Quick Guide to using The Australian Bed & Breakfast Book

Listing Information
The 2006 edition is arranged alphabetically in states and territories starting with Australian Capital Territory and concluding with Western Australian. Accommodation listings are arranged alphabetically by location - city or region. Each listing includes a photograph and description written by the hosts and in some cases a guest comment written by an earlier guest.

Quick Reference:

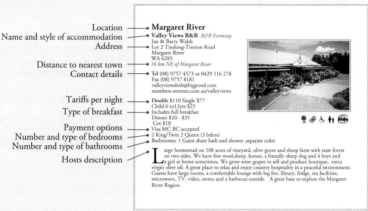

Location	**Margaret River**
Name and style of accommodation	**Valley Views B&B** *B&B Farmstay*
	Jan & Barry Walsh
Address	Lot 2 Tindong-Treeton Road
	Margaret River
	WA 6285
	16 km NE of Margaret River
Distance to nearest town	
Contact details	Tel (08) 9757 4573 or 0429 116 278
	Fax (08) 9757 8181
	valleyviewsbnb@bigpond.com
	members.westnet.com.au/valleyviews
Tariffs per night	Double $110 Single $77
	Child 6 to12yrs $25
Type of breakfast	Includes full breakfast
	Dinner $20 - $35
	Cot $10
Payment options	Visa MC BC accepted
Number and type of bedrooms	2 King/Twin 2 Queen (3 bdrm)
Number and type of bathrooms	Bathrooms: 1 Guest share bath and shower ,separate toilet

Hosts description

Large homestead on 108 acres of vineyard, olive grove and sheep farm with state forest on two sides. We have fine wool,sheep ,horses, a friendly sheep dog and 4 boys and a girl at home sometimes. We grow wine grapes to sell and produce boutique, extra virgin olive oil. A great place to relax and enjoy country hospitality in a peaceful environment. Guests have large rooms, a comfortable lounge with log fire, library, fridge, tea facilities, microwave, TV, video, stereo and a barbecue outside.   A great base to explore the Margaret River Region.

Style of Accommodation
B&B Accommodation has challenged traditional hotel and motel accommodation head on by offering wonderful accommodation, great hospitality and splendid breakfasts. It is now a diverse style of accommodation with no two B&Bs quite alike. We have classified them for ease of selecting a style to suit your requirements.

Bed & Breakfast: Welcoming accommodation with private guest living and dining areas

Homestay: Similar to B&B where guests are invited to share dining and living areas with their hosts

Farmstay: Country accommodation with farm activities

Self-Contained: Separate self-contained accommodation, with kitchen and living/ dining room

Separate/Suite: Similar to self-contained but without kitchen facilities. living/ dining facilities may be limited

Guesthouse or Small Hotel: Larger style accommodation but retaining the warm hospitality found in B&Bs, often with restaurants

You will find other categories such as Retreat or Historic Home, which are often self-explanatory. If you are unsure or new to B&B accommodation we suggest you ask your hosts to describe the facilities when booking your stay.

Location
The location enables you to find your accommodation. You may also refer to the maps at the beginning of each chapter.

Contact Details
Listings include hosts' names, location address, telephone and fax numbers, email and web addresses.

Tariffs
B&Bs offer great value accommodation and room tariffs or rates cover a broad range reflecting the quality of the accommodation, location and facilities offered. Tariffs are listed in Australian dollars and are for two persons (ie double, queen, king or twin share) and include breakfast unless indicated otherwise. Listings show if they have facilities for children or a third adult sharing the same room at an additional charge. Tariffs shown are for 2006, but are subject to change and should always be confirmed with your hosts when booking. A 10% Goods and Service Tax (GST) is included in rates where applicable.

Payments
Most hosts accept cash, personal cheques and major credit cards (ie Visa Card, MasterCard, Bankcard). Some will accept payment by others cards including American Express or Diners Card, eftpos, direct deposit or travellers cheques.

Breakfast
Breakfast is one of the pleasures of a good B&B. Your breakfast is included in the tariff unless otherwise indicated and you can be sure they will be generous. More and more B&Bs are now offering a wider variety of options for breakfast quite removed from a traditional hot breakfast of bacon and eggs. This may include fresh fruit juice, home made bread and preserves and fresh tropical fruits. B&B hosts are very understanding about your breakfast, which is served at a reasonable time to make your stay as comfortable as possible. We suggest you advise your host if you need to get away early and would like an early breakfast or even if you would like to sleep in and take a late breakfast. Some B&Bs request a small additional charge for hot breakfasts.

Options available include
Continental or Light: A light breakfast such as a selection of cereals, bread or toast, fruit juice, tea or coffee.
Full: A light breakfast with a cooked course.
Special: Many hosts love cooking and will offer you a Special Breakfast. It may be a wide cold selection or gourmet cooked meals that would do any great chefs proud. With a little advance notice hosts are able to cater for special diets. Some self-contained properties offer breakfast provisions or a breakfast hamper to prepare yourself.

Additional Meals
Some accommodations particularly farmstays, rural B&Bs, guesthouses as well as boutique style properties offer evening meals. Others offer barbecue packages or picnic hampers. You may need to request meals in advance or by arrangement (B/A).

Dining and Lounge areas

An attractive feature of B&Bs is their uniqueness. Homestays may invite you to share the dining and living rooms with hosts. Most, however, have separate and private dining and lounge rooms where you can either dine uninterrupted or choose to join other guests for a friendly chat. Others may have no separate facilities but offer breakfast in the privacy of your own room or a private courtyard.

Beds and Bedrooms

Guide listings indicate the number and size of beds, how many bedrooms and number of guests that can be accommodated. Beds are usually standard sizes: single, double, queen or king. Some hosts offer twin beds (ie two single beds) or King Twin (ie 2 king size single beds or a King Size bed that can be unzipped to 2 large single beds. Advise your host when making a reservation if you have special requirements.

Bathrooms

Most accommodations provide ensuite bathrooms for your exclusive use, that is a bathroom leading directly from your bedroom. Many B&Bs now offer luxurious bathrooms with spas and maybe even candlelight and Champagne! Older or historic B&Bs may offer private facilities, that is a bathroom for your exclusive use but off the hallway. Shared bathrooms are available at some properties, but if the accommodation is not full you will still have exclusive use. If in doubt confirm details with your hosts when booking your stay.

Smoking

It is now accepted that smoking is not permitted inside. Many hosts will provide outside facilities for guests wishing to smoke. Some hosts have a definite no smoking policy and indicate in their listing text that there is no smoking anywhere on the property.

Icons

We have used a few icons to assist you in selecting the best accommodation to suit your needs.

Easy Access &

Use of this icon indicates access to a wheelchair user or less able travellers. Some properties are accredited, others may be 'disabled friendly.' Check with hosts to confirm details.

Children

Children are now welcomed at most accommodations whether a traditional B&B or in a small guesthouse. Many hosts, particularly farmstays cater mainly for families or guests with children whereas others cater more for the 'adult retreat' market. Properties displaying this icon welcome children, but as they may not have facilities for younger children or babies ask that you first contact the hosts to confirm details.

Pets

Many properties welcome pets and mention this in their text. Some hosts allow small pets such as cats or small dogs inside, while others have a run or kennel. Properties displaying this icon are able to offer facilities for some pets, but guests should first contact the hosts to confirm details.

Swimming Pool

After a day travelling in the heat of summer, there is nothing better than a dip in a refreshing swimming pool! Properties displaying this icon have a swimming pool available for guests

Outstanding Garden

For many hosts their garden is a major attraction of their accommodation. Some properties participate in the open garden scheme for others it is just an enjoyable pastime. Hosts displaying this icon take pride in the garden and believe it offers outstanding qualities

B&B Association Logo

Most states and territories have established a B&B Association to represent their members. Use of the logos indicates hosts are members.

AAA Tourism

Properties displaying 'the stars' symbol are independently assessed by AAA Tourism, the national body of the Australian motoring organisation. 'The stars' are trademarks of AAA Tourism Pty Ltd.

Australian Tourism Accreditation

This symbol indicates an Accredited Tourism Business. Accredited operators have a commitment to professional and ethical conduct in all areas of their business. (Note: Not all states are yet able to offer Accreditation.)

Vouchers

Guests may order Bed & Breakfast Book Vouchers in attractive presentation cards. Each Voucher comes with a Free Copy of The Bed & Breakfast Book. There is a small postage and handling charge of only $10 per voucher. You may use the Vouchers at any accommodation displaying the icon.

Privacy for Guests

Your privacy will be respected in B&Bs just as in any hotel or motel. You will be given a key to your accommodation and bedrooms will have locks (or secure storage for valuables).

Independence For Hosts

B&B hosts will not necessarily be at home all the time. Generally, if hosts go out they will advise guests of their contact details in case of an emergency.

Reservations

Contact your hosts well in advance to be sure of confirming your accommodation. You may also book accommodation through some travel agents or through specialised B&B reservation services.

Be sure to give your date of arrival, how many days you are staying and how many guests in your party. Other details you may need to check include time of arrival, tariffs, deposit required and any special requirements, such as style of room, special diets, directions, parking facilities, and whether you are travelling with children or pets. Some B&Bs have minimum stays during peak periods. Check the details with your host.

Booking and Cancellation Policy

You will find most accommodations offer a clear booking and cancellation policy. This makes good sense, particularly if you need to cancel. For short stays you may need to pay in advance, some hosts accept a deposit by credit card others may request you to send a cheque.

When booking it's good to ask how much deposit is due, when full payment is required and what is the cancellation policy.

Checking In

Hosts are often flexible with check in and check out times but if guests are leaving the day you arrive you will understand why check in or check out times are requested. Times vary but usually check in is around 1.00–3.00 in the afternoon with check out 10.00–12.00 in the morning.

Standards

All hosts included in The Bed & Breakfast Book are committed to ensuring your stay is enjoyable. Hosts must meet a Quality Assurance, that is a self-appraisal by the hosts to guarantee high standards of hospitality and housekeeping. Many have also been inspected independently by AAA Tourism and awarded a Star rating. Many are also members of State or Territory B&B and Farmstay Associations meeting a further set of standards and a code of conduct, or requiring inspections.

Committed to Generous Hospitality

B&Bs included in The Bed & Breakfast Book are committed to Generous Hospitality - Traditional rating systems have given credit to the level of facilities available but have been unable able to give due credit to the special qualities of a B&B and the hosts - Guest Comment cards available from hosts (copies are also located at the back of the book) give you the opportunity to comment about the features, which made your stay special: The warm welcome, the outstanding hospitality, special location or just simple good value. *The People's Choice Awards for Great Accommodation* are selected solely by Guests returning *Guest Feedback Cards*. Likewise, if you find your experience not meeting your expectations, do first discuss your concerns with your host, who will most likely be able to rectify the situation to your satisfaction. If necessary drop us a line.

Eden Bed & Breakfast, Eden NSW

The People's Choice Awards for Great Accommodation 2005

"What makes Great Accommodation?"   Hospitality!

Guests staying at each of the accommodations included in The Bed & Breakfast Book are offered wonderful accommodation with great hospitality. That means welcoming hosts, comfortable beds and a generous breakfast. Many guests find that their hosts exceed all expectations and write and tell us about it. Some visit our website at www.bbbook.com.au and record comments online, others take the time to write us a letter, but most complete the Guest Comment Cards available at B&Bs or from the back of the B&B Book and mail them to us.
In the last few years we have received thousands of Comment Cards from guests who have thoroughly enjoyed their stays.

The People's Choice Awards for Great Accommodation our way of praising the industry as a whole. Award Winners are selected from each state determined by a minimum number of positive comments we receive. We also 'Commend' properties receiving a significant number of comments.

Award Winners
Shackleton B&B, Mawson
Frankfield Guest House, Gunning
Cudgerie Homestead, Cooroy
Arabella Country House, Princetown
The Temple Tree B&B, Broome

Commended
Ossian Hall, Colo
Ninderry Manor Luxury B&B, Ninderry
Jireh, Stanthorpe,
Arrowee House, Gloucester
Magnolia House, Hunters Hill

Hall of Fame
For the past three years several B&Bs have constantly rated very highly and they have now been admitted to our Hall of Fame.
Congratulations to:
Shackleton B&B, Mawson
Cudgerie Homestead, Cooroy
The Temple Tree B&B, Broome

Shackleton Bed & Breakfast, Mawson ACT   *Cudgerie Homestead,* Mawson QLD   *The Temple Tree Bed & Breakfast,* Broome WA

Guest Comments 2006.

Hospitality is the word

Harolden, Glebe, NSW.
"Everything including the hostess, the breakfast and the surroundings are heaven sent."
Naomi Blick, Griffith, ACT.

Edwil House B&B, Kambah, ACT.
"We have stayed in a lot of places in Australia and overseas. This B&B has been the best by far. Hospitality – the Best."
Glen & Deidre Edmonds, Bray Park, Qld.

Rooftops B&B Ulmarra, NSW.
We were at home for 2 days and nights and so relaxed. We would have loved to stay longer".
Ian & Phil Lawrence, Somerset, England.

Mango Meadows Homestay, Humpty Doo, NT.
"After this wonderful experience (even a birthday cake) who would stay at a hotel/motel again?"
Denis and Denise Brown, Rosanna, Vic.

Lilybank, Kambah, ACT.
"Very helpful hosts right from the first contact. Fantastic breakfasts. Great location."
Barb Anderssen, Missouri, USA.

Sandiacre House B&B, North Tamborine, Qld.
"A wonderfully peaceful place with caring, friendly and very personable hosts – excellent amenities and food."
Ian & Cheryl Feeney, Toowoomba, Qld.

Homestay Brighton, Seacliffe Park, SA.
"I have stayed here several times and am always made to feel very welcome and at home. It is terrific value for the tariff charged."
Graham Baker, Brighton, Vic.

Somewhere Special

Clovelly House, Metung, Vic.
"Simply the best B&B we have experienced in Australia."
Mikal Ponder, Kureelpa, Qld.

Green Mango Hideaway, Bangalow, NSW.
"Thank you very much for sharing your "heaven" with us – we loved it."
Angus & Kaylene Glenn, Santa Barbara, Queensland.

Orangewood B&B, Alice Springs, NT.
"Why didn't our travel agent give us more time here."
Jean & John Darnell, Surrey, England.

Ninderry Manor Luxury B&B, Ninderry, Qld.

"Beautiful view and many kinds of flowers! Especially breakfast is delicious and healthy. In the room, it's elegant and well matched."
Takeo Mizumura, Miyamoto, Japan.

Watervilla House, Strathalbyn, SA.
"Very beautiful house, perfect breakfasts, very nice host, just a reason to travel to Australia again."
Marianne and Peter Staub, Riggisberg, Switzerland

Riseley Cottage Dover, Tas.
"Sometimes if you are fortunate, you may experience tranquillity beautiful surroundings and superb food. This is it."
Mr & Mrs Gardiner, County Wicklow, Ireland.

A little bit of history

The Bank B&B, Hay, NSW.
"Had a wonderful time, very historic building, beautiful breakfast, cosy sitting room (open fires)."
Colleen & John Howard, Wagga Wagga, NSW.

Boonara Homestead, Goomeri, Qld.
"It was truly a fantastic experience. Great hosts, great food, great hospitality. Everything to make a great B&B. A piece of history."
Mr & Mrs Reilly, Tewantin, Qld.

Great Value

Bella Vista, Merimbula, NSW.
"5* plus accommodation at a reasonable cost – the best B&B we have stayed in . . . warm welcome . . .superb decoration . . . beautiful views . . . brilliant breakfast . . . excellent host."
Brenda & Robin Smith, Surrey, England.

Self Contained Cottages, Apartment and Suites

Cherry Plum Cottages B&B, Port Fairy, Vic.
"Wonderful small touches make this an exceptional and so comfortable."
Dr Sandra Sedgwick, Bognor Regis, England.

Bernadette's B&B, Lyons, ACT.
"A warm and cosy studio apartment with excellent bathroom and kitchen. A very kind and welcoming host and the best breakfast in town."
Rachel Carter, Leichhardt, NSW.

Gibson's by the Beach, Eden, NSW.
"Simply the best, wonderful food, so very friendly and helpful."
Wendy Clint, Bedford, England.

We love children

Kathy's Place, Alice Springs, NT.
"So happy to find a family style B&B. Kathy & Karl made my daughter welcome and even celebrated 12/31 with us."
Alice T, Milan, Italy.

We like pets!

Orara Valley View, Upper Orara, NSW.
"A little part of heaven hosted by two perfect angels and titch (the dog)."
Gail & Barry Fletcher, Nana Glen, NSW.

Pub Hill Farm, Narooma, NSW.
"Wonderful break away – lovely people, relaxing for dog and owners, great location."
Jennifer Stanford, Narrabeen, NSW.

Carinya Highgate Hill B&B, Highgate Hill, Qld.
"The box rating say it all [5 out of 5]! Even the dog was worth a 5!."
Robert Channon, Stanthorpe, Qld.

Close to Vineyards

Holroyd B&B, Rutherglen, Vic.
"If this is the standard of Bed & Breakfasts, who needs hotels and motel?"
Alison & Bill Fry, Mitcham, Vic.

Bellevue Bed & Breakfast, McLaren Vale, SA.
"Upmost privacy – discretion. Fantastic food and plenty of it."
Ina & Debra Klingberg, Stirling North, SA.

By the Ocean

North Haven by the Sea, Williamstown, Vic.
"Margaret's hospitality is overwhelmingly excellent."
Michael Webster, Tauranga, New Zealand.

Arabella Country House, Princetown, Vic.
"This is the perfect stay and the best in all our travels in Australia. The hosts Lynne and Neil are so hospitable ane we enjoy our stay here.."
Prudence Kee, Singapore.

B&B by the Sea, Albany, WA.
"First time at a B&B, fantastic food, was just over the top, tremendous."
Kelvin Blair, Kilsyth, Vic.

Pelican's Rest, Victor Harbor, SA.
"A truly wonderful B&B so professionally presented. Exquisitely relaxing."
Jen Roberts, Plympton Park, SA.

Quality Assurance

Properties included in The Australian Bed & Breakfast Book offer a commitment to generous hospitality and guarantee to offer the following standards

Housekeeping
◊ The Property is well maintained internally and externally
◊ Absolute cleanliness in all guest areas
◊ Absolute cleanliness in the kitchen, refrigerator and food storage areas
◊ All inside rooms are non-smoking unless indicated in the text

Hospitality
◊ Hosts present to welcome and farewell guests (unless advised in self-contained accommodation)
◊ Guests treated with courtesy and respect
◊ Guests have contact details if hosts leave the premises
◊ Room rates, booking and cancellation policy advised to guests
◊ Local tourism and transport information available.

Bedrooms
Bedrooms solely dedicated to guests with -
◊ bedroom heating and cooling appropriate to the climate
◊ fans and heating (alternatively reverse cycle air-conditioning)
◊ quality mattresses in sound condition on a sound base
◊ clean bedding appropriate to the climate, with extra available
◊ clean pillows with extra available
◊ bedside lighting for each guest
◊ blinds or curtains on all windows where appropriate
◊ night light or torch in case of power failures
◊ wardrobe space with selection of hangers
◊ adequate storage space
◊ good quality floor coverings in good condition
◊ adequate sized mirror
◊ power point
◊ alarm clock
◊ waste bin
◊ drinking glasses

Bathrooms
Sufficient bathroom and toilet facilities for all guests -
◊ bath or shower
◊ hand basin and mirror
◊ waste bin in bathroom
◊ extra toilet roll
◊ privacy lock on bathroom and toilet doors
◊ power point
◊ soap, towels, bathmat, facecloths, for each guest
◊ towels changed or dried daily for guests staying more than one night
◊ Towel rail/hook per guest in the bathroom or bedroom

Meals
◊ Drinks: water, tea and coffee offered or available
◊ Breakfast: A generous breakfast is provided (unless advised otherwise in self-contained accommodation)
◊ Breakfast: Self Contained Accommodation indicates if Hamper/Breakfast provisions are provided or Accommodation Only.

General
◊ Roadside identification of property
◊ An honest and accurate description of listing details and facilities
◊ Hosts accept responsibility to comply with government regulations
◊ Description includes if hosts' pets and young children are sharing a common area with guests
◊ Operational Smoke Alarms
◊ Adequate Public and Product Liability under a B&B Insurance Policy

Optional Extras
◊ Lock on guest rooms or secure storage facilities available
◊ Air-conditioning, particularly in hotter areas
◊ Laundry facilities for guests
◊ Bathroom/toilet - air freshener, tissues
◊ Television, radio, fresh flowers, magazines, books, fresh fruit
◊ Membership of State B&B Association
◊ Accredited Tourism Business (Green Tick)
◊ Independently inspected B&B (eg, by AAATourism or B&B Association)

B&B Gift Vouchers

Guests may order *Bed & Breakfast Book* vouchers in attractive presentation cards. Each voucher comes with a free copy of *The Australian Bed & Breakfast Book*. There is a small postage and handling charge of only $10 per voucher. You may use the vouchers at any accommodation displaying the logo.

Orders to:
Inn Australia
PO Box 8003
Coffs Harbour 2450
Tel: 02 6658 5701
vouchers@inn.com.au

B&B Services

Ayr House Residential School of Bed & Breakfast
If you are contemplating a 'Sea Change' by venturing into the B& B industry, what better training than to sign up for one of Ayr House's three night/two day courses where you will be expertly guided through many of the pitfalls which can catch the unwary.
Ayr House
Echuca
03 5482 1973
ayrhouse@innhouse.com.au

Insiders Melbourne
Melbourne - stately and conservative yet vibrant and exciting if you know where to look. Insiders Melbourne will help you discover the established, iconic and hidden treasures that make Melbourne one of the most cosmopolitan cities in the world. Check out the CBD and neighbourhood precincts for some of Melbourne's best - including five-star and bohemian accommodation, fine dining and hip cafes, chic retail and specialty shops, and a wide range of fringe and mainstream art and culture.
www.insidersmelbourne.com
03 9428 8134
0412 068 855

www.insiders*melbourne*.com
uncover Melbourne's iconic & hidden treasures

Accommodation
Dining
Shopping
Attractions
www.insidersmelbourne.com

Bed & Breakfast Associations

Bed & Breakfast and Farmstay Australia
Bed & Breakfast and Farmstay Australia (BBFA) represents 1500 properties all distinguished by their commitment to quality product and excellence in customer care. Each one of our state and territory member associations agrees, as a condition of their membership, to a minimum standard of presentation and service. Increasingly this standard is being independently assessed providing that essential guarantee that member properties will meet the increasing expectations of the travelling public.

Accommodation Getaways Victoria
03 9431 5417
info@agv.net.au
www.agv.net.au
Accommodation Getaways Victoria represents a wide range of bed & breakfasts, farmstays and all types of hosted and self-catering B&Bs throughout Victoria. Whether you want to indulge in a weekend of pampering, a farm holiday for the family or a fun getaway for a group, AGV members can provide you with excellent service and a memorable stay. For a comprehensive listing of all AGV members, please see our website.

Bed & Breakfast and Boutique Association of Tasmania
03 6394 8477
exec@tasmanianbedandbreakfast.com
www.tasmanianbedandbreakfast.com

Bed & Breakfast and Farmstay NSW - ACT
. . . a warm welcome . . . a special experience!
1300 888 862
chair@bedandbreakfast.org.au
www.bedandbreakfast.org.au
Look for the Association's logo as a sign for the highest quality of Bed & Breakfast and Farmstay properties in Sydney and Rural New South Wales, Canberra and the Australian Capital Territory. You will find friendly hosts that are committed to ensuring your stay is an experience to remember. Bed & Breakfast and Farmstay NSW & ACT is a non profit member association of B&B and Farmstay owners abiding by a code of practise with an independently assessed quality checklist.

Bed & Breakfast and Farmstay Northern Territory
(08) 8981 3900
info@bed-and-breakfast.au.com
www.bed-and-breakfast.au.com
The members of the NTBBC host the friendliest accommodation for visitors to the Northern Territory. Make your stay more relaxed and enjoyable by staying with our members.

Bed & Breakfast and Farmstay Queensland
1800 205 030
info@bbfq.com.au
www.bbfq.com.au

Bed & Breakfast and Farmstay Far North Queensland

07 4097 7022
info@bnbnq.com.au
www.bnbnq.com.au
Our hosts offer a wide choice of styles of accommodation or lodgings, from traditional bed & breakfasts, farmstays, ruralstays, homestays, retreats, self contained cottages, spas and Outback Stations.

Bed & Breakfast and Farmstay South Australia

1300 559 943
contact@bandbfsa.com.au
www.bandbfsa.com.au
Bed & Breakfast and Farmstay South Australia members offer some of the most unique and outstanding accommodation opportunities in the State. Look for this logo when choosing accommodation and you can rest assured that these properties operate under a strict Code of Conduct, and have their properties assessed on a regular basis. From the Limestone Coast to the Flinders Ranges, Metropolitan Adelaide and throughout all major wine growing areas you will find our member properties offer great hospitality. Why settle for a key to a room when you can unlock a whole experience with one of our B&Bs or Farmstays.

Bed & Breakfast and Farmstay Western Australia

admin@bedbreakfastfarmstay.com
www.bedbreakfastfarmstay.com
Bed & Breakfast and Farmstay Western Australia represents members who are owners/managers of a varied selection of Bed & Breakfasts and farmstays throughout Western Australia. Bed & Breakfast accommodation comes in varying styles, some in private homes, country retreats, or self-contained apartments and cottages. Whatever the style, very high standards and quality are expected of BBFWA members. B&B operators are keen to offer their hospitality and properties to travellers who are seeking out accommodation that's "more than just a place to stay".

Inn.House Bed and Breakfast Australia Inc

president@innhouse.com.au
www.innhouse.com.au
At an INN.HOUSE Bed & Breakfast property you can depend on a warm welcome, excellent accommodation and friendly attention from your hosts. Each member must meet the high standards set by INN.HOUSE for hospitality, comfort and cleanliness. Our high standards are your assurance of a quality bed and breakfast experience.

Award Winner - *Frankfield Guest House,* Gunning NSW

Australian Capital Territory

ACT and the Canberra Region

Canberra, is one of the more beautiful capital cities of the world.

Canberra boasts more than a million trees and shrubs, mostly exotic. As a result on a clear spring or autumn day it is a captivating and gracious capital. Canberra was designed by the American Walter Burley Griffin based on a series of geometrically precise circles, similar to the street patterns of Washington and Paris.

Drift over the city in a hot air balloon, bush walk through the national parks, ride a bike around the lakes, visit the many cold climate vineyards in the area, or just simply do an embassy tour or a leisurely Lookouts Tour.

In the evening you can enjoy a meal from mountain top restaurants serving local seasonal produce or join the café-set that abounds in the city centre.

Enjoy historical, cultural, sporting, outdoor and culinary experiences including The Australian War Memorial, The National Museum of Australia and the National Gallery, The National Library, the old and new Parliament Houses, the High Court and the Botanic Gardens. There is also our National Zoo and Aquarium and Questacon to enthral the children.

Joe & Sue Sciberras, Ginninderry Homestead B&B, Ginninderra Falls and Leon and Kate Norgate, Birch Corner B&B, Curtin.

The old Parliament House

Sheep shearing and a colonial era oven from Ginninderry Homestead

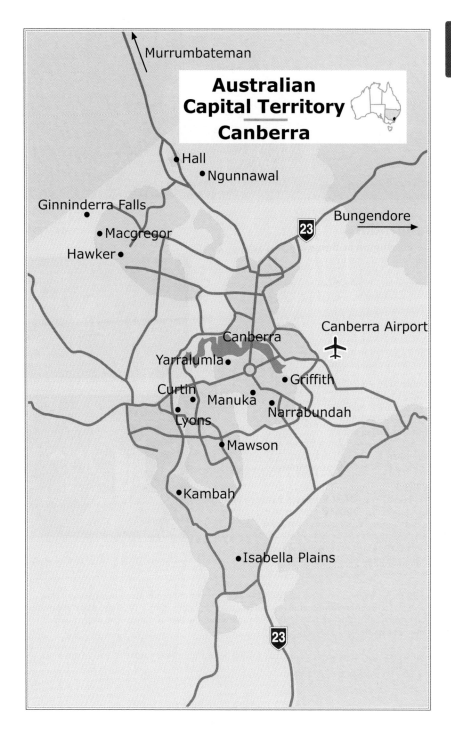

Murrumbateman

**Australian
Capital Territory
Canberra**

Hall
Ngunnawal

Ginninderra Falls

Bungendore

23

Macgregor

Hawker

Canberra Airport

Canberra

Yarralumla

Griffith

Curtin

Manuka

Lyons

Narrabundah

Mawson

Kambah

Isabella Plains

23

Bungendore

The Carrington at Bungendore *Boutique Hotel*
Toni Dale and Nicki Baxter
21 Malbon Street
Bungendore   NSW 2621
30 km E Canberra

Tel (02) 6238 1044
or 1800 046 079
Fax (02) 6238 1636
enquiries@thecarrington.com
www.thecarrington.com

Double $185 - $ 235 Single $135
Child $15-$30
Includes Full Breakfast
Extra Person $35-$45
Dinner at Restaurant
Visa MC BC Diners Amex Eftpos accepted
5 Kingtwin 21 Queen (26 bdrm)
Bathrooms: 26 Ensuite 5 Spa Suites

The Carrington of Bungendore.
For 22 years The Carrington has been creating a special ambience for guests to enjoy, from the moment they arrive until they leave. From the presentation and atmosphere of the historic building and gardens, to the ever changing innovative menus, to the dedication of staff to spoiling guests – attention to detail is the key. This is what keeps guests coming back again... and again!

The 26 individually decorated accommodation suites have been built to complement the historic restaurant building, whilst providing many modern luxury touches. Each room has it's very own individual character and colour scheme, further adding to the charm of this unique destination.

What a great way to relax or enjoy that special occasion.....spoil yourself - you deserve it!

Bungendore

Birchfield *B&B Homestay*
Gary & Kathy Royal
34 Turallo Terrace
Bungendore
NSW 2621
30 km E of Canberra

Tel (02) 6238 0607
or 0418 620 571
Fax (02) 6238 0607
kathy.royal@bigpond.com
www.bbbook.com.au/birchfield.html

Double $130 Single $90
Includes full breakfast
Open weekends Only
1 Double 1 Single (1 bdrm)
Bathrooms: 2 Private

Romantic and peaceful attic accommodation in historic "Birchfield". Double attic bedroom, sitting room, bathroom with spa and private entrance. Breakfast is served in the delightful cottage garden in warm weather or by cosy wood fire in winter. "Birchfield" is a Victorian Gothic-style house built in the 1880's by Father Patrick Birch. Recently operated as "Birchfield Herbs". Restored to its former beauty, complimented by the fragrant, rambling cottage gardens. Located in Bungendore, a friendly, historic rural village, on the Kings Highway, just 30 minutes drive to Canberra. On Sydney to Canberra rail line.

Bungendore

The Old Stone House *B&B*
Geoff and Carolyn Banbury
41 Molonglo Street
Bungendore
NSW 2621
30 km E of Canberra

Tel (02) 6238 1888
Fax (02) 6238 1888
stnhsebb@tpg.com.au
www.theoldstonehouse.com.au

Double $180 Single $125
Includes full breakfast
Dinner by arrangement
No smoking on property
Visa MC BC accepted
2 Queen 2 Double 1 Single (4 bdrm)
Bathrooms: 3 Ensuite 1 Private

The Old Stone House has attracted admiration since 1867. Now charmingly extended and furnished with fine antiques, guests can relax by firelight with "Tiggy" the dog. Behind the gate lies an acre of delightful garden. Down the steps to Giverny-inspired rose arches, discover the reflective pool, kitchen garden and wisteria walk. Leave the car and stroll to village attractions or drive to spring-time gardens and wineries close by. Retreat from the Nation's Capital half an hour away to life in a country village. Small celebrations/ functions.

Canberra - Curtin

Birch Corner *B&B Homestay*
Leon and Kate Norgate
31 Parker Street
Curtin
ACT 2605
6 km S of Canberra City

Tel (02) 6281 4421
Fax (02) 6260 4641
info@birchbb.com
www.birchbb.com

Double $110 Single $80
Child negotiable
Includes full breakfast
Dinner from $25 to $35
Visa MC BC accepted
1 King 1 Queen 1 Double 1 Twin (4 bdrm)
Bathrooms: 2 Guest share

Welcome to our award winning B&B, in a quiet leafy area, where we aim to provide superb home hospitality at an affordable price. Enjoy modern air-conditioned rooms, each with internet access, innovative meals, tea and coffee making facilities, in-ground heated pool and laundry facilities. Our central location allows easy access to Canberra's major attractions, shops, restaurants, hospitals and sporting venues. Leon and Kate, sports and travel enthusiasts, are keen to ensure your stay in the National Capital is memorable. Complimentary transfers are available from airport, train/coach terminals.

Canberra - Hall

Last Stop Ambledown Brook *B&B Cottage with Kitchen*
David & Jenny Kilby
198 Brooklands Road
Hall
ACT 2618
25 km N of Canberra

Tel (02) 6230 2280
laststopambledownbrook@apex.net.au
www.laststop.com.au

Double $120 Single $88
Child $15
Includes full breakfast
No smoking on property
3 Double 4 Single (4 bdrm)
Bathrooms: 3 Ensuite

Last Stop Ambledown Brook. Just 20 minutes from Canberra, on our 40 acres, we have renovated a 1929 Melbourne Tram and a 1935 Train Carriage. They are fully self contained and are decorated with leadlights, posters and other memorabilia. A barbecue, tennis court (weather permitting) and swimming pool are available and there are three wineries within walking distance. We have been featured on "Getaway", "The Great Outdoors" and Postcards".

Canberra - Hall

Surveyor's Hill Winery and B&B *B&B Farmstay Cottage with Kitchen*

Leigh Hobba
215 Brooklands Road
Wallaroo (near Hall)
NSW 2618
25 km N of Canberra

Tel (02) 6230 2046
or 0400 564 050
survhill@oalink.com.au
www.survhill.com.au

Double $130 Single $90
Child $20
Includes full breakfast
Dinner $55 incl. GST per person
Visa MC BC accepted
2 Queen 1 Double (2 bdrm)
Bathrooms: 1 Private

B ed & Breakfast and Farmstay, in a 1930's farmstead surrounded by vineyards and olive groves. Located on a 230 acre property with extensive vineyards, overlooking the Murrumbidgee River and Brindabella Ranges. Easy 20 minute drive to central Canberra. Guests enjoy exclusive use of the cottage, fully private, self contained and separate from the host's residence. Open fire in loungeroom, and heaters in all rooms ensure cosy warmth. Gourmet meals featuring farm and local produce and our own premium wines are provided in the cottage dining room. A fully equipped kitchen enables self catering.

Canberra - Hall

Redbrow Garden B&B *B&B Farmstay Guest House*

David & Elisabeth Judge
1143 Nanima Road
Hall via Canberra
ACT 2618
28 km W of Canberra

Tel (02) 6226 8166
Fax (02) 6226 8166
info@redbrowgarden.com.au
www.redbrowgarden.com.au

Double $120-$160 Single $80-$120
Child $30
Includes full breakfast
Dinner $35
Visa MC BC Amex Eftpos accepted
1 King 2 Queen 1 Twin (5 bdrm)
Bathrooms: 4 Ensuite 1 Guest share

AAA Tourism
★★★★☆

S et in the midst of scenic undulating farmland, wineries and gourmet eateries, our colourful and productive rambling rural garden and tranquil lakeside B&B are just 20 minutes to the nations capital, Canberra. All ensuite rooms have queen/king beds, double showers, bar fridge, tea and coffee making facilities and air conditioning/heating. Log fires in the recreation room in winter for year round comfort. Guests have exclusive use of facilities including television, pool table, jacuzzi and we are able to provide transport to/from local restaurants. Pet enclosures available.

Canberra - Kambah

Edwil House Bed & Breakfast *B&B Homestay*
Judith Simpson
6 Rudder Place
Kambah, ACT 2902
3 km N of Tuggeranong Town Centre

Tel (02) 6231 4001
or 0418 863 193
Fax (02) 6231 4001
judy@edwil.com
www.edwil.com

Double $110-$130 Single $80-$90
Child $12
Includes full breakfast
Dinner from $20 B/A
Visa MC BC accepted
2 Queen 1 Double 1 Twin (4 bdrm)
Bathrooms: 2 Ensuite 1 Private

S et against the backdrop of the Tuggeranong Valley and within minutes to shops, walking trails, clubs, major attractions, Edwil B&B provides quality and comfort with friendly personalised service and home cooked food. Enjoy scrumptious breakfasts served in front of the open fire in winter. Relax in the games room, play the piano, find your favourite record, play snooker or air hockey. In summer take a refreshing dip in the solar-heated pool. Children welcome. Let us make your stay at Edwil an experience to be remembered.

Canberra - MacGregor

Grevillea Lodge *B&B*
Merrill Moore
1 Florey Drive
Macgregor
ACT 2615
13 km NW of Canberra GPO

Tel (02) 6161 7646 or 0414 418 374
Fax (02) 6161 7646
merrill@grevillealodge.com
www.grevillealodge.com

Double $110 Single $90
Includes full breakfast
Extra adult $50.
Weekly and self-catered rates on application.
No smoking on property
Visa MC BC accepted
2 Queen 1 Single (2 bdrm)
Bathrooms: 2 Ensuite

G revillea Lodge offers informal country hospitality in suburban Canberra. Comfortable accommodation in new energy-efficient guest wing with sitting room and private courtyard; access to large deck and native gardens, and the company of our beautiful malamute Nikki if you choose. Selection of teas, coffee, delicious treats always available. Generous breakfast includes hot dishes, fruit platter, homemade muesli, jams and muffins. Quality bedding, ducted heating, internet connection in rooms, kitchenette, BBQ. Nature reserve, walking/bike tracks 100m. Bus stop 50m. Short drive to all Canberra attractions.

Canberra - Manuka - Griffith

La Perouse Bed & Breakfast *B&B*
Heather Gaskell
22 La Perouse Street
Griffith
ACT 2603
200m km SW of Manuka

Tel (02) 6295 2857
or 0407 952 857
Fax (02) 6295 2657
laperousebb@hotmail.com
www.koala-link.net/laperouseb&b

Double $160-$220 Single $130-$180
Includes special breakfast
No smoking on property
Visa MC accepted
1 King 1 Queen 1 Twin (3 bdrm)
Bathrooms: 2 Private

Tourism Awards, 2002, 2003 & 2004 Canberra and Capital Region. Elegantly restored with Edwardian flair, this heritage B&B is two blocks from Manuka Village renowned for its boutiques, restaurants and sidewalk cafes. A few minutes away are the Nation's iconic institutions and Parliament Houses. Treasured antiques, fireplaces, chandeliers, homemade soaps and chocolates, fluffy robes, rose petal baths, fine food, delicious refreshments, a fountain and saltwater pool, create a tranquil, charming and romantic ambience, with personal pampering, complimentary tourism itineraries and 2 sweet little poodles.

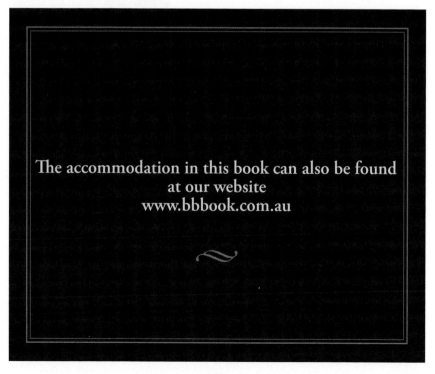

The accommodation in this book can also be found at our website
www.bbbook.com.au

Canberra - Mawson

Shackleton B&B *B&B Homestay*
Wendy & John Whatson
113 Shackleton Circuit
Mawson   ACT 2607
10 km S of Parliament House

Tel (02) 6286 2193
Fax (02) 6286 4720
wendy@shackletonbnb.com.au
www.shackleton.citysearch.com.au

Double $110-$130 Single $90-$110
Includes full breakfast
Visa MC BC accepted
2 Queen 1 Double 1 Twin (2 bdrm)
Bathrooms: 1 Ensuite 1 Private

Shackleton Bed and Breakfast has been the ACT winner of The Peoples Choice Award for Great Accommodation 2003, 2004 and 2005. You are invited to experience our welcoming hospitality, quality accommodation and excellent food. The sensational breakfasts at Shackleton have become legendary. Enjoy the seasonal garden produce, home made breads, jams and other gourmet delights. Relax in the large sunny lounge room with your afternoon tea, or have drinks and savouries on the balcony and enjoy the beauty of the extensive gardens, the native birds feeding, and the panorama of the Brindabella Mountains. We can assist you plan your holiday, weekend away, or business trip to get the most out of a visit to Canberra. Mawson is centrally located, close to many restaurants and only 10 - 15 minutes from all the venues and attractions that our amazing city has to offer. "Shackleton Bed and Breakfast is a great place to stay." *Bruce Elder*. Sydney Morning Herald.

Canberra - Narrabundah

Narrabundah B&B *Homestay*
John & Esther
5 Mosman Place
Narrabundah
ACT 2604
3 km SE of Parliament House

Tel (02) 6295 2837
or 0419 276 231
info@narbb.com
www.narbb.com

Double $105 **Single** $85
Continental Breakfast
Dinner $25pp by arrangement
No smoking on property
Visa MC BC accepted
1 King/Twin (1 bdrm)
Bathrooms: 1 Ensuite

C omfortable, renovated home in quiet street. Conveniently located in relation to Canberra's main tourist attractions, such as Parliament House, National Gallery and War Memorial. Short drive to restaurants in Manuka. Close to public transport and to train station and airport. Air-conditioned (heating and cooling). Hosts are semi-retired and interests include history, genealogy, computing, music, gardening and embroidery.

Canberra - Ngunnawal

Gungahlin Homestay B&B *B&B Homestay*
Lynn and Harold Skinner
36 Leita Court
Ngunnawal
ACT 2913
13 km N of CBD

Tel (02) 6241 0776
or 0410 641 077
ghbandb@bigpond.net.au
www.gungahlinbb.com.au

Double $100 **Single** $80
Child $10 over 5yrs   Includes full breakfast
Visa MC BC accepted
1 Queen (1 bdrm)
Bathrooms: 1 Ensuite

AAA Tourism
★★★★

M odern contemporary family home in quiet northern suburb. Backs reserve. Sweeping views. Guest room features TV/DVD, Foxtel with library of DVD's books and magazines, complementary Lindor chocolates, shortbreads, port and Twinings teas. Take our legendary breakfast at your leisure. BBQ and Internet available for guests use. Children welcome by arrangement. Your friendly hosts guarantee to have you feeling relaxed and refreshed by the end of your stay. Stay one night or a week. You'll be glad you did! We'll show you the warm heart of Canberra!

Canberra - Yarralumla

Annies@Yarralumla *B&B*
Annie Collins
27 Mueller Street
Yarralumla
ACT 2600
3 km SW of Parliament House

Tel 0408 669 631
or (02) 6161 9681
annies.yarralumla@bigfoot.com
www.bigfoot.com/~annies.yarralumla

Double $145-$155 Single $105-$115
Includes full breakfast
1 Queen (1 bdrm)
Bathrooms: 1 Private

Enjoy the comfort and privacy of our contemporary home in the inner Canberra suburb of Yarralumla, on the southern shores of lake Burley Griffin. Yarralumla is home to the majority of Canberra's international embassies, the Royal Canberra Golf Course and Government House. Only 3kms from Parliament, and close to all the major attractions. The Yarralumla village, including restaurants, cafes and a bakery, are only 100m from Annies. Enjoy a private dining room and lounge with satellite TV. Help yourself to endless fresh coffee, a selection of teas and home baked cookies.

Murrumbateman

Country Guesthouse Schönegg *B&B*
Evelyn & Richard Everson
381 Hillview Drive
Murrumbateman
NSW 2582
4 km E of Murrumbateman

Tel (02) 6227 0344
or 0408 673 494
Fax (02) 6227 0361
info@schonegg.com.au
www.schonegg.com.au

Double $150 Single $130
Child $30 Includes full breakfast
Dinner $49
2 Queen (2 bdrm)
Bathrooms: 2 Ensuite

Country tranquillity, culinary bliss, modern elegance. The garnet room features a double spa. The amethyst room is discreetly disabled friendly, featuring a double shower. The lounge offers guests a private retreat. Enjoy the slow-combustion fire or shaded terraces. Indulge in a hearty breakfast buffet and cooked breakfast. Experience fine dining without leaving Schönegg. We offer a 3-course menu for $49.00 per person. We're a BYO venue, fine wineries nearby. Children welcome, trundle beds available. Outdoor pets (including horses) comfortably accommodated. 'Winner Hosted Accommodation 2004 Rhodium Canberra and Capital Region Tourism Awards'.

New South Wales

Armidale New

Armidale is set high on the Northern Tablelands halfway between Sydney and Brisbane. Mild summers, glorious autumn colours, soft, colourful springs and crisp winter days with occasional snowfalls provide many opportunities for seasonal activities. Enjoy bushwalking in National Parks, horse riding, trout fishing, golfing, scenic helicopter flights and waterfalls. Wander through museums, galleries, Cathedrals, restaurants and coffee shops.

Marg Hadfield, Armidale.

Bathurst

Bathurst is Australia's oldest inland city with many significant historic buildings. Machattie Park and King's Parade in the centre of town have fine gardens and memorial fountains. The Sommerville Collection is regarded as one of the top three collections of fossils, palaeontologic specimens and gemmology in the world. The Bathurst region is famous as an artists' colony and the Regional Gallery is home to an outstanding collection of Australian art.

Vineyards, orchards and farms provide the region with fine food and wine. The Farmers Markets are held on the fourth Saturday of the month and have a lively atmosphere and wonderful gourmet food, wine, flowers and music. Bird watching enthusiasts will enjoy the abundance of bird life in the region as well as trout fishing in the local streams and dams.

Bathurst is also home to one of Australia's prime car racing tracks - Mount Panorama and is an ideal base for exploring the Central West being about an hours drive from the Blue Mountains, Jenolan Caves, Cowra, Orange and many historic goldmining villages.

Lyn Boshier, Elm Tree Cottage, Bathurst.

Bermagui and Wallaga Lake

Enjoy the beautiful beaches, marvel at Mt. Dromedary. Bermagui offers the delights of a true Australian beachside holiday. Rock-pools to explore and safe beaches that are patrolled in summer and swimming in our unique rock pool. Enticing and invigorating walks long enough to exhaust the liveliest youngster. Climb Mt. Dromedary to experience the stunning views from the summit.

The waterways of the Bermagui River, Wallaga Lake and Cuttagee Lake provide tranquil waters for fishing, boating, sailing, canoeing and a whole host of other water related activities.

The small diverse shopping centre operates seven days a week with much of the fresh seafood, meat, dairy products and vegetables being produced locally. Recent years have seen the opening of several restaurants and cafes to satisfy many a discerning taste.

Bev Bray, Bimbimbi House, Bermagui, NSW.

Blue Mountains

The Blue Mountains World Heritage area is one of Australia's natural wonders. Stretching for over one million hectares, it is an inspiring mixture of canyons, towering cliffs, streams, waterfalls, limestone caves and forest. Less than one hour from central Sydney, the region has some of the most breathtaking landscapes in Australia. From the upper mountains villages of Wentworth Falls, Leura, Katoomba and Blackheath, to the awe imposing vistas of the mighty Jamison and Grose Valleys and beyond. Mountain streams flow through beautiful river gorges or tumble over the escarpment in stunning waterfall displays - most entwined with both exciting and serene walking trails.

On the western side of the Blue Mountains, the beautiful countryside and lakes around Oberon are a haven for fishing and picnics. Nearby Kanangra Falls are some of the largest cliffs in Australia. Further to the west are The Jenolan Caves - one of the most extensive and beautiful limestone cave networks in the world with much of it fully accessible to tourists.

Bill McCabe, Whispering Pines B&B, Wentworth Falls.

Byron Bay Hinterland

Nestled in the hills behind Australia's most easterly point of Byron Bay is a sub-tropical hinterland with a diverse and beautiful landscape. Drive through lush rolling hills dotted with macadamia orchards, stop at quaint villages and visit the Nightcap National Park with bush walks and waterfalls. Come and share this experience and soak up the atmosphere of peace, tranquillity and relaxed hospitality.

Suzanne McGuinness, Suzanne's Hideaway, Clunes.

Central Coast

Most people know the Central Coast is from north of the Hawkesbury River to South of Newcastle, Gosford is a rapid growing City 79 Km to the north of Sydney, The Entrance, Wyong, Terrigal, Avoca Beach, Woy Woy are just a few well known suburbs on the Coast. The Central Coast is a holiday playground with vast attractions, and ever increasing unique and stylish B&Bs,, trendy markets, al fresco cafes, classy boutique shops. For some family entertainment visit the award winning National Australian Reptile Park, discover the magic of the Australian Rainforest Sanctuary, visitors flock to see the pelican feeding 3pm daily at The Entrance. Or interested in experiencing a contemporary garden, then visit Mt Penang Gardens, Yarramalong & Dooralong Valleys or take a scenic drive through the lush valleys and feel the natural beauty of the hinterlands.

Elizabeth & John Fairweather, Greenacres Bed & Breakfast, Mardi.

Coffs Coast

Coffs Harbour as a holiday destination or a romantic escape has it all! Located mid-way between Sydney and Brisbane on the sub-tropical North Coast of NSW. With beautiful golden beaches, fine restaurants and an abundance of activities and adventures … 'Coffs' is the idyllic holiday paradise! The Coffs Coast Region is renowned for its' great weather, shopping, arts and craft

Coffs Coast Tourism

galleries, water sports, top quality golf courses, markets, fresh seafood, historic harbour/marina, and a casual lifestyle. An hour in a cruise boat or dive boat will give you a great view of the Solitary Islands Marine Reserve or less than an hour by car you can visit the World Heritage area /Dorrigo National Park.

Ben Howell, Santa Fe Luxury B&B, Coffs Harbour, NSW.

Cowra

Cowra –a different slice of country life, situated on the banks of the Lachlan River where the landscape varies from rich river flats to fertile rolling hills to rugged wilderness areas. Cowra is a scenic four hour drive from Sydney and two hours from Canberra.

Cowra is an attractive, friendly and unpretentious town that delivers the visitor a unique experience by offering fine wines and delicious food right in the heart of where it is actually produced. Cellar doors and excellent restaurants, using local foods products, are one of the great highlights of the town.

Peter and Barbara Carne, Conargo B&B, Woodstock.

Crookwell

Crookwell is well known for its revitalizing climate. Because of the altitude, gardens in this high country are spectacular. Fabulous displays of massed bulbs in the spring and glorious changes in the trees during autumn. Superb accommodation is available with a selection of Farmstays and B&Bs providing country charm and hospitality With Santa's Hideaway, Mt Wayo Lavender Farm, the renowned Lindner Sock Factory and great browsing shops there is always something that will catch your eye. For the more adventurous we have Abercrombie and Wombeyan Caves and Grabine Lakeside State Park. With detailed historic and scenic tourist drives you won't get lost whilst investigating the quaint villages of Binda. Laggan, Tuena, Bigga and Grabben Gullen where bushranger history abounds.

Mary Prell, Minnamurra Farmstay, Crookwell.

Dorrigo

Dorrigo - "Where the mountains reach the sky". Perched on the dramatic eastern escarpment of the Great Dividing Range and only 40 km from the coast, Dorrigo offers spectacular scenery, bushwalking and abundant bird life. Dorrigo is the gateway to the most accessible World Heritage Rainforest in New South Wales with spectacular scenery with easy walking tracks leading to a different world beneath the canopy of waterfalls and lush subtropical rainforest. Take the skywalk and experience a unique close up view of the rainforest canopy with views over the beautiful Bellinger Valley to the distant coastline beyond.

Di McDonald, Tallawalla Retreat, Dorrigo.

Eden

Historic Eden is truly paradise! Situated on the magnificent Sapphire Coast, surrounded by National Parks and State Forests, it is the last town on the South Coast of New South Wales before you enter Victoria. Eden is now a popular whale watching destination with migrating whales pausing to feed offshore here during October. The famous Killer Whale Museum tells the unique story of Tom the Killer Whale who used to work with the whalers in days gone by. Dolphin and Whale watching cruises are popular. The fishing charter operators know where to catch 'a big one' or your can scuba dive on one of the wrecks that litter the coast. Eden is centrally located for excellent bushwalking in the National Parks. One of the more popular is the Light to Light walk where you can walk along

 the rugged coast from Boyds Tower to Greencape Lighthouse, pausing at magnificent beaches for a swim and camping along the way.

Gail and David Ward, Cocora Cottage B&B, Eden

Glen Innes

Glen Innes is a country town consumed by all things Celtic. Originally settled by Scottish, Welsh and Cornish folk, Glen Innes is dedicated to celebrating its heritage. The annual Celtic Festival held the first weekend in May each year and is a major event on the national calendar. The Australian Standing Stones at Glen Innes are based on the first solar aligned megalithic stone circles

erected thousands of years ago during the peak of Celtic civilisation. Over thirty Heritage-listed buildings dress the main street of Glen Innes in colonial charm. The romance of the past is recaptured in the tranquil rural villages of Emmaville, Deepwater, Torrington and Ben Lomond. This area is the richest mineral belt in the world as far as concentration and diversity are concerned - sapphires, topaz and quartz crystals. Emmaville Mining Museum traces the history of local mining back to the once flourishing Chinese community. Minerama, on the second weekend in March, is the largest annual Mineral and Gem Show in NSW. Discover the World Heritage Way and explore National Parks that will amaze you with their rugged beauty and pristine wilderness.

Genevieve Barrett, Glen Innes Visitor Information Centre.

Gloucester

Northern Gateway to the World Heritage Barrington Tops, Top Tourist Town and home of country hospitality. Nestled in the foothills of the Bucketts Mountains and acclaimed for its friendliness and serene surroundings, Gloucester, base camp to World Heritage Barrington Tops, is the perfect place to relax and unwind. Go for a drive and enjoy breathtaking views, dramatic mountain ranges, beautiful rivers and valleys.

Boasting a range of outdoor activities including fishing, horse riding, 4WD tours, skydiving or canoeing, visit the Folk Museum or Gloucester Gallery to learn more about local history and culture, call into the Visitor Information Centre and pick up a copy of the Farm Trail map. Events in Gloucester include the Shakespeare on Avon Festival, Mountain Man Tri Challenge, Gloucester Ceilidh, Rodeos, Country Music camps and community markets.

Almost every palate is catered for in our extensive choice of eating houses.

Kyoko Sakamoto, Arrowee House B&B, Gloucester.

Hawkesbury and Hawkesbury Valley

Forming the northern border of Sydney is the majestic Hawkesbury River. From the waterfront retreat of Brooklyn you can dine at riverfront restaurants or ride Australia's only Riverboat Postman. Catch a ferry to the car-free Dangar Island or hire a boat to tour the local oyster farms.

The Hawkesbury Valley extends from Historic towns like St Albans, Ebenezer and on to Windsor, and Richmond then climbing the mountains through Kurrajong Hills to Bilpin and beyond. This beautiful picturesque rural setting and its local community creates an atmosphere of peace and serenity for those who venture to taste the hospitality offered. Wisemans Ferry is a serene river town set beneath

towering cliffs of Hawkesbury sandstone. The ferry master still operates the punt 24 hours a day for vehicles to cross the Hawkesbury River – a time honoured tradition since 1827.

Matt McDonell, Sydney Hills and Jim Swaisland, Ossian Hall B&B, Colo.

Jervis Bay

Experience the dramatic beauty of Jervis Bay and it's pleasant coastal climate. It's an unspoilt paradise just 2 - 3 hrs away from Sydney or Canberra, and the perfect place for a getaway or as the first or last stop for overseas travellers visiting the south coast of NSW.
Come and listen to the Kookaburras laugh, walk on the beach and look for dolphins playing in the surf, go fishing, swimming or diving, a dolphin-watch cruise (year round) or a whale-watch cruise (June-July, September-October). Be dazzled by the whitest sand in the world, play golf on scenic courses, or hire bikes and explore the bike trails. One of the must-see places is Booderee National Park, where you can go walking, visit the amazing ruined lighthouse, picnic in the botanical gardens, see kangaroos and marvel at the many beautiful parrots.

Bill Rogers, Jervis Bay Guesthouse, Jervis Bay.

Snowy Mountains – Khancoban

Visit beautiful Khancoban at the foot of Kosciuzko and half way between Sydney and Melbourne. The picturesque township of Khancoban is the spectacular western face of The Snowy Mountains. Local activities include, trout fishing, golf, bowls and tennis. Take The Alpine Way from Thredbo to Khancoban - one of Australia's best scenic drives with much to see including lookouts with the best views over the main range, the historic hut and kangaroo colony at Geehi and M1 Power Station.

Kathleen Cossettini, Cossettini B&B, Khancoban.

Kiama Region - Kiama, Jamberoo, Gerringong, Gerroa and Minnamurra

Kiama is a small seaside town 90 minutes drive south of Sydney. Remnants of the rainforest can be seen in the dairy farms, where ancient cabbage palms dot the scenery and historic dry stone walls fringe the farms and roadsides.
Within a few minutes drive of the beachside and through the dairy farming area are the beautiful rainforests and waterfalls of the Jamberoo escarpment.
Kiama Blowhole is perhaps the most

famous attraction to the region. Jamberoo Recreation Park is a terrific fun park for all the family. Award-winning wineries with cafes and restaurants are just a few minutes drive. Walking trails include coastal trails, Minnamurra Rainforest, Barren Grounds Nature Reserve, lookouts and Historic town walks.
Kiama has a mild climate – it boasts many other activities such as surfing, swimming, fishing, boating, golfing, bird watching, whale watching, sightseeing tours, shopping and, of course, indulging in it's many good quality cafes and restaurants.

Marian & Tony van Zanen, Kiama B&B, Kiama.

Moruya

Moruya's location on the banks of the picturesque Moruya River midway between Batemans Bay and Narooma makes it the ideal centre for exploring the beauties of the increasingly popular Eurobodalla Nature Coast, plus the Deua National Parks and wilderness areas.

The township maintains its country town atmosphere with heritage buildings, museum, craft and antique shops, plus the unique display of wood carvings in the main street.

Saturday brings the popular country markets located close to the riverbank. You are never far from beaches, golf courses, fishing, boating and riding, or quality restaurants.

Within easy travelling are Tuross, Narooma, Tilba and Bermagui to the South, with Mogo, Broulee, Batemans Bay, Nelligen and Durass to the North.

By road Sydney is 5 hours away and Melbourne 9 hours, making an ideal overnight stop. The airport is serviced by Regional Express to Sydney and Melbourne, the Aero Club offer wonderful scenic flights.

John Spencer, Bryn Glas B&B, Moruya.

Newcastle

Newcastle, capital of the Hunter, has thrown off its old image as an industrial city and emerged as a sought-after week-end getaway and holiday destination. Almost as old as Sydney, Newcastle impresses by its beauty, cleanliness, parks and facilities. Beautiful old buildings are a reminder of our rich architectural heritage. Beaches to die for, vibrant harbour and great restaurants are all within easy access of the centre. Nature

reserves like Blackbutt, the Wetlands and the Botanic Gardens are worth a visit as is the Art Gallery, the leading regional gallery in Australia. A stroll along the Foreshore and on the Hill gives a vivid reflection of life then and now.

Rosemary Bunker, Newcomen B&B Newcastle.

Northern Rivers - The Tweed Shire

Jewel in the Crown of the Northern Rivers. Nestled between the NSW/ Queensland Border and Byron Shire, the Tweed enchants those lucky enough to stumble upon this largely undiscovered area. Whilst other shires claim to be the gateway to the rainforests, in the Tweed you have actually arrived. Home to 5 World Heritage listed National Parks, including Mt Warning, the eroded central chamber of the world's largest extinct shield volcano and the spot where the dawn sun first touches Australia, pristine beaches, untouched rainforests, world class artisans, golf, horse-riding, scenic joyflights, multi-million dollar art gallery and more. From the Tweed coastal region, dotted with small towns offering a range of eateries and resorts, to the spectacular hinterland mountains and valleys, with quaint villages, sidewalk cafés, galleries, arts and crafts, the Tweed has something to satisfy all tastes and pockets.

Tracy and Clive Parker,
Hillcrest Mountain View,
Murwillumbah, NSW.

Sydney's Hills District

Stretching from North Parramatta to historic Wisemans Ferry on The Hawkesbury River is Sydney's Hills District where you'll discover the mystique of colonial history mixed with cosmopolitan life. It's a great way to experience Sydney without the bustle of busy city streets. The villages of Galston, Kenthurst and Dural hide a myriad of fruit orchards, hobby farms, antique and craft stalls. With over 60 nurseries in the area covering everything from bonsai to herbs and roses, this really is gardeners' heaven. Break your day with a meal amongst the spring scents at one of the many garden cafes and restaurants.

All this gives way to the modern amenities and vibrant events of Castle Hill. The Hills District is now a cosmopolitan hub with acclaimed shopping and entertainment precincts. A smorgasbord of quality restaurants and cafes cover the region. The leafy streets border open bushland and the area hosts Sydney's only State Forest.

Matt McDonell, Sydney Hills.

39

Tilba

Tolkienesque rocky outcrops among rolling green hills entice visitors to the National Trust villages of Central Tilba and Tilba Tilba. Set in the Tilba Valley with the majesty of Gulaga (Mt Dromedary) as a backdrop, the area is well known for its cheese, gold mining past, gardens and more recently art, craft, heritage and indigenous culture. Within easy driving distance from Narooma and Bermagui the area has access to a pristine coastline with many secluded beaches. The temperate climate – the area's best kept secret – means that visitors can discover, explore and enjoy what's on offer all year round.

Stuart Absalom, Green Gables Bed & Breakfast, Tilba Tilba.

Walcha

Walcha, with a population of 3500, is one of the friendliest rural towns and a perfect stopover to Brisbane. It lies 1067metres above sea level on the Northern Tablelands of New South Wales, an easy 447 km drive from Sydney on the New England Highway or via "Thunderbolts Way" through Gloucester and then climbing up to fresh mountain air with majestic vistas. Walcha is the gateway to the Oxley Wild Rivers National Park and world heritage listed, Werrikimbie National Park home to the spectacular Aplsey Falls with a gorge is 360m deep. Tia Falls, not to be missed, is ideal for easy walks and perfect photo opportunities. Summers in Walcha are short and mild, Winters can be "crisp" with occasional snow falls!

Louise Gill, Country Mood Bed & Breakfast, Walcha.

Wallendbeen and Temora

Wallendbeen is very close to Temora, a wonderful town because of its amazing Aviation Museum of Vintage Aircraft and its voluntary run Farm Heritage Museum with one of the largest collections of tractors in the world.

The Aviation Museum belongs to David Lowie, son of Frank Lowie, of Sydney and houses the only flying Gloucester F8 Meteor war plane in the world and the oldest flying Spitfire in Australia.

It also showcases many other vintage aircraft such as the Wirraway, the first ex-military aircraft permitted to fly on the Civil Aircraft Register, the oldest flying Tiger Moth in Australia, the only flying Canberra Bomber, an Australian built Vampire and a wooden propeller Ryan, which was used to train Australian Troops during WWII. All the aircraft are taken from the museum and flown on two consecutive days about once a month.

Colleen Hines, Colleen & Old Sil's Farmhouse B&B, Corang, Wallendbeen.

Wellington

Wellington is a set in a delightful valley of colour, shape and texture of trees, rural landscapes and historic buildings. Set between the magic of two well-known rivers, the Bell and the Macquarie, these rivers meet in the older section of Wellington, better known as Montefiores or Mountain of Flowers. Originally, Wellington made its mark by being one of the first Convict Settlements in New South Wales. The Convict settlement disbanded in early 1832, but remnants remain on the outskirts south of town. Now hosting a Caves and Japanese Garden complex, the most scenic Golf Course for miles, and a wonderful scenic Burrendong Dam and Burrendong Botanic Garden and Arboretum.

Helen O'Brien, Carinya Bed & Breakfast, Wellington.

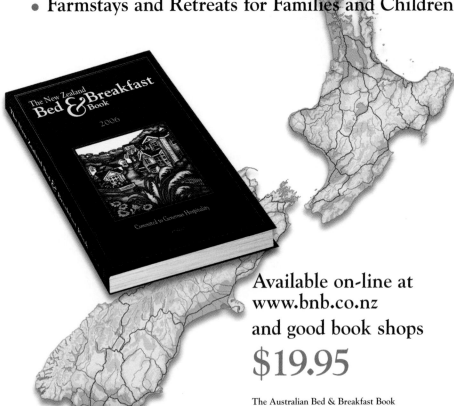

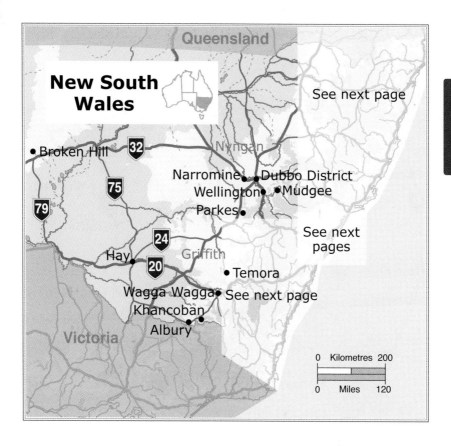

New South Wales

Queensland

See next page

Broken Hill · 32

Nyngan

Narromine · Dubbo District

Wellington · Mudgee

Parkes ·

24

Hay · 20 · Griffith

Temora

See next pages

Wagga Wagga · See next page

Khancoban

Albury

Victoria

0 Kilometres 200

0 Miles 120

75

79

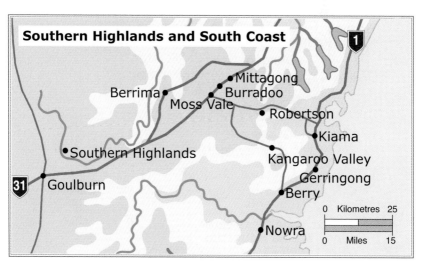

Southern Highlands and South Coast

1

Berrima · Mittagong · Burradoo

Moss Vale · Robertson

Southern Highlands

Kiama

Kangaroo Valley

Gerringong

31 · Goulburn

Berry

Nowra

0 Kilometres 25

0 Miles 15

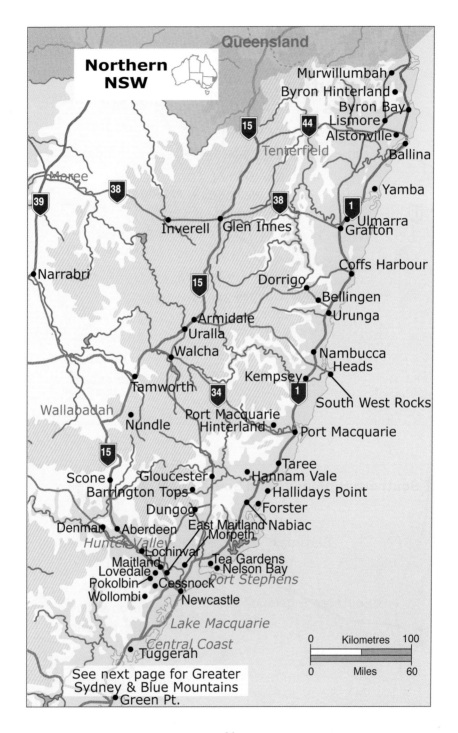

Northern
NSW

Queensland

Murwillumbah
Byron Hinterland
Byron Bay
Lismore
Alstonville
Ballina

Tenterfield

Moree

Yamba

Inverell   Glen Innes   Ulmarra
Grafton

Narrabri

Dorrigo   Coffs Harbour

Bellingen
Urunga

Armidale
Uralla
Walcha   Nambucca
Heads
Kempsey
South West Rocks

Tamworth

Wallabadah   Port Macquarie
Nundle   Hinterland   Port Macquarie

Taree
Scone   Gloucester   Hannam Vale
Barrington Tops   Hallidays Point
Dungog   Forster
Denman   Aberdeen   East Maitland   Nabiac
Morpeth
Hunter Valley   Lochinvar
Maitland   Tea Gardens
Lovedale   Nelson Bay
Pokolbin   Cessnock   Port Stephens
Wollombi   Newcastle

Lake Macquarie
Central Coast
Tuggerah

See next page for Greater
Sydney & Blue Mountains
Green Pt.

0   Kilometres   100
0   Miles   60

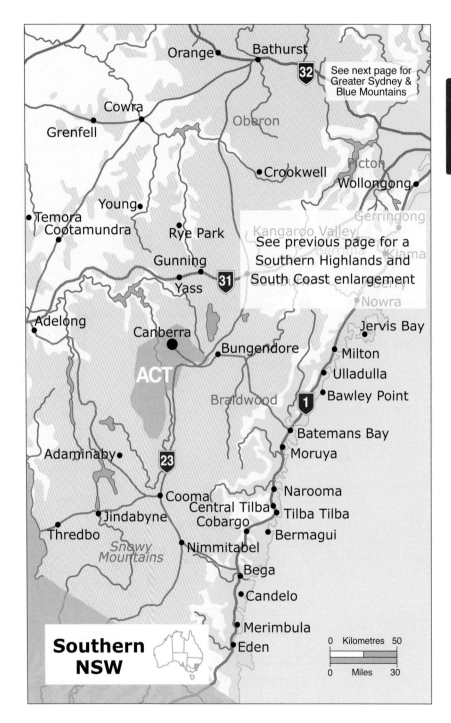

New South Wales

Orange
Bathurst

32

See next page for
Greater Sydney &
Blue Mountains

Cowra

Grenfell

Oberon

Crookwell

Picton

Wollongong

Young

Gerringong

Temora
Cootamundra

Rye Park

Kangaroo Valley

Gunning

Berrima

See previous page for a
Southern Highlands and
South Coast enlargement

Yass

31

Goulburn

Berry

Nowra

Adelong

Canberra

Jervis Bay

ACT

Bungendore

Milton

Braidwood

Ulladulla

1

Bawley Point

Batemans Bay

Adaminaby

23

Moruya

Cooma

Narooma

Central Tilba

Tilba Tilba

Jindabyne

Cobargo

Thredbo

Bermagui

Snowy
Mountains

Nimmitabel

Bega

Candelo

Merimbula

Southern
NSW

Eden

0   Kilometres   50

0   Miles   30

45

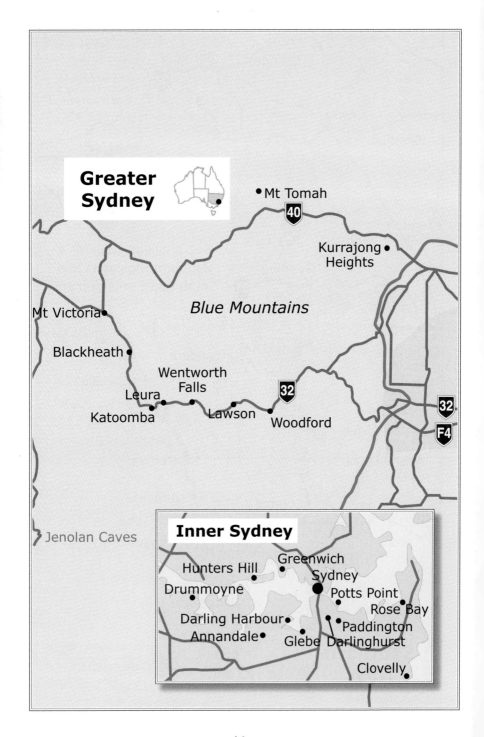

Greater Sydney

- Mt Tomah
- **40**
- Kurrajong Heights
- *Blue Mountains*
- Mt Victoria
- Blackheath
- Wentworth Falls
- Leura
- **32**
- Katoomba
- Lawson
- Woodford
- **32**
- **F4**
- Jenolan Caves

Inner Sydney

- Hunters Hill
- Greenwich
- Sydney
- Drummoyne
- Potts Point
- Rose Bay
- Darling Harbour
- Paddington
- Annandale
- Glebe
- Darlinghurst
- Clovelly

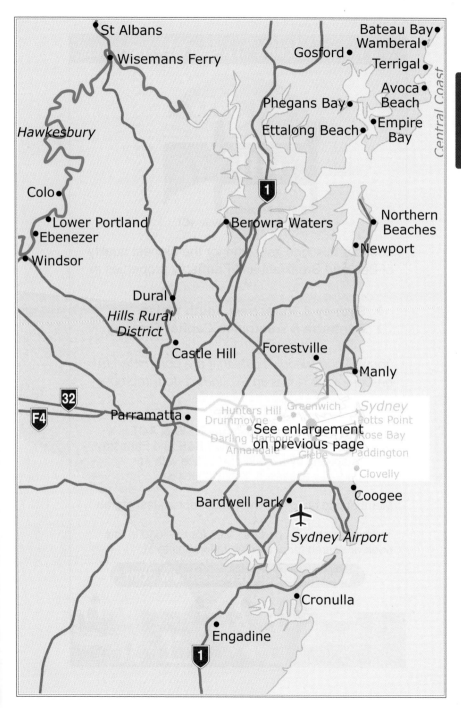

Adelong

Yavendale Garden Cottage *B&B Farmstay Cottage with Kitchen*

Susan & Patrick Roche
Yavendale
Adelong
NSW 2729
16 km SW of Adelong

Tel (02) 6946 4259
Fax (02) 6946 4269
susan.roche@bigpond.com
www.bbbook.com.au/yavendale.html

Double $100 Single $60
Includes full breakfast
Dinner B/A
No smoking on property
1 Double 2 Single (2 bdrm)
Bathrooms: 1 Private

Approximately half-way between Sydney and Melbourne Yavendale Garden Cottage offers the traveller or visitor charming private accommodation on a cattle and sheep property in classic grazing country. On arrival guests are warmly welcomed with tea or coffee and home-made cake. Delicious breakfasts featuring home-made jams and preserves, local produce and farm eggs, are served in the homestead overlooking the garden, or supplies may be provided to prepare at your leisure. Explore interesting places or we invite you to relax in the peaceful garden and surrounds. "Had a wonderful time, hospitality exceptional, food delightful." UC, Paris.

Adelong

Beaufort Guesthouse *B&B Guest House Luxury master bedroom*

Mike Matthews
77 Tumut Street
Adelong
NSW 2729
21 km SW of Tumut

Tel (02) 6946 2273
Fax (02) 6946 2553
info@beaufort-guesthouse.com.au
www.beaufort-guesthouse.com.au

Double $105-$150 Single $72.50-$110
Includes full breakfast
Dinner $35
Packages available
Visa MC BC Amex accepted
2 Queen 4 Double 5 Twin 3 Single (14 bdrm)
Bathrooms: 5 Ensuite 9 Guest share 4 motels ensuite, 1 master bedroom ensuite, 9 bedrooms with shared bathrooms

Half way between Sydney and Melbourne and two hours from Canberra, "Beaufort Guesthouse & Motel" offers elegant accommodation with personalised care, hospitality and country-style cuisine. Situated in the historic Heritage listed, old gold mining town of Adelong NSW, a warm welcome awaits our guests and visitors. Sample home made fare in Granny's Kitchen coffee shop or our leafy courtyard. Dine at night in style in our restaurant. Our function centre specialises in private lunches and dinner parties, weddings and small seminars. Many special packages are available please check our web page.

Albury

Elizabeth's Manor *B&B Cottage Kitchen*
Larry & Betty Kendall
531 Lyne Street
Lavington, North Albury
NSW 2641
1.5 km E of North Albury Post Office

Tel (02) 6040 4412
Fax (02) 6040 5166
bookins@elizabethsmanor.com.au
www.elizabethsmanor.com.au

Double $160 **Single** $130
Child $22
Includes full breakfast   Dinner $44 - $55
No smoking on property
Visa MC BC Diners Amex Eftpos accepted
3 Queen 1 Double (3 bdrm)
Bathrooms: 3 Ensuite

AAA Tourism
★★★★★

E lizabeth's Manor would have to be the most luxurious and romantic adults only accommodation in Australia. On arrival guests will be presented with complimentary Champagne and a box of chocolates. Breakfast is a true English gourmet delight and can be served in your suite or the Gallery. Although we have a "No Smoking" policy in the house, smoking is permitted anywhere outside. We also have a late check-out, twelve PM. A three course dinner with complimentary wine can be arranged during booking the accommodation. As seen on 'Getaway'& "Sydney Weekender".

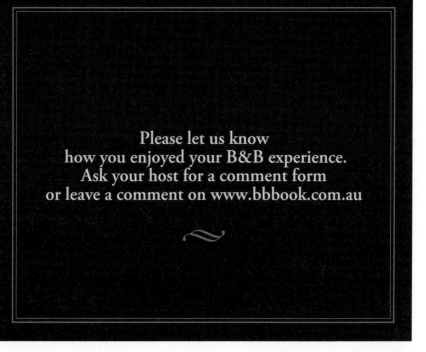

Please let us know
how you enjoyed your B&B experience.
Ask your host for a comment form
or leave a comment on www.bbbook.com.au

Alstonville - Ballina

Hume's Hovell *Luxury B&B Separate Suite*
Peter & Suzanne Hume
333 Dalwood Road
Alstonville
NSW 2477
8 km S of Alstonville

Tel (02) 6629 5371
Fax (02) 6629 5471
stay@humes-hovell.com
www.bed-and-breakfast.com.au

Double $165-$231 Single $115-$160
Child $25   Includes full breakfast   Dinner $35
Visa MC BC accepted
2 King/Twin2 King 3 Single (3 bdrm)
Bathrooms: 3 Ensuite 1 Private

Hume's Hovell, one of the State's Best Short Break destinations" - NRMA Open Road Magazine review. Located south of Byron Bay, in the rolling green hills above Ballina, Hume's Hovell provides fine boutique accommodation amidst the trees of a Macadamia Plantation. Spacious suites provide maximum privacy with luxurious comfort, featuring King size beds, air-conditioning, cosy lounges, TV/CD/video, guest toiletries, and hand-made soap. The Plantation Spa Suite is wheelchair friendly. Enjoy afternoon tea on arrival, plus complementary macadamias, plunger coffee, various teas, and chocolates in your suite. Our rates include sumptuous breakfasts, afternoon tea, and in the evening savouries and pre-dinner drinks. Guests can then choose from dining at local restaurants, by candlelight in your suite or in the Poolside Pavilion (with prior arrangement). BBQ's and Seafood Platters are other delicious popular alternatives. Enjoy the beautiful beaches and World Heritage Wilderness Areas, stroll the country lanes, play tennis, swim in the salt-water pool, visit local galleries and markets. Do it all - or do nothing. For a secluded honeymoon, a place to unwind, or simply overnight, Suzanne and Peter will welcome you warmly.

Armidale

Cox's on South Hill *B&B*
Leanne & Col Cox
44 The Avenue
Armidale
NSW 2380
3 km S of City Centre

Tel (02) 6772 3994
or 0402 091 036
Fax (02) 6772 3994
colinc@northnet.com.au
www.bbbook.com.au.coxsonsouthhill.html

Double $80-$120 **Single** $60-$80
Child $20 - $40
Continental Breakfast
1 Queen 1 Double 2 Twin (4 bdrm)
Bathrooms: 1 Guest share 1 Private

R elax and enjoy the picturesque city and rural views of Armidale at Cox's on South Hill. Centrally located, you can enjoy all that Armidale offers only minutes from the CBD, hospital, UNI and golf course. After a day travelling, studying, business or just visiting dine at the many local restaurants or enjoy the use of the dining room. Relax in the luxurious bath and spacious bathroom. Then snuggle in a comfy bed with electric blankets and heated rooms. Included in your accommodation are a continental breakfast, tea/coffee facilities, fridge, microwave and BBQ. Buster is our friendly dog. Come as a visitor, leave as a friend.

∼

Armidale

Poppys Cottage *B&B Farmstay Cottage No Kitchen*
Jake & Poppy Abbott
Malvern Hill
Dangarsleigh Road, ARMIDALE
NSW 2350
6 km S of Armidale

Tel (02) 6775 1277
or 0412 153 819
Fax (02) 6775 1308
poppyscottage@bluepin.net.au
home.bluepin.net.au/poppyscottage

Double $120 **Single** $95
Child $40
Includes special breakfast
Dinner $48
2 Double 2 Single (2 bdrm)
Bathrooms: 1 Ensuite 1 Private

W INNER TOURISM AWARD FOR EXCELLENCE in CUSTOMER SERVICE - an unforgettable, warm and friendly B&B experience with romantic, cosy atmosphere in enchanting garden. Friendly farm animals. Guests enjoy peace, tranquillity and privacy. Beautiful Gourmet breakfasts enjoyed beneath canopy of fruit trees a speciality. Delicious intimate candlelit dinner with complimentary wine. Relax and enjoy country hospitality at its best - warm, friendly and generous. "At last a B&B as we hoped it would be. You obviously enjoy providing such gracious hospitality and it shows". G.& N. B. Canberra, January 2005

Armidale

Wattleton *Farmstay Cottage with Kitchen*
Lea & Allan Waters
845 Sandon Road
Metz via Armidale
NSW 2350
35 km SE of Armidale

Tel (02) 6775 3731
www.bluepin.net.au/wattleton

Double $90 Single $70
Child $25
Continental Breakfast
Dinner $25
1 Queen 1 Double 3 Single (2 bdrm)
Bathrooms: 1 Private

C ome to Wattleton Farmstay and experience the real country life of the Australian sheep and cattle grazier. Wattleton is nestled amongst the spectacular and scenic New England Gorges near Armidale. Families and couples are made to feel most welcome enjoying farm life, bushwalking, horse riding, tennis, swimming and a barbeque in the large all weather B.B.Q shed. Children have the opportunity to interact with the many farm animals close to the cottage. The fully self-contained cottage has wood fires and all mod-cons. "Came as guests, left as friends." KF.

Armidale

Glenhope Alpacas - B&B *Luxury B&B Farmstay Separate suite with cooking facilities*
Bronwyn and David Mitchell
Red Gum Lane, off Boorolong Road
Armidale
NSW 2350
3.5 km W of Armidale & University

Tel (02) 6772 1940
or 0422 969 310
Fax (02) 6772 0889
info@glenhopealpacas.com
www.glenhopealpacas.com

Double $120-$140 Single $90-$100
Child $15 - $30
Includes full breakfast
S/C From $90
Visa MC BC accepted
1 King 1 Double 2 Twin (3 bdrm)
Bathrooms: 2 Ensuite

A touch of luxury...in the bush. Located 4kms Armidale and the University. Accommodation consists of two self-contained suites with cooking facilities suitable for up to four people. Indulge in some alpaca gazing or bird watching over breakfast and soak up the relaxing atmosphere of this unique property. We offer generous hospitality and all the creature comforts of home. Our own alpaca products are available for sale. Experience the changing seasons of Armidale and enjoy its many cultural and historical attractions. Explore the natural wonders of World Heritage National Parkes and waterfalls.

Ballina

Landfall *B&B Homestay*
Gaye & Roger Ibbotson
109 Links Ave
East Ballina
NSW 2478
In Ballina East

Tel (02) 6686 7555
or 0428 642 077
Fax (02) 6686 7377
landfall@spot.com.au
www.bbbook.com.au/landfall.html

Double $95 Single $55
Includes full breakfast
No smoking on property
Visa MC BC accepted
1 Queen 2 Single (2 bdrm)
Bathrooms: 1 Guest share

"Landfall" You're welcome in our home.

This home was the residence of Captain Tom Martin and his wife; he named this home "Landfall" when he retired to Ballina after many years at sea. "Landfall" is situated in East Ballina overlooking the golf course. You are invited to relax in our courtyard with its indoor solar heated pool and spa. Perhaps you'd prefer to read in the "chart-room" library. "Landfall" is a "non smoking" home. We offer you a relaxed stay with warm, friendly hospitality. The main part of our home is air conditioned as is the Queen Bedroom for the comfort of our guests. Your hosts Gaye and Roger Ibbotson.

Ballina

The Yabsley B & B *B&B*
Judee Whittaker and David Clark
5 Yabsley Street
East Ballina
NSW 2478
3 km NE of Ballina

Tel (02) 6681 1505
or 0407 811 505
Fax (02) 6681 1505
yabsley@bigpond.com
www.tropicalnsw.com.au/yabsley

Double $120-$130 Single $100
Includes full breakfast
Dinner 3 courses - $40 per person
No smoking on property
Visa MC BC accepted
2 Queen (2 bdrm)
Bathrooms: 2 Private

AAA Tourism
★★★★☆

The Yabsley is a two minute walk to Lighthouse Beach, Richmond River and Shaws Bay Lagoon. Also within easy walking distance to a hotel, a resort and three restaurants. The house has been refurbished and contains private guest suites, guest lounge and delightful courtyards. Watch the whales and dolphins or play tennis and golf. East Ballina gives access to day trips to Byron Bay, the Border Ranges or the Gold Coast. You can negotiate a superb meal of your choice cooked by David who specialises in seafood cuisine. Unfortunately we cannot cater for children.

Ballina

Brundah B&B *Luxury B&B*
Ros & Mal Lewis
37 Norton Street
Ballina
NSW 2478
In Centre of Ballina

Tel (02) 6686 8166
or 0414 861 066
Fax (02) 6686 8164
stay@brundah.com.au
www.brundah.com.au

Double $165-$195 Single $120-$165
Includes full breakfast
Visa MC BC Diners Amex accepted
3 Queen 1 Single (3 bdrm)
Bathrooms: 3 Ensuite

B rundah B&B . . . an elegant National Trust Heritage Home (circa 1908), set on half an acre of peaceful and secluded gardens. Take the time to sip afternoon tea or a cool drink on the wide verandahs, utilise the guest library, lounge or dining rooms all tastefully furnished for your comfort. Enjoy a large gourmet breakfast and on arrival complimentary afternoon tea or glass of wine. A short stroll will take you to the town centre, restaurants, river or beaches. Three Queen rooms each with ensuites. Hosts: Mal & Ros Lewis.

Barrington Tops - Gloucester

Valley View Homestead B&B *B&B Farmstay Cottage with Kitchen*
John & Denise Glew
1783 Bucketts Way
Wards River
NSW 2422
30 km S of Gloucester

Tel (02) 4994 7066
or 0417 409 729
Fax (02) 4994 7066
sales@valleyviewbnb.com
www.valleyviewbnb.com

Double $110-$120 Single $70
Includes full breakfast
extra persons $20
Visa MC BC accepted
1 King/Twin 3 Queen 2 Twin (3 bdrm)
Bathrooms: 1 Ensuite 2 Guest share

E njoy the relaxed atmosphere at this tranquil retreat set in 30 acres at the foothills of The Barrington Tops. Included in your accommodation is our sumptuous full country breakfast. Listen to the sounds of the native birdlife while you relax around the pool or have a BBQ and just sit back and enjoy the magnificent views. The Barrington area caters for many varied activities - horseriding, 4x4 driving. Sightseeing around historic Stroud and Gloucester. Bushwalking. Golf. Mountain biking. Canoeing and Kayaking. We also have the self-contained Bower Bird cottage where children and pets are most welcome.

Batemans Bay

Chalet Swisse Spa *B&B Self Contained*
Herbert and Elizabeth Mayer
676 The Ridge Road
Surf Beach, Batemans Bay
NSW 2536
10 km S of Batemans Bay

Tel (02) 4471 3671
Fax (02) 4471 1671
info@chaletswissespa.com.au
www.chaletswissespa.com.au

Double $120-$295 **Single** $90-$250
Child $40
Continental Breakfast
Self Contained Cabins incl Linen $120 - $245
Visa MC BC Diners Amex accepted

Deluxe 4.5 * 2 King, 6 Queen **Lodge** 3.5 * 2 family (4) **Self Contained** 2 family (5)
Bathrooms: 17 Ensuite

Situated on top of "Hero's Hill" above Surf Beach our 85 ac Retreat & Health Spa offers you:- our own mineral spring water, fresh clean air, tranquillity, 120 degree ocean views from our Cafe-verandah, visits by birds and wallabies. Facilities: Indoor heated pool (28 degrees C), Spa, revitalising therapies and massages, rainforest walks, tennis, table tennis, archery. Guest lounge with large open fireplace, games corner. Friendly, widely travelled hosts. A place for you to relax, wind down and get pampered.

~

Bathurst

Cherrywood-by-the-River *B&B*
Belinda Mansell
238 Eglinton Road
Bathurst
NSW 2795
3 km NW of Bathurst

Tel (02) 6331 9427
www.bbbook.com.au/cherrywood.html

Double $100-$120 **Single** $70-$80
Child $30
Dinner $20-$25 by arrangement
1 Queen 2 Single (2 bdrm)
Bathrooms: 1 Guest share

Our delightful home with a rural garden nestles in two acres. Beyond the ponies paddock, stroll beside the Macquarie River, capture scenic views from our wide verandahs. Large lounge and family rooms have cheerful log fires, TV, coffee and tea making facilities. Gracious dining room, enjoy homemade stylish breakie, recommending my speciality: "Eggs Benedict"! Charming large bedrooms have comfortable beds and electric blankets. Help groom and feed Neffie our Welsh pony, Kiri the shy Burmese cat prefers the fire side. Smokers: verandah please.

Bathurst

Elm Tree Cottage *B&B Cottage with Kitchen*
Lyn Boshier
270 Keppel Street
Bathurst
NSW 2795

Tel (02) 6332 4920
or 0407 890 445
Fax (02) 6331 8566
elmtree@ix.net.au
www.bathurstheritage.com.au

Double $143-$165 **Single** $132-$143
Child $33
Includes breakfast by arrangement
3 adults $187-198
Visa MC BC accepted
1 Queen 2 Single (1 bdrm)
Bathrooms: 1 Ensuite

Quiet and peaceful yet close to town Elm Tree Cottage offers warm country hospitality in the privacy of your own self contained cottage. Set in a beautiful garden, the sun streams in through french windows, Freshly brewed coffee and tea can be enjoyed in the walled garden overlooking the hills while the fountain plays gently in the background.

Bega

The Pickled Pear *B&B*
Wendy and Bob Gornall
60-62 Carp Street
Bega
NSW 2550
In Bega Central

Tel (02) 6492 1393
Fax (02) 6492 0030
info@thepickledpear.com.au
www.thepickledpear.com.au

Double $110-$170 **Single** $99-$130
Child over 12 years
Includes special breakfast
Dinner pre-arranged
Visa MC BC Amex accepted
1 King/Twin 1 Queen 1 Twin (3 bdrm)
Bathrooms: 3 Ensuite

AAA Tourism
★★★★

Special features of our renovated 1870's house include: scrumptious food, charming ensuites (one with spa), private suite available, candlelight dinners - (prearranged), weekend markets, old wares, secluded beaches, national parks surround us, the aura of history, tranquillity and warmth, main street location (walk to restaurants, clubs, shops), read, sleep, walk, fish, paint, golf, or whale watch, no facilities for children, smoking on open verandah, a good stopping off point between Sydney/Melbourne.

Bellingen

Rivendell *B&B*
Janet Hosking
10 Hyde Street
Bellingen
NSW 2454
In Bellingen

Tel (02) 6655 0060
or 0403 238 409
Fax (02) 6655 0060
rivendell@midcoast.com.au
www.rivendellguesthouse.com.au

Double $115-$140 **Single** $99-$140
Includes full breakfast
No smoking on property
Visa MC BC Eftpos accepted
3 Queen 2 Twin (4 bdrm)
Bathrooms: 3 Ensuite 1 Private

AAA Tourism
★★★★

In the heart of the heritage village of Bellingen, Rivendell is a beautifully decorated Federation style home. Luxurious rooms furnished with antiques, feather & down doonas and fluffy bathrobes, open to shady verandahs and picturesque gardens. Take a refreshing dip in the freshwater pool, or in winter, relax by the log fire. After dinner settle back with complimentary port and chocolates. TV, stereo, books, games, magazines and tea/coffee making is provided in the guest lounge. "A warm & homely ambience in a marvellous old home." T & J, Kotara South.

Bellingen

Bellingen Heritage Cottages *Luxury Cottage with Kitchen Self Contained*
Gail and Gus Raymond
7 William Street
Bellingen
NSW 2454
0.25 km W of PO

Tel (02) 6655 1311
or 0428 551 311
Fax (02) 6655 1311
contact@auntylils.com.au
www.auntylils.com.au

Double $150-$160 **Single** $140
Continental Breakfast provisions
$25 extra person
1 King/Twin 2 Queen (3 bdrm)
Bathrooms: 1 Private

Aunty Lil's cottage was built by the Raymond family circa 1910 and lovingly restored to the period with all the comforts of home and beyond. Enjoy fascinating family memorabilia. Lots of pillows and feather doonas and warm cosy atmosphere. In the heart of Bellingen in a quiet street. Self contained - including lounge, dining, full kitchen, 3 bedrooms, bathroom, laundry and verandahs front and back. Cottage garden and off street parking. Walking distance in minutes to Heritage and craft shops, restaurants, the Bellinger River, Markets, and attractions. TV, VCR, sound system, washing machine, line undercover.

Bellingen

CasaBelle Country Guest House *Luxury B&B Guest House*
Suzanne & Fritz
Gleniffer Road
Bellingen
NSW 2454
1.2 km N of Bellingen

Tel (02) 6655 9311
or 0427 550 155
Fax (02) 6655 0166
enquiries@casabelle.com
www.casabelle.com

Double From $195 Single $165
Includes full breakfast
Dinner $60 p.h.
Visa MC BC Eftpos accepted
1 King 2 Queen 2 Single (3 bdrm)
Bathrooms: 3 Ensuite

   AAA Tourism ★★★★☆

CasaBelle invites you to enjoy a very special B&B experience. Step into a tranquil Tuscan courtyard with vibrant bougainvillea and bubbling fountain. Enjoy acres of forest and garden views from your beautifully appointed room furnished with all luxury comforts including TV/DVD, hairdryer, fresh flowers, bowls of fruit and nuts, filter coffees and home-made cakes. Candlelit spa baths, log fires, complimentary port and chocolates, a library of books, CD/DVD's and games. Sumptuous breakfasts served until noon. The perfect indulgence in an idyllic setting. Midway Sydney/Brisbane

Bermagui

Bimbimbi House *B&B Self Contained*
Peter and Beverley Bray
62 Nutleys Creek Road
Bermagui
NSW 2546
32 km S of Narooma

Tel (02) 6493 4456
or 0428 569 803
Fax (02) 6493 4456
bimbimbihouse@bigfoot.com.au
www.bimbimbihouse.com.au

Double $130-$170 Single $100-$120
Child neg
Full Breakfast Provisions
No smoking on property
1 King 1 Queen 2 Double 1 Twin 1 Single (4 bdrm)
Bathrooms: 3 Private

Bimbimbi House accommodation consists of a luxurious suite, cottage and garden room with private bathrooms. Hearty breakfast provisions provided. Access to the verandah or gardens offer peaceful views through magnificent spotted gums overlooking paddocks, river and distant Mt Dromedary. Guests such as Billy Connolly, Ken Done "Today Show" and "Postcards" have all enjoyed the many beautiful birds that visit our Edna Walling style garden. We are located two kilometres from the picturesque township of Bermagui, with restaurants, beaches and golf club. Your stay will always be relaxing, private and memorable.

Bermagui

Bellbird Cottage *B&B*
Laurel & Edwin Lloyd-Jones
88 Nutleys Creek Road
Bermagui
NSW 2546
32 km S of Narooma

Tel (02) 6493 5511
or 0403 772 392
Fax (02) 6493 5511
bellbird@asitis.net.au
www.bellbirdcottage-bnb.com

Double $130 Single $110
Child $20-$40
Includes full breakfast
1 Queen 1 Double 1 Twin (3 bdrm)
Bathrooms: 2 Ensuite Twin room needs to share parent's bathroom.

Tucked into a majestic spotted gum forest, Bellbird Cottage is a bird-lovers paradise allowing tranquil privacy. Close to local fresh fish and oysters, cafes, restaurants, wineries, galleries, golf, fishing, walks and beaches. Two comfortable suites with private entrances. LIBRARY ROOM - own sitting room/library with open fire and attic bedroom for 2 children. COURTYARD ROOM; large suite opening to garden. Heaters, fans, electric blankets, refrigerators, TVs/videos. Home-baked afternoon tea. Full breakfast includes local produce. We share our home with a small dog. A warm welcome is assured.

Bermagui - Tanja

Ngairin on Tanja Lagoon *B&B*
Libby & David Bright
144 Haighs Road
Tanja
NSW 2550
30 km S of Bermagui

Tel (02) 6494 0033
Fax (02) 6494 0023
info@ngairin.com
www.ngairin.com

Double $100 per person
Includes full breakfast
Dinner Luncheons and Dinner $25 - $50
Child by arrangement
2 King 4 Queen 2 Twin (8 bdrm)
Bathrooms: 5 Ensuite

Whales, walks, wallabies, woodfires - birds, books, bandicoots, barbeques - fishing, freshment, food, fun - gliders, gulls, games, 'goodies - canoes, crepes, coots, cheese - sea eagles, music and more are found at "Ngairin" inside coastal Mimosa Rocks National Park. One quiet pair or up to eight couples celebrating can create wonderful memories here. Visiting New Zealand artist pair reported in last year's Christmas newsletter to friends "And the best B&B ever - Ngairin on Tanja Lagoon. Libby and David Bright have a unique place, and they broke the mould with David!"

Berrima

Berrima Guest House *B&B Cottage with Kitchen*
Wendy & Michael Roodbeen
Cnr Oxley & Wilkinson Streets
Berrima
NSW 2577
In Berrima

Tel (02) 4877 2277
Fax (02) 4877 2345
hillside@hinet.net.au
www.berrimaguesthouse.com

Double $135-$220 Single $110-$210
Includes full breakfast
Cottage $300-$420
Visa MC BC accepted
1 King/Twin 5 Queen (6 bdrm)
Bathrooms: 6 Ensuite

O verlooking the historic Southern Highlands picturesque village of Berrima. Built around the original stone cottage tack room stables and old well. Circa 1843 this carefully restored boutique country guesthouse will enchant you. Start the day viewing the platypus in their natural habitat only 500m away, followed by a leisurely gourmet breakfast in the dining room or out on the deck. Stay in one of the six well-appointed centrally heated rooms or pamper yourself in the self contained studio including spa and gas log fire.

Berry

Willowvale Berry *Luxury Separate Suite*
David & Lorna Wardle
290 Woodhill Mountain Road
Berry
NSW 2535
10 km S of Kiama

Tel (02) 4464 1968
Fax (02) 4464 1968
lornawardle_6@hotmail.com
www.willowvaleberry.com.au

Double $160-$220
Full Breakfast Provisions
Visa MC BC Eftpos accepted
2 Queen (1 in each suite bdrm)
Bathrooms: 2 Ensuite

L orna and David are sea changes from Sydney and have travelled extensively to know what is needed for that special weekend away, Willowvale offers glorious views and privacy in your self contained suite with fireplace and all the best of facilities to make your stay special.

Berry - Jaspers Brush

Jaspers Brush B & B and Alpaca Farm
B&B
Leonie and Ian Winlaw
465 Strongs Road
Jaspers Brush
NSW 2535
5 km S of Berry

Tel (02) 4448 6194
or 0418 116 655
Fax (02) 4448 6254
iwinlaw@ozemail.com.au
jaspersbrushbandb.com.au

Double $220
Includes full breakfast
No smoking on property
Visa MC Amex accepted
2 Queen 2 Single (3 bdrm)
Bathrooms: 2 Ensuite 1 Private

AAA Tourism
★★★★☆

Come take breakfast overlooking one of nature's most spectacular creations. Our property, located on the Berry escarpment, commands views that stretch from Jervis Bay to Gerringong, taking in the Shoalhaven River, Mt Coolangatta and the lush green pastures of the coastal plain. The bedrooms, opening onto the wrap around verandah and the view, have private facilities, electric blankets, alpaca fleece doonas, heaters, ceiling fans and fresh flowers from the garden. The house boasts an eclectic art collection and the guest lounge has an open fire with great art, travel, wine and garden books for browsing. A gourmet breakfast is served in the lounge overlooking the views and our herd of alpacas.

Blue Mountains - Katoomba

Melba House *Luxury B&B*
Marion Hall
98 Waratah Street
Katoomba
NSW 2780
In Katoomba

Tel (02) 4782 4141
or 0403 021 074
Fax (02) 4782 7957
stay@melbahouse.com
www.melbahouse.com

Double $195-$249 Single $175-$229
Includes full breakfast
Visa MC BC accepted
1 King/Twin 2 Queen (3 bdrm)
Bathrooms: 3 Ensuite (2 Spas & showers and 1 shower)

AAA Tourism
★★★★☆

Imagine your own open log fire and spa, central-heating, electric blankets, large comfortable suites with own sitting and dining areas, sumptuous breakfasts, that's historical 4.5* Melba House. Luxury at affordable prices. Quiet and secluded yet close to many restaurants, galleries, antique and craftshops and walking tracks. Also, close to the best-loved attractions of Katoomba and Leura. See our website www.melbahouse.com. "Of the B&Bs around the world we have stayed, this is our best experience, it's exquisite." (W, Dallas Texas). Stay 3 consecutive nights Midweek and only pay for 2.

Blue Mountains - Lawson

Araluen *B&B*
George & Gai Sprague
59 Wilson Street
Lawson
NSW 2783
15 km E of Katoomba

Tel (02) 4759 1610
relax@araluen.com
www.araluen.com

Double $135-$220 Single $95-$130
Includes special breakfast
Dinner $35 - 55
No smoking on property
Visa MC BC accepted
3 Queen (3 bdrm)
Bathrooms: 3 Ensuite

  AAA Tourism
★★★★☆

Perfect balance of pampering and privacy. Large, superbly furnished home overlooking mountain bushland. "Perfect beds," modern ensuites, one with double spa-bath. Sumptuous breakfasts. Sunny living room; romantic log-fire. Quiet reading room. Huge games room (pool/billiards, piano, DVD library). Heating/cooling throughout. Prize gardens. Secluded waterfalls nearby. (Candlelit dinners/picnic baskets by arrangement.) Handy all Blue Mountains attractions. Attractive golf packages. "Excellent hosts." "Ideal getaway for up to 3 couples". Reviewed "Australian Good Taste" Dec 2001. SM Herald "Reader Recommendation" 16/03/02. "Qantas Magazine" Oct 2003.

Blue Mountains - Leura

Woodford of Leura *B&B*
John & Lesley Kendall
48 Woodford Street
Leura
NSW 2780
0.75 km E of Leura

Tel (02) 4784 2240
or 0427 410 625
Fax (02) 4784 2240
woodford@leura.com
www.leura.com

Double $135-$190 Single $100-$150
Includes full breakfast
Visa MC BC accepted
1 King 2 Queen 1 Double 2 Twin 1 Single (4 bdrm)
Bathrooms: 4 Ensuite

AAA Tourism
★★★★☆

E legant retreat located in one of Leura's quietest country lanes and set in tranquil, spacious gardens with towering pines. This grand old home offers both suites and standard rooms, all with en-suites, TV and tea making facilities. Woodford is renowned for its sumptuous breakfasts and complimentary afternoon tea on arrival. It also features central heating, indoor heated 4-person spa/jacuzzi and cosy guest lounge with log fire. Winner of 2000 Blue Mountains Regional Award for Excellence in Tourism - Hosted Accommodation. Finalist, 2000 NSW Tourism Awards.

Blue Mountains - Leura

Broomelea *B&B*
Bryan & Denise Keith
273 Leura Mall
Leura
NSW 2780
0.5 km S of Leura

Tel (02) 4784 2940
or 0419 478 400
Fax (02) 4784 2611
info@broomelea.com.au
www.broomelea.com.au

Double $154-$215 Single $130-$190
Includes full breakfast
No smoking on property
Visa MC BC Diners Amex Eftpos accepted
3 Queen 2 Twin (4 bdrm)
Bathrooms: 4 Ensuite

AAA Tourism
★★★★☆

A beautiful 1909 mountain home for guests who would like more than simply a bed and a breakfast. We offer spacious ensuite rooms with 4 poster beds, open fires, lounges, TV, Video, CD Players, a freshly prepared gourmet breakfast each morning and most importantly local knowledge. Broomelea is perfectly located in the Living Heritage precinct of Leura just a 10 minute stroll to famous cliff top walks with great views or our beautiful village with numerous restaurants and galleries.

Blue Mountains - Leura

Bethany Manor Bed & Breakfast *B&B*

Greg & Jill Haigh
8 East View Avenue
Leura
NSW 2780
0.8 km NW of Leura

Tel (02) 4782 9215
or 0402 068 208
Fax (02) 4782 1962
bmanor@optusnet.com.au
www.bethanymanor.com.au

Double $120-$200 Single $100-$170
Includes full breakfast
Visa MC BC accepted
3 Queen (3 bdrm)
Bathrooms: 3 Ensuite

AAA Tourism
★★★★☆

Looking for a welcoming place to call home when visiting the World Heritage Blue Mountains? Bethany Manor is a Federation style home set on over an acre of parklike grounds, with tennis court. Your ensuite bedroom incorporates a spa-bath and verandah access while the Garden View room provides the perfect setting for enjoying a sumptuous breakfast in any season. Centrally heated with a wood fire in the guest's lounge. We're an easy walk to Leura village with its speciality shops, restaurants and railway station.

Blue Mountains - Leura

The Greens of Leura *B&B*

Noel McCarthy & Trish Collinson
26 Grose Street
Leura
NSW 2780
0.15 km SE of Leura

Tel (02) 4784 3241
Fax (02) 4784 3241
greens@hermes.net.au
www.bluemts.com.au/greens

Double $125-$175 Single $105-$125
Includes special breakfast
Visa MC BC Eftpos accepted
4 Queen 1 Twin (5 bdrm)
Bathrooms: 3 Ensuite 2 Guest share

AAA Tourism
★★★★☆

The Greens built in the early 1920's was originally a pair of semi-detached cottages, now converted into a B&B adults retreat. The literary theme is throughout our home focusing on poets and writers inspired by their love of romance and nature. High ceilings, chandeliers, marble fireplace, library (with secret door), full size billiard table and heritage style bedrooms create an ambience of cosy comfort. Only 150 metres to Leura Village Mall, restaurants and cafes. - Central heating - non smoking indoors - sorry, no pets - 4 poster beds.

Blue Mountains - Mount Tomah - Bells Line of Road

Tomah Mountain Lodge *B&B*
Bill & Gai Johns
25 Skyline Road
Mount Tomah via Bilpin
NSW 2758
14 km W of Bilpin

Tel (02) 4567 2111
or 0419 908 724
tomahlodge@ozemail.com.au
www.tomahmountainlodge.com.au

Double $200 Single $170
Includes full breakfast
Dinner $50 each
Visa MC BC Diners Amex Eftpos accepted
1 King/Twin 2 Queen (3 bdrm)
Bathrooms: 3 Ensuite

AAA Tourism
★★★★☆

Tomah Mountain Lodge is situated in the World Heritage Blue Mountains National Park and offers prestige executive style accommodation. Mount Tomah is 1000 metres above sea level with extensive mountain views. This secluded setting is only two minutes drive to Mount Tomah Botanic Garden, and a short drive to the historic gardens at Mount Wilson. The lodge offers spacious & comfortable lounge rooms with log fires. Gourmet three course candlelit dinners are a speciality.

Blue Mountains - Mount Victoria

The Manor House *Guest House Apartment with Kitchen*
Colin and Annette Lenton
Montgomery Street
Mount Victoria
NSW 2786
15 km NW of Katoomba

Tel (02) 4787 1369
Fax (02) 4787 1585
info@themanorhouse.com.au
www.themanorhouse.com.au

Double $155-$230 Single $105-$175
Child 20
Includes full breakfast
Dinner $24-$46
Visa MC BC Amex Eftpos accepted
2 King 13 Queen 3 Double 6 Single (13 in guesthouse, 2 in one apart bdrm)
Bathrooms: 13 Ensuite 2 Private 13 ensuite rooms, 2 apartments

AAA Tourism
★★★☆

Magnificent country house, circa 1876, on 2 quiet acres of lawns and gardens. All facilities are for guests. Heritage ensuite guest rooms or The Servants Quarters, a 4-bedroom self-contained apartment or Orchard View, a 2-bedroom self-contained apartment. Several sitting rooms, billiards room, croquet, large indoor jacuzzi and licensed restaurant.

Blue Mountains - Wentworth Falls

Whispering Pines by the Falls *B&B Country House & Cottages*

Maria & Bill McCabe
178 Falls Road
Wentworth Falls
NSW 2782
8 km E of Katoomba

Tel (02) 4757 1449
or 0412 144 917
Fax (02) 4757 1219
wpines@bigpond.com
www.whisperingpines.com.au

Double $165-$290 Single $120-$290
Includes full breakfast
Cottages $150 - $440
No smoking on property
Visa MC BC Diners Amex Eftpos accepted
3 Queen 1 Double (4 bdrm)
Bathrooms: 3 Ensuite 1 Private

AAA Tourism ★★★★☆

Enjoy the delights of our luxurious heritage-listed B&B set in 4 acres of rambling woodland gardens, and perched on the escarpment at the head of the most spectacular waterfall in the beautiful Blue Mountains. Over 600,000 acres of unspoilt wilderness on our doorstep for you to explore. Our bedrooms are warm and spacious with feather doonas, electric blankets and luxury appointments. Our guests have use of a large lounge with open fire, sunny breakfast room (tea & coffee available at all times) and barbecue facilities.

Blue Mountains - Wentworth Falls

Dove Cottage *Cottage with Kitchen*

Bill & Maria McCabe
c/- 178 Falls Road
Wentworth Falls
NSW 2782
2 km S of Wentworth Falls

Tel (02) 4757 1449
or 0412 144 917
Fax (02) 4757 1219
wpines@bigpond.com
www.whisperingpines.com.au

Double $150-$250
Child $50
Accommodation Only
Extra person $50. B&B from $240.
Visa MC BC Diners Amex Eftpos accepted
2 Queen 2 Single (3 bdrm)
Bathrooms: 1 Ensuite 1 Guest share Double corner spa bath and showers

Built in traditional mountains' style, this ultra-modern 3 bedroom cottage has every amenity and luxury essential for you to enjoy your holiday. The main bedroom opens onto the front deck and has an enormous ensuite with double corner spa bath. Two large bedrooms upstairs allow others to escape to their own private retreat. Fireplace, central heating/air conditioning, stereo system, surround sound home entertainment room, natural gas BBQ, large modem kitchen and dining room for 8 people. Very close to the National Park walking trails.

Blue Mountains - Wentworth Falls

Blue Mountains Lakeside *B&B New Self Contained Spa Suite*
Michaela Russell
30 Bellevue Road
Wentworth Falls
NSW 2782
1 km N of Wentworth Falls

Tel (02) 4757 3777
Fax (02) 4757 3444
stay@lakesidebandb.com.au
www.lakesidebandb.com.au

Double $155-$210 **Single** $125-$180
Includes special breakfast
Ask about our mid-week specials
Visa MC BC accepted
2 Queen (2 bdrm)
Bathrooms: 2 Ensuite

Blue Mountains' only waterfront Bed & Breakfast.
At the edge of the Lake in the heart of the mountains. Looking for somewhere special with a log fire and spa? Choose the new self contained Reflections Spa Suite with living room and verandah or the traditional Lake Suite - both suites with amazing views. Your personal walking guide and or pamper packages available or soothing in-house massage. Perhaps a delicious picnic by the Lake, hampers organised. Complimentary boat and fishing gear. Delicious cooked breakfasts with home grown produce. Minutes to Echo Point and the Three Sisters. "An amazing piece of paradise." Michael and Ashley. (From our Visitors' Book)

Blue Mountains - Wentworth Falls

Monique's Bed & Breakfast Establishment *B&B Cottage with Kitchen*
Ian Williamson
31 Falls Road
Wentworth Falls
NSW 2782
0.4 km S of Wentworth Falls

Tel (02) 4757 1646
Fax (02) 4757 2498
moniques@ram.net.au
www.moniques.com.au

Double $100-$180
Full Breakfast Provisions
Whole Cottage $300-$390
No smoking on property
1 King 1 Queen 1 Double 1 Single (3 bdrm)
Bathrooms: 3 Ensuite

Guests stay in the private, self-contained cottage. There are three bedrooms (king, queen/twin, double), each with ensuite, a large comfortable lounge/dining room with enclosed log fire, TV/video, a fully-equipped kitchen and a sunny terrace. The French Provincial style house and cottage are set in a quiet, mature garden. Features include:

* generous provisions for self prepared breakfast
* walking distance to village shops and cafes
* suitable for couples, groups of friends, families

* close to famous bushwalks
* log fire, heating, electric blankets
* attractive longer-stay rates.

Blue Mountains - Woodford

Braeside *B&B*
Robyn Wilkinson & Rex Fardon
97 Bedford Road
Woodford
NSW 2778
18 km E of Katoomba

Tel (02) 4758 6279
or 0414 542 860
Fax (02) 4758 8210
Braeside.BandB@bigpond.com
www.bluemts.com.au/braeside

Double $110-$130 Single $75-$85
Child by arrangement
Includes full breakfast
Dinner available
Visa MC BC accepted
1 King/Twin 1 Queen 1 Double (3 bdrm)
Bathrooms: 2 Ensuite 1 Private

Situated in the heart of the mountains Braeside offers a quiet escape as well as being central to all the attractions of the upper mountains. Bedrooms include one king/twin room with a private bathroom and air conditioning; a queensized room with ensuite and air conditioning. The double "family" room has an ensuite and small adjoining room for children. All beds have electric blankets and the guests lounge has an open log fire for colder weather. No smoking indoors. Dinner available.

Broken Hill

Royal Exchange Hotel *Art Deco Boutique Hotel*
Michael & Carol Robinson
320 Argent Street
Broken Hill
NSW 2880
In Town Centre

Tel (08) 8087 2308
or 1800 670 160
Fax (08) 8087 2191
info@RoyalExchangeHotel.com
www.RoyalExchangeHotel.com

Double $215-$265 Single $195-$245
Includes full breakfast
Visa MC BC Diners Amex Eftpos accepted
22 King/Twin 2 Queen (24 bdrm)
Bathrooms: 24 Ensuite

This Art Deco Boutique Hotel has the charm of a bygone era while incorporating all refinements of a modern, first class establishment. It is the ideal base - whether one is visiting for business or for pleasure - and occupies a prime location close to public transport, shops, banks, post office, travel agencies, tourist information, car rental offices, the Convention Centre, cafEs, restaurants and the town's nightlife with its innumerable pubs and clubs. Guests may relax in a large, handsomely furnished lounge, divided into intimate fire-placed nooks.

Byron Bay
Baystay *B&B Homestay*
John Witham
30 Marvell Street
Byron Bay
NSW 2481
0.4 km E of town

Tel 0418 857 509
Fax (02) 6685 7609
baystay@nor.com.au

Double $98-$118 Single $77-$88
Child $25
Includes special breakfast
Visa MC BC accepted
1 Queen 3 Double 3 Twin 1 Single (4 bdrm)
Bathrooms: 2 Ensuite 1 Family share 1 Guest share 2 Private

Quiet, yet only a short stroll to beach and town. Set in a lush native garden, Baystay is a lovely modern beach house offering great value and great breakfasts. With delightful and comfortable guestrooms, spa, sauna, BBQ, bikes, a beautiful spotty poodle and an amusing Gizmo, your stay will be relaxing and enjoyable. Your host, John, has lived in the area for over 18 years and can guide you on wonderful bush tours in and around town or just assist you to relax.

Byron Bay
Sandals B&B *B&B*
Sue & David Shearer
1/11 Carlyle Street
Byron Bay
NSW 2481
In Byron Bay Central

Tel (02) 6685 8025
or 0414 658 025
Fax (02) 6685 8599
baysand@linknet.com.au
www.byron-bay.com/sandals

Double $110-$120 Single $95
Includes full breakfast
Surcharge during holidays
Visa MC BC accepted
2 Queen 2 Twin 1 Single (5 bdrm)
Bathrooms: 2 Ensuite 2 Guest share

AAA Tourism
★★★★

Nestled in a quiet cul-de-sac in the heart of Byron, close to the many attractions, Sandals is a short stroll past the many and varied high quality shops and restaurants to the town centre and Main Beach. Sandals is more than just another Bed & Breakfast - it is a home away from home.....a place to unwind, soak in the sunlight, put your feet up and enjoy our complimentary tea, coffee and home-made biscuits any time of the day. To your charming hosts, your comfort, relaxation and every need is their only priority. Winter Specials.

Byron Bay

Victoria's at Ewingsdale & Victoria's at Watego's *B&B*

Victoria McEwen
Marine Parade & McGettigans Lane
Byron Bay
NSW 2481
2 km E & 6 km W of Byron Bay

Tel (02) 6684 7047
or (02) 6685 5388
Fax (02) 6684 7687
indulge@victorias.net.au
www.victorias.net.au

Double $225-$599
Includes full breakfast
Visa MC BC Diners Amex accepted
10 Queen (10 bdrm)
Bathrooms: 10 Ensuite

Only minutes from Byron Bay, is the multi-award winning "Victoria's At Ewingsdale" (formerly "Ewingsdale Country Guest House"). This stately country manor is situated on 3 acres of landscaped gardens, and features panoramic ocean, mountain and rural views. "Victoria's at Wategos", is a stunning Tuscan style guest house, nestled in an exclusive ocean front valley at beautiful Wategos beach, just under the famous Cape Byron lighthouse, Experience personalised service in our small and exclusive boutique retreats, dedicated to providing the best in first class hospitality, quality and style.

Byron Bay Hinterland

Green Mango Hideaway *B&B*

Susie Briscoe
Lofts Road, off Coolamon Scenic Drive
Coorabell
NSW 2479
12 km W of Byron Bay

Tel (02) 6684 7171
relax@greenmango.com.au
www.greenmango.com.au

Double $165-$250 Single $140-$220
Includes full breakfast
Visa MC BC Eftpos accepted
2 King 2 Queen (4 bdrm)
Bathrooms: 4 Ensuite

From the moment you walk down its leafy path, you'll be captivated by the tropical atmosphere of this peaceful & secluded B&B set in the spectacular country behind Byron Bay. With just four guestrooms, each with ensuite & verandah, you'll be escaping the crowds and yet be within 10 minutes of fabulous shops & cafes and glorious beaches. The muslin-draped beds & Oriental decor, sparkling palm-fringed pool, sitting room with log fire, lush gardens with abundant birdlife and the wonderful breakfasts & warm hospitality all guarantee you a relaxing memorable stay.

Byron Bay Hinterland

The Tin Dog *B&B*
Sue and Mark Kelly
Macadamia Lane
Federal
NSW 2480
23 km W of Byron Bay

Tel (02) 6688 4465
Fax (02) 6688 4436
relax@thetindog.com.au
thetindog.com.au

Double $160-$220 **Single** $125-$165
Includes full breakfast
Visa MC BC accepted
1 King/Twin 3 Queen (4 bdrm)
Bathrooms: 4 Ensuite

A luxury haven within a wonderful tropical setting where uncompromising but uncomplicated service provides guests with a peaceful escape. Relax on the palm fringed deck by the pool or next to a log fire in the cooler months. Enjoy a fabulous gourmet breakfast made from local produce served on the sunny verandahs. Stylishly furnished with four large guestrooms, spa & clawfoot bath available. Two pavilion style rooms adjoin the main building, all have private verandahs. Only a 20 min drive to Byron Bay and Bangalow.

Byron Hinterland - Clunes via Byron Bay

Suzanne's Hideaway *Cottage with Kitchen*
Peter & Suzanne McGuinness
20 Elliot Road,
Clunes via Byron Bay
NSW 2480
18 km NE of Lismore

Tel (02) 6629 1228
Fax (02) 6629 1756
suzanne@suzanneshideaway.com.au
www.suzanneshideaway.com.au

Double $130-$240 **Single** $130-$240
Child $10
Accommodation Only only
Extra adult $20
Visa MC BC accepted
2 King/Twin2 King 6 Queen 4 Single (6 bdrm)
Bathrooms: 1 Ensuite 6 Private villas have own large spa baths each

4 star AAA rated. Your own private resort. Large 1, 2, or 3 bedroom S/C villas with spa baths or S/C studio. Set on hill in sub-tropical gardens and vast panorama. Walk to our rain forest lined river and swim or fish. Enjoy the use of our salt water swimming pool, floodlit synthetic grass tennis court and gym equipment. Linen included, A/C TV/VCR or DVD, CD/radio. BBQ. Laundry. Licensed general store, cafes and butcher nearby. Byron Bay/ Lismore/National Park 20 mins. drive. Treat yourself to a luxurious quiet hideaway. Children welcome.

Candelo - Bega Valley

Bumblebrook Farm *B&B Homestay Farmstay Apartment with Kitchen*
Rick & Ann Patten
Kemps Lane
Candelo
NSW 2550
20 km SW of Bega

Tel (02) 6493 2238
Fax (02) 6493 2299
stay@bumblebrook.com.au

Double $100-$115 Single $80-$110
Child under 13 free
Includes full breakfast
Dinner $40
Visa MC BC accepted
1 King/Twin 1 Queen 3 Double 4 Single (4 bdrm)
Bathrooms: 4 Ensuite

A 100 acre beef property on top of a hill with magnificent views and lovely bush walks, fronting Tantawangalo Creek. We have four well equipped self-contained units. Breakfast is a "cook-your-own" from our fresh farm ingredients. Children are welcome and can often help feed the farm animals. With prior notice guests are welcome to a friendly, candlelit, family dinner in the homestead. BBQs are provided by the creek and in the rustic playground near the units. Beaches and National Parks nearby. Pets welcome with prior arrangement.

~

Central Coast - Avoca Beach - Terrigal

Avoca Valley Bed & Breakfast *Luxury B&B*
Robin & Dennis Eyre
243 Avoca Drive
Avoca Beach
NSW 2251
3 km W of Avoca Beach

Tel 0404 240 463
or 02 4368 6316
Fax 02 4368 6316
relax@avocavalleybnb.com.au
www.avocavalleybnb.com.au

Double $150-$220 Single $110-$160
Includes full breakfast
Visa MC BC Diners Eftpos accepted
3 Queen 1 Twin (3 bdrm)
Bathrooms: 3 Ensuite Double spa

A voca Valley is a 4.5 star luxury, romantic retreat for couples, located in a tranquil valley on the Central Coast of NSW. It is five minutes from Avoca and Terrigal beaches, yet only one hour from Sydney and Newcastle. French doors lead to private, sunny terraces offering stunning valley views from each elegant suite. Gourmet breakfasts, stylish marble ensuites, spa, and a cosy fireplace ensure you'll want to return time and time again. Ask about our packages & complimentary transfers to local restaurants.

Central Coast - Bateau Bay

Bateau Bay Beachfront Luxury Spa Accommodation for Couples *Luxury-Spa-Suites-Opposite-the-Beach.*

Lyn Rundle
22 Reserve Drive
Bateau Bay
NSW 2261
0.25 km E of Bateau Bay -Post Office

Tel (02) 4332 6887
or 0414 326 887
Fax (02) 4333 3667
info@bateaubaybeachfront.com.au
www.bateaubaybeachfront.com.au

Double $220-$300   Includes full breakfast
Visa MC BC Amex Eftpos accepted
1 King 2 Queen (3 bdrm)
Bathrooms: 3 Ensuite 3 Private 2 person Oval Spas

Bateau-Bay-Beachfront-Luxury-Romantic-Couples-Spa-Accomm-90min North of Sydney-60min South of Newcastle-Ocean-Views-Beach-Opposite-Heated -Saltwater-10 mtr-Pool. Beachfront-King-Spa-Suite-Poolside-Queen-Spa-Suites. Large-Bathrooms-En-suites-Oval-Spas-Separate-Shower-Toilet-Heated Towel Rails Bath Robes-Massage Roller-Candles around Spa-Comp DVDs.Linen-Towels-R/c-AirCon-Ceiling Fans- Large Screen TV/DVD/CD-Fridge-Microwave Oven-Elec Jug-Toaster-Crockery- Cutlery-Tea/Coffee-Crystal Glasses-Lounge-Dining Table & Chairs-Iron-Ironing Board-Elec Safe-Clock Radio-BBQ on Deck overlooking Ocean. Special- Breakfast delivered to suites.

Central Coast - Empire Bay

The Getaway Place *B&B*
Kathleen Smith
20 Pomona Road
Empire Bay
NSW 2257
10 km W of Woy Woy

Tel (02) 4363 1238
or 0415 785 814
Fax (02) 4369 3126
thegetawayplace@zipworld.com.au
www.thegetawayplace.com.au

Double $135-$190
Child On application
Includes full breakfast
Visa MC BC Diners accepted
1 King/Twin1 King 1 Queen (2 bdrm)
Bathrooms: 1 Ensuite 1 Private

The Getaway Place provides premier bed & breakfast accommodation in the heart of the beautiful NSW Central Coast. Nestled in an acre plus of secluded landscaped gardens, the residence is just minutes away from Bouddi National Park, beautiful beaches (including Killcare) and the cosmopolitan centres of Terrigal and Avoca. The Getaway Place provides a memorable and enjoyable experience for a well deserved respite. Your hosts are dedicated to being available at all times to ensure you have a relaxing break in an atmosphere without resident pets or children.

Central Coast - Green Point

Binawee Bed & Breakfast *Luxury B&B*
Kevin & Patricia O'Donnell
295 Avoca Drive
Green Point
NSW 2251
7 km E of Gosford

Tel (02) 4369 0981
or 0418 203 671
Fax (02) 4369 0997
info@binawee.com.au
www.binawee.com.au

Double $150-$230 Single $100
Includes full breakfast
Dinner B/A
Visa MC BC Amex accepted
3 Queen 1 Twin (4 bdrm)
Bathrooms: 3 Ensuite 1 Family share 1 spa bath

Luxury accommodation featuring three theme rooms Baywatch, Titanic family suite, Barrier Reef & Lighthouse. Hosts Kevin & Patricia greet guests with aperitifs and welcoming drinks whilst overlooking extensive water views. Guests can wander in the gardens, relax by the solar pool or indulge in the therapeutic spa. In winter enjoy the open fire and sunroom where we offer full video, CD, DVD and Foxtel. Binawee offers Gourmet Breakfasts, barbeque and tea making trolley. We are close to Terrigal, Erina, arts, cinemas, restaurants, beaches, Bushwalking, Reptile Park. Free pickup from Rail, Bus or Ferry.

Central Coast - Terrigal - Avoca

The Acreage B&B - Avoca Beach *Luxury B&B*
Leonie Lovell
110 Picketts Valley Road
Avoca Beach
NSW 2251
3 km N of Avoca Beach/Terrigal

Tel (02) 4382 4651
or 0419 133 334
Fax (02) 4382 6084
avoca.acreage@bigpond.com
www.theacreagebb.com.au

Double $150-$220 Includes full breakfast
Visa MC BC Eftpos accepted
4 Queen 1 Double (4 bdrm)
Bathrooms: 4 Private 3 suites with Spa baths

The perfect short break solution . . . enjoy the best of both worlds. The Acreage B&B is an Award Winning retreat providing luxury accommodation in rural surroundings, only minutes to Avoca and Terrigal Beaches. 1.5 hour's drive north of Sydney. This luxury B&B offers privacy combined with the highest level of hospitality and service. The elegantly decorated Queen sized air conditioned suites are designed for maximum comfort and privacy. Each suite offers magnificent views and has a luxurious marble bathroom with Spa bath, bathrobes and aromatherapy products. Four Course breakfast daily. Wine/champagne on arrival, morning newspapers.

Central Coast - Tuggerah

Greenacres B&B *B&B Cottage with Kitchen*
Elizabeth & John Fairweather
8 Carpenters Lane
Mardi
NSW 2259
1 km W of Tuggerah

Tel (02) 4353 0643
or (02) 4353 0309
jl_f@tpg.com.au
www.greenacres-bb.com

Double $125-$160 **Single** $110-$145
Full Breakfast Provisions
1 Queen (1 bdrm)
Bathrooms: 1 Ensuite

W elcome to Greenacres B&B, a unique tranquil retreat set on 3.5 evergreen acres, yet only minutes from Westfield Tuggerah, the railway station and factory outlet stores. Relax in your fully self contained air conditioned suite with queen bed, sofa bed, television, VCR & DVD. The Property offers for your enjoyment a 14m salt water swimming pool, outdoor spa, Bali style gazebo's, extensive landscaped gardens with waterfalls, fountains, ponds, dam, bushwalking trails and a 7 hole novice golf course. We are also pet friendly with a pet enclosure located next to the suite.

Central Tilba

The Stay at Tintagel *Farmstay Cottage with Kitchen*
Peter and Kathryn Essex
228 Armitage Road
Central Tilba - Tilba Tilba
NSW 2546
10 km N of Central Tilba

Tel (02) 4476 3952
thestayattintagel@home.netspeed.com.au
www.bbbook.com.au/thestayatfintagel.
html

Double $110-$130 **Single** $100-$110
Full Breakfast Provisions
Dinner From $35
Visa MC BC accepted
1 Queen (1 bdrm)
Bathrooms: 1 Ensuite 1 Private Cottage has two bathrooms,
one with bath and other with shower

N ot just a room, it's a home and it's all yours. Watched over by sacred Gulaga Mountain The Stay offers a haven of privacy and tranquillity for anyone looking for a quiet, romantic escape. The self-contained cottage offers unique features including two bathrooms,(one with a claw-foot bath for two) spacious lounge, full kitchen and private courtyard with barbecue. Set on 50 acres The Stay is a wonderful place to bushwalk, picnic by the dams or gather fruit, herbs and vegies from the seasonal organic garden. Pristine beaches and historic Tilba are minutes away.

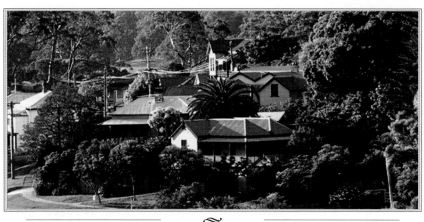

Central Tilba - Tilba Tilba - Narooma

The Two Story B&B *B&B*
Ken & Linda Jamieson
Bate Street
Central Tilba
NSW 2546
In Central Tilba

Tel (02) 4473 7290 or 1800 355 850
Fax (02) 4473 7290
stay@tilbatwostory.com
www.babs.com.au/twostory

Double $105-$110 Single $85-$95
Includes full breakfast
Visa MC BC Eftpos accepted
2 Queen 1 Double 1 Single (3 bdrm)
Bathrooms: 3 Ensuite

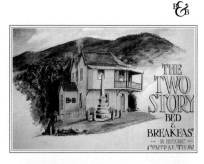

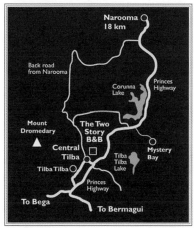

A warm welcome awaits you from Aussie hosts Ken and Linda Jamieson and family at the Two Story B&B. Nestled in foothills of Mt Dromedary situated in National Trust Village of Central Tilba. Our building is 108 years old built 1894 and was originally the Post Office and residence, it has great character and views overlook a superb valley of rolling hills and lush greenness, enjoy atmosphere and warmth, a glass of Tilba Port in front of our log fire. Our weather is temperate and beaches are close by. Situated 300km south of Sydney. The Craft Village of Central Tilba is extensive, businesses include: leather shop, tea rooms, alpaca shop, cheese factory, woodturning gallery and more. A short scenic drive takes you to a local winery, short drives to Bermagui and Cobargo, bushwalking, fishing and swimming. We offer our guests a choice of continental and full cooked breakfasts with tea/coffee facilities, off street parking, in a total relaxed atmosphere in pleasant old world charm and non smoking environment. Enquire about our package: 2 nights at The Two Story B&B and 3 nights at Bateman's Bay.

Cobargo

Old Cobargo Convent *Homestay Cottage with Kitchen*
Bob & Dianne Saunders
Wandella Road
Cobargo
NSW 2550
0.5 km W of Cobargo

Tel (02) 6493 6419
or 0413 362 812
Fax (02) 6493 6419
oldconvent@asitis.net.au
www.cobargoconvent.com.au

Double $120-$130 Single $65
Includes full breakfast   Dinner $20
No smoking on property
Visa MC BC accepted
2 Queen 2 Single (3 bdrm)
Bathrooms: 2 Ensuite 1 Guest share 1 Private

AAA Tourism ★★★★

Experience the ambience of yesteryear, built in 1917 our historic Old Convent is restored and with antiques. French doors lead onto the verandah where you can admire unspoilt rural views. Choose from 3 tastefully decorated bedrooms or the fully self contained Old Schoolhouse, peaceful and private with 2 bedrooms, claw footed bath, wood heater and loads of charm and character. Only a short stroll to the historic working village of Cobargo with much of its original architecture and many unique shops. A short drive to Tilba, Narooma or Bermagui. We have a friendly cat.

~

Cobargo

Eilancroft Country Retreat *B&B Homestay*
Margaret and George Law
County Boundary Road
Cobargo
NSW 2550
8 km W of Cobargo

Tel (02) 6493 7362
or 0438 628 689
glaw2@bigpond.com.au
www.bbbook.com.au/eilancroft.html

Double $120 Single $90
Includes full breakfast
Visa MC BC accepted
2 Queen (2 bdrm)
Bathrooms: 2 Ensuite

Welcome to our lovely 100 year old home, located amidst spectacular mountain scenery, overlooking the historic village of Cobargo. Our rooms have comfortable Queen beds, electric blankets, ensuites and private verandahs. We offer intimate B&B accommodation with two guest rooms both with ensuite bathrooms, a guest lounge/ dining room with wood fire, tea & coffee making facilities. We have a smoke free interior. Nearby, beautiful Bermagui and Narooma beaches, historic Tilba, cheese factories and wineries. We look forward to meeting you and sharing our love of this beautiful area with you.

Coffs Harbour

Mount Boambee Retreat *Luxury B&B*
Eva & Carl Southern
200C Ayrshire Park Drive
Coffs Harbour
NSW 2450
9 km S of Coffs Harbour

Tel (02) 6658 5701
or 0414 327 545
Fax (02) 6658 5702
book@mbr.com.au   www.mbr.com.au

Double $120-$220 Single $120-$190
Includes special breakfast
Dinner By Arrangement
Seasonal rates. Specials for extended stays.
Extra person $60
Visa MC BC Diners Amex Eftpos accepted
1 King 1 Queen (2 bdrm)
Bathrooms: 2 Ensuite Queen room with deluxe soaking bath

Welcoming, relaxed and comfortable. Mount Boambee Retreat offers stylish, secluded accommodation only minutes from the centre of Coffs Harbour. Two deluxe air conditioned suites each with ensuite bathrooms, one with a luxury soaking bath, in the character of cast iron claw footed baths - contemporary but chic. Thoughtful landscaping and a creative touch with furnishings and decorating has created a sympathetic harmony in design.
Guests are welcomed with complementary drinks in the fridge, chocolates, quality toiletries and fine bed linen. Eva is a fully qualified Aromatherapist and is able to offer treatments on request. Both suites overlook the beautiful Boambee Valley with views over banana plantations to Sawtell and the Pacific Ocean. Private entrances from each suite lead into the garden and to the swimming pool - pick fresh fruit in season straight from the tree, including mangoes, paw paws and avocados. Climb Boambee Ridge for spectacular mountains and ocean views or take a bush walk into the Koala habitat eucalypt forest.
We welcome couples as well as families (we have twin boys ourselves) to enjoy the semi tropical north coast.
Located west of the Pacific Highway and only minutes to beaches, restaurants, the city centre, University, Sawtell and Bonville International Golf Club and transport links - airport, train and bus stations. Complementary pick up.

Coffs Harbour

Sapphire Beach House *Luxury B&B Cottage No Kitchen*
Julie & Ron Pike
16A Elouera Drive
Sapphire Beach
NSW 2450
9 km N of Coffs Harbour

Tel (02) 6653 7554
or 0407 231 787
Fax (02) 6653 7856
pikey@wxc.com.au
www.sapphirebeachretreat.com.au

Double $170-$220 Single $130-$180
Includes full breakfast
Visa MC BC Diners Amex accepted
1 King 1 Queen (2 bdrm)
Bathrooms: 2 Ensuite

Sapphire Beach House - Luxury Beachfront B&B that enjoys magnificent 180-degree ocean views, that allow you to relax and enjoy the ocean's ambience.
The SeaView Room has a king size bed, large private ensuite and magnificent ocean views from all the windows. The Studio, separate from the main house is delightfully intimate, with queen size bed, private ensuite, CD player, mini frig, microwave, tea/coffee making facilities, air conditioning and it too has magical ocean views. Each room features huge windows that capture the ever changing seascape, luxury cotton bed linen, glass walled double shower and wall mounted remote TV/VCR.

A further walk downstairs and along a private walkway of sub-tropical vegetation and you are on the sands of the beautiful Sapphire Beach. Walk to nearby restaurant or a short drive to the centre of the coastal resort town of Coffs Harbour with its many cafes, restaurants and diverse local attractions.

COFFS HARBOUR
BEST BED & BREAKFASTS

Wonderful accomodation
Unique locations
Welcoming hospitality
Generous breakfasts
Discover Coffs Harbour, New South Wales
www.coffsharbourbb.com.au
stay@coffsharbourbb.com.au

Coffs Harbour

Santa Fe Luxury Bed & Breakfast *B&B Cottage No Kitchen*

Sharon Howell
235 Gaudrons Road
Coffs Harbour
NSW 2450
9 km N of Coffs Harbour

Tel (02) 6653 7700
Fax (02) 6653 7050
info@santafe.net.au
www.santafe.net.au

Double $165-$250
Includes full breakfast
Visa MC BC Diners Amex accepted
1 King 2 Queen 1 Twin (3 bdrm)
Bathrooms: 3 Ensuite

SANTA FE is not only the romance of Santa Fe but the irresistible appeal of it's lifestyle . . . a casual elegance. Tucked away in a secluded valley just 10 minutes nth of Coffs Harbour & 2 minutes to Beautiful Sapphire Beach. Discover 6 acres of total luxury . . . adobe walls, vibrant colours, hammocks, textures & fragrances. Guest suites are each a haven, lavishly and romantically furnished with gorgeous ensuites, TV/DVD, plunger coffee, toiletries, hair dryers & pool towels. All have private entrances & decks with table & chairs. 'Navajo' suite has a covered outdoor spa overlooking the lagoon & valley.

Coffs Harbour - Hinterland

Orara Valley View *B&B*
Judi & Bob Bray-Ferguson
553 Upper Orara Road
Upper Orara
NSW 2450
17 km W of Coffs Harbour

Tel (02) 6653 8603
or 0408 194 812
Fax (02) 6643 5767
info@OraraValleyView.com
www.oraravalleyview.com

Double $150-$165 Single $130
Includes full breakfast
Dinner $40-$50
Visa MC BC accepted
1 Queen (1 bdrm)
Bathrooms: 1 Ensuite

An exclusive Bed & Breakfast Experience to remember. Set in the Coffs Hinterland. Orara Valley is a beautiful fifteen minute drive winding up into the foothills of one of Australia's most treasured valleys. Be welcomed by your hosts Bob & Judi. Experience the serenity of your own private balcony take in the sunset swim in the saltwater pool soak in your private heated spa relax in your own separate lounge. Awaken to the bird songs and feast on our delicious gourmet breakfasts.

Coffs Harbour - Sawtell
Woodlands Beach House B&B *B&B*
Ron & Judy Woodlands
4 Boronia Street
Sawtell
NSW 2452
8 km S of Coffs Harbour

Tel (02) 6658 9177
or 0410 543 824
Fax (02) 6658 9177
juron727@ecopost.com.au
www.woodlandsbeachouse.com.au

Double $120-$165 Single up to$125
Includes special breakfast
Visa MC BC accepted
2 Queen (2 bdrm)
Bathrooms: 2 Ensuite

Woodlands is situated near the southern headland of Sawtell with beautiful views of the ocean, creek estuary and Bongil Bongil National Park. The surf beach, rock pool and lookout are nearby. Sawtell is an unspoilt seaside village, containing popular restaurants, heritage cinema, shops and clubs. Activities available include surfing, fishing, boating and golf. Coffs Harbour and its attractions are only 10 minutes away. We have two rooms, both tastefully decorated and with private ensuites. One has ocean views. Airport, rail or coach transfers are available.

Coffs Harbour - Sawtell
Alamanda Lodge Sawtell *B&B*
Sue & Wal Midgley
59 Boronia Street
Sawtell
NSW 2452
In Sawtell

Tel (02) 6658 9099
sue@alamanda.com.au
www.alamanda.com.au

Double $95-$150 Single $85-$120
Includes special breakfast
Visa MC BC accepted
4 Queen (4 bdrm)
Bathrooms: 4 Ensuite

Alamanda Lodge is 4 Star accommodation situated within 5 minutes of Sawtell Beach, BYO restaurants and unique cinema. A stylish B&B purpose built for couples. Four queen rooms with private bathrooms and balconies. Whether it's a short getaway, a relaxing holiday, or a stopover our "rather special place" provides our guests with an atmosphere in which to spoil themselves. Breakfast included in tariff is buffet style with a selection of fresh fruits, cereals, eggs, toasts and spreads. A full cooked breakfast is an optional extra.

Coffs Harbour - Sawtell

Boambee Palms Bed & Breakfast *B&B*

Marcus and Colleen Blackwell
5 Kasch Road
Coffs Harbour
NSW 2450
6 km S of Coffs Harbour

Tel (02) 6658 4545
or 0417 787 790
Fax (02) 6658 4545
info@boambeepalms.com.au
www.boambeepalms.com.au

Double $130-$205 **Single** $100-$205
Includes full breakfast
Visa MC BC accepted
1 King/Twin2 King 2 Queen (5 bdrm)
Bathrooms: 4 Ensuite 1 Private

AAA Tourism
★★★★☆

The perfect couples only escape. Everything a guest could wish for is here, 4 acres of lush landscaped gardens abundant with bird life. Facilities include floodlit tennis court, large sub tropical pool with BBQ area. There are four well appointed King and queen ensuite rooms some with double spas. All rooms have private entrances, outside seating areas, TV, CD, DVD, mini fridges, bathrobes, tea/plunger coffee, hair dryers and complimentary fruit bowls. A luxurious 3 course gourmet breakfast is served daily on the balcony overlooking the pool.

Cooma - Snowy Mountains - Nimmitabel

Royal Arms *B&B*

Bernadette Green
Snowy Mountains Highway
Nimmitabel
NSW 2631
In Nimmitabel Central

Tel (02) 6454 6422
Fax (02) 6454 6433
stay@royalarms.com.au
www.royalarms.com.au

Double From $75 per person
Includes full breakfast
Dinner $20 -$30
Visa MC BC Eftpos accepted
4 Double 4 Twin (8 bdrm)
Bathrooms: 2 Ensuite 2 Private

 AAA Tourism
★★★★

Historic Royal Arms in pioneering village of Nimmitabel, restored featuring modern facilities whilst retaining its olde world charm with antique furnishings. Since 1989, family-staff have provided weary travellers with a friendly atmosphere plus hearty country meals (a tradition that began back in the 1850's when it played host to horse drawn carriages), picnic baskets on request. Our delightful building was used as the hotel in 1960' film "The Sundowners". Central, trout fishing, bird watching, bush walks, wineries, ski fields, beaches. Come on home to the Royal Arms. 20 min Cooma, only 1 1/2 hours Canberra. Group Bookings, car and bike clubs welcome.

Cowra

Conargo B&B Woodstock *B&B Cottage with Kitchen*

Barbara & Peter Carne
Conargo, 286 Nargong Road
Woodstock
NSW 2793
30 km N of Cowra

Tel (02) 6345 0365
or 0429 848 232
Fax (02) 6345 0004
conargo_woodstock@hotmail.com
www.bbbook.com.au/conargo.html

Double $121 Single $88
Includes full breakfast
Dinner $30 B/A
Visa MC BC accepted
1 King/Twin 1 Queen (2 bdrm)
Bathrooms: 2 Ensuite

A quiet friendly stylish Bed & Breakfast where our guests enjoy comfort and privacy of this purpose-built cottage on a fine wool Merino property on sealed road - between Blayney and Cowra (30km from Cowra) in the beautiful clean air of the Central Tablelands. Bedrooms have ensuites and all rooms open onto a wide verandahs with spectacular views of rolling hills, trees and pastures. Birds and wildlife abound. Delicious breakfasts served or self-cater if preferred. Dinners are a speciality on request.

Cowra - Mandurama

Millamolong *Homestay Farmstay*

James and Sue Ashton
Millamolong Station
Mandurama
NSW 2792
16 km W of Mandurama

Tel (02) 6367 5241
or 0418 635 143
Fax (02) 6367 5120
millamolong@ix.net.au
www.millamolong.com.au

Double $160-$240 Single $45-$150
Child $0-$80
Includes full breakfast
from $45 per person
No smoking on property
8 Queen 8 Double (8 bdrm)
Bathrooms: 3 Ensuite 3 Family share

M illamolong is a large working station in the central west of NSW famous for its leisurely and relaxing atmosphere. It has thousands of sheep and cattle and hundreds of horses. Millamolong offers luxury accommodation at the homestead and budget accommodation at the historic slab farmhouse. Enjoy country cuisine in our fully licensed restaurant with a wide range of local wines. Horse riding, children, polo are all a feature. A tennis court and swimming pool are available and guests can fish in the beautiful Belubula River.

Crookwell

Minnamurra Farmstay *B&B Homestay Farmstay*
Tony & Mary Prell
Minnamurra
Crookwell
NSW 2583
15 km SE of Crookwell

Tel (02) 4848 1226
Fax (02) 4848 1288
tprell@wirefree.net.au
www.bbbook.com.au/minnamurra.html

Double $180 Single $80
Child $40, 5 - 12yrs
Includes special breakfast
Dinner $65
1 Double 2 Twin 1 Single (4 bdrm)
Bathrooms: 1 Ensuite 1 Guest share 1 in guest bathroom

Multiple award winning Minnamurra Farmstay is a 1080 hectare farm, 3 hours from Sydney. Our home is warm, friendly and comfortable with fresh flowers in every room and tender loving care always on hand. Special breakfast - other meals by arrangement. Good homestyle country cooking. Laundry facilities available. Smoke-free and quiet - no children under 5. Walk where you will over undulating and picturesque country. Tennis. Trout fishing. Farm activities at certain times. Fresh air and blue skies. Rest and Relaxation. Gracious Living. AussieHost accredited. Winner of Awards for Excellence in Tourism.

~

Crookwell

Markdale Homestead *B&B Farmstay Cottage with Kitchen*
Geoff & Mary Ashton
Mulgowrie Road
Binda
NSW 2583
40 km NW of Crookwell

Tel (02) 4835 3146
or (02) 9327 2191
Fax (02) 4835 3160
g_ashton@bigpond.com
www.markdale.com

Tariff $60-$100pp
Full Breakfast Provisions
Dinner $30 - $40
Visa MC BC accepted
2 Queen 3 Double 7 Twin (12 bdrm)
Bathrooms: 1 Ensuite 3 Private

Food for the soul. A beautiful landscape, 6000 acres, trout stocked streams, solar heated pool and all weather tennis. The Markdale Homestead and Garden combine the talents of two Australia Icons; Edna Walling, garden designer, and Professor Wilkinson, architect. Live in two adjoining, self contained, beautifully renovated, stone houses. Both have central heating, open fire, sitting room, kitchen, laundry, TV, CD Player, phone and internet access. Or stay in the comfortable Shearers' Quarters at cheaper rates.

Dorrigo
Fernbrook Lodge *B&B*
Ross & Sue Erickson
4705 Waterfall Way
Dorrigo
NSW 2453
6 km W of Dorrigo

Tel (02) 6657 2573
Fax (02) 6657 2573
fernbrooklodge@midcoast.com.au
www.midcoast.com.au/~fernbrooklodge

Double $95-$110 Single $65
Child $25
Includes full breakfast
Dinner $25 - $30
2 Queen 1 Double 2 Single (4 bdrm)
Bathrooms: 4 Ensuite

I f you would enjoy quality comfort, thoughtful consideration of your needs, fresh mountain air, fresh flowers, books, cushions and comfy chairs, afternoon tea on arrival, magnificent views to the sea, a rambling old garden of sighing pines, tree ferns and great birdlife, we would be delighted to welcome you. Two verandah rooms have garden access. Dinner by arrangement features local produce and dietary needs are respected. 10 minutes Dorrigo Rainforest, Dangar Falls, excellent craft & art. Within 1 hour drive - 4 National Parks, surf beaches, rivers, Ebor Falls, Wollomombi Gorge, trout fishing. "Established 11 years."

Dorrigo
Tallawalla Retreat B&B *B&B*
Paul & Di McDonald
113 Old Coramba Road
Dorrigo
NSW 2453
2 km SE of Dorrigo

Tel (02) 6657 2315
or 0412 750 773
Fax (02) 6657 2315
info@tallawalla.com
www.tallawalla.com

Double $120-$125 Single $75-$85
Child $30
Includes special breakfast
Dinner $15-$35
Visa MC BC accepted
3 Queen 1 Double 2 Twin 3 Single (5 bdrm)
Bathrooms: 3 Ensuite 1 Private

T allawalla Retreat is situated on a ridge overlooking the Dorrigo Plateau with panoramic views to distant mountains. We have five acres of beautiful gardens and our own rainforest. Bird life abounds. Relax by the pool or on our full size tennis court. Our dining room, with floor to ceiling windows, allows guests to view the natural beauty of the plateau whilst enjoying country-style cooking. The nearby World Heritage National Park provides breathtaking scenery and interesting walks. Enjoy a cup of tea in our specialty Tea House. Your hosts Paul & Di McDonald look forward to spoiling you.

Dubbo

Walls Court B&B *B&B Farmstay Separate Suite*
Neil and Nancy Lander
11L Belgravia Heights Road
Dubbo
NSW 2830
12 km S of Dubbo

Tel (02) 6887 3823
or 0407 226 606
(02) 6887 3606
Fax (02) 6887 3602
nlander@bigpond.com
www.bbbook.com.au/wallscourt.html

Double $150 Single $125 Child $30
Includes full breakfast   Dinner $15-$30
Visa MC BC accepted
1 Queen (1 bdrm)
Bathrooms: 1 Ensuite

Relish the tranquillity and comfort of your Walls Court suite as you laze on the veranda with a drink observing the birds in the garden. See your children's joy as they feed sheep and chooks, pat dogs and gather eggs. Gain more from your visit to the zoo; we are volunteer guides. Revel in crowd free shopping precincts or savour the tastings at nearby wineries. Explore attractions yourself or take advantage of our familiarity with the area. Your pet is welcome by arrangement. Learn a new craft - make a pair of silver earrings for a small additional cost.

Dubbo District - Tottenham

Meadow View Farmstay *B&B Farmstay Cottage No Kitchen*
Meryl Boothby
Meadow View
Tottenham
NSW 2873
20 km S of Tottenham

Tel (02) 6892 8205
Fax (02) 6892 8244
merylboothby@optusnet.com.au
www.bbbook.com.au/meadowview.html

Double $90-$120 Single $60
Child $15 (under 13)
Includes full breakfast
Dinner $18, $10 (under 13)
Extra $25, $15 (under 13)
1 Queen 2 Twin 1 Single (3 bdrm)
Bathrooms: 1 Private

Meadow View Farmstay,in the centre of New South Wales, specialises in family, farm holidays. Enjoy true country hospitality and scrumptious home cooked meals. Take in the sunshine, relax in the garden and tranquil surroundings. Plenty of farm animals - gather eggs for breakfast, feed ducks, baby chicks and goats. Accommodation is modern with lots of facilities - TV, DVD, laundry, electric blankets, gas heating, air conditioning - all linen supplied. Most pets welcome - take some of our adventure and sightseeing tours.

Eden

Crown & Anchor Inn B&B *B&B*

Mauro and Judy Maurilli
239 Imlay Street
Eden
NSW 2551
In Eden Central

Tel (02) 6496 1017
Fax (02) 6496 3878
info@crownandanchoreden.com.au
www.crownandanchoreden.com.au

Double $140-$170 **Single** $120-$160
Includes full breakfast
Visa MC accepted
5 Double (5 bdrm)
Bathrooms: 5 Ensuite

As seen on "Getaway" and the "Today Show". Step back in time. Experience romantic early Australian charm in an original 1840's Inn. Breathtaking ocean and bay views, antiques and open fires. Watch the whales from the veranda or the back deck during October and November. Central to Eden and wonderfully quiet; walk to restaurants, beaches and the working wharf. Enjoy a champagne watching the sun-set over the waters of Twofld Bay. Watch the sun-rise whilst breakfasting on the sunny veranda.

Eden

Gibsons by the Beach *B&B Homestay Apartment with Kitchen*

Allan and Ruth Gibson
10 Bay Street
Eden
NSW 2551
In Eden Central

Tel (02) 6496 1414
or 0427 649 614
gibsons@asitis.net.au
www.gibsonsbythebeach.com.au

Double $120-$220 **Single** $95-$120
Child $20 - $40
Continental/Full Breakfast
Visa MC BC accepted
2 Queen 3 Single (2 bdrm)
Bathrooms: 1 Ensuite 1 Private spa bath (1)

Nature Lover's Paradise. Self-contained garden apartment (sleeps up to 5), cosy, beach atmosphere with full kitchen and spa bath. Also available Q-bed room with ensuite. 2 minute bush descent to protected Cocora Beach. Come and explore the magnificent beauty of Twofold Bay, beaches and surrounding National Parks. Excellent Bay Cruises or fishing trips with whale watching Oct/Nov. Enjoy bushwalking, golf, fishing, swimming, snorkelling, diving or just relaxing, here or at the wharves. Great restaurants. Children are welcome.

Eden

Cocora Cottage *B&B*
Gail and David Ward
2 Cocora Street
Eden
NSW 2551
In Centre of Eden

Tel (02) 6496 1241
or 0427 218 859
Fax (02) 6496 1137
wardg@acr.net.au
www.cocoracottage.com

Double $135-$150 Single $115
Includes full breakfast
2 Queen (2 bdrm)
Bathrooms: 2 Ensuite

AAA Tourism
★★★★

Heritage listed Cocora Cottage was the original Police Station in Eden. It is centrally located in a quiet area close to Eden's famous Killer Whale Museum, the Wharf and Eden's fine restaurants. Breakfast is served upstairs with spectacular views down to the Wharf and across Twofold Bay to the foothills of Mt Imlay. Both bedrooms have a Queen sized bed, a television and an ensuite with a spa. The front bedroom features the original open fireplace while the back bedroom offers bay views.

Forster - Green Point

Lakeside Escape B&B *B&B Homestay*
Denise & Rob Dunsterville
85 Green Point Drive
Green Point, Forster
NSW 2428
5 km S of Forster

Tel (02) 6557 6400
or 0412 314 426
Fax (02) 6557 6401
lakesideescapebnb@tsn.cc
lakesideescape.com.au

Double $150-$165 Single $135-$125
Includes special breakfast
Dinner $30 - $45pp
Extra person $50
Visa MC BC Diners accepted
1 King/Twin 2 Queen (3 bdrm)
Bathrooms: 3 Ensuite

AAA Tourism
★★★★☆

Indulge in tranquillity and luxury at our purpose-built, bush-setting, waterfront home. Choose from undisturbed intimacy or harmony with your hosts. Unwind in the outdoor heated spa among the trees or around the cosy fire. Close, stunning water views of Wallis Lake from every room. Observe the changing moods and colours of the lake and awesome sunsets. See our website for special packages. Five minutes to cafes, restaurants, shops, safe beaches and a huge variety of sport, recreational and relaxing activities to suit all requirements.

Gerringong

Tumblegum Inn *B&B Homestay*

Heather Williams
141C Belinda Street
Gerringong
NSW 2534
In Gerringong

Tel (02) 4234 3555
or 0419 469 099
Fax (02) 4234 3888
tumbleguminn@hotmail.com
www.tumbleguminn.com.au

Double $100-$130 Single $90-$110
Includes full breakfast
No smoking on property   Visa MC BC accepted
2 Queen 1 Twin (3 bdrm)
Bathrooms: 3 Ensuite

AAA Tourism
★★★★

With rolling green hills that lap to pristine beaches, Gerringong reminds visitors of Ireland. Tumblegum Inn is a newly-built Federation style home featuring antique furnishings and warm hospitality. Two queen and one twin share bedrooms each contain ensuites, electric blankets, fans, clock radios and remote TV. Separate guest lounge has fridge, tea and coffee facilities, and home baked goodies. Only 1 1/2 hour south of Sydney, local attractions include beach side golf course, saltwater pools, boutique wineries, Minnamurra Rainforest and Kiama blowhole. Older children welcome, no pets. Winner, Illawarra Tourism Award for Accommodation.

~

Glen Innes

Sharron Park Farmstay B&B *B&B Homestay Farmstay*

Cathryn & John Crosby
Sharron Park
Glencoe
NSW 2365
15 km S of Glen Innes

Tel (02) 6732 3858
or 0427 024 494
Fax (02) 6732 3858
crosby@northnet.com.au
www.bbbook.com.au/sharronpark.html

Double $100-$120 Single $65
Includes full breakfast
1 King 1 Queen 1 Double 2 Single (3 bdrm)
Bathrooms: 1 Ensuite 1 Private

Set in beautiful gardens, this federation style home has spacious bedrooms, ensuite bathrooms and is furnished throughout the house with genuine antiques. The King room and the guest lounge rooms have log fires and all rooms have electric blankets, TVs and vanities. The homestead at Sharron Park is part of a functioning cattle property. Take a farm tour and see the cattle, horses, kangaroos and birdlife or enjoy colonial style camp oven cooking (by request). All additional meals available on request.

Glen Innes

Mackenzie House *B&B*
Beth and Bruce McGrath
92 West Avenue
Glen Innes
NSW 2370
In Glen Innes Central

Tel (02) 6732 1679
or 0409 122 679
mackenzie.house@bigpond.com
www.mackenziehouse.com.au

Double $100-$150 Single $70-$95
Child $25-35
Includes full breakfast
Dinner $25-40 pp
1 King 1 Queen 1 Double (3 bdrm)
Bathrooms: 2 Ensuite

Peace and quiet at Mackenzie House, one of the finest homes in Glen Innes. Enjoy the gorgeous gardens free from highway noise, opening as part of Australia's Open Garden Scheme. Smell the roses. Enjoy the wonderful New England climate. Luxuriate in beautiful bedrooms, enjoy music in the oak-panelled lounge, relax in front of open fires, wonder at magnificent stained glass windows. Modern Australian breakfast. Opposite beautiful parkland and very easy stroll to restaurants, clubs and shops. Phoebe, our outside golden retriever loves tummy tickles!

Glen Innes

Queenswood - The Quiet One *B&B*
The Sim Family
82 Wentworth Street
Glen Innes
NSW 2370
In Mid town Glen Innes

Tel (02) 6732 3025
or 0428 121 929
www.bbboook.com.au/
queenswoodthequietone.html

Double $90-$100 Single $70-$75
Child $30 - $35
Includes full breakfast
Dinner $25 - $30 B/A
1 King 1 Queen 1 Twin (3 bdrm)
Bathrooms: 1 Ensuite 1 Guest share

Formally the residence of "Queenswood Girls Grammar" opened in 1899, now an old style family home which welcomes you. Conveniently situated in town opposite the Bowling Club. Comfortable beds, electric blankets and room heaters, wood fires plus fully cooked breakfast. Experience our mild summers, invigorating winters (occasional snow), glorious spring and autumn. Visit the only Celtic Stones in Australia, National Parks. Fossicking, fishing and frolicking for everyone. Reservations please. Children over six welcome, not suitable for little children. No pets. Dinner by arrangement. BYO. Off street parking.

Glen Innes

Glen Innes Bed & Breakfast *B&B*

Bill & Joyce Stringer
95 Church Street
Glen Innes
NSW 2370
In Glen Innes Central

Tel (02) 6732 4226
or 0421 310 900
Fax (02) 6732 6578
gibandb@bigpond.com.au
www.gleninnes.com/gibandb

Double $90 **Single** $55
Child $25-$50 (depending on age)
Includes full breakfast
No smoking on property
1 Queen 1 Double 2 Single (3 bdrm)
Bathrooms: 1 Guest share

This quaint two storey Cape Cod cottage is set in half an acre of gardens and has all the old fashion comforts and genuine hospitality you could wish for. We are located on the New England highway just a short leisurely stroll to the historic main street, the majority of buildings being heritage listed, the remaining legacy of our past colonial charm. Picturesque Glen Innes is Australia's Celtic capital nestled in the Northern Tablelands of the delightful New England district. A perfect place to rest while travelling between NSW and Queensland.

Glen Innes

Glen Waverly *B&B Cottage No Kitchen*

Betty & Adrian Whitten
Lot 1 Fawcett Road
Glen Innes
NSW 2370
3 km S of Glen Innes

Tel (02) 6732 3314
or 0408 482 158
bawhitten@bigpond.com
www.glenwaverly.gleninnes.biz

Double $100
 $15.00 basket breakfast per couple
Visa MC BC accepted
1 Queen 1 Double (1 bdrm)
Bathrooms: 1 Ensuite

Modern Self contained one bedroom cottage on Hobby Farm, only 5 minutes south of Glen Innes, off the New England Highway. Relax and enjoy country hospitality in a quiet garden setting with sweeping valley views and wonderful sunsets. The cottage is well appointed, light and airy with cooking facilities. These include microwave, electric kettle bar-b-que and electric kettle. The sunny bedroom has a queen size bed and there is a sofa bed in the lounge room. The wood heater and electric blankets ensure comfort in the winter. Pets under control and children welcome.

Glen Innes - Ben Lomond

Silent Grove Farmstay B&B *B&B Homestay Farmstay Cottage with Kitchen*

John & Dorothy Every
Silent Grove
Ben Lomond
NSW 2365
32 km N of Guyra

Tel (02) 6733 2117 or 0427 936 799
Fax (02) 6733 2117
silentgr@northnet.com.au
www.silentgrovefarmstay-bandb.com.au

Double $85-$85 Single $45-$50
Child $15
Includes full breakfast   Dinner $18
Visa MC accepted
1 Queen 1 Double 2 Single (3 bdrm)
Bathrooms: 2 Guest share

Enjoy country hospitality in a peaceful rural setting, short detour by sealed road from the New England Highway. Top of the Tablelands. Working sheep and cattle property. Farm activities. 4WD tour through property to see Kangaroos & Birdlife (fee applies). Panoramic views, scenic walks, yabbying (seasonal), tennis court, trout fishing, occasional snow fall. Easy access to new England, Gibraltar Range, Washpool National Parks. Glen Innes Australian Stones. Smoking outdoors. Have a cat. Winner of 2001 Big Sky Regional Tourism Hosted Accommodation. Campervans welcome. "Lovely peaceful atmosphere, friendly hospitality couldn't be better." WC.

Gloucester - Barrington Tops

Arrowee House B&B *B&B Homestay Separate Suite*

Kyoko Sakamoto
152 Thunderbolts Way
Gloucester
NSW 2422
1 km N of Gloucester

Tel (02) 6558 2050
Fax (02) 6558 2050
information@gloucester.nsw.gov.au
www.gloucester.org.au/

Double $55 per person
Includes full breakfast
Dinner $30
Child 1-11 yrs $1 per yr, Child 12-16 yrs $25
No smoking on property
Visa MC BC accepted
3 Queen 6 Single (Baby cot available. bdrm)
Bathrooms: 1 Ensuite 1 Guest share 3 Private

The longest established B&B in Gloucester with sealed road to the front door. Walking distance to shops, cafes, restaurants and mountain walks on The Buckett Mountains. Open scenic views of rolling hills, Buckett Mountains and Mograni Mountains. Local activities include bush walking, canoeing, horse riding, scenic drives, golf, swimming, tennis, sky diving or just take in the views. During winter months a 2-3 hour Japanese dinner is available for only $30 per person. Pre book 2 weeks. Bring the children to feed our friendly cow and chickens after breakfast. Courtesy XPT Country Link pick up.

Grafton

Rest Your Case *B&B*
Pattie Morton
136 Victoria Street
Grafton
NSW 2460
In Grafton

Tel (02) 6642 6631
Fax (02) 6642 6631
www.graftononline.com.au/restyourcase.
htm

Double $100 Single $75
Child $15
Includes full breakfast
1 King/Twin 1 Queen (2 bdrm)
Bathrooms: 1 Ensuite 1 Guest share

Quiet, restful accommodation including 2 bedrooms, 1 queen with full bathroom and 1 twin with king singles. The rooms are light and airy with cotton bed linen, air conditioning, ceiling fans and heaters. The second bedroom is reserved for your family or travelling companion to ensure privacy. Elegant sitting room for relaxing, reading or watching television. Stroll across the road to the Clarence River or a short walk to Grafton's best restaurants, cafes and gallery. Breakfast is served at your convenience. Amenities include fridge, microwave over, jug and toaster. Smoking permitted in the garden, children are welcome with notification.

Grafton

Seeview Farm *B&B Homestay Farmstay*
Mona Ibbott
440 Rogans Bridge Road
Seelands Grafton
NSW 2460
10 km N of Grafton

Tel (02) 6644 9270
or 0429 004 872
Fax (02) 6644 9270
www.bbbook.com.au/seeviewfarm,html

Double $90-$110 Single $70-$80
Child $17.50
Includes full breakfast
Dinner $20
1 Queen 1 Twin (2 bdrm)
Bathrooms: 1 Family share 1 Private

AAA Tourism
★★★☆

Seeview Farm is a pretty cattle property on the banks of the Clarence River which is noted for river boat and water skiing. Grafton is famous for its Jacaranda Festival and its historical buildings. Close to beaches and mountains. Enjoy peaceful countryside - many overseas students have visited the farm, where pets are welcome. Kangaroos and bird life to watch. Good stopover from Sydney or Brisbane. Relaxing and friendly. Children are welcome.

Grafton - Ulmarra

Rooftops *B&B*
Sandra Grogan
6 Coldstream Street
Ulmarra
NSW 2462
In Ulmarra

Tel (02) 6644 5159
rooftops@ceinternet.com.au
www.bbbook.com.au/rooftops.html

Double $110 Single
Includes full breakfast
2 Queen (2 bdrm)
Bathrooms: 2 Ensuite

U lmarra is an Historic Village classified by the National Trust, situated on the Pacific Highway and the mighty Clarence River. Grafton the 'Jacaranda City' is 12 km south. Rooftops B&B is conveniently sited in the CBD amongst antique shops, art gallery and collectable antique glass. Rooftops B&B is a boutique accommodation atop a warehouse. Views of the river and the town can be viewed from the balcony. Our accommodation is distinctive and modern. Take a stroll to the river or walk the heritage walk around the village. Fresh seafood restaurant and local pub meals are available next door. Not suitable for people with a problems with heights and stairs. Not suitable for young children and pets.

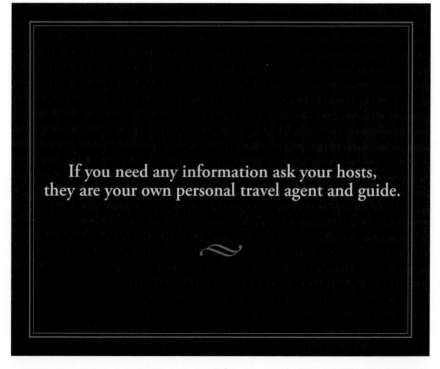

If you need any information ask your hosts, they are your own personal travel agent and guide.

Gunning

Frankfield Guest House *B&B Guest House*
Andrew Neville
1-3 Warrataw Street
Gunning
NSW 2581
45 km W of Goulburn

Tel (02) 4845 1200
or 0419 214 940
Fax (02) 4845 1490
enquiries@frankfield.com.au
www.frankfield.com.au

Double $90-$140 Single $55-$95
Child B/A
Includes full breakfast
Dinner $25 - $35
 $175 - $390
Visa MC BC Amex accepted
10 Double (10 bdrm)
Bathrooms: 2 Ensuite 3 Guest share

B uilt in 1870 as the Frankfield Hotel now a charming Guest House. Each bedroom is fitted out with antique furniture, brass and four poster beds. Relax in front of an open fire or outside in award winning gardens. Enjoy a gourmet meal in our period dining room. 2 1/2 hours from Sydney, 50 mins from Canberra, Gunning is only minutes from the new Highway. Visit cold climate vineyards and historic townships all within 30 minutes drive. Local facilities include golf, tennis and swimming.

Hawkesbury - Colo

Ossian Hall *Luxury B&B Farmstay Cottage with Kitchen*
Diane & Jim Swaisland
1928 Singleton Road
Colo, NSW 2756
26 km NE of Windsor

Tel (02) 4575 5250or 0428 640 435
Fax (02) 4575 5169
info@ossianhall.com.au
www.ossianhall.com.au

Double $185 **Single** $185
Full Breakfast Provisions
Dinner by arrangement
Packages available
Visa MC BC Amex accepted
3 Queen (3 bdrm)
Bathrooms: 3 Ensuite 3 Private 2 person spas

Ossian Hall located on 86 acres in a secluded valley fronting the beautiful Colo River and surrounded by natural bush filled with abundant bird life. Accommodation is self contained with quality inclusions, designed for couples with full kitchen facilities, ensuite, air conditioned, TV, video, DVD & CD stereo. Log fire and 2 person spa in cottages. 4 person hot tub spa, solar heated pool, games room, bikes and rowing on the river- available to all guests. Complete privacy with beautiful outlook. Breakfast basket supplied. Picnic/BBQ and evening meals available on request. Romantic horse drawn interludes and picnic packages.

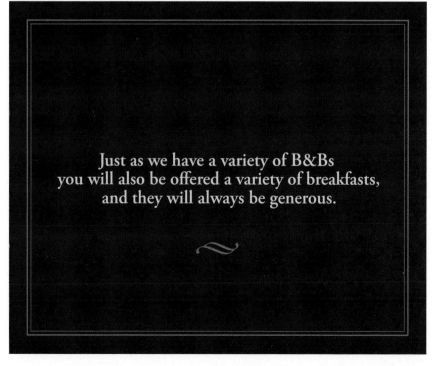

Just as we have a variety of B&Bs
you will also be offered a variety of breakfasts,
and they will always be generous.

Hawkesbury - Lower Portland

Jerimuda *B&B Cottage No Kitchen*
Jenny and Kevin O'Shea
72 Laws Farm Road
Lower Portland
NSW 2756
22 km N of Windsor

Tel (02) 4579 1028
or 0425 289 367
0425 289 366
Fax (02) 4579 1029
jerimudabb@bigpond.com
www.guesthouse.au.com

Double $155-$125
Includes full breakfast
1 King 2 Queen 2 Double (5 bdrm)
Bathrooms: 1 Ensuite 1 Private

Jerimuda B&B is peaceful and tranquil for the ideal weekend or romantic getaway set on 37 acres of bushland and Hawkesbury River views. We have one King size bed with spa, one Queen size bed with ensuite and one Queen and two double rooms with share bathroom. All rooms have tea/coffee making facilities, television, radio, CD and video players. We have a heated swimming pool as well as log fires in the winter months. We have a family labrador. Dinner is available on request.

Hawkesbury - St Albans

Price Morris Cottage *Cottage with Kitchen B&B/Heritage Cottage/Rural/Self Contained*
Joyce Stepto
37 Upper Macdonald Road
St Albans
NSW 2775
50 km NW of Windsor

Tel (02) 4568 2121
or 0412 766 597
Fax (02) 4568 2121
bookings@pricemorris.com.au
www.pricemorris.com.au

Double $140-$220 Single $100-$120
Continental Breakfast provisions
1 Queen 1 Double 4 Single (4 bdrm)
Bathrooms: 1 Guest share Toilet, Vanity & Shower

Featured in Sunday Telegraph's "Escape" Magazine, our 1837, Heritage Listed, slab, wattle and daub cottage, located on 50 acres of farmland, reflects the lifestyle of 6 generations of the early pioneering Morris family. With restoration completed the Cottage is becoming a popular short break venue, two hours from Sydney, Newcastle or Gosford. Open sandstone fireplaces, modern kitchen, bathroom, Loo with a View, etc gives that comfortable, traditional feeling. Bushwalking, tennis, golf, fishing nearby. Self cater, BBQ or dine out cafe, hotel, restaurant close proximity.

Hay

Bank Bed & Breakfast *B&B*

Sally Smith
86 Lachlan Street
Hay
NSW 2711
In Hay Central

Tel (02) 6993 1730
or 0429 931 730
Fax (02) 6993 3440
ttsk@tpg.com.au
www1.tpg.com.au/users/ttsk

Double $120 Single $80
Includes full breakfast
1 King 1 Twin (2 bdrm)
Bathrooms: 1 Private

This National Trust classified mansion was built in 1891 to house the London Chartered Bank, one of the historic buildings restored to its original condition in Lachlan Street. The residence consists of a large dining room complete with period furniture and decor. The cedar staircase leads to the guest suite of two bedrooms and a fully modernised bathroom (complete with spa). The guest sitting room opens onto the balcony overlooking the main street. We look forward to you experiencing the hospitality of Hay with us.

Hunter Valley - Aberdeen - Scone

Craigmhor Mountain Retreat *Luxury B&B Homestay Apartment with Kitchen*

Gay Hoskings
Upper Rouchel Road
Upper Rouchel
NSW 2336
48 km E of Aberdeen

Tel (02) 6543 6393
Fax (02) 65436394
bnb@craigmhor.com.au
www.craigmhor.com.au

Double $130-$160 Single $70-$85
Child $35-$45
Includes full breakfast
Dinner $30- $50
Visa MC BC accepted
3 Queen 1 Twin (4 bdrm)
Bathrooms: 1 Ensuite 1 Guest share 1 Private

Total contrast to city living - seclusion, splendid views, crisp mountain air. Peace, privacy and tranquillity assured -just you, your host, 1000 ha of Australian bush and all its wildlife. Fully Catered; B&B; Self Catered; Mix & Match to suit. Possible activities: doing absolutely nothing, picnicking by mountain streams, bush walking (50 km of forest trails-from gentle strolls to climbing mountains, mountain biking, fishing stocked dams, Lake Glenbawn, 4-WD touring (optional extra), exploring Upper Hunter Country,- magnificent horse studs, historic towns, wineries, vast National Parks.

Hunter Valley - Cessnock

Cessnock Heritage Inn *B&B*
Donna & Mark McTiernan
167 Vincent Street
Cessnock
NSW 2325
0.5 km S of PO

Tel (02) 4991 2744
or 0427 907 338
Fax (02) 4991 2720
cessnockheritageinn@dodo.com.au
www.hunterweb.com.au/heritageinn.html

Double $100-$130 Single $80-$100
Child On application
Includes full breakfast
Visa MC BC Eftpos accepted
9 Queen 4 Double 7 Single (13 bdrm)
Bathrooms: 13 Ensuite

We are a comfortable and friendly B&B in the heart of Cessnock, just a leisurely stroll from clubs, pubs, restaurants, shops and cinema. Only a few minutes away are the famous Hunter Valley vineyards and a host of attractions that Hunter Valley Wine Country offers. Guests enjoy a delicious breakfast in the dining room, while our spacious lounge is ideal for relaxing with friends old and new. Our Inn has character and charm that keeps guest coming back time and again.

Hunter Valley - East Maitland

The Old George and Dragon Guesthouse *Guest House*
Nicolena & Martin Hurley
50 Melbourne Street
East Maitland
NSW 2323
5 km E of Maitland

Tel (02) 4934 6080
or 0412 995 639
Fax (02) 4933 6076
reservations@oldgeorgedragonguesthouse.
com.au
www.oldgeorgedragonguesthouse.com.au

Double $140-$200 Single $130-$180
Includes full breakfast
Dinner $340-$380 per couple
Visa MC BC Amex Eftpos accepted
2 King 3 Queen (5 bdrm)
Bathrooms: 5 Ensuite

Your hosts Nicolena and Martin will greet you on arrival. Our service is discreet and professional. The guesthouse is centrally located in the heart of the Hunter Valley just minutes away from the historic township of Morpeth and just 90 minutes north of Sydney. The perfect base for touring nearby historic houses, the famous wineries of Pokolbin or for day excursions to Barrington Tops and Port Stephens. Dine next door at the Good Food Guide 2004/2005 restaurant or there are many other options available within close proximity to the guesthouse.

Hunter Valley - Lochinvar

Lochinvar House *B&B Cottage No Kitchen*
James Gould & Corryne Parkhill
1204 New England Highway
Lochinvar
NSW 2321
3 km W of Lochinvar
(turn off Hwy Kaludah Ck)

Tel (02) 4930 7873 or 0439 802 526
Fax (02) 4930 7798
lochinvarhouse@dodo.com.au
www.geocities.com/lochinvarhse

Double $110-$165 **Single** $88-$140
Includes full breakfast
Dinner by arrangement
1 King/Twin 4 Queen 1 Double (6 bdrm)
Bathrooms: 2 Guest share 1 Private

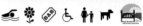

Historic Georgian-Victorian country homestead circa 1841 on Kaludah Estate, an 88 acre grazing property on the Hunter River. With grand entrance and dining room, luxuriously appointed rooms featuring 13 foot ceilings and antique furnishings, Lochinvar House overlooks beautiful Loch Katrine with views over the surrounding countryside. A large swimming pool and spa with BBQ area are available. Situated 1 km north of the New England Highway, close to restaurants, Wyndham Estate and other vineyards, equestrian centre, historic Maitland and Greta for antiques. Kennels available. Ideal for small groups, conferences etc.

Hunter Valley - Lovedale - Pokolbin

Hill Top Country Guest House *Luxury B&B Homestay Farmstay Cottage No Kitchen*
Guest House
Margaret Bancroft
288 Talga Road
Rothbury
NSW 2320
17 km N of Cessnock

Tel (02) 4930 7111
Fax (02) 4930 9048
stay@hilltopguesthouse.com.au
www.hilltopguesthouse.com.au

Double $88-$240 **Single** $85-$230
Includes full breakfast
2 King/Twin1 King 3 Queen (6 bdrm)
Bathrooms: 4 Ensuite 2 Private

AAA Tourism
★★★☆

The picturesque 300 acres abounds with wildlife. The 4WD Night Wildlife Tour lets you be with kangaroos, wombats, possums feeding in their natural environment. Horse riding is a favourite activity capturing spectacular views of wine country below. Ride mountain bikes to wineries, self-drive bush buggies, walk scenic bush trails, canoes on site. Fly a kite, winery and rainforest tours. The luxury accommodation offers spa suites, wood fires, Queen, King and single beds. 10' billiard table, grand piano, delicious meals. In-house massage, beauty treatments, sauna, pool, reverse-cycle air-conditioning. Selected by leading international tourist guides.

Hunter Valley - Maitland

Peacock Grove Biodynamic Olive Farm *B&B Homestay*
Chris & Gloria Peacock
84 Valley Street
Gosforth, via Maitland
NSW 2320
10 km NW of Maitland

Tel (02) 4932 8596
or 0417 292 642
Fax (02) 4932 5359
peacock@hunterlink.net.au
www.peacockgrove.com.au

Double $135-$145 Single $115-$125
Child Under 5, free, 5-12 $25
Includes full breakfast
Extra adult $40
Visa MC BC accepted
2 Queen (2 bdrm)
Bathrooms: 2 Ensuite

P eacock Grove is secluded tranquillity on a 150 acre olive farm just 12 minutes from Maitland. Your full country breakfast is served on the verandah overlooking tree covered hills on the far side of the Hunter River. The queen-sized rooms have ensuites and split system reverse cycle air conditioning. Visit nearby vineyards, historic Morpeth, Maitland Jail, go whale watching or deep sea fishing in Port Stevens or explore the Barrington tops area.

Hunter Valley - Maitland

Daniel's B&B *B&B Homestay Cottage with Kitchen*
Daniel Shaunessy
1 Brisbane Street
Lorn, Maitland
NSW 2320
0.5 km N of Maitland

Tel (02) 4934 2494
or 0410 483 424
daniel1@hypermax.net.au
www.bbbook.com.au/daniels.html

Double $80-$120 Single $60-$80
Child $30
Includes full breakfast
Bicycles $10/hr
2 Queen (2 bdrm)
Bathrooms: 1 Ensuite 1 Private

D aniel's B&B is located in the garden suburb of Lorn in the Historic town of Maitland. Built in 1896 it has been lovingly restored to its former Victorian style. A 10.5 metre heated pool and self-contained accommodation has been added. Pressed metal ceilings and polished hardwood floors are feature of our home. We are located 20 minutes from the vineyards and less than 60 minutes from beautiful mountains and beaches. Let us make you feel at home away from home.

Hunter Valley - Morpeth

Bronte Guesthouse *Guest House*
Nicolena & Martin Hurley
147 Swan Street
Morpeth
NSW 2321
10 km E of Maitland

Tel (02) 4934 6080 or 0412 995 639
Fax (02) 4933 6076
reservations@bronteguesthouse.com.au
www.bronteguesthouse.com.au

Double $120-$190 Single $110-$180
Includes full breakfast
Dinner Light dinner available - Sun to
Wed $35.00 per person
Visa MC BC Amex Eftpos accepted
3 King 3 Queen (6 bdrm)
Bathrooms: 6 Ensuite One room has a bath

Historic, charming, chic and comfortable, welcoming service with attention to detail. All rooms are themed to reflect the needs of the sophisticated traveller and offer complete luxury with ensuites, individually controlled air conditioning and televisions. Located in the heart of Morpeth, within walking distance to cafes, craft, antique and homeware shops. Our location is ideal for the overnight stay guest, those simply on vacation or the business and corporate traveller. Children over 12 years welcome upon arrangement.

Hunter Valley - Pokolbin

Catersfield House *Guest House*
Rosemary & Alec Cater
96 Mistletoe Lane
Pokolbin
NSW 2320
23 km NW of Cessnock

Tel (02) 4998 7220   Fax (02) 4998 7558
catersfield@catersfield.com.au
www.catersfield.com.au

Double $140-$225   Extra Adult $35
Includes full breakfast
Dinner $50 for 3 course. $35 for 2 course
Weekend package from $420
Visa MC BC Diners Amex Eftpos accepted
7 King 1 Queen 14 Twin (8 bdrm)
Bathrooms: 8 Ensuite

A Boutique Country Resort situated amongst the vineyards of Pokolbin with spectacular views of the Brokenback Ranges. A total of eight guestrooms comprised of five luxurious bedrooms with king-size or twin beds, two with two-person spas, a special French room with a traditional four poster bed, a separate Summerhouse also with a two person spa. Rooms have reverse cycle A/C, TVs, VCRs, fridges, tea/coffee facilities, irons/boards and hairdryers. There is a log fire in the Guests lounge, a salt-water swimming pool, petanque, fishing and BBQ facilities. A hot country breakfast is included in the tariff and Dinner is available. Guests can also enjoy gourmet coffee and fine food from Catersfield's Cafe Monteverdi. Catersfield House specialises in Estate Weddings.

Hunter Valley - Pokolbin

Elfin Hill *B&B Farmstay Separate Suite*
Marie & Mark Blackmore
Marrowbone Road
Pokolbin
NSW 2320
5 km W of Cessnock

Tel (02) 4998 7543
or 0412 199 373
Fax (02) 4998 7817
relax@elfinhill.com.au
www.elfinhill.com.au

Double $110-$180 Single $98-$180
Child $20
Continental Breakfast
Visa MC BC Amex Eftpos accepted
6 Queen 1 Double 5 Single (6 bdrm)
Bathrooms: 6 Ensuite

Enjoy delightful country accommodation, serenely nestled atop a foothill of Brokenback Range. Elfin Hill has breathtaking views to Lindeman Winery. Delightfully enhanced by the birdlife in tall Spotted Gum trees, Rooms are freshly refurbished in log cabin style, with covered barbecue area right beside the salt water swimming pool. Simple delicious breakfasts, plenty of car free walking tracks and the nearby State Forest compliment the renowned Wine Tasting and Fantastic Cuisine! All the advantages of a B&B with the benefit of private rooms.

~

Hunter Valley - Upper Hunter - Denman

The Old Dairy *Luxury Cottage with Kitchen*
Sarah Windybank
430 Mt Dangar Road
Baerami (via Denman)
NSW 2333
20 km W of Denman

Tel (02) 6547 5033 or 0409 429 656
Fax (02) 6547 5033
sarah@windybankestate.com.au
www.windybankestate.com.au

Double $120-$150   Child $30
Continental breakfast provisions supplied
No smoking inside
Visa MC BC accepted
1 Queen (1 Bedroom)   Total capacity for 4 guests (with day bed)
Bathrooms: 1 Private Claw foot bath

Luxurious accommodation in the Upper Hunter Valley. The Old Dairy offers self catering facilities & lots of privacy. We have thought of everything to help you truly unwind. Gorgeous French Provincial-themed styling throughout, reverse cycle air-conditioning, cosy slow combustion log fire, BBQ facilities, fully equipped kitchen/laundry, claw foot bath, with a wonderfully romantic bedroom you will never want to leave! Located in an idyllic rural setting beneath Mt Dangar, with stunning views of surrounding farmland and the Goulburn River & Wollemi National Parks. A perfect base for visiting the wineries, horse studs & restaurants of The Upper Hunter, and ideally situated on the scenic route between Pokolbin/Cessnock, Broke/Fordwich, the Upper Hunter and Mudgee vineyards..

Hunter Valley - Wine Country - Wollombi

Capers Guesthouse *B&B Cottage with Kitchen Guest House*
Jane Young
6 Wollombi Road
Wollombi
NSW 2325
29 km SW of Cessnock

AAA Tourism
★★★★★ B&B

Tel (02) 4998 3211 or 0409 305 285
Fax (02) 4998 3458
stay@capers.com.au
www.capers.com.au

Double $200-$330 Single $200-$330
Includes full breakfast   Dinner $55-$65
Cottage from $75 per person per night
Visa MC BC accepted
1 King 5 Queen 2 Double 1 Twin (9 bdrm)
Bathrooms: 8 Ensuite

The Hunter's finest luxury Sandstone Guest House in Wine Country. This beautiful and unique 1850's convict hewn sandstone house was transported from Macquarie Street, Sydney and re-built in Wollombi. Magnificent views, fabulous breakfasts and attention to detail have become the hallmark of Capers. All suites have been individually designed for maximum comfort and have ensuites, some with spa baths. French doors lead from each bedroom to wide stone paved verandahs with stunning views. All are air conditioned, centrally heated and have tea coffee facilities, mini bar and in-house licence.Enjoy the romance in the chilly winter months in front of a roaring fire, and wake to a gourmet breakfast served on the terrace which in winter is heated for your comfort. Wollombi is perfectly situated in the Wine Region of the Hunter Valley. Only 90 minutes from Sydney and minutes to world famous wineries. Our staff can arrange wine tours, 4 wheel drive experiences in the Mt Yengo National Park and the Barrington Tops, tennis, horse riding at the local stables, numerous bush walks, and for the more adventurous - sky diving and hot air ballooning. We also have a delightful 3 bedroom luxury cottage for families and small groups. Our website is extensive so please take a visit and wet your appetite.

Hunter Valley - Wollombi - Laguna

Judsons at Laguna *Luxury Separate Suite Guest House*
Di & Adrian Judson
3868 Great North Road
Laguna, NSW 2325
8 km S of Wollombi

Tel (02) 4998 8085   Fax (02) 4998 8563
judsonsatlaguna@bigpond.com.au
www.judsonsatlaguna.com.au

Double $190-$320
Includes special breakfast   Dinner $25 - $60
Visa MC BC Amex Eftpos accepted
4 Queen (4 bdrm)
Bathrooms: 4 Ensuite Spa Baths

From the moment you leave the Great North Road and thread along the private drive that winds up the valley, you're in for a special experience that combines the best of country living with style and sophistication. The sprawling, modern homestead overlooks a pretty garden and lawns that dip down to the bottom of the valley, with timbered slope forming a rugged backdrop on the far side. The 4 guest suites are arranged side-by-side, in two separate cottages tucked back into the hills.

Each is bright and meticulously kept, with a lounge/dining room separate from the bedroom and includes:
*Open wood fire
*Spa baths (3 double)
*CD/DVD players
*Comprehensive DVD library (complimentary)
*Complimentary antipasto platter on arrival
*Complimentary beer and decanter of sherry
*Kitchenette tucked behind folding doors
*Reverse cycle air-conditioning
*In-ground pool in bush setting

A variety of meals is available in the luxurious guest lounge/dining room or in the privacy of your suite. The 100-acre property has its own bush walks and Yango & Watagan National Parks are nearby. Touring wineries of the Wollombi and Hunter Valleys or simply exploring the nearby historic village of Wollombi are just some of the pleasures available.

Jervis Bay - Huskisson

Sandholme Guesthouse *Luxury B&B Guest House, The Fine Art of Hospitality*
Alan & Christine Burrows
2 Jervis Street
Huskisson
NSW 2540
1 km S of Huskisson

Tel (02) 4441 8855
Fax (02) 4441 8866
guesthouse@sandholme.com.au
www.sandholme.com.au

Double $200-$280
Child under 15 not catered for
Includes full breakfast
Dinner by arrangement
Visa MC BC Eftpos accepted
King dble or twin, 2 with single (5 bdrm)
Bathrooms: 5 Ensuite, 4 with Spa bath

Sandholme Guesthouse. Offering couples a romantic getaway at Huskisson on Jervis Bay just 2 hours south of Sydney. Experience the natural beauty of Jervis Bay and be pampered in a luxurious and spacious guestroom retreat with en-suite and spa. Enjoy a sumptuous cooked breakfast, relax on the verandah with a delicious espresso coffee or that bottle of champagne, watch a favourite movie in the theatre or your room. Only 200 meters from the waters edge and a 12 minute walk to the Village centre, Sandholme is a holiday destination in its own right.

Jervis Bay - Huskisson

Jervis Bay Guesthouse *Luxury B&B Guest House*
Bill Rogers
1 Beach Street (Cnr Nowra/Beach St)
Huskisson
NSW 2540
0.5 km SE of Huskisson

Tel (02) 4441 7658
Fax (02) 4441 7659
info@jervisbayguesthouse.com.au
www.jervisbayguesthouse.com.au

Double $145-$235 Single $130-$220
Includes full breakfast
Visa MC BC Diners Amex Eftpos accepted
3 Queen 1 Twin (4 bdrm)
Bathrooms: 4 Ensuite 1 room has spa bath

Experience Jervis Bay at our multi-award winning B&B, just 50 metres from a beautiful white-sand beach. Sydney/Canberra are just 2.5-3 hrs away, and we're walking distance from Huskisson's shops and restaurants. Perfect for a weekend-away, or as the first or last stop for visitors to NSW. There are four beautiful guest rooms, all with Queen-size beds and ensuites (one with a spa). French doors lead onto the verandah, where there are spectacular views of the bay, and you can hear the sound of the surf.

Jervis Bay - Huskisson

Dolphin Sands Jervis Bay *B&B Cottage with Kitchen*
Wayne and Beatrice Whitten
6 Tomerong Street
Jervis Bay/Huskisson
NSW 2540
25 km S of Nowra

Tel (02) 4441 5511
or 0418 476 280
Fax (02) 4441 7712
info@dolphinsands.com
www.dolphinsands.com

Double $175-$295
Includes full breakfast
Visa MC BC Amex Eftpos accepted
4 Queen 1 Twin (5 bdrm)
Bathrooms: 5 Ensuite 2 Spa Queen Rooms, 1 queen room with bath and shower.

Dolphin Sands is what life by the ocean is all about. Dolphin Sands is a tranquil couples retreat, only minutes from the White Sands, Dolphins, and Clear Blue Waters of Jervis Bay at Huskisson. Hosts Wayne and Beatrice Whitten designed your luxury accommodations creating an intimate and relaxing atmosphere, while maintaining guest room privacy. Each room has the features expected of a luxury retreat; mini-fridge, TV, queen beds, bathrobes, tea/coffee facilities, aircon and ensuites. A twin and 2 spa rooms are available. Also Dolphin Cottage, an original Creswell Cottage. S/C accommodation. Two queen rooms and a sleep out suitable for two young adults (children).

Jervis Bay - Vincentia

Nelson Beach Lodge *B&B*
Robyn Brown
404 Elizabeth Drive
Vincentia
NSW 2540
30 km S of Nowra

Tel (02) 4441 6006
or 0402 263 997
Fax (02) 4441 6006
rbrown303@hotmail.com
www.bbbook.com.au/nelson.html

Double $95-$130 Single $55-$95
Child 1/2 price
Includes special breakfast
Dinner $25
Visa MC BC accepted
1 King/Twin 3 Queen 2 Twin (4 bdrm) Beds have electric blankets
Bathrooms: 1 Ensuite 1 Guest share 1 Private

Just two minutes walk from white sands

Enjoy a relaxing weekend or stopover at Nelson Beach Lodge. Ideally situated 2 1/2 hours from Sydney and Canberra. A cozy comfortable home, with guest lounge and balcony overlooking Jervis Bay and secluded garden. Just two minutes walk from white sands, red cliffs and crystal clear waters of Nelson Beach. Baywatch cruises see the dolphins, seals and penguins. Also diving, fishing, swimming, sailing, golf, bike riding and bush walking tracks around the waterfront and many picnic spots in local National and Marine Park, Botanic Gardens, Winery, and historic towns nearby. Aussie Host Business.

Jervis Bay - Woollamia

Woollamia Village Retreat *Cottage with Kitchen*

Brian & Suzanne Brown
21 Pritchard Avenue
Woollamia
NSW 2540
5 km NW of Huskisson

Tel (02) 4441 6108
or 0408 428 633
Fax (02) 4441 7055
wvr@shoalhaven.net.au
www.wvr.com.au

Double $130-$250 Single $130-$250
Child $25
Includes full breakfast
1 King/Twin 6 Queen 1 Double (8 bdrm)
Bathrooms: 8 Private

We offer self-contained cottages representative of an Australian village at Federation time. You may stay in our Church, Bank, General Store, School, Police Station, Post Office, The Overseas Cottage, which is suitable for disabled with carer, or the Village Inn. A unique experience in a high standard of accommodation awaits you, along with a touch of history, nostalgia, seclusion and romance in a quiet bush setting close to Jervis bay. We are also pet friendly. Dolphin and Whale watching packages available.

Jindabyne - Snowy Mountains

Troldhaugen Lodge *B&B*

John and Sandra Bradshaw
13 Cobbodah Street
Jindabyne
NSW 2627
In Central Jindabyne

Tel (02) 6456 2718
or 0409 562 718
Fax (02) 6456 2718
troldhaugen@ozemail.com.au
www.troldhaugen.com.au

Double $75-$150 Single $50-$120
Child $15- $40
Continental Breakfast
Cooked breakfast $6-$10
Visa MC BC accepted
1 Queen 8 Double 1 Single (10 bdrm)
Bathrooms: 10 Ensuite 10 Private

Centrally located in Jindabyne within walking distance to shops, hotels, restaurants, club and lake. Troldhaugen is situated at the end of a quiet cul-de-sac. A friendly owner/operated lodge catering for the family or couples, holiday. Facilities include guest lounge with open fireplace, TV and videos. Game room with tennis & pool tables, drying room & ski racks. All rooms are centrally heated and have own ensuites. Features include mountain and lake views.

Kangaroo Valley

Laurel Bank *B&B*
Chris and Christine Bult
2501 Moss Vale Road
Kangaroo Valley
NSW 2577
5 km N of Kangaroo Valley

Tel (02) 4465 1616
or 0429 647 398
laurelbank@shoal.net.au
www.laurelbank-bnb.com

Double $130-$220 Single $90-$120
Includes full breakfast
4 Queen (4 bdrm)
Bathrooms: 4 Ensuite

Established in 1920, Laurel Bank nestles at the base of Barrengarry Mountain, midway between Bowral in the beautiful Southern Highlands and Nowra on the South Coast. Surrounded by lush green pastures gently climbing into eucalyptus forest before reaching the soaring 600 metre escarpment, Kangaroo Valley is among the most stunning scenery in NSW. Guests enjoy spacious rooms and are served delicious breakfasts by welcoming friendly hosts. "We have done a lot of overseas travel, why bother when there's Laurel Bank. Great ambience. Great service. Beautiful food." KE, Hurstville, NSW.

Kempsey

Benbullen Farmstay *B&B Farmstay*
Marion Rudkin
171 Swan Lane
Collombatti, NSW 2440
21 km W of Kempsey

Tel (02) 6566 8448
or 0428 682 944
Fax (02) 6566 8448
info@benbullenfarmstay.com.au
www.bbbook.com.au/benbullen.html

Double $130-$170 Single $65-$85
Child $15-$25
Includes special breakfast
Dinner $10-$55
Mention the B&B Book and stay two
nights for the price of one.
3 Queen 2 Twin (3 bdrm)
Bathrooms: 2 Guest share 1 Private

Benbullen is a new colonial style farming property, yet still retains the charms of the true rural Australian environment. We are a Hereford stud farm with farm and native animals set on 69 hectares of undulating countryside. Only 20 minutes from Kempsey, Benbullen provides excellent accommodation with panoramic views of mountain and valleys. Guests have full use of the house which features large living areas with open fireplaces for winter evenings and a barbecue area. Hat Head National Park, South West Rocks and the Picturesque Trial Bay Gaol are a short drive. Go canoeing on the Macleay River or ask about supervised horse trail rides.

Kiama

Kiama Bed & Breakfast *Guest House Self-catering cottage with Kitchen*
Tony and Marian van Zanen
15 Riversdale Road   Kiama   NSW 2533
2.5 km W of Kiama

AAA Tourism
★★★★★

Tel (02) 4232 2844   **Fax** (02) 4232 2868
kiamabnb@kbb.com.au   www.kbb.com.au

Double $150-$240   **Single** $100-$150   **Child** $33
Includes special breakfast
Visa MC BC Diners Eftpos accepted
2 King 2 Queen 1 Double 4 Single (4 bdrm)
Bathrooms: 4 Ensuite

Multi Award-winning Kiama Bed & Breakfast (as seen on TVs Sydney Weekender) provides luxurious boutique-style 5-star accommodation on the outskirts of the picturesque seaside township of Kiama, overlooking the spectacular rural scenery of Jamberoo Valley and scenic rainforest escarpment. The two Guest House B&B suites, two Cottage B&B suites, or the self-catering Cottage (sleeps 8), provide the traveller with everything necessary from an overnight corporate stopover, to a romantic wedding night or extended family holiday. All rooms have ensuites, air-conditioning, TV/VCR in rooms and free movies for guest use. Guest areas include a sun-drenched dining room, comfortable lounge area with 24hr tea and coffee making, and huge furnished verandahs with spectacular views. Specially designed, the 2-bedroom cottage is available for couples, families or groups of up to 8 people with their own personal choice of full bed and breakfast, a "do it yourself" breakfast hamper, or fully self-contained accommodation, complete with fully functional kitchen and dishwasher. Scrumptious Breakfasts can be tailored to suit fussy tastes and dietary requirements. Kiama is only 90 minutes drive south of Sydney and boasts many tourist attractions including the Kiama Blowhole, clean surf beaches, harbour, wineries, Minnamurra Rainforest, Jamberoo Recreation Park, fishing, golfing, walking trails, art galleries, great shopping and many excellent quality cafes and restaurants. Afternoon tea, a bottle of bubbly and a Vintage Chevrolet car ride to the Blowhole (weather permitting) can be included to enhance your experience of Kiama Bed & Breakfast. A free Jaunt is included for return guests. Meet Maysha, the playful B&B toy poodle, wander in the gardens and discover the koi pond. Treat yourself or someone you love to a little decadence. We specialize in Wedding nights, Specialty Packages and Gift Vouchers. For more information, see our website on www.kbb.com.au.

Kiama

Bed and Views Kiama *B&B*
Sabine & Rudi Dux
69 Riversdale Road
Kiama
NSW 2533
3 km W of Kiama

Tel (02) 4232 3662
Fax (02) 4232 3662
admin@bedandviewskiama.com.au
www.bedandviewskiama.com.au

Double $140-$160
Includes special breakfast
Lovebird Suite from $180
Visa MC BC accepted
1 King/Twin 2 King 1 Queen (4 bdrm)
Bathrooms: 4 Ensuite one with spa

Enjoy crystal clear waters at various beaches, see the world`s famous Blow Hole, walk the nearby rainforest or find your favourite spot in the garden with unspoilt ocean and rural views. Only 2 min. away from the seaside town Kiama this B&B offers modern king and queen-bed rooms, ensuites, some with spa, all air-conditioned (cool/heat). Welcoming European hospitality invites to a "spoilt for choice" breakfast. Day-tour suggestions and booking assistance provided.
"What a remarkable combination of stunning views, most comfortable bed, delicious breakfast and a warm and friendly welcome." L&D Wilson, Melbourne

Kiama

Kiama Sea Mist Cottage *Cottage with Kitchen*
Marilyn Richardson
37 Tingira Crecent
Kiama
NSW 2533
In Kiama

Tel 0408 332 118
or (02) 4233 2116
seamistcottage@optusnet.com.au
www.kiama.com.au/seamist

Double $160-$350   Child $25
Includes provisions first night
$850-$2500pw
Visa MC BC accepted
1 Queen 1 Double 2 Single (3 bdrm)
Bathrooms: 1 Ensuite 1 Private

Waterfront Cottage near the Little Blowhole. Panoramic ocean views from spacious living areas. Relax and unwind on the deck or take a stroll along the Coastal Walk to the beach. Dolphin & whale watch (seasonal). Self-cater facilities with light breakfast hamper for your first night. Modern kitchen, microwave, dishwasher. Internal laundry. 2 TVs/VCR/CD/DVD/Videos. BBQ.A/C. Weekend Check-in 2.30pm Friday Check-out 2.30pm Sunday (if available). Sleeps 6. Sydney 90 minutes, Canberra 2.5 hours. "Medicine for the soul" NS Sydney. "The house and location were perfect" CS St. Ives.

Kiama

Elli's Bed & Breakfast *B&B*
Elli Lipton
126 Manning Street
Kiama
NSW 2533
In Kiama

Tel (02) 4232 2879
Fax (02) 4232 4338
elli@ellisbnb.com.au
www.ellisbnb.com.au

Double $120-$155
Includes full breakfast
Extra person $40
Visa MC BC accepted
2 Queen 2 Single (2 bdrm)
Bathrooms: 2 Ensuite one with spa

AAA Tourism
★★★★☆

A spacious welcoming home with everything close by... walk to magnificent beaches, coastal walking track, The Blowhole, railway station, town centre, shops,cafes, clubs, restaurants and much more... Enjoy well appointed ensuite rooms (1 with spa) each with own tea/coffee making facilities. Wake to a continental buffet followed by a delicious freshly cooked hot breakfast served in the sunny dining room which opens on to a palm shaded courtyard and saltwater pool. Fully air-conditioned. Quality accommodation. Friendly ambience. "My favourite oasis" F.J.Northcote,VIC.

Kiama

Seashells Kiama *Cottage with Kitchen*
Dianne Rendel
72 Bong Bong Street   Kiama NSW 2533
In Central Kiama

Tel (02) 4232 2504 or 0414 423 225
Fax (02) 4232 3419
dianne@seashellskiama.com.au
www.seashellskiama.com.au

Double $180-$350 Accommodation Only
only
Rates based on min stay 2 nights for one
couple   School & P/H POA
1 Queen 1 Double 2 Single (3 bdrm)
Bathrooms: 3 Private

AAA Tourism
★★★★☆

U nwind. Relax. and enjoy the delights of Kiama from this thoughtfully renovated holiday home. The spacious living area with sweeping town and ocean views is sunroom by day and cosy living room by night. Self-cater with the fully equipped kitchen and BBQ or eat out at the nearby cafes and restaurants. Tea, coffee, biscuits, fresh milk and fruit are provided for you on arrival. Stroll to shops, beaches, blowholes and leisure centre. There are TV, VCR/DVD Stereo and Game Cube as well as books and traditional board games providing in house entertainment for all ages. Three tastefully appointed bedrooms and bathrooms accommodate 2-6 guests in absolute comfort. Other features include gas log fire r/c air-conditioning, second TV/VCR and full internal laundry. Whether looking for a weekend away or a longer stay Seashells Kiama is the ideal choice for a summer holiday or winter retreat - the perfect getaway for couples, families and friends.

Kiama

Spring Creek Retreat Country House & Cottages *Luxury B&B Farmstay Cottage with Kitchen Guest House*
Sue & Jack Stoertz
41 Jerrara Road
Kiama NSW 2533
2.7 km W of Kiama

Tel (02) 4232 2700   Fax (02) 4232 2600
springcreekret@bigpond.com
www.springcreekret.com

Double $195-$500   Includes full breakfast
Visa MC BC Eftpos accepted
1 King/Twin1 King 3 Queen 5 Double 3 Single
(5 bdrm)
Bathrooms: 8 Ensuite

A country retreat by the sea offering 5 King/Queen bedroom Bed & Breakfast and 3 one/two bedroom Cottages. Tranquil 20 acre rural retreat in rolling green hills on a ridge overlooking Kiama and the Pacific Ocean, in magnificent landscaped grounds bounded by dry-stone walls. Walks, a swimming hole in the creek and private picnic spots on the property make it very easy to drive in the gate, park the car and throw away the key. All of this can be combined with either:
* The five star luxury of the guest house, which has five exquisite suites (3 with spas), satellite TV, CD, VCR,DVD, bathrobes, complimentary Port and chocolates, and gourmet breakfast in the French quarter dining room OR * 3 self-contained cottages, (two with spas in the bathroom), featuring lounge/dining room, full kitchens and large verandah with barbecues. Air conditioning and ceiling fans cool summer days and nights. Honeymooners and small group functions of up to 10 couples catered for. Winners of the 2001 Innovation Award in the Illawarra Tourism Awards for Business Excellence and finalists in the 2001 NSW Tourism Awards. Winners Tourism & Hospitality 2001 SIBTA. Winners 2003 Illawarra Tourism Award for Hosted Accommodation. For lovers young and old, Spring Creek sets the scene for special experiences. Winner of 2003 NSW Award Distinction.

Merimbula

Bella Vista *B&B*
Judy Hori
16 Main Street
Merimbula
NSW 2548
In Town Centre

Tel (02) 6495 1373
Fax (02) 6495 2344
bellavista@asitis.net.au
www.bbbook.com.au/bellavista.html

Double $150-$200
Includes full breakfast
2 King/Twin (2 bdrm)
Bathrooms: 2 Ensuite

AAA Tourism
★★★★☆

Bella Vista is an Award Winning designed boutique B&B with entrance to your private area with king size bed, bathroom, under-floor heating, tea and coffee making facilities. Private access to the lake. Enjoy a delicious breakfast while admiring the spectacular views from the large deck, watch the pelicans, swans and bird life go by. Minutes walk to shops, restaurants and clubs. Minutes drive to pristine beaches, golf clubs, whale watching and fishing. We are half way between Sydney and Melbourne with daily flights taking just over an hour. Also 2 hours to the snow fields. You will enjoy Bella Vista.

Merimbula

Robyn's Nest Guest House *Luxury B&B Cottages with Kitchen and Spa*
Guest House Fully Self Contained Units
Robyn Britten
188 Merimbula Drive
Merimbula
NSW 2548
3 km N of Merimbula

Tel (02) 6495 4956
Fax (02) 6495 2426
enquiries@robynsnest.com.au
www.robynsnest.com.au

Double $165-$250 Single $132-$165
Child $25 - $50
Includes full breakfast
S/C Cottages
Visa MC BC Amex Eftpos accepted
5 King/Twin 10 King 11 Queen 2 Twin (26 bdrm - Total capacity for 58 guests)
Bathrooms: 26 Ensuite

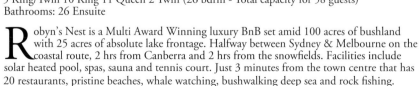

AAA Tourism
★★★★★

Robyn's Nest is a Multi Award Winning luxury BnB set amid 100 acres of bushland with 25 acres of absolute lake frontage. Halfway between Sydney & Melbourne on the coastal route, 2 hrs from Canberra and 2 hrs from the snowfields. Facilities include solar heated pool, spas, sauna and tennis court. Just 3 minutes from the town centre that has 20 restaurants, pristine beaches, whale watching, bushwalking deep sea and rock fishing.

Merimbula - Pambula

McKell's Cottage *B&B Homestay*
Robyn Cooper
47 Toalla Street
Pambula NSW 2549
10 km N of Merimbula

Tel 0438 063 790 or (02) 6495 7910
Fax (02) 6495 7910
robynfcooper@hotmail.com
www.southcoastbnbs.com.au

Double $115-$130 Single $90-$110
Child $20 -$35 over 5 yrs
Includes full breakfast
Dinner $50 ---$80 seasonal   Picnic
basket/morning &afternoon tea
2 Double (2 bdrm)
Bathrooms: 1 Guest share 1 Private ensuite available on request

Birthplace of former Governor General of Australia, Sir William McKell, McKell's Cottage is restored with rustic charm. A "home away from home" or a "romantic getaway." Our homely atmosphere is a haven for children and a respite for parents.A full country breakfast is included in the tariff and other meals are available on request. Alternatively, the kitchen is available for the use of guests. Free port and chocolates in each room, TV/DVD, heaters, electric blankets and open fires add to the ambiant detail. Transportation to and from local restaurants is available also. Robyn looks forward to meeting and greeting and is available to assist with any special requirements.

Milton - Ulladulla

Meadowlake Lodge *Luxury B&B*
Diana & Peter Falloon
318 Wilfords Lane
Milton
NSW 2538
3 km S of Milton

Tel (02) 4455 7722
Fax (02) 4455 7733
meadowlake@bigpond.com
www.meadowlakelodge.com.au

Double $160-$220 Single $120-$180
Includes full breakfast   Dinner B/A
No smoking on property
Visa MC BC Amex accepted
1 King/Twin 2 Queen (3 bdrm)
Bathrooms: 3 Ensuite

Meadowlake Lodge has won the South Coast Award for Excellence in Tourism in both 2004 and 2005. The category was Accommodation Up to Five Stars. The Lodge is a luxurious and relaxing country house overlooking lakes and wetlands which have prolific birdlife. We are only 3 hours from Sydney, 2 1/2 from Canberra and 3 minutes from historic Milton. We are close to the beaches at Mollymook and bush walks in the Budawangs. Spacious and elegant rooms have en suites with baths. Dinners and picnics by arrangement. At Meadowlake Lodge luxury is a way of life. Come and listen to the sounds of nature on the beautiful South Coast.

Moruya

Bryn Glas *Luxury B&B plus S/C Cottage*
Sandra & John Spencer
19 Valley View Lane
Moruya
NSW 2537
3 km S of Moruya PO

Tel (02) 4474 0826 or 0427 740 826
info@brynglas.com.au
www.brynglas.com.au

Double $120-$160 **Single** $120-$140
Child $10 per stay in cottage
Includes full breakfast
Childen welcome in Cottage only.
Visa MC BC accepted
2 Queen (+ Cottage bdrm)
Bathrooms: 2 Ensuite 1 Bathroom in Cottage

Four and a Half Star Quality with Rural Tranquility.Bryn Glas is a modern homestead style residence situated on 15 rural acres,plus s/c cottage sleeping 4. Within a short driving distance are Batemans Bay, Mogo, Tuross and Narooma, wonderful beaches and National Parks, fishing and boating.Bryn Glas is rated 4 Star plus, has Air Conditioned ensuite bedrooms with TV, guest sitting/dining/TV room, wide verandas with magnificent mountain views and country landscape.Stroll round the property and see our young calves, chickens and 300 lavender plants in our developing gardens which give a wonderful show.

Moruya

Post & Telegraph Bed & Breakfast *B&B*
Ruth Fred Spasic and Arlene Liang
Cnr 52 Page & Campbell Streets
Moruya
NSW 2537
0.5 km N of Moruya PO

Tel (02) 4474 5745
or 0427 099 718
Fax (02) 4474 5745
pandtbb@hotmail.com
www.southcoast.com.au/postandtel

Double $120-$135 **Single** $80-$90
Includes full breakfast
Visa MC BC Amex accepted
3 Queen 1 Single (3 bdrm)
Bathrooms: 1 Ensuite 1 Guest share

The Post & Telegraph Bed & Breakfast invites you to partake in the pleasures of this beautifully restored, heritage building which offers luxury accommodation in a warm and friendly atmosphere.
* Cosy sitting room with open fire and teamaking
* Sunny verandahs
* Wholesome cooked breakfast served in dining room
* Easy walk to river, shops and restaurants
* Close to beaches, National Parks<
* 2 hours drive from Canberra.

Mudgee

Riverlea B&B *B&B*
Pauline & Robert Betts
63 Riverlea Road
Apple Tree Flat, via Mudgee
NSW 2850
17 km SE of Mudgee

Tel (02) 6373 1386
Fax (02) 6373 1387
riverlea@hwy.com.au
www.riverlea-bnb.com.au

Double $140-$180
Includes full breakfast
Dinner By arrangement
3 Queen (3 bdrm)
Bathrooms: 3 Ensuite

R iverlea is an intimate and luxurious boutique B&B famous for its comfort, hospitality and sumptuous country breakfasts. Riverlea's 3 double bedrooms (each with ensuites and queen-size beds) are complemented by spacious dining, lounge and courtyard areas for the exclusive use of guests. Set on 16 tranquil acres in the scenic Cudgegong Valley, Riverlea is only a 12-minute drive from Mudgee. It is an ideal weekend getaway location for three couples.

Mudgee

The Mudgee Homestead Guesthouse *B&B Cottage with Kitchen Guest House*
Sean Wolfson and Karen Webb
3 Coorumbene Court (off Buckaroo Road)
Mudgee
NSW 2850
6 km N of Mudgee

Tel (02) 6373 3786
Fax (02) 6373 3086
welcome@mudgeehomestead.com.au
www.mudgeehomestead.com.au

Double $195.00-$297 Single $175.00-
Includes full breakfast
Dinner package available
Breakfast & afternoon tea included for guesthouse bookings
Visa MC BC accepted
2 King/Twin2 King 4 Queen (6 bdrm)
Bathrooms: 6 Ensuite

N estled on the flanks of Mount Buckaroo, the Mudgee Homestead Guesthouse is a stunning, purpose-built, Federation-style guesthouse ideally situated on 40 acres only 5 minutes from town. The guesthouse boasts six delightful guestrooms with private ensuites. Each guestroom features French doors which open onto the sweeping verandah, offering the area's most spectacular panoramic views of the valley and surrounding vineyards. A grand dining room, cosy fireside lounge and spacious billiards lounge are yours to enjoy. Please also enquire about our self-contained cottage on the property.

Mudgee

Lauralla Guest House & Grapevine Restaurant *B&B Guest House*

Vinh Van Lam & Stuart Horrex
25 Lewis Street
Mudgee NSW 2850
0.4 km S of Mudgee Post Office

Tel (02) 6372 4480
BednBreakfast@lauralla.com.au
www.lauralla.com.au

Double $149-$199 Single $99-$190
Includes full breakfast
Dinner Seven Stage Regional
Degustation dinner from $77 per person
Visa MC BC Eftpos accepted
1 King/Twin 2 Queen 3 Double (6 bdrm)
Bathrooms: 6 Ensuite

Lauralla Guest House and Grapevine Restaurant is a Mudgee landmark with a 100 year history. Built at the turn of last century, Lauralla is a fine example of the Late Victorian architectural style. Food and wine is the passion that partners/ proprietors, Vinh Van Lam & Stuart Horrex love to share with guests, and it's central to the experience that they offer. Lauralla the perfect place to enjoy a romantic getaway together. Drink fantastic local wines beside warming winter fires... Dine on exquisite regional flavours... Dream in cosy, intimate bedrooms... Discover a valley you'll want to return to time again... The restaurant is the showcase for regional produce and local wines. Open on Friday and Saturday nights they specialise in a seven-stage regional degustation menu.

Murwillumbah - Crystal Creek

Hillcrest Mountain View Retreat *Luxury B&B Farmstay Cottage with Kitchen*

Fully Air-conditioned
Clive & Tracy Parker
Upper Crystal Creek Road
Murwillumbah
NSW 2484
12 km NW of Murwillumbah

Tel (02) 6679 1023
info@hillcrestbb.com
www.hillcrestbb.com

Double $155-$295
Includes full breakfast
Dinner from $55pp
Visa MC BC accepted
3 Queen (3 bdrm)
Bathrooms: 3 Ensuite 2 with Spa Baths

Multi Tourism Award winning specialists in romantic getaways for couples offering peace, privacy, spectacular views from Mt Warning to the rainforests of Springbrook Ranges, solar heated pool, luxury double spa baths, massage, wood fire, air-conditioning & jolly good food. Choose from 2 B&B suites in a private guest wing of the main house, or 1 fully self contained cottage in its own secluded garden. Centrally located to 5 World Heritage listed National Parks, golf, horse-riding, arts & crafts galleries and more. Only 35 minutes from Gold Coast airport and 90 minutes from Brisbane.

Nambucca Heads

Beilbys Beach House *B&B Guest House*
Eric Mayer & Maita van Stockum
1 Ocean Street
Nambucca Heads
NSW 2448
0.9 km E of Nambucca Heads

Tel (02) 6568 6466
or 0431 732 200
beilbys@midcoast.com.au
www.beilbys.com.au

Double $60-$98 **Single** $50-$78
Includes special breakfast
Visa MC BC Diners Eftpos accepted
1 King/Twin 2 Queen 2 Double (5 bdrm)
Bathrooms: 3 Ensuite 2 Private

You will feel relaxed and comfortable at idyllic Beilbys Beach House, in its quiet, traffic-free hideaway location surrounded by tropical gardens. A 4-minute stroll through the bushland walkway to the warm golden sands of Nambucca's famous beaches, 900 meters to town, restaurants in walking or short drive distance. Comfortable rooms, all with verandah, TV, ceiling fan, heating, electric blankets, polished floors. Sumptuous buffet breakfast, fully equipped guest kitchen and dining room, large swimming pool, covered barbecue area, Internet facilities, laundry. Off-street parking. Three-night specials.

Nambucca Heads

Nambucca Riverview Lodge *B&B*
Veronica Buchanan
4 Wellington Drive
Nambucca Heads
NSW 2448
0.5 km SE of Nambucca Heads

Tel (02) 6568 6386
Fax (02) 6569 4169
riverview@here.com.au
www.here.com.au\riverview

Double $90-$140
Continental Breakfast
Room only $75 -$125.
Extra person $15 or $23 with B/F
Visa MC BC Amex Eftpos accepted
7 Queen 1 Double 5 Single (8 bdrm)
Bathrooms: 8 Ensuite

Nambucca Riverview Lodge is in the perfect seaside location. Originally a Historic Hotel, it has been charmingly refurbished with all the comforts of home. All rooms are air conditioned and feature ensuites and private balconies to enjoy breathtaking ocean and river views. It is a stone's throw from fantastic seafood restaurants, children's playground, tennis courts, boating, rainforest and boardwalks. Short stroll to clubs and shops. Quiet and private with undercover parking, wonderfully spacious rooms and genuine country hospitality will ensure a most memorable stay. Outdoor Hot Tub Spa available to all guests. "We will always remember this best kept secret." MN, Atlanta, USA.

Nambucca Heads - Macksville

Jacaranda Country Lodge *B&B*
Jude Rhoades
PO Box 364
Macksville
NSW 2447
3 km W of Macksville

Tel (02) 6568 2737
Fax (02) 6568 2769
jacaranda@midcoast.com.au
www.jaclodge.com.au

Double $110-$135 Single $90-$120
Child $15 - $25
Continental Breakfast   Dinner $25
Extra Adult $25 - $35
Visa MC BC accepted
9 Queen 2 Double 1 Twin (12 bdrm)
Bathrooms: 12 Ensuite

Country club facilities with B & B hospitality. Gracious accommodation set amidst pastures, wetlands and lily-filled ponds. Savour home baking and local fruit on our breakfast buffet. Relax in the lounge with its over-stuffed sofas, TV, billiard table and fireplace. Enjoy the pool, sauna, spa, tennis court, or fish from our Nambucca River jetty. Be entertained by the resident band of thoroughbreds and the prolific bird life. An idyllic place for a quiet night's rest or a base for exploring the scenic delights of the Nambucca Valley.

Narooma

The Grove *B&B*
Patricia and Brian Gorman
290 Riverview Road
Narooma
NSW 2546
3 km N of Narooma

Tel (02) 4476 1311
or 0407 936 050
Fax (02) 4476 1322
bpgorman@bigpond.com
www.thegrovebb.com.au

Double $149-$159 Single $99
Child $50
Includes full breakfast
Visa MC BC accepted
2 Queen 1 Twin (3 bdrm)
Bathrooms: 3 Ensuite 1 with spa

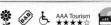

The Grove offers guests the highest standards of comfort in stunning natural surroundings. Situated on 50 hectares overlooking the pristine waters of Wagonga Inlet, 3 kilometres from Narooma. Wake to the calls of birds and frogs, enjoy a gourmet breakfast on the verandah, or sip wine in front of the fire. Walk in forests and on beaches, play golf, fish or dive, whale watch or simply relax in our extensive gardens. "A truly beautiful and tranquil setting. Absolutely luxurious accommodation. Natural surrounds superb. Such warm hospitality!" AI Dover Heights. Friendly dog in residence.

Narromine

Camerons Farmstay *B&B Homestay Farmstay Self Contained Cottage*
Ian and Kerry Cameron
Nundoone Park, 213 Ceres Road
Narromine NSW 2821
6 km W of Narromine

Tel (02) 6889 2978
Fax (02) 6889 5229
www.bbbook.com.au/camerons.html

Double $110-$130 Single $90-$80
Child $40
Continental Breakfast
Dinner B/A
No smoking on property
2 Queen 2 Double 1 Twin 4 Single (5 bdrm)
Bathrooms: 1 Ensuite 1 Guest share

Our home, 30 minutes west of Dubbo. We offer 4 1/2 star S/C cottage and B&B. Our house. is modern and spacious with reverse cycle air-conditioning with each bedroom having a fan/heater; guest lounge has television, video, books, tea/coffee making facilities, fridge etc. It is surrounded by large gardens, all weather tennis court, and pool. Ian and Kerry run a successful Border Leicester Sheep stud - see lambs, shearing, haymaking, cotton growing and harvesting (seasonal), tour cotton gin. Visit: Rose Nursery, Iris Farm, Aviation Museum and Gliding Centre. " Excellent, comfortable accommodation and great hospitality. So good to come back." P&G, Belgium.

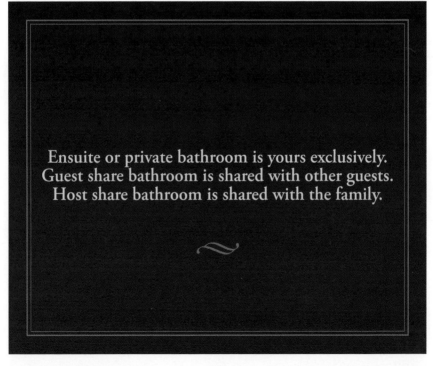

Ensuite or private bathroom is yours exclusively.
Guest share bathroom is shared with other guests.
Host share bathroom is shared with the family.

New England Bed &
Breakfast/Farmstays
Over 30 of the finest & friendliest

www.ruralstay.com

our **NEB&B/Farmstays booklets** *are available at*
Armidale Visitor's Information Centre - 02 6772 4655

Narooma - Tilba

Pub Hill Farm *B&B Self Contained Farm Cottage*
Micki & Ian Thomlinson
566 Scenic Drive or Box 227
Narooma
NSW 2546
8 km W of Narooma

Tel (02) 4476 3177
Fax (02) 4476 3177
pubhill@austarnet.com.au
www.pubhillfarm.com

Double $100-$125 Single $90-$100
Includes full breakfast
Karibu Cottage $150 per day
1 King/Twin 3 Queen 1 Double 2 Single
(4 bdrm)
Bathrooms: 5 Ensuite

AAA Tourism ★★★★☆

Pub Hill Farm is a small farm running beef cattle. It is situated high on a hill on the original site of the old Wagonga Hotel, overlooking the beautiful Wagonga Inlet with views over Mt. Dromedary to the South. Pub Hill has over one and a half kilometres of absolute water frontage onto the Inlet and also Punkallah Creek. The delightful seaside town of Narooma is just ten minutes away. The Wagonga Inlet enters the sea at Narooma and the magnificent turquoise colour of the water is a stunning sight to greet guests as they arrive by car. Narooma's incredible 18 hole golf course is renowned throughout Australia; The heritage villages of Central Tilba and Tilba Tilba are just 11 kms from Pub Hill. Here you can browse in interesting shops, visit the beautiful Foxglove Spires open garden and enjoy a great cup of coffee or a wonderful light lunch at Love at First Bite Cafe. The popular whale watch tours to Montague Island depart from Narooma daily in Spring. The birdlife at Pub Hill is both abundant and varied . Over 100 different birds have been sighted and listed at Pub Hill and the extreme quiet makes it an ideal place to bird watch. Small mobs of Eastern Grey kangaroos and Swamp wallabies also live on the property and can usually be seen at dusk.

Continued next page »

This is also a fishermen's paradise. Those keen to fish can do so in the estuary or they may simply throw a line in while sitting on the bank of our creek which runs through the farm. Cook the catch for dinner on one of our barbecues! Bushwalking in the quiet forests surrounding the farm is an ideal way to walk off the hearty breakfast. Our aim is to make guests feel at home and to relax and enjoy our large gardens. All four rooms have water views and each has a private sitting-out area and private entrance. All rooms have ensuite bathrooms, microwaves and fridges, colour TV and tea and coffee making equipment. We welcome guests' pets if they are well behaved and our large garden is fully fenced. Pub Hill is a non-smoking household but guests may, of course, smoke whilst sitting outside enjoying the views. We provide breakfast only but will happily recommend any of Narooma's excellent restaurants. We have travelled extensively and have lived abroad in both U K and North and East Africa for many years. We love sharing our

beautiful property, as we have been doing happily for 16 years, with guests from Australia and overseas, and enjoy swapping travellers tales with our new friends. Because of Narooma's very pleasant and mild winter climate we have no real low season at Pub Hill Farm and it is recommended that you make advance bookings to avoid disappointment. Opening in October 2005 is our brand new self contained "Karibu Cottage" (Karibu is Swahili for "welcome"). Karibu is simply gorgeous. Just for two people with mezzanine bedroom and views to die for over Wagonga Inlet. Beautifully appointed with everything you will need for a short or longer stay it sits in its own secluded garden and lawns where you can enjoy water or mountain views in complete privacy and quiet. Bookings being taken now. Four very friendly Border Collies live at Pub Hill. "Quite the best B&B we have ever stayed at, anywhere. Superb hospitality" J and P J, Woodham, Surrey, England. "Am speechless - loved every minute - your hospitality was warm and wonderful" Mary and Bill R, Los Osos, California USA."Just as relaxing 6th time around - thank you." Trish and Phil R and David N, East Ryde, Sydney. "A home away from home but in the country, what more could you want? We love it and always want to return. Thank you Micki and Ian". Ann B, Petersham, Sydney.

Newcastle

Newcomen B&B *B&B Studio accommdation*
Rosemary Bunker
70 Newcomen Street
Newcastle
NSW 2300
In Newcastle Central

Tel (02) 4929 7313
or 0412 145 104
Fax (02) 4929 7645
newcomen_bb@hotmail.com
www.newcomen-bb.com.au

Double $120 Single $90
Child $15
Includes full breakfast
Visa MC BC accepted
1 Queen 1 Single (1 bdrm)
Bathrooms: 1 Private

Nestling in Newcastle's historic precinct with ocean and city views, Newcomen offers personalised accommodation with absolute privacy and warm hospitality. The heritage ambience of the decor complements essentials for contemporary away-from-home living, including a sumptuous breakfast treat. It's a short stroll to beaches, galleries, harbour and cafes.

Newcastle - Hamilton

Hamilton Heritage *B&B*
Laraine & Colin Bunt
178 Denison Street
Hamilton, NSW 2303
6 km N of Newcastle

Tel (02) 4961 1242 or 0414 717 688
Fax (02) 4969 4758
colaine@iprimus.com.au
www.theholidayhost.com/
hamiltonheritage

Double $95-$130 Single $89-$100
Child $10-$20 (under 3 free)
Includes special breakfast
Wedding night champagne $185
Visa MC BC accepted
2 Queen 1 Double 1 Single (3 bdrm)
Bathrooms: 3 Ensuite

Hamilton Heritage B&B, "Old World Charm", situated on Historic Cameron Hill. Close to Broadmeadow Station, Broadmeadow Race Course, Newcastle Entertainment Centre & All Major Sporting Venues. Beaumont Street the Cosmopolitan Heart of Newcastle famous for its Restaurants, Newcastle CBD, Foreshore and Beaches. Feel free to enjoy the serenity of the garden or the verandah. Breakfast of choice and time served in the Breakfast Room overlooking garden Laundry facilities available. Fax and e-mail access. We also offer a unique and memorable place to stay for newlyweds, before heading off on their honeymoon.

Newcastle - Merewether

Merewether Beach B&B *B&B*

Jane & Alf Scott
60 Hickson Street
Merewether
NSW 2291
5 km S of Newcastle PO

Tel (02) 4963 3526 or 0407 921 670
Fax (02) 4963 7926
janescott@bigpond.com
www.merewetherbeachbandb.com

Double $130 Single $100
Child by arrangement
Includes full breakfast
Visa MC BC accepted
1 Double 3 Single (2 bdrm)
Bathrooms: 1 Ensuite

Wake up to this view! Go to sleep with only the sound of waves breaking on shore. Three minutes stroll to beach, 5 km from CBD, 1000 km from care. Featured on "Getaway", air-conditioned, self-contained studio with kitchenette, glassed-in verandah, private entrance and garden. Children welcome. Not suitable for pets. Alf's ceramics and paintings lovingly adorn the rooms. With Jane's passion for cooking, expect a breakfast extravaganza. You are our only guests. Let us spoil you! "The view is as rare as the B&B itself. Superb cooking by Jane and like living in an Art Gallery thanks to Alf." L&DF, Bowral.

Nundle

Jenkins Street Guest House B&B *B&B Guest House*

Judy Howarth
85 Jenkins Street
Nundle
NSW 2340
In Nundle

Tel (02) 6769 3239
Fax (02) 9769 3239
jenkinsstreetguesthouse@bigpond.com
www.nundle.info

Double $140-$180 Single $99
Includes full breakfast
Dinner $40 - $60
Visa MC BC Eftpos accepted
7 Queen (7 bdrm)
Bathrooms: 4 Ensuite 3 Guest share

Nundle is a tiny historic mining village of just 150 people nested in the foot hills of the Great Dividing Range. Jenkins Street Guest House is a superbly renovated Bank building with sitting room, library and verandahs overlooking extensive gardens. Open fire places, damask linen and antiques surround you. We welcome weddings. Fully licensed restaurant - Cha Cha Cha - open 7 days. Horse riding, bush walks, farm tours, craft and antique shops and Nundle Woollen Mill nearby golf and tennis.

Orange

Cotehele: The Magistrates House *B&B*

Marie Eedy
177 Anson Street
Orange
NSW 2800
0.4 km SW of PO

Tel (02) 6361 2520
or 0431 256 090
Fax (02) 6361 2521
info@cotehele.com.au
www.cotehele.com.au

Double $175 Single $110-$120
Includes full breakfast
Visa MC BC Eftpos accepted
5 Queen 1 Single (5 bdrm) Total Capacity for 11 guests
Bathrooms: 5 Ensuite, 1 room with Spa

The Magistrate's House - Cotehele is a well established Bed & Breakfast in a quiet and convenient location, close to shops and restaurants and just 3 minutes walk to Orange CBD. Built in 1878 as the Magistrate's town house, Cotehele has recently been restored to its Victorian grandeur and offers luxury accommodation for guests. Guest rooms have been immaculately furnished for a comfortable stay including guest lounge with log fire, cosy dining room for sumptuous breakfasts and the sunny courtyard for afternoon teas. The cottage garden is also a feature of this property.

Orange

Acacia Grove *B&B Self Contained*

Margaret Johnson
33 Neal's Lane, off Cargo Road
Orange
NSW 2800
2 km W of Orange

Tel (02) 6365 3336
or 0419 653 336
Fax (02) 6365 3000
bnb@acaciagrove.com.au
www.acaciagrove.com.au

Double $105-$125 Single $90-110
Child B/A
Includes full breakfast
Dinner by arrangement $20- $25
Self Contained - Double $125 per night then reductions after first night
Visa MC BC Diners Amex accepted
1 Queen 1 Double 1 Twin (3 bdrm)
Bathrooms: 2 Ensuite 1 Private

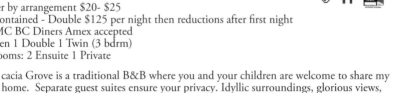

Acacia Grove is a traditional B&B where you and your children are welcome to share my home. Separate guest suites ensure your privacy. Idyllic surroundings, glorious views, and sumptuous breakfasts imperceptibly generate feelings of wellbeing and relaxation. Home grown and local produce served when possible.

Orange

Cloudgap *Luxury B&B*
Susan & Tony Doe
224 Strathnook Lane
Orange
NSW 2800
9 km E of Town

Tel (02) 6365 1231
cloudgap@cloudgap.com.au
www.cloudgap.com.au

Double $165-$225 Single $145
Includes full breakfast   Dinner $55
No smoking on property
Visa MC BC Diners Amex accepted
3 King (3 bdrm)
Bathrooms: 3 Ensuite with hydrotherapy spa bath

AAA Tourism
★★★★☆

Embrace the luxury and be pampered at Cloudgap, a new luxury boutique retreat set in 150 acres of magnificent gardens and unspoilt bushland. Three fully air-conditioned & heated, spacious, luxurious, private king bed and deep hydrotherapy spa ensuites are inspirationally designed for couples seeking privacy and modern comfort. Rooms include soft, fluffy king bath sheets, crisp fresh linen, soft doonas, electric blankets, toiletries, hair dryer, iron/board, refrigerator, tea/coffee, safe & direct-dial phone for Internet access. Surrounded by abundant bird and wildlife, Cloudgap is a very special, irresistibly romantic and magical hideaway, the perfect environment to soothe and relax tired souls and rejuvenate energies. From your balcony watch the kangaroos hop by and be amused by the antics of the parrots, kookaburras and wild duck that call Cloudgap home. To discover an appetite for dinner, take a short walk along meandering paths in the midst of tall eucalyptus & listen to the bird calls distinct in the silence. Our delightful four-course dinners - accompanied by complimentary fine wines - are prepared using fresh home grown and local produce and are served in the elegant guest dining room. The dinner menus are influenced by European cuisine especially French and Portuguese. Special diets too, are catered for. Following a perfect night's sleep, wake up a full gourmet breakfast served in the dining room at a time of your choice. Choose from our wide selection of multiple night packages offered on our website or call us.

Orange

Greentrees *B&B Separate Suite Apartment with Kitchen Guest House*
Jasmin Bond
33 Pinnacle Road
Orange   NSW 2800
4.5 km SW of Orange

Tel (02) 6361 4546
Fax (02) 6361 4566
jasmin.bond@bigpond.com
www.greentreeshouse.com.au

Double $120-$225 Single $95-$225   Child $14
Includes full breakfast   Dinner from $30
Visa MC BC accepted
1 King/Twin 8 Queen (9 bdrm)
Bathrooms: 9 Ensuite

Greentrees is a very comfortable country home with peaceful valley views. Extensive lawns, flower beds, shrubs and trees combine to create a peaceful garden and serene atmosphere. Informal friendly hospitality is the theme at Greentrees. Homemade jams, jellies and marmalades and preserved peaches, pears, plums, apricots and other luscious fruit are offered to guests in season. There are eight rooms - all with ensuites - and one very luxurious suite. The gold and pink rooms (both sleep three people

each) are very prettily furnished and are located in the original home, which is set out with comfortable old fashioned and antique furniture and is centrally heated. The new guest wing, which has six rooms and one suite, is very attractively furnished. Each room has its own theme, colour, decor, design and shape. Spring and Autumn sleep four people each. Summer, Harvest and Birdsong sleep five people each with the latter two having kitchenettes. Barnyard sleeps six people and has its own kitchenette. All six guest rooms have their own very large ensuites, private balcony or verandah, beautiful valley views, split system air conditioners, colour TVs, fridges, irons and ironing boards and tea making facilities. The Rose Suite, the premier suite, features all the above facilities. It also has a small sitting room, king bed, and enormous bathroom with a large spa, double shower, double vanity, toilet and bidet. The BYO restaurant seats some 55 people and is ideal for special occasions and family celebrations. Bookings are essential. Disabled facilities are available for The Guesthouse and the restaurant.

Orange

Killarney Homestead *Homestay*
Beth & Colin Magick
Darley Road
Nashdale
NSW 2800
10 km W of Orange

Tel (02) 6365 3419 or 0417 283 762
Fax (02) 6365 3419
KillarneyBandB@aol.com
cww.octec.org.au/killarney

Double $100-$120 Single $80
Child $20 under 12 yrs
Includes full breakfast Dinner $25 B/A
No smoking on property Visa MC BC accepted
1 Queen 1 Double 2 Single (3 bdrm)
Bathrooms: 1 Ensuite 1 Guest share

Relax in a restored Federation homestead set amongst rambling gardens and orchards on slopes of Mt Canobolas. Only minutes from wineries, great bushwalking and Orange's parks, historic buildings galleries, gardens and golf courses. An ideal spot to use as a base when visiting Orange, the Central West or just passing through. Enjoy top hospitality and great cooking with friendly hosts who have an interest in antiques and a good knowledge of local attractions and places of interest. Log fire. No pets. No smoking.

Parkes

Kadina B&B *B&B*
Helen and Malcolm Westcott
22 Mengarvie Road
Parkes
NSW 2870
1.5 km E of Parkes CBD

Tel (02) 6862 3995
or 0412 444 452
Fax (02) 6862 6451
kadinabb@bigpond.net.au
www.kadinabnb.com

Double $110 Single $80
Child B/A
Includes full breakfast
Dinner B/A
Visa MC BC Diners accepted
2 Queen 1 Single (2 bdrm)
Bathrooms: 2 Ensuite

AAA Tourism
★★★★☆

Come and enjoy the tranquillity and ambience of this lovely modern spacious home. Watch TV, listen to music, play piano, read or just soak in the views. Dine in our traditionally furnished dining room, patio or secluded back garden. Mal is involved in cereal growing and merino sheep farming. Guests may visit when convenient. Come and see "The Dish". Relax in our luxurious therapeutic Hot Tub. Winner of Explorer Country Tourism Award for Hosted Accommodation and Finalists in NSW 2002. Finalist in 2004 Inland Tourism Awards.

Port Macquarie

Woodlands Bed & Breakfast *B&B*
Ian & Gretel McGinnigle
348 Oxley Highway
Port Macquarie
NSW 2444
3 km W of town centre

Tel (02) 6581 3913 or 0412 443 277
info@woodlandsbnb.com.au
www.woodlandsbnb.com.au

Double $130-$150 **Single** $110-$130
Includes full breakfast
Visa MC BC accepted
1 King/Twin 4 Queen (3 suites bdrm)
Bathrooms: 1 Ensuite 2 Private

Woodlands B&B Port Macquarie offers luxury accommodation and hospitality in a relaxed setting of gardens and trees where guests can relax in quiet comfort and seclusion with easy access to all the attractions of the area. Luxury air-conditioned accommodation options include the two bedroom Frangipani Suite which is partly self contained with lounge and equiped kitchen area, the two bedroom Magnolia Suite with its magnificently large bathroom and the Verandah Room, a ensuited queen size bedroom which opens out to the verandah and landscaped front gardens. Both the suites can be booked as double rooms only - the same rates as the Verandah Room apply. All rooms have the full complement of expected comforts. Great dinner/accommodation package deals are available for couples and groups.

Port Macquarie - Bonny Hills

Kookaburras Bed and Breakfast *B&B*
Deborah and Robert Buchanan
1121 Ocean Drive
Bonny Hills
NSW 2445
6 km N of North Haven

Tel (02) 6585 5841
or 0405 159 329
Fax (02) 6586 3586
bandb@kookaburras.com.au
www.kookaburras.com.au

Double $150-$200
Includes full breakfast
No smoking on property
Visa MC BC accepted
2 Queen (2 bdrm)
Bathrooms: 2 Ensuite

Set on a leafy half acre close to the beach, this new B&B, in a separate wing, comprises two deluxe A/C queen bedrooms, each with en-suite bathroom, TV, DVD and private entrance. The comfy guests' lounge/dining room with 'fridge, microwave and tea making facilities. We are just a couple of minutes from beaches, shops and tavern. The area boasts wineries, golf courses, restaurants, galleries and national parks. We welcome children and pets by arrangement and are a non-smoking establishment.

Port Macquarie Hinterland - Ellenborough

Toms Creek Retreat *Cottage with Kitchen*

Margaret and Stewart Williams
223 Toms Creek Road
Ellenborough
NSW 2446
45 km W of Port Macquarie

Tel (02) 6587 4313
or 0412 199 484
Fax (02) 6587 4313
tomscreekretreat@bigpond.com
www.tomscreekretreat.com.au

Double $130-$165
Child $30
Accommodation Only only
Visa MC BC Eftpos accepted
3 Queen 3 Double 2 Single (3 bdrm)
Bathrooms: 3 Private

W inner 2004 NSW North Coast Tourism Award for Best Hosted Accommodation. Ecotourism accredited. 3 private s/c cottages on 160 acres in a magnificent mountain setting. Fully equipped for self-catering plus bbq facilities. Walk and enjoy the extensive bird and wildlife or simply relax and observe nature from your spacious deck. River frontage provides a natural spa and swimming as well as possible sightings of our resident platypus. Perfectly located for exploring the cafes, galleries and wineries of the beautiful Port Macquarie Hinterland.

Port Macquarie Hinterland - Wauchope

Auntie Ann's Bed & Breakfast *B&B*

Ann Pereira
19 Bruxner Avenue
Wauchope
NSW 2446
0.5 km W of Wauchope PO

Tel (02) 6586 4420
www.bbbook.com.au/auntieanns.html

Double $77 Single $55
Includes full breakfast
No smoking on property
Visa MC BC accepted
1 Double 4 Twin (3 bdrm)
Bathrooms: 1 Guest share

W auchope is the gateway to Port Macquarie's Hinterland. Within easy driving are several national parks, nature reserves and vineyards as well as the largest single drop waterfall in the Southern Hemisphere. Overlooking the golf course, Auntie Ann's is close to clubs, restaurants and shops. Visit Timbertown Heritage Park, art, pottery and furniture galleries or just relax by the pool with some locally made fudge. Also available: Air-conditioning, TV room, BBQ, tea/coffee making facilities, heaters and/or fans each room.

Escape to...
"a high quiet place"...

Hannam Vale

One of nature's great secrets, Hannam Vale is tucked away just off the Pacific Hwy., between Taree and Port Macquarie...and yet only thirty minutes from the beaches of the Pacific Ocean. It is closer still to the Cooranbakh National Park with its vistas of the hinterland escarpment and a spread of countryside from Wingham through Lansdowne to Comboyne.

With its roller-coaster country lanes, rattling wooden bridges and the rich green pastures of the early twentieth century, Hannam Vale reminds its many visitors of rural England.

Hannam Vale is under four hours drive from Sydney and an easy eight hours from Brisbane; it is half way between Sydney and Byron Bay on the Mid North Coast of New South Wales.

B&B Farmstay and Self Contained B&B Cottages
Port Macquarie / Taree Hinterland - Hannam Vale
20 km South of Laurieton

Sherry Stumm & Peter Wildblood
Cherry Tree Lane - Hannam Vale 2443
Phone: 02 6556 7788 - Freecall: 1800 187 888

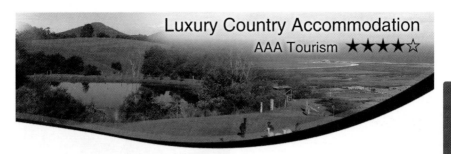

Luxury Country Accommodation
AAA Tourism ★★★★☆

Benbellen Country Retreat (B&B Farmstay)
Double: $145-$175 Single: $110-$135 (Full Breakfast) Dinner $35+
3 Queen (3 bdrm) - all ensuite

Revitalise yourself with fresh air, the peaceful relaxed atmosphere and our country hospitality. The large open-plan homestead, with its solar passive design and its quietly stated elegance, is purpose built with your privacy and comfort in mind.

Benbellen Country Retreat is a small working alpaca and [Wagyu] beef producing farm tucked away high in a lush valley just 40 minutes from Port Macquarie, 25 minutes from Laurieton and 30 minutes from Taree.

You will fall in love with the farm itself, with its magical landscape of rolling hills, lily strewn dams and lush pastures.

Cherry Tree Cottage (Self Contained B&B Cottage)
Double: $145-$205 Extra people: $5-$35 Single: $110-$165
1 Queen (1bdrm) 1 Ensuite

Located on Benbellen farm, Cherry Tree Cottage is some 100 metres from the homestead, adjacent to the alpaca paddocks. It has two ample sized bedrooms and a large lounge/dining area that spills onto a huge open verandah that captures the early sun and provides access to the wonderful views over the large dam on the property and to South Brother Mountain. Cherry Tree Cottage is suited to small families (2+3) looking for on-farm experiences. Pets are only by arrangement.

Penlan Cottage (Self Contained B&B Cottage)
Double: $145-$205 Extra people: $5-$35 Single: $110-$165
1 Queen (1bdrm) 1 Ensuite

Penlan Cottage is a delightful Queenslander-style "home away from home" on an acre and a half adjacent to a dairy where black and white Friesian heifers wander across green pastures that roll on down the valley. Its large living areas and open verandahs provide "space" for relaxing and enjoying the country life free of the cares of the world. Sleeping up to six people, Penlan Cottage is also an excellent jumping off point for visiting the beaches, national parks and other considerable attractions of the area. Pets are most welcome.

www.bbfarmstay.com.au

Port Stephens - Nelson Bay

Croft Haven B&B *B&B Homestay*
Dian Cox
202 Salamander Way
Nelson Bay
NSW 2317
4 km S of Nelson Bay

Tel (02) 4984 1799
or 0405 257 914
Fax (02) 4984 1799
crofthav@bigpond.net.au
www.crofthaven-nelsonbay.com

Double $110-$150 Single $85
Child $45
Includes full breakfast
$55 extra adult
Visa MC BC accepted
1 King/Twin1 King 1 Queen 1 Double 1 Twin 1 Single (3 bdrm)
Bathrooms: 2 Ensuite 1 Private

AAA Tourism
★★★★

R elax, Reflect & Rejuvenate. Our bushland retreat by the sea is so close but so far
from the hustle & bustle of city life. Croft Haven is central to all Port Stephens
major attractions with beautifully appointed guest rooms and surrounds. Enjoy
our sumptuous buffet & specialty breakfasts served in the courtyard, at your leisure. With
fireplaces for winter comfort and barbecue area for summer sizzles, let the stress of everyday
life drift away. Ask about our packages for the ultimate in fun, rest & relaxation.

Scone - Hunter Valley

Willowgate Hall Luxury *B&B & Guest house*
Theresa
91 Kingdon Street
Scone
NSW 2337
In Scone

Tel (02) 6545 9378
Fax (02) 6545 9378
enquiries@willowgatehall.com.au
www.willowgatehall.com.au

Double $135-$200 Single: $80
Includes full breakfast
Gourmet Dinner B/A $25-$40
Bridal & Business functions, Cocktail parties B/A
Visa MC BC accepted
4 Queen 1 Double 1 Single (5 Bedrooms, 1 with private sitting room)
Total capacity for 11 guests.
Bathrooms: 2 Ensuite 1 Guest share

W illowgate Hall offers luxury bed and breakfast accommodation right in the heart of
Scone NSW. We have five rooms, one with Queen bed, bathroom & private sitting.
You will be in luxurious comfort, luxury linen and towels, gourmet meals, beautiful
gardens, in ground pool and hosts that want to make your stay a memorable one. Afternoon
tea or pre-dinner drink on arrival and a full breakfast. Enjoy a break in relaxed and friendly
atmosphere with all the comforts of home only 3 hours from Sydney, on the New England
highway.

Snowy Mountains - Khancoban

Cossettini B&B *B&B Homestay Farmstay Self Contained*
Joe and Kathleen Cossettini
Alpine Way
Khancoban
NSW 2642
7 km N of Khancoban

Tel (02) 6076 9332
Fax (02) 6076 9332
www.bbbook.com.au/cossettini.html

Double $70-$90 Single $60
Child $20
Includes special breakfast
$250-$300 per week
2 King/Twin 2 Queen (2 bdrm)
Bathrooms: 1 Ensuite 1 Private

Escape to peace and tranquillity in delightful Khancoban, with spectacular views of the Snowy Mountains, half way between Sydney and Melbourne. Enjoy warmth and hospitality in this centrally heated home. Relax in your private spa, sleep in crisp white linen and wake to the delicious aroma of freshly made cappuccino and a generous gourmet country breakfast. Access to a wide range of activities including fishing, golf, bush-walking, horse-riding, rock-climbing, white water rafting, skiing.

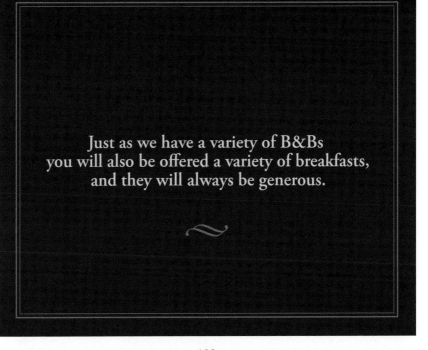

Just as we have a variety of B&Bs
you will also be offered a variety of breakfasts,
and they will always be generous.

South Coast
Accommodation South Coast (NSW) Association (ASCA)

Tel (02) 4464 3335
info@accommodationsouthcoast.com.au
www.accommodationsouthcoast.com.au

Accommodation South Coast (NSW) Association (ASCA) offers accommodation for everyone visiting the beautiful South Coast. Choose from bed and breakfast guesthouses, self contained cottages, entire houses, hotel or motel accommodation. If you desire privacy for your romantic getaway for two, if you crave a luxurious pampered weekend away, or if you want to take the children and the dog away for a holiday - ASCA can provide an accommodation venue perfect for you. Only 2 hours drive from Sydney or Canberra, the South Coast of NSW is a treasure trove for adults and children alike. Offering pristine beaches, rugged headlands, rainforests and mountain escapes. ASCA Members have catering down to a fine art - from your picnic basket, romantic dinner, formal or casual dining, corporate events, functions, weddings and other special occasions. Spend your days as organised as you like or as relaxed as you prefer; treat yourself to the plethora of cafés, antiques, shops, gift stores, markets and inviting coffee houses. Enjoy spectacular scenery on one of hundreds of walks, relax on the whitest beaches or cosy up in front of an open fire. From Minnamurra Falls to Seven Mile Beach, from Berry to Jervis Bay, you will want to return again and again. Romantic dinner for two, a short stay, a long holiday, or perhaps just to getaway; Accommodation South Coast (NSW) Association endeavours to ensure your visit to the South Coast of NSW is one you will never want to forget.

South West Rocks - Yarrahapinni

Yarrahapinni Homestead *Luxury B&B*
Kevin & Glenda Wilson
340 Stuarts Point Rd
Yarrahapinni
NSW 2441
5 km S of Stuarts Point

Tel (02) 6569 0240
or 0418 225 810
Fax (02) 6569 0160
yarrahome@bigpond.com
yarrahome.com.au

Double $120-$135 Single $100-$110
Includes full breakfast
Dinner $22.00 per head by arrangement
Visa MC BC accepted
3 Queen (3 bdrm)
Bathrooms: 3 Ensuite

Nestled at the foot of Yarrahapinni Mountain you will find the perfect place to stay and relax. The architect designed Yarrahapinni Homestead is located on a 10-acre parkland setting, close to unspoilt beaches and spectacular national parks. The Homestead includes three spacious and tastefully decorated air-conditioned bedrooms with en-suites and open verandas. The Pool Patio, Pool and Spa provide the perfect location for those balmy summer afternoons. A sumptuous breakfast with your choice of full cooked or continental meals made from the finest of local ingredients is served in the Breakfast Room or on the Mountain Patio.

Southern Highlands - Burradoo - Bowral

Hartnoll Park *Cottage with Kitchen*
Julie & Bill Flemming
8 Ranelagh Road
Burradoo
NSW 2576
2 km S of Bowral

Tel (02) 4861 7282
or 0429 001 042
Fax (02) 4861 7252
stay@hartnollpark.com.au
www.hartnollpark.com.au

Double $150-$200 Single
Full Breakfast Provisions
Visa MC BC accepted
2 Queen (2 bdrm)
Bathrooms: 1 Private

I ndulge yourself in our tranquil self-contained 2 bedroom cottage nestled in the old part of Burradoo. Plan your romantic escape to this inviting country cottage that features queen size beds, comfortable lounge, full kitchen, bathroom, separate laundry, relaxing outdoor area and private garden. Quality linen, TV/DVD/video, gas log heating, electric blankets and all those little luxuries for a relaxing break in the Southern Highlands. Only 75 minutes from Sydney - we look forward to welcoming you.

Southern Highlands - Goulburn

Mandelson's of Goulburn *B&B Guest House*
Noel and Renate Johnson-Barrett
160 Sloane Street
Goulburn
NSW 2580
In Goulburn. On the edge of CBD

Tel (02) 4821 0707
or 0414 813 601
Fax (02) 4821 0225
reception@mandelsons.com.au
www.mandelsons.com.au

Double $150-$215 Single $115-$205
Child $40
Includes full breakfast
Dinner With prior arrangement only
8 Queen 1 Double 5 Single (8 bdrm)
Bathrooms: 8 Ensuite

AAA Tourism
★★★★☆

A splendid example of colonial architecture, Noel and Renate have passionately restored and refurbished Mandelson's into an elegant and luxurious yet homely boutique style B&B. A complementary decanter of port and chocolates, superior bedding, electric blankets, central heating, air conditioning, bathrobes and more are signs of the world class, warm and friendly hospitality all guests will receive. Your hosts are happy to recommend a number of restaurants within easy walking distance and a delicious full breakfast with homemade jam is served in the Dining Room.

Southern Highlands - Moss Vale

Heronswood House *B&B*
Brian & Tina Davis
165 Argyle Street
Moss Vale
NSW 2577
1 km N of Moss Vale

Tel (02) 4869 1477
Fax (02) 4869 4079
heron@acenet.com.au
www.heronswood.com.au

Double $137.50-$198.00
Includes full breakfast
No smoking on property
Visa MC BC accepted
2 King/Twin 3 Queen 1 Single (5 bdrm)
Bathrooms: 4 Ensuite 1 Private

This beautiful 19th century home, on the North side of town, in the heart of the Highlands, offers you friendly, comfortable accommodation. The five bedrooms are tastefully decorated with one adapted for the physically disabled. The lounge, sunroom and kitchenette are available to guests. Greeted with afternoon tea on arrival. Breakfast each morning is varied and generous, ranging from traditional to house specials eg "Herons Nest". The wide verandahs and one acre of grounds encourage you to relax and enjoy the delights of the Highlands. *"Arrive as a visitor, leave as a friend."*

Southern Highlands - Robertson

Ranelagh House *B&B Guesthouse, Conference Centre*
Vera Menday
Illawarra Highway
Robertson
NSW 2577
25 km SE of Bowral

Tel (02) 4885 1111
Fax (02) 4885 1130
ranelagh@hinet.net.au
www.ranelagh-house.com.au

Double $95-$130 **Single** $55-$90
Child $10 - half price
Includes full breakfast
Dinner Additional meals $10-$40
Dinner, B&B from $95-$135 per person
Visa MC BC accepted
6 King 10 Queen 18 Double 7 Twin (26 bdrm)
Bathrooms: 16 Ensuite 6 Guest share

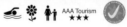

Ranelagh House (circa 1924), is a 3-4 storey English manor House operating as a Guest House, B&B and Function Centre. Set on 13.5 acres of landscaped grounds, rainforest, weir and swimming pool. Deer and peacocks roam the grounds. Built as Hotel Robertson, then used as a Country Club, WRAAF depot in WWII, then a Franciscan Friary, when the beautiful stained glass windows were installed. Enjoy meals in our formal dining room or relax in front of one of the several open fires with our special Devonshire Tea.

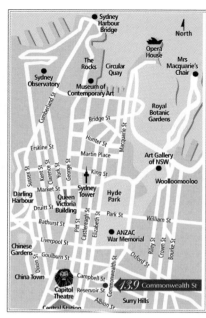

Sydney

Bed and Breakfast Sydney Central *B&B Homestay 2 bedroom suite available*

Julie Stevenson
139 Commonwealth Street
Surry Hills, NSW 2010
In Sydney Central

Tel (02) 9211 9920
or 0419 202 779
Fax (02) 9212 2450
jas@bedandbreakfastsydney.com.au
www.bedandbreakfastsydney.com.au

Double $130-$160
Includes Continental Breakfast
2 bedroom suite available
No smoking on property
3 King/Twin (3 bdrm)
Bathrooms: 1 Guest share 2 Private

Guests, David Lucus & Pat Woodley

An elegant Terrace house set in the heart of the best Sydney has to offer. Relax in the tranquillity and comfort of your 'home away from home'. A short walk to the The Capitol Theatre, Imax and all Theatres, Chinatown, Darling Harbour, Aquarium, Paddys and Fish Markets, Star City Casino, Chinese Garden of Friendship, Centrepoint Tower, Queen Victoria Building, Art Gallery of NSW, Museums, Law Courts, Hyde Park, Oxford Street, The Rocks, Circular Quay, the Opera House, the exciting harbour BridgeClimb. Board ferry to Manly, Zoo, Parramatta and Darling Harbour. Walk or drive to Fox Studios, the Sydney Cricket Ground, Universities, Cathedrals, Race Courses, Centennial Park, Beaches. Major attractions are Elizabeth Bay and Vaucluse House, Watsons Bay Beach 'Doyles' famous seafood restaurants. 3 Bedrooms (2) with balconies TV and Air-Conditioned A pretty patio garden off breakfast room One resident cat Not suitable for young children KST Sydney Airporter door to door.

Sydney

AAA Tourism
★★★★☆

Arcadia House Bed & Breakfast *B&B*
Donna & Gary Abbott
5 Toxteth Road
Glebe NSW 2037
3 km W of CDB

Tel (02) 9552 1941 or 0416 005 795
Fax (02) 9660 1594
reservations@arcadiahouse.com.au
www.arcadiahouse.com.au

Double $150-$250 Single $150-$250
Includes full breakfast
Visa MC BC Eftpos accepted
1 King/Twin 3 Queen (4 bdrm)
Bathrooms: 3 Ensuite 1 Private

Whether you are travelling to Sydney on business or pleasure Arcadia House offers the finest bed and breakfast accommodation in a fully restored Victorian home. Arcadia House offers the discerning guest the best of both worlds. Located in Glebe, a charming suburb full of character and history, surroundings are tranquil, yet the city is only five minutes away. Your spacious accommodation has old-world charm with all the modern comforts and conveniences. All bedrooms have ensuites/private bathrooms with heated floors, airconditioning, TVs, DVD/CD players, tea/coffee making facilities, irons/ ironing boards and internet connections. Other facilities include a guest lounge, library and email facilities. An exceptional breakfast is provided. Regular public transport to the city and Darling Harbour is 200 metres away. It is an easy walk to a multitude of restaurants, cafes, shops and movie theatres. Sydney University & RPA Hospital are within walking distant. Guest comments:
Kevin & Michelle, Philadelphia USA "Thank you so much for making our stay in Sydney so wonderful. The location is fantastic, your home is wonderful and hospitality incredible."
Leon & Kaaren, Canberra "Can't stop coming back! Arcadia House has everything that is fantastic about Sydney' heritage accommodation in a great Sydney location, all the comforts of home with lashings of luxury and with the most wonderful hosts." Arcadia House - Close to everything yet truly a world apart.

Sydney - Potts Point

Victoria Court Sydney *B&B*
Manager
122 Victoria Street
Sydney, Potts Point
NSW 2011
Within Sydney

AAA Tourism
★★★★

Tel (02) 9357 3200
Fax (02) 9357 7606
info@VictoriaCourt.com.au
www.VictoriaCourt.com.au

Double $99-$250 Single $60-$250
Includes full breakfast
Visa MC BC Diners Amex accepted
22 King/Twin 3 Single (25 bdrm)
Bathrooms: 25 Ensuite

Victoria Court, whose charming terrace house dates from 1881, is centrally located on quiet, leafy Victoria Street in Sydney's elegant Potts Point; the ideal base from which to explore Sydney. It is within minutes of the Opera House, the Central Business District and Beaches. Friendly and personalised service is offered in an informal atmosphere and amidst Victorian charm. No two rooms are alike; most have marble fireplaces, some have four-poster beds and others feature balconies with views over National Trust classified Victoria Street. All rooms have en-suite bathrooms, hairdryers, air-conditioning, colour television, a safe, radio-clock, coffee/tea making facilities and direct dial telephones. In the immediate vicinity are some of Sydney's most renowned restaurants and countless cafes with menus priced to suit all budgets. Public transport, car rental, travel agencies and banks are nearby. An airport shuttle bus operates to and from Victoria Court and security parking are available.

Sydney - Parramatta

Harborne Bed & Breakfast *B&B*
Josephine Assaf
21 Boundary Street
Parramatta
NSW 2150
2 km S of Parramatta

Tel (02) 9687 8988
Fax (02) 9687 8998
www.bbbook.com.au/harborne

Double $105-$140 **Single** $95-$130
Includes continental breakfast
Dinner from $20
$10 extra person
Visa MC BC Amex Diner Eftpos accepted
7 Queen 1 Single (8 bdrm) Family suite up to 7 adults
Bathrooms: 3 Ensuite 1 Guest share 1 Private

AAA Tourism ★★★★

H arborne is a magnificent 1858 Georgian sandstone mansion. Harborne has recently been restored as a charming 8 room B&B. The beautiful home and the lush gardens have been classified by the National Trust. A glazed breakfast atrium with Tea & coffee facilities is available. Harborne is ideal for a relaxed stay or business or team stay. Harborne, Your Home Away From Home.

Sydney - Annandale

Bet's B&B *B&B Self-contained studio*
Bet Dalton
176 Johnston Street
Annandale
NSW 2038
3 km W of Sydney

Tel (02) 9660 8265
Fax (02) 9660 8265
stay@betsbandb.com.au
www.betsbandb.com.au

Double $120-$130
Full Breakfast Provisions
Book for one week, pay for six nights
Visa MC BC accepted
1 Queen (1 bdrm)
Bathrooms: 1 Private

B et's B&B is a modern, comfortable and spacious artist-style studio-apartment. It's light and airy, roomy and clean. Self-contained and with its own private entrance, Bet's B&B is just 15 minutes by bus or light rail to the sights and attractions of Sydney and a three-minute stroll to the restaurants, cafes and shops of Annandale Village. Queen-size bed, a lounge area, dining table, fully-equipped kitchenette, washing machine, pullout clothes dryer and ironing facilities, reverse cycle air-conditioning and TV. Bet's B&B is private and quiet, clean and comfortable, cosy and convenient.

Sydney - Annandale

Aronui *B&B Homestay Cottage with Kitchen*
Pamela Bond
72A Johnston Street
Annandale
NSW 2038
3 km W of Sydney CBD

Tel (02) 9564 1992
or 0432 426 514
pamela.aronui@pocketmail.com
www.aronui.com

Double $120-$130 Single $100
Includes special breakfast
Visa MC BC accepted
1 King/Twin 1 Double (2 bdrm)
Bathrooms: 2 Ensuite

Built in 1895, Aronui is a superb example of Australian Victorian architecture, with high ceilings, ornate plasterwork, leadlight windows and marble fireplaces. The house is surrounded by lush rain forest gardens and has a solar saltwater swimming pool, bbq and delightful Koi fish pond. Aronui is close to restaurants, shops, Sydney University, RPA Hospital, Italian Forum. Historical walking tours available on request, also evening meals and picnic lunches. Open log fire in separate formal lounge. Reverse cycle a/c and cable TV in family room. We have a pet on property. Close to good public transport to the City Centre by bus or light rail.

Sydney - Castle Hill

Glenhope Bed & Breakfast *B&B*
Keith and Lyn Stapley
113 Castle Hill Road
West Pennant Hills
NSW 2125
3 km E of Castle Hill

Tel (02) 9634 2508
Fax (02) 9659 1674
admin@glenhope-bnb.com.au
www.glenhope-bnb.com.au

Double $165-$209 Single $121-$165
Includes full breakfast
3 Queen 1 Double (4 bdrm)
Bathrooms: 4 Ensuite

AAA Tourism
★★★★☆

Glenhope is a heritage listed former farmhouse set on the ridge at Castle Hill offering warm hospitality and personal attention in a comfortable, old world setting. There are 4 bedrooms upstairs, each with ensuite, full air conditioning, tv, phone. One bedroom even has a tower. Downstairs is the drawing room and formal dining room where we serve a wide range of breakfast fare. Evening dining available by arrangement. Set in more than an acre of gardens, Glenhope is conveniently located about 30 km NW of Sydney CBD in the attractive Hills area.

Sydney - Clovelly

Clovelly Bed & Breakfast *B&B*
Tony & Shirley Murray
2 Pacific Street
Clovelly
NSW 2031
6 km SE of Sydney

Tel (02) 9665 0009
or 0419 609 276
clovellybandb@yahoo.com
www.bbbook.com.au/clovelly.html

Double $130-$160 Single $100-$130
Includes full breakfast
Visa MC BC accepted
1 Queen 1 Double 2 Twin (3 bdrm)
Bathrooms: 1 Ensuite 2 Private

AAA Tourism
★★★★

C lovelly, Coogee and Bronte beaches and cafes/restaurants are within walking distance. We are close to transport to many of Sydney's tourist attractions. Afternoon tea will be served on arrival. Tea and coffee available all day. Breakfast includes fresh fruit and juices, home made bread and a hot dish. The air conditioned bedrooms are located upstairs and each has a television, hairdryer and bathrobes. Rooms are serviced daily. Guests have a separate sitting room. Unable to accommodate pets. "Immaculately clean, tastefully decorated accommodation . . . hosts attentive to our needs." RC, Qld.

Sydney - Coogee

Coogee Beachouse *Luxury B&B*
Didier and Diane Guerriau
15 Garnet Street
Coogee NSW 2034
6 km SE of Central Sydney

Tel (02) 9340 7311
or 0412 113 999
Fax (02) 9665 8636
info@coogeebeachouse.com.au
www.coogeebeachouse.com.au

Double $275-$395
Includes full breakfast
Visa MC BC accepted
1 Queen (1 bdrm)
Bathrooms: 1 Private double Spa Bath

C oogee Beachouse is the ultimate in luxury ocean-front accommodation, offering guests spectacular views of the Pacific Ocean. We're walking distance from the beach and Coogee's restaurants and night life. It's the perfect place to unwind on the weekend or a mid-week break. Foxtel digital television included. Only 15 minutes by car will bring you to the heart of Sydney. Gourmet breakfasts are our speciality to be savoured against a backdrop of breathtaking ocean views. Bon appetit . . .

AAA Tourism
★★★★☆

Sydney - Cronulla

Cronulla Seabreeze B&B *B&B Homestay*
Maria & Richard Morey
6 Boronia Street
Cronulla NSW 2230
28 km S of Sydney

Tel (02) 9523 4908 or 0407 774 426
Fax (02) 9501 5950
seabreezebnb@optusnet.com.au
www.seabreezebnb.com.au

Double $110-$155 Single $100-$135
Child B/A
Includes full breakfast
Extra person $30.00
Visa MC BC accepted
1 King/Twin 1 Queen (2 bdrm)
Bathrooms: 2 Ensuite

A warm welcome awaits you at "Seabreeze" on quiet, picturesque Cronulla Peninsula. Guests enjoy private use of the upper level of our home, offering inviting bedrooms, guest lounge with delightful ocean outlook, fridge, TV/Video. Stroll to beaches, ocean pools, bayside parks, shops, cinemas and restaurants. Beachcombing, surfing, bushwalking, bird watching, whale watching, kayaking, scuba diving, horse riding, golf, Botany Bay National Park & ferry to Royal National Park. Train to central Sydney & Airport. Friendly pointer dog. German spoken. "Thanks for your wonderful hospitality and friendliness. Everything about the room was wonderful, and breakfast too."

Sydney - Darling Harbour

The Imperial *B&B*
Elizabeth Dennison
11 Pyrmont Bridge Road
Pyrmont
NSW 2008
0.5 km W of CBD Sydney

Tel (02) 9692 0058
or 0438 317 604
Fax (02) 9331 0183
lucie1@bigpond.com
www.bbbook.com.au/theimperial.html

Double $90-$110 Single $65-$80
Continental Breakfast
Family room from $135
3 King/Twin3 King 3 Queen 2 Double (11 bdrm)
Bathrooms: 9 Ensuite

The Imperial is located in an historic building only 30 metres to Darling Harbour, a short walk via Pyrmont Bridge Road to the CBD and only one block to Star City Casino. Tea and coffee facilities, television and refrigerator are provided. The ground floor cafe restaurant opens out onto a leafy courtyard. Harbour and city views from the roof top terrace. The Imperial is 10 minutes from Central Station via light rail and just 2 minutes walk to the monorail. There is a guest kitchen and guest laundry..

Sydney - Darlinghurst

The Chelsea Guesthouse *B&B Boutique Hotel*
Paul Petersen
49 Womerah Avenue
Darlinghurst
NSW 2010
2 km NE of City

Tel (02) 9380 5994
Fax (02) 9332 2491
reservations@chelseaguesthouse.com.au
www.chelsea.citysearch.com.au

Double $143-$195 Single $93.50
Continental Breakfast
Visa MC BC Amex accepted
2 King/Twin 7 Queen 4 Single (13 bdrm)
Bathrooms: 9 Ensuite 4 Guest share

Located in two glorious 1870s terrace houses on a quiet, leafy avenue in Sydney's vibrant suburb of Darlinghurst. The interior décor has been designed so as to mix and match French provincial style with cutting edge modernity. All Queen and King Rooms feature contemporary limestone and tile ensuite bathrooms. Continental breakfast is served in the rustic dining room or around the huge stone table in the Mediterranean influenced courtyard. With an enviable location to the CBD and Sydney's many attractions, restaurants, cafes, bars, shops and theatres, the Chelsea makes a wonderful choice that's both homely but yet offers something very special.

Sydney - Drummoyne

Eboracum *B&B Homestay*
Jeannette & Michael York
18A Drummoyne Avenue
Drummoyne
NSW 2047
5 km W of Sydney

Tel (02) 9181 3541
or 0414 920 975
mjyork@bigpond.com
www.bbbook.com.au/eboracum.html

Double $120 Single $95
Includes full breakfast
Dinner B/A
1 King/Twin 1 Double (2 bdrm)
Bathrooms: 1 Family share 1 Private

Charming water frontage home by the Parramatta River, amid beautiful trees, with glorious views. Boatshed and wharf at waters edge. Handy to transport, Water Taxi at the door, short stroll to the bus or Rivercat ferry wharf, off street under cover parking. Ideal central location for business or pleasure, close to city CBD, Darling Harbour, Opera House, museums, theatres and sporting venues. Many restaurants and clubs, nearby... Enjoy, the hospitality of Jeannette and Michael, with their two cats and the ambience of their comfortable home.

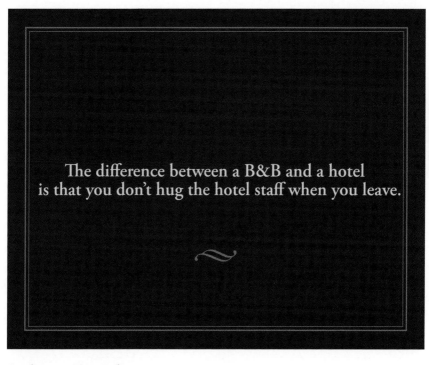

The difference between a B&B and a hotel
is that you don't hug the hotel staff when you leave.

Sydney - Engadine

Engadine Bed & Breakfast *Luxury B&B 2 Separate Self contained suites with kitchenette*

Pamela and Philip Pearse
33 Jerrara Street
Engadine   NSW 2233
28 km S of Sydney

Tel (02) 9520 7009 or 0412 950 606
0419 950 606
Fax (02) 9520 7009
engadinebnb@bigpond.com.au
www.engadinebnb.com

Double $145-$180 Single $125-$155
Child U12 $25.00 -
Includes special breakfast
Dinner $55 per person
Self Cater from $790 p/w
1 King/Twin1 King 1 Queen 2 Single (3 bdrm)
Bathrooms: 1 Ensuite 1 Private 1 double bathroom, 1 hot spa jacuzzi

Nestled amidst trees in leafy Sutherland Shire, Engadine Bed and Breakfast surrounded by The Royal & Heathcote National Parks. Beaches, walking tracks and restaurants are close by. We are 2km from Southern Freeway. We offer 2 fully self contained suites. An intimate King Bed suite or a family garden apartment with Queen, double and single beds. Both suites feature, heated bathrooms, kitchenettes, bar fridges well stocked with goodies. Also tv, dvd, cd, lounge/dining, bbq, private furnished courtyard, separate entrances with bushland valley views. Blending antiques & modern conveniences, quiet secluded oasis. Complimentary breakfast hamper first night. U/C parking. AussieHost Accredited. Sutherland Shire Tourism Association.

Sydney - Forestville - Manly

Jan's Forestville B&B *B&B Homestay Apartment with Kitchen*
Jan Fujak
49 Keldie Street
Forestville
NSW 2087
10 km N of Sydney CBD

Tel (02) 9975 6703
or 0414 351 399
Fax (02) 9975 6703
jan@accommodation-sydney.com
www.accommodation-sydney.com

Double $80 Single $60
Child Negotiable
Continental Breakfast
Visa MC BC accepted
1 Queen 1 Twin 1 Single (3 bdrm)
Bathrooms: 1 Guest share

Relax in the comfort and privacy of our forest getaway. There are three bedrooms (queen, twin and single), a fully equipped kitchen, bathroom and lounge/dining room. There are no carpets and the furnishing is child friendly. The deck overlooks the national park and the tropical pool, which guests are welcome to use. Off-street parking is available. We are just a twenty minute drive from Sydney CBD, a fifteen minute drive to the beach and a ten minute drive to Chatswood Shopping Centre.

Sydney - Glebe

Bellevue Terrace *Homestay*
Jan
19 Bellevue Street
Glebe
NSW 2037
3 km W of Sydney Central

Tel (02) 9660 6096
Fax (02) 9660 6096
bellevuebnb@pocketmail.com.au
www.babs.com.au/bellevue

Double $100 Single $80
Includes full breakfast
1 Queen 1 Double 2 Single (3 bdrm)
Bathrooms: 2 Guest share

My spacious, elegant townhouse is situated on a quiet residential street in the inner city suburb of Glebe, where you will find a great variety of restaurants, boutiques, galleries, pubs, and the Sydney University campus. Walk to Darling Harbour, Chinatown, Paddy's Market and the Powerhouse Museum, or take a bus to the City centre, just 3 kms away. We are happy to supply maps, brochures and lots of ideas for things to see and do in Sydney.

Sydney - Glebe

Cathie Lesslie Bed & Breakfast *Homestay*
Cathie Lesslie
18 Boyce Street
Glebe
NSW 2037
3 km SW of Sydney

Tel (02) 9692 0548
cathie@cathielesslie.net
www.cathielesslie.net

Double $100 Single $70
Child $15
Includes full breakfast
3 Double 2 Single (4 bdrm)
Bathrooms: 1 Family share 1 Guest share

Quiet leafy inner city, close to transport, cafes, cinemas, universities and Darling Harbour. Large comfortable room with cable TV, fridge and tea and coffee facilities. Hot "bacon and eggs" breakfast, your choice including fruit, juiced oranges and freshly baked croissants. We want you to feel welcome and at ease. Please phone first for bookings.

Sydney - Glebe

Harolden *Homestay*
Leonie Dawes
Address Please Phone (02) 9660 5881
3 km W of Sydney Central

Tel (02) 9660 5881
or 0414 481 881
harolden@senet.com.au

Double $100-$110 Single $70-$80
Includes full breakfast
1 Double 1 Single (2 bdrm)
Bathrooms: 1 Guest share

Built in 1895 "Harolden" a comfortable Victorian home in historic Glebe, minutes from the many restaurants of cosmopolitan Glebe Point Road. Public transport outside the door to Universities of Sydney and NSW, major hospitals and City Centre and a comfortable walk to the Fish Market, Darling Harbour and Light Rail. Your host, a descendant from the First Fleet to arrive at Sydney Cove in 1788 is well travelled and knowledgeable about Sydney. Unwind to warmth of log fires or breakfast in the garden. Tea and coffee available.

Sydney - Glebe

Tricketts *B&B Guest House*
Elizabeth Trickett
270 Glebe Point Road
Glebe   NSW 2037
2.5 km W of Sydney Central

Tel (02) 9552 1141
Fax (02) 9692 9462
trickettsbandb@hotmail.com
www.tricketts.com.au

Double $198 Single $176
Continental Breakfast
Garden Apartment from $220
Visa MC BC Diners Amex Eftpos accepted
1 King 6 Queen 1 Twin (7 bdrm)
Bathrooms: 7 Ensuite

Tricketts is a lovely Victorian mansion whose magnificent ballroom was once used as the Children's Court. Today this historic building has been fully restored to its original splendour. Large bedrooms with high ceilings, all beautifully decorated, all with ensuite, have top range Sealy beds. Breakfast is served in the conservatory and in summer out on the secluded deck overlooking the garden with bottle brush trees providing a wonderful splash of colour. The tranquillity makes one forget the city is a short 431 bus ride away and Darling Harbour, Fish Markets, Power House Museum, the Chinese Temple and Sydney University are close by. Glebe is an historic suburb full of interesting old homes that have been lovingly restored; and old fashioned gardens giving strong overtones of a bygone era. We are at the quieter "waterend" of Glebe Point Road, and a little further up lies the restaurant heart of Glebe, well known all over Sydney. Off street parking is available. We enjoy providing a luxury homestay for travellers and business people. Also at Tricketts, the resident cat is Bandit, who ignores us all. Children over 12 in B&B. Tricketts is fully centrally heated and air-conditioned. All ages accepted in comfortable self-contained one bedroom garden apartment which sleeps four. We ask guests to smoke outside on the verandahs.

Sydney - Greenwich

Greenwich B&B *B&B Homestay Apartment with Kitchen*
Jeanette & David Lloyd
15 Hinkler Street
Greenwich
NSW 2065
5 km N of Sydney

Tel (02) 9438 1204
or 0411 409 716
Fax (02) 9438 1484
info@greenwichbandb.com.au
www.greenwichbandb.com.au

Double $99-$140 Single $77-$120
Continental Breakfast provisions
Visa MC BC Amex accepted
1 King/Twin 1 Queen 1 Double (3 bdrm)
Bathrooms: 1 Ensuite 2 Private

Relaxed and friendly hosted accommodation in leafy Greenwich just 5km from the Sydney CBD. Enjoy spacious and private guests air-conditioned lounge/dinning areas in a classic Australian Federation home. Internet and E-mail access is available. Ample off street parking. Greenwich B&B is ideal for business or leisure stays and is conveniently located to public transport (Bus, Train, Ferry) shopping, entertainment and restaurants. Pick up and delivery to St Leonard's railway station can be arranged. Airport shuttle bus also available.

Sydney - Greenwich

Lofthouse Bed and Breakfast *B&B Homestay Apartment with Kitchen*
Leslie and David Bottomley
17 Seaman Street
Greenwich
NSW 2065
5 km NW of Sydney CBD

Tel (02) 9437 3316
or 0418 238 058
Fax (02) 9437 3383
leslie@lofthousebandb.com.au
www.lofthousebandb.com.au

Double $150-$200 Single $140-$190
Continental Breakfast
Visa MC BC accepted
1 Queen 1 Double 1 Twin (3 bdrm)
Bathrooms: 1 Ensuite 1 Private

Lofthouse B&B built in 1913 in true Edwardian style. Situated in quiet, leafy harbourside setting with water views. Landscaped gardens

 AAA Tourism ★★★★

feature fountains, fishponds, waterfalls and glass pavilion enclosed heated lap-pool. Two friendly dogs greet all our guests. It really is A Country House in the City. Your choice of luxurious queen bedroom self-contained apartment, a twin or double room with private bathroom. Lofthouse B&B is close to train, buses and ferry only 5kms - Sydney downtown, 2kms - North Sydney, 3kms - Chatswood and 1km - Royal North Shore Hospital.

a Sydney
stay...

...with a
Country feel

Sydney's Beautiful Hills District

www.
hillshavens
.com.au

Ph: 1300 884 881

Sydney - Hunters Hill

Magnolia House Bed and Breakfast *B&B Homestay*
Fofie Lau
20 John Street
Hunters Hill   NSW 2110
7 km NW of Sydney

B&B   AAA Tourism
★★★★☆

Tel (02) 9879 7078 or 0418 999 553
Fax (02) 9817 3705
fofie@magnoliahouse.com.au
www.magnoliahouse.com.au

Double $145-$210 Single $132
Includes full breakfast
Visa MC BC accepted
1 King/Twin 1 Queen (2 bdrm)
Bathrooms: 2 Ensuite

Set in the quiet and leafy surrounds of Sydney's historic Hunters Hill, Magnolia House offers traditional homestay bed and breakfast accommodation. Our Federation style family home is fully air conditioned and features elegant decor, antique furnishings and fine art pieces. A guest foyer and sitting room with lounge, writing desk and television are provided for guests. Telephone and computer access is available. Guest bedrooms also have their own televisions. The spacious and airy Rustica Room with king or twin beds is richly furnished with an old world charm and opens onto a private balcony with outdoor furniture setting. The balcony overlooks the front garden and the quiet, leafy street. Private ensuite bathroom facilities with a double shower feature. The Verdi Room is elegantly furnished and offers a queen size bed with ensuite bathroom and looks through a large bay window to the front garden. Guests are welcome to share the dining and living rooms with your hosts. All the rooms are beautifully furnished with many antiques. The dining room opens onto a comfortable rear deck overlooking the huge backyard. Coffee and tea making facilities are available for guests in the kitchen. Magnolia House is conveniently located only 7 km from the heart of Sydney and is placed within easy reach of transport that takes you directly to the city centre. Bus or ferry transport is close by. Sydney Airport, The Sydney Opera House, Sydney Harbour and The Harbour Bridge, the CBD, galleries, museums, are all within easy reach. Taking the ferry to Sydney Harbour and The Opera House is a memorable trip. Hunters Hill is one of Australia's oldest residential areas. Located on a peninsula between the Lane Cove and Parramatta Rivers, much of the suburb enjoys spectacular views over Sydney Harbour. Transfers from the airport can be easily arranged.

Sydney - Hunters Hill

Magnolia House *B&B Homestay*
Fofie Lau
20 John Street
Hunters Hill
NSW 2110
7 km NW of Sydney

Tel (02) 9879 7078 or 0418 999 553
Fax (02) 9817 3705
fofie@magnoliahouse.com.au
www.magnoliahouse.com.au

Double $145-$210 Single $132
Includes full breakfast
1 King/Twin 1 Queen (2 bdrm)
Bathrooms: 2 Ensuite

S et in the quiet and leafy surrounds of Sydney's historic Hunters Hill only 7 km from the heart of Sydney, Magnolia House offers traditional homestay bed and breakfast accommodation. Our Federation style family home is fully air conditioned and features elegant decor, antique furnishings and fine art pieces. A guest foyer and sitting room with lounge, writing desk, telephone and computer access and television. Guest bedrooms also have televisions. Guests are welcome to share the dining and living rooms with your hosts. Coffee and tea making facilities are available for guests in the kitchen. Transfers from the airport can be easily arranged.

Sydney - Northern Beaches Peninsula

The Pittwater Bed & Breakfast *B&B*
Colette and James Campbell
15 Farview Road
Bilgola Plateau NSW 2106
1 m km N of Newport Beach

Tel (02) 9918 6932
or 0418 407 228
Fax (02) 9918 6485
colette@thepittwater.com.au
www.thepittwater.com.au

Double $165-$180 Single $165-$180
Includes special breakfast   Dinner $55
per person
No smoking on property Visa MC BC accepted
2 King/Twin 2 Queen (2 bdrm)
Bathrooms: 2 Ensuite

C omfortable beds, ensuite bathrooms, full gourmet breakfast, peace, quiet and privacy. Close to Sydney's famous Palm Beach and great local restaurants, Colette and James would be delighted to welcome you to The Pittwater. Our family home is situated on the high plateau above Newport Beach. The guest areas have spectacular panoramic views of the ocean and coastline, including an attractive garden and large solar heated swimming pool. The Pittwater offer a range of complimentary services and may include airport pickup after a long haul flight.

Sydney - Ebenezer
Tizzana Winery Bed & Breakfast *B&B*
Peter & Carolyn Auld
518 Tizzana Road
Ebenezer
NSW 2576
15 km NW of Windsor

Tel (02) 4579 1150
Fax (02) 4579 1216
enquiries@tizzana.com.au
www.accommodation.tizzana.com.au

Double $175-$220
Includes full breakfast
Dinner $60-$130
Visa MC BC Diners Amex Eftpos accepted
2 King (2 bdrm)
Bathrooms: 2 Ensuite

 AAA Tourism ★★★★★

Romantic getaway with a sense of history in one of the Windsor district's outstanding buildings (c1887). Nestled in a valley overlooking a lake of waterlilies and in walking distance of historic churches, vineyard and olive grove. The tranquil setting offers luxurious 5 star accommodation to share with you. Tizzana is a National Trust listed building, an imposing two-storied building with a Mediterranean feel, built of local sandstone . A unique working winery and vineyard. The luxury rooms (king sized beds and ensuites) are comfortably appointed with many extras to make your stay a memorable one.

Sydney - Parramatta
Harborne Bed & Breakfast *B&B*
Josephine Assaf
21 Boundary Street
Parramatta
NSW 2150
2 km S of Parramatta

Tel (02) 9687 8988
Fax (02) 9687 8998
www.bbbook.com.au/harborne

Double $105-$140 Single $95-$130
Includes continental breakfast
Dinner from $20
$10 extra person
Visa MC BC Amex Diner Eftpos accepted
7 Queen 1 Single (8 bdrm) Family suite up to 7 adults
Bathrooms: 3 Ensuite 1 Guest share 1 Private

 AAA Tourism ★★★★

Harborne is a magnificent 1858 Georgian sandstone mansion. Harborne has recently been restored as a charming 8 room B&B. The beautiful home and the lush gardens have been classified by the National Trust. A glazed breakfast atrium with Tea & coffee facilities is available. Harborne is ideal for a relaxed stay or business or team stay. Harborne, Your Home Away From Home.

Sydney - Manly
Cecil Street B&B *B&B*

Linda Hart
18 Cecil Street
Fairlight
NSW 2094
1 km W of Manly

Tel (02) 9977 8036
or 0415 359 388
Fax (02) 9977 4701
linda@cecilstreetbb.com.au
www.cecilstreetbb.com.au

Double $90-$130 **Single** $70-$90
Child 12 yrs and under $35
Continental Breakfast
1 Queen 2 Single (2 bdrm)
Bathrooms: 1 Guest share

elightful Federation residence nestled in quiet, secluded cul-de-sac, 10 minute walk from the thriving beachside suburb Manly. Local attractions include beautiful beaches, bush and harbourside walks, Manly Aquarium, art gallery and historic Quarantine Station. Close to Manly Wharf and 15 minute Jetcat ride to Sydney City. Cosy breakfast/sitting room with TV, video, tea/coffee making, fridge and toaster. Delicious continental breakfast including fresh seasonal fruits. Linda will transport guests to and from Manly Wharf. Children welcome. "What a delight! Both Linda and her home, my new place in Manly."Keri.

~

Sydney - Manly
The Periwinkle Guesthouse *B&B*

Guest House
Rhonda Roth
18/19 East Esplanade
Manly Cove   NSW 2095
In Manly Cove

Tel (02) 9977 4668
Fax (02) 9977 6308
periwinkle.manly@bigpond.com
www.periwinkle.citysearch.com.au

Double $135-$190 **Single** $110-$165
Continental Breakfast
Visa MC BC accepted
6 Queen 6 Double 4 Twin 2 Single (18 bdrm)
Bathrooms: 12 Ensuite 6 Guest share

uilt in 1895 the Periwinkle Guesthouse is one of a few surviving buildings from the Federation era and is one of the most charming places to stay in Manly. It features high ceilings, elegant staircases, original wrought iron lacework verandahs overlooking either the delightful courtyard or picturesque Manly Cove. A short stroll takes you to The Corso, Manly Oceanarium, Art Gallery, Museum, a wide range of restaurants, bars. a cinema and Manly's world famous Ocean Beach. From Sydney's Circular Quay it is only a 15 minute ride on the high speed Jetcat. On arrival it is just a five minute stroll to the Periwinkle.

Sydney - Paddington

Harts *Homestay*
Katherine Hart
91 Stewart Street, nearest cross street - Gordon.
Paddington 2021
NSW 2021
2.8 km E of Sydney Central

Tel (02) 9380 5516
paddington91@bigpond.com
www.atn.com.au/harts

Double $115-$150 Single $85-$110
Includes special breakfast
No smoking on property
1 King 1 Queen 2 Twin 1 Single (4 bdrm)
Bathrooms: 1 Ensuite 1 Guest share 1 Private

Tastefully decorated 19th Century Cottage in Sydney's Historic Paddington, courtyard garden, two minutes from Oxford Street and the bus service to the CBD, Sydney Harbour, Circular Quay, The Rocks, The Opera House, Botanical Gardens, Sydney Casino, Chinatown, and Bondi Beach. Nearby Centennial Park, Fox Studios, Aussie Stadium, Sydney Cricket Ground, Art Galleries, Antique Shops, Pubs, Restaurants, Fashion Boutiques, Cinemas, Paddington Markets. All rooms with T.V, clock radios, electric blankets and feather quilts. Ironing facilities, varied breakfasts, fruit platters, special requests catered for, complimentary teas and coffee. Two resident cats. "Dear Katherine, I remember you with a great pleasure. You are so kind and your breakfasts so good. My stay in your home was a great happiness." Michel, France. "I'm missing your magnificent breakfasts which will stand out in my memory. Thank you for all your care of us." Jeanne, UK.

Sydney - Paddington
Marshalls of Paddington *B&B Homestay*
David & Donna Marshall
73 Goodhope Street
Paddington
NSW 2021
2.5 km E of Sydney City

Tel (02) 9361 6217
Fax (02) 9361 6986
dmarsh@zipworld.com.au
www.marshallsbnb.net

Double From $160
Includes full breakfast
Additional person
Visa MC accepted
1 Queen 1 Single (2 bdrm)
Bathrooms: 1 Ensuite

AAA Tourism
★★★★☆

This historic terrace offers exclusive use of two levels including master bedroom with ensuite and balcony with city skyline views. As part of Fiveways, a local landmark, we are within an easy walk of cosmopolitan Oxford Street, art galleries, boutiques, restaurants and pubs. Centennial Park, Paddington Markets, Fox Studios, SCG, CYC and Double Bay provide a cross section of local places of interest. Watsons Bay, Bondi Beach, The Rocks, Darling Harbour, Sydney Opera House and the CBD are a short bus trip away.

Sydney - Paddington
The Secret Garden *B&B*
Janna & Jamie Thomson
58A Goodhope Street
Paddington
NSW 2021
2.5 km E of Sydney

Tel (02) 9357 4560
or 0401 555 068
Fax (02) 9357 4560
jammytom@hotmail.com
www.babs.com.au/secretgarden

Double $135 **Single** $100
Includes full breakfast
Reduced rates for extended stays
1 King/Twin (1 bdrm)
Bathrooms: 1 Ensuite 1 Private

French Mediterranean-inspired cottage in a tranquil and private off-street walled garden. Choice of breakfast on your terrace or indoors. Ensuite accommodation includes a fan, heater, refrigerator, TV, laundry and separate access to allow you to come and go as you please. We have a small poodle called Audrey who adores people - but also knows her place. We are just minutes to cafes, pub, restaurants, galleries, gym and tennis courts. Nearby Fox Studios, Aussie Stadium, the Sydney Cricket Ground, cinemas and Paddington Markets. Ten-minute stroll to the Harbour, Rushcutters Bay and yacht clubs.

Sydney - Paddington

Paddington B&B *B&B Homestay*
Mary J de Merindol
7 Stewart Place
Paddington
NSW 2021
2.8 km E of Sydney Central

Tel (02) 9331 5777
Fax (02) 9331 5777
stay@paddingtonbandb.com.au
www.paddingtonbandb.com.au

Double $85-$130 Single $60-$90
Includes full breakfast
Dble/Twin: First night $130, then $85/nt.
Sgl: $90, then $60/nt
1 Double 1 Twin 2 Single (4 bdrm)
Bathrooms: 2 Guest share

Your hosts, originally from England, are recent 'empty nesters' who have travelled widely. The comfortable 5 bedroom family home dating from 1880 is furnished in traditional style and located in a tranquil cul-de-sac. It is 20 minutes from the Airport, a few minutes walk to the Football Stadium and Cricket Ground and 20 minutes by frequent bus service to the City Centre, Opera House, harbour ferries and Bondi Beach. Paddington is a residential area of heritage architecture enlivened by many galleries, boutiques, restaurants and cafes.

Sydney - Potts Point

Simpsons of Potts Point Boutique Hotel *B&B Guest House*
Keith Wherry
8 Challis Avenue
Potts Point Sydney
NSW 2011
2 km E of Sydney City

Tel (02) 9356 2199
or 0408 282 802
0402 765 507
0408 292 802
Fax (02) 9356 4476
info@simpsonshotel.com
www.simpsonspottspoint.com.au

Double $165-$285 Single $145-$215
Continental Breakfast
Visa MC BC Amex accepted
4 King/Twin 4 King 6 Queen 2 Twin (12 bdrm)
Bathrooms: 12 Ensuite 3 of King-bed rooms also have bath-tub

An historic 1892 mansion, the bedrooms have private bathrooms, air-conditioning and all modern conveniences. The building itself has high ceilings, spacious rooms, stained glass windows and grand hallways. Located in quiet, exclusive tree-lined Potts Point, less than one mile (leisurely 15min. stroll along the water) from the heart of Sydney or through the beautiful Botanical Gardens to The Opera House, Circular Quay Harbour Ferries or the historic Rocks area. It's within walking distance of some of the city's finest restaurants as well as the Oxford Street bars, clubs and night life.

Sydney - Rose Bay

Syl's Sydney Homestay *Homestay*
Sylvia & Paul Ure
75 Beresford Road
Rose Bay
NSW 2029
6 km E of Sydney

Tel (02) 9327 7079
or 0411 350 010
Fax (02) 9362 9292
homestay@infolearn.com.au
www.sylssydneyhomestay.com.au

Double $120-$145 Single $85-$95
Continental Breakfast
 $160 Double, extra person $40
Visa MC BC accepted
1 Queen 2 Double 3 Twin 4 Single (3 bdrm)
Bathrooms: 1 Ensuite 1 Guest share 1 Private

Rose Bay is one of Sydney's most beautiful harbourside suburbs and hospitality and friendliness are the essence of our modern, spacious family B&B with bush and harbour views, pet dogs and that real home away from home atmosphere. We are just a short stroll from cafes, restaurants, tennis, golf, sailing and the most beautiful harbour in the world and on excellent bus and ferry routes to the City and Opera House, Bondi Beach, train stations and shopping centres. Our B&B was featured on British TV in 1991 and we were one of Sydney's first B & Bs operating since 1980. Syl and Paul are well travelled and always ready to share their local knowledge and hospitality in a relaxed informal setting to help travellers enjoy our wonderful city. So if formality is what you seek, then Syl's is not for you! All rooms have TV and the self contained garden apartment is ideal for families. Guests are requested not to smoke inside the house.

Tamworth

Jacaranda Cottage Bed and Breakfast *B&B*

Elizabeth Maclean Charles Cox
105 Carthage Street
Tamworth
NSW 2340
0.5 km E of Tamworth

Tel (02) 6766 4281
or 0412 297 472
Fax (02) 6766 4281
lizzymcharlesc@optusnet.com.au
www.bbbook.com.au/jacaranda.html

Double $100-$150 Single $80-$120
Includes full breakfast
3 Queen (3 bdrm)
Bathrooms: 1 Ensuite 1 Guest share

Located in the heart of leafy East Tamworth, only 500m from the CBD, Jacaranda Cottage offers large comfortable bedrooms with queen sized beds, lead light windows, heating and cooling. The guest lounge offers a comfortable area to relax in with TV, fridge and coffee making facilities. Delicious home cooked breakfasts are served either in the family dining room or on the leafy verandah. At the bottom of the cottage garden is the private studio loft, well suited for either your business needs or romantic weekends.

Tamworth

The Retreat at Froog Moore Park *Luxury B&B*

Sandy and Peter Moore
78 Bligh Street
Tamworth
NSW 2340
2.3 km N of Town

Tel (02) 6766 3353
Fax (02) 6766 5326
retreat@froogmoorepark.com.au
www.froogmoorepark.com.au

Double $165-$255 Single $130-$200
Includes full breakfast
Visa MC BC accepted
2 King/Twin1 King 2 Queen (5 bdrm)
Bathrooms: 5 Ensuite 1 claw foot bath

Luxurious, artistic and romantic as seen on Getaway. Your experience will be unforgettable at this private adult retreat . . . Come and awaken all your senses. Designed around extensive travel experiences Amazing and artistic interiors and exteriors, 6000 sq meters of award winning gardens and modern gourmet food feeds the mind, body and soul. Distinctly different spacious air-conditioned rooms with full size bathrooms capture the essence of international luxury. Enjoy the large secluded Spa Tub, have a massage, play badminton or relax in the library or the deck.

Taree

Tallowood Ridge *B&B Farmstay Self Contained*
Shirley Smith
79 Mooral Creek Road
Cedar Party via Wingham
NSW 2429
8 km NW of Wingham

Tel (02) 6557 0438
or 0411 035 945
Fax (02) 6557 0438
twr@ceinternet.com.au
www.bbbook.com.au/tallowoodridge.html

Double $90-$100 Single $60-$70
Child $20
Continental Breakfast
2 Double 4 Single (3 bdrm)
Bathrooms: 1 Ensuite 1 Private

Come and share the country lifestyle. Enjoy the comforts of an a/c modern home set on 33 hectares of undulating hills, magnificent views, colourful birds, friendly cows and Jessie the dog. There is also a fully equipped a/c, s/c cabin acc. 4. No smoking inside please. Relax by the pool or visit the many attractions in the area, historic buildings, a museum of past history, picturesque rainforest area alongside the Manning river or visit Ellenborough Falls. Clubs, pubs and restaurants in town. "Very hospitable - scenery fantastic - so peaceful - could stay longer." M&NC, Nthn Ireland.

~

Tea Gardens - Hawks Nest

Lavender Grove Farm *B&B Farmstay*
Chris(tine) Townsley & Tony Irvine
55 Viney Creek Road
Tea Gardens
NSW 2324
15 km W of Tea Gardens

Tel (02) 4997 1411
or 0414 461 101
Fax (02) 4997 2001
info@nsw-accommodation.com.au
www.nsw-accommodation.com.au

Double $125-$185 Single $45-$145
Child $22 - $55
Includes special breakfast
Dinner $16.50-$55+ B/A
Mid-week specials
Visa MC BC accepted
1 King/Twin 1 Queen 1 Double 2 Single (3 bdrm)
Bathrooms: 3 Ensuite 1 spa bath, 2 pvt outdoor spas

AAA Tourism
★★★★☆

Only 2 hours easy drive north of Sydney, our B&B is ideal for romantic getaways or family stays. Indulge in relaxed, luxury, rural surroundings including solar heated salt water pool, orchard, vege patches and extensive native plantings. National Parks, Beaches & Port Stephens are all only a 10 minute drive or stay here and watch kangaroos grazing and sunsets from the verandah (or the spa) or curl up in front of the log fire. All meals are prepared by host/chef Tony. (Sorry no pets).

Temora

Cedar Farm Guesthouse *Cottage with Kitchen*
Ann Brace
323 Cedar Road
Temora
NSW 2666
15 km N of Temora

Tel (02) 6978 0368
or 0432 306 178
Fax (02) 6978 0368
ann68@bigpond.com
www.bbbook.com.au/cedarfarm.html

Double $100-$200
Continental Breakfast provisions
Full breakfast basket $5 per person
1 Queen 1 Double 4 Single (3 bdrm cot provided on request.)
Bathrooms: 1 Private

Cedar Farm Guest House is a self contained house on 280 acres of crop land, nestled against the Big Bush Nature Reserve. This unique house is totally powered by solar electricity. There is a gas heater, cooktop and wood stove. One large bedroom with a balcony overlooks the farm, with two spacious downstairs bedrooms. A timbered paddock with a small dam may be used for horses. Temora is renowned for it's flying weekends at the aviation museum, and has many old planes including Australia's only flying spitfire. Temora has a reputation of being NSW's friendliest town.

Terrigal

Terrigal Lagoon Bed & Breakfast *B&B*
Roz Fuller & Bruce Fitzpatrick
58A Willoughby Road
Terrigal
NSW 2260
1.5 km N of Terrigal

Tel (02) 4384 7393
or 0414 230 895
Fax (02) 4385 9763
enquiries@terrigalbnb.com.au
www.terrigalbnb.com.au

Double $140-$200 Single $100-$160
Includes full breakfast
Visa MC accepted
3 Queen (3 bdrm)
Bathrooms: 3 Ensuite

The comfortable, private facilities of this modern B&B provide the perfect base for exploring the magnificent beaches, lakes and National Parks of the Central Coast, or Sydney, Newcastle, and the Hunter Valley Wineries. The cosmopolitan seaside resort of Terrigal offers an extensive range of restaurants, speciality shops, galleries and entertainment in a picturesque setting. Queen rooms, ensuites, fans, TV, A/C. Separate guest entry and sitting room. Pool. Smoking outside only. No pets. Facilities not suitable for children. Parking. Public transport. Delicious breakfasts. Warm, friendly hospitality.

Tilba Tilba - Narooma

Green Gables *B&B*
Stuart Absalom & Philip Mawer
269 Corkhill Drive
Tilba Tilba
NSW 2546
16 km S of Narooma

Tel (02) 4473 7435 or 0419 589 404
Fax (02) 4473 7835
relax@greengables.com.au
www.greengables.com.au

Double $130-$150 Single $90-$110
Child $20 - $40
Includes full breakfast
Dinner $30 - $40 B/A
Visa MC BC Diners Amex accepted
3 Queen 1 Twin (3 bdrm)
Bathrooms: 2 Ensuite 1 Private

Green Gables (c.1879) at Tilba Tilba is nestled in the green undulating foothills beneath sacred Gulaga (Mt Dromedary). With generous hospitality, fine food and great views accommodation includes three guests rooms, ensuite/private bathrooms, guest sitting room and wide verandahs where you can linger. A popular option is dinner by prior arrangement served on the verandah or in the private dining room. Take time to relax and explore what the area has to offer - heritage, bushwalking, fishing, beaches, craft, local cheese and wine, Foxglove Spires garden. The perfect getaway.

Ulladulla - Bawley Point

Interludes at Bawley *B&B*
Sandra Worth & Ken Purves
103 Forster Drive
Bawley Point
NSW 2539
26 km S of Ulladulla

Tel (02) 4457 1494 or 0418 665 735
interludes@bigblue.net.au
www.southcoast.com.au/interludes

Double $120-$180
Includes full breakfast
Dinner By arrangement
Visa MC BC accepted
3 Queen (3 bdrm)
Bathrooms: 2 Ensuite 1 Private
2 Bedrooms have ensuites, one has sole use of bathroom

Interludes is set in 26 secluded acres of bushland with magnificent panoramic ocean views. Be lulled to sleep by the murmur of the sea in one of our three comfortable guest rooms and waken to a dazzling ocean sunrise with the gentle sounds of surf, morning birdsong and the rustle of leaves in the trees. Verandahs on three sides of the house allow guests to laze away the day enjoying their view of choice, from the inspiring changing moods of the ocean to the glorious romantic sunsets over the mountains. The unsurpassed beauty of the local beaches is only a 5 minute drive away. Swimming, surfing, sorkeling, fishing or boating are all activities available to the energetic. Finish the day with a romantic candlelit dinner for two, enhanced by silvery moonlight gleaming on the water to the background song of the sea.

Ulladulla

Ulladulla Guest House *B&B Apartment with Kitchen Guest House*
Andrew & Elizabeth Nowosad
39 Burrill Street Ulladulla NSW 2539
0.1 km S of Ulladulla

Tel (02) 4455 1796 or 1800 700 905
Fax (02) 4454 4660
ugh@guesthouse.com.au   www.guesthouse.com.au

Double $180-$278 Single $100-$248 Child $50
Includes full breakfast   Dinner $40 - $90
Visa MC BC Diners Amex Eftpos accepted
3 King/Twin 6 Queen 1 Double 3 Single (10 bdrm)
Bathrooms: 10 Ensuite

Ulladulla Guest House consists of 5 star (AAAT) accommodation, Elizans French Restaurant and Art Gallery and is located within minutes to town centre and picturesque harbour of Ulladulla.
Accommodation - All rooms are spacious and well-equipped with custom-designed furniture, warm carpeting and original artwork. Executive suites have marble bathrooms with private spas and king size beds. Two self-contained units have private entrances from the garden and cooking facilities.
Restaurant - Our executive chef presents French cuisine utilizing local fresh produce, including seafood straight from fishing harbour 100 metres away, local cheeses and world famous Milton beef.

Best Restaurant South Coast 2002, 3 & 4

Art Gallery – The Gallery has permanent exhibiting Artists: David Benson, Dianne Gee and Tracey Creighton. With the current by Judy Trick. Also exhibiting are potters Lee Casey and Celia Lenton. Surrounded by lush sub-tropical gardens, the Guest House caters to any requirement for a perfect relaxing holiday. After a leisurely gourmet breakfast, guests have the choice of lingering in the lounges surrounded by African artwork: ambling outside with a book to browse in a secluded nook; plunging into the heated pool or one of the spas; or enjoying a sauna after a work out in the gym. Ulladulla Guest House won 2003, 02, 01, 00, 99, 98, 97 Tourism Awards for Excellence and is recommended by number of reputable guides Frommers (US), Rough (UK), Time-Out (London), Johansens. Elizans Restaurant also won best Restaurant south coast 2004,03,02.

Wagga Wagga

Wagga Wagga Country Cottages *B&B Cottage with Kitchen*
Lyn Burgmann
Hillary Street
Wagga Wagga
NSW 2650
4 km NE of Wagga

Tel (02) 6921 1539
or 0417 216 697
Fax (02) 6921 1503
cntycott@bigpond.net.au
www.bbbook.com.au/waggacottages.html

Double $125 Single $95 Child $22
Continental Breakfast
Visa MC BC Amex accepted
1 Queen 2 Single (2 bdrm)
Bathrooms: 1 Private

In the language of the local Wiradjuri people, the name historically has meant 'the place of many crows'. We are famous for producing many champions in sport. Wagga Wagga is a great place to use as a base, and travel the Riverina. We have some of the finest wineries in Griffith, a beautiful old haunted homestead in Junee along with a Liquorice & Chocolate factory. Wagga Wagga offers fantastic golf courses and a River Boat that travels up and down the Murrumbidgee. You will find plenty do in our beautiful farm region. If you haven't been to Wagga Wagga before come and let us show you some real hospitality.

Walcha

Country Mood B&B *B&B*
Louise & Alec Gill
PO Box 51
Walcha
NSW 2354
4 km W of Walcha

Tel (02) 6777 2877
or 0413 905 391
Fax (02) 6777 2877
algill@northnet.com.au
www.bbbook.com.au/countrymoodbb.
html

Double $95 Single $75
Child $15
Includes full breakfast
Dinner $25 B/A
1 Queen 1 Double 1 Single (1 bdrm)
Bathrooms: 1 Private

Perfect place to escape in quiet country garden - close town, golf, National Parks, Apsley Gorge, trout and kangaroos. We run cattle and offer views, tranquillity and warmth - private access. Tea/coffee, TV, CD, iron, fresh flowers, comfortable Queen bed, undercover parking. Delicious meals served. Perfect stopover, Sydney (5 hrs), a scenic drive via Gloucester - Brisbane (6 hrs) - or stay longer - only 1 hour Tamworth and 45 minutes Armidale. We also have a self contained cottage in town."Our first B&B. Can the others be as good? Many thanks - so comfortable, lovely food"..

Wellington

Carinya B&B *B&B*
Miceal & Helen O'Brien
111 Arthur Street (Mitchell Highway)
Wellington
NSW 2820
0.5 km S of Wellington

Tel (02) 6845 4320
or 0427 459 794
Fax (02) 6845 3089
carinya@well-com.net.au
www.bbbook.com.au/carinyabb.html

Double $79-$94 Single $75-$84
Child $12 - $15
Includes full breakfast
Visa MC BC accepted
1 King/Twin 2 Queen 3 Single (3 bdrm)
Bathrooms: 2 Guest share

Carinya is an old homestead in a lovely garden setting. Pool and tennis court available. Off street parking a plus. Situated Sydney side of Wellington, on the Mitchell Highway. Family friendly. Billiard table is always popular. Close to everything, especially Wellington Caves and Japanese Garden. Walk Mt Arthur or inspect significant historic buildings and acclaimed Cameron Park. Drives to Burrendong Botanic Garden & Arboretum and Burrendong Dam make Wellington a pleasant stopover. Other attractions; Dubbo Zoo, Mudgee and Parkes are ideal for short excursions

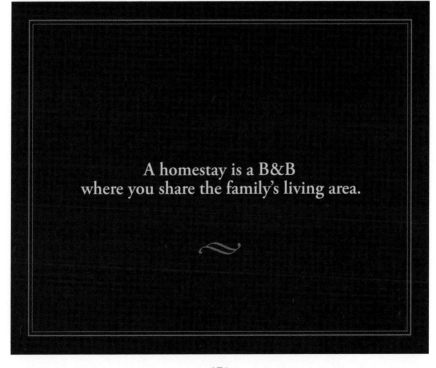

A homestay is a B&B
where you share the family's living area.

Wollongong - Mount Pleasant - South Coast

Above Wollongong at Pleasant Heights B&B *Luxury b&b - suites with kitchenette*
John & Tracey Groeneveld
77 New Mt Pleasant Road
Mount Pleasant
Wollongong   NSW 2519
5 km NW of Wollongong

Tel (02) 4283 3355
or 0415 428 950
info@pleasantheights.com.au
www.pleasantheights.com.au

Double $185-$420
Child by arrangement
midweek specials available
Includes breakfast hamper (Not special breakfast)
Dinner by arrangement
Visa MC BC Amex Diners accepted
1 King/Twin 2 Queen (3 bdrm)
Bathrooms: 1 Ensuite 2 Spa suites

A boutique B&B on the NSW South Coast, 'Above Wollongong at Pleasant Heights' provides exquisite accommodation which opens into a lush, bushland setting, complete with sweeping coastal views.

Guests choose between an eclectic trio of suites: two stylish spa suites in exotic, modern themes, and our chic, adorable studio with The View......serentity - harmony - solitude

This is high quality accomodation offering privacy and relaxation. . . each suite has its own entrance with either a courtyard, terrace or balcony and also offers a range of indulgences, including aromatherapy massage. And of course, a lavish breakfast hamper is provided for each stay.

Above Wollongong is a popular wedding destination and also great for pampering weekends We are within minutes of local restaurants, beaches , 5 kilometres from the Wollongong CBD, University and The Nan Tien Temple

Just one hour from Sydney, Southern Highlands, Jervis Bay, Kangaroo Valley and another one to The Blue Mountains - all this makes Pleasant Heights the perfect base for day tripping!!

Yamba

Wynyabbie House *B&B Homestay*
Greg & Kay Perry
Yamba Road
Palmers Island
NSW 2463
50 km N of Grafton

Tel (02) 6646 0168
Fax (02) 6646 0167
gregjp@tpg.com.au
www.bbbook.com.au/wynyabbiehouse.
html

Double $95-$120 Single $60-$75
Child $10-30
Includes full breakfast
Visa MC BC accepted
2 Queen 1 Double 2 Single (3 bdrm)
Bathrooms: 1 Ensuite 2 Guest share

Wynyabbie House is a century old farmhouse sitting on the banks of The Clarence River. Located just 10 km west of Yamba and 6 km east of Maclean, Wynyabbie House is ideally placed to take advantage of the area's many attractions. These include the popular beaches of Yamba and Angourie, Yuraygir National Park and fishing for the keen angler. There are several fine restaurants in Yamba and Maclean to cater for all tastes.

Yass

Kerrowgair *B&B*
Judy Gray & John Heggart
24 Grampian Street
Yass
NSW 2582
1.5 km N of Yass

Tel (02) 6226 4932
or 0417 259 982
Fax (02) 6226 4931
info@kerrowgair.com.au
www.kerrowgair.com.au

Double
Includes full breakfast
$130 - $150
Visa MC BC Diners Amex Eftpos accepted
1 King/Twin 3 Queen (4 bdrm)
Bathrooms: 4 Ensuite

Kerrowgair - A beautifully restored Georgian house (C.1853), in historic Yass, one hour from the Nation's capital. This outstanding heritage house has large bedrooms, all with ensuites, and gracious sitting and dining rooms, with open fires, for the use of guests. It is complimented by the shady verandahs and covered terrace. Set in over an acre of beautiful gardens, guests can enjoy the peace and tranquillity of the ancient trees, rose gardens and pond. Kerrowgair has become renowned for it's warm hospitality and superb breakfasts.

Yass - Rye Park
The Old School *B&B Country House (self-contained)*
Margaret Emery
Yass Street
Rye Park
NSW 2586
20 km SE of Boorowa, 40 km N of Yass

Tel (02) 4845 1230 or 0418 483 613
(02) 6227 2243
Fax (02) 4845 1260
theoldschool@bigpond.com
www.theoldschool.com.au

Double $120-$150 Single $90-$100
Child $25
Includes special breakfast Dinner $60
Country House: per week: $1,500
Visa MC BC Diners accepted
1 King 2 Queen 1 Double 1 Twin 2 Single (5 bdrm)
Bathrooms: 2 Ensuite 1 Family share 1 Private Orchard Wing suite has a bath

AAA Tourism
★★★★

Fine food, warm fires, good books and a piano make this retreat a return to life's simple pleasures. Set on four acres amidst trees, roses, gardens and ponds an atmosphere is created that encourages relaxation. Margaret has built a reputation for her food and offers a seasonal menu, with influences from Belgium, the Mediterranean and Asia. The Old School won an Award of Distinction in the 2000 Capital Country Awards for Excellence in Tourism. Rye Park is half an hour north of Yass.

≈

Young - Cootamundra
Old Nubba Schoolhouse *Cottage with Kitchen*
Fred & Genine Clark
Old Nubba
Wallendbeen
NSW 2588
3 km N of Wallendbeen

Tel (02) 6943 2513
or 0438 432513
Fax (02) 6943 2590
nubba@dragnet.com.au
www.bbbook.com.au/
oldnubbaschoolhouse.html

Double $95-$120 Single $75-$95
Child $10-$20
Full Breakfast Provisions
2 Queen 2 Double 8 Single (7 bdrm)
Bathrooms: 3 Private

Old Nubba is a sheep/grain farm midway between Cootamumdra and Young, 3 1/2 hours SW of Sydney, 1 1/2 hours west of Canberra. The Schoolhouse, Killarney Cottage and Peppertree Cottage are all fully self-contained and have heating, cooling, electric blankets and linen provided. They sleep 4-8. Children will love the chickens, ducks, geese, dogs and pet lambs and will be able to help with farm activities. Other farm attractions include peace and quiet, bush walks, birdlife, bike riding, fishing and olive picking (in season). Well behaved doggies and cats welcome.

Young - Cootamundra

Colleen & Old Sils Farmhouse *Luxury B&B Homestay Farmstay Separate Suite Guest*
House Luxury B&B & Guesthouse
Greg & Colleen Hines
Burley Griffin Way, Corang
Wallendbeen
NSW 2588
4.5 km W of Wallendbeen Village

Tel (02) 6943 2546 or 0429 432 546
0408 695 213
Fax (02) 6943 2573
colleenhines@bigpond.com
www.aussiefarmstay.com

Double $150-$160 Single $120-$160
Child B/A
Includes special breakfast
Dinner Aprox. $50.00 B/A Or, BBQ your own
1 King/Twin 1 Queen 1 Double 1 Twin 6 Single (4 bdrm)
Bathrooms: 1 Ensuite 3 Private 3 private, 1 en-suite

Corang, is a friendly Australian home, built in 1924 in a lovely rural setting. You will enjoy spacious, luxurious accommodation in parkland atmosphere, ideal for small groups, and conferences and small corporate dinners. Luxurious suites, 24 hr. tea/coffee, Stereo, TV etc. Our beautiful Louis XV dining room, resplendent in the family silver and crystal is the setting for many memorable dinners. Guests' Comment:"Like the elite and famous English Wolesley chain." Cynthia and Bruce Hestelow.

Take time to enjoy your journey and the company of your hosts.

Northern Territory

Alice Springs

Overwhelmed by the awesome splendour of skyscrapers made of rock, not steel, the centre captures the imagination of all its spectators. Admission to one of the best shows is Free - the spectacular multimillion-star night-time display of the Milky Way. The Centre's arid environment is home to a large population of unique animals, birds and reptiles.

Its beauty calls to an inner part of you, to do the Centre, and yourself, justice you'll need 5 to 7 days to explore the region. Visit her hidden jewels, explore her rugged terrain, try to unravel her hidden mysteries. But even if you can only spare three or four days to see the highlights, you'll have a fantastic time. Be warned though, it will leave you wanting to come back again.

Pauline Haden, The Hideaway, Alice Springs.

Humpty Doo

Humpty Doo is a rural area 35km South of Darwin, on the Arnhem Highway which leads to Kakadu National Park. We are well known for our crocodiles, glorious sunsets, abundance of birds and wildlife, mangoes and friendly people. We have two seasons the tropical wet which turns our brown earth into lush green grass from October to March and the dry season bringing cooler nights and low humidity from April to September. The locals take advantage of the ideal conditions for outdoor living, BBQs, festivals and camping.

Humpty Doo and the rural area is an ideal place to base yourself to visit the many attractions nearby. The jumping crocodile tours, Fogg Dam with it abundance of wildlife, Windows on the wetland, The Territory Wildlife Park, Berry Springs and Howard Springs Reserves are all a easy 20 minute drive or less away. Litchfield National Park is only a half day trip.

Brian and Joyce Maden, Humpty Doo Homestay, Humpty Doo.

Photos supplied by Suzy Forwod, Bonrook Country Stay.

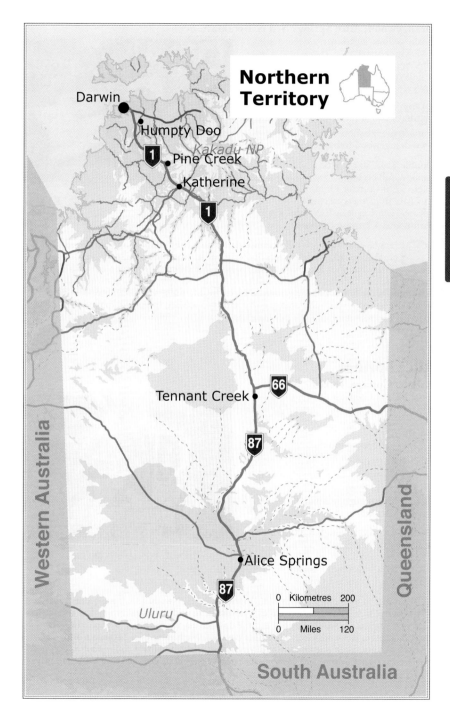

Alice Springs
Orangewood, Alice Springs Bed & Breakfast *B&B*

Lynne & Ross Peterkin
9 McMinn Street
Alice Springs
NT 0870
1 km E of Alice Springs town centre

Tel (08) 8952 4114
Fax (08) 8952 4664
orange@orangewood-bnb.au.com
www.orangewood-bnb.au.com

Double $187 Single $165
Includes full breakfast
Triple $220 Cotttage Only
Visa MC BC Diners accepted
2 King/Twin 1 Queen 1 Double (4 bdrm)
Bathrooms: 3 Ensuite 1 Private

O rangewood offers quality accommodation in a comfortable home furnished with antiques, special family pieces and original art works. The guest sitting room and library has open fire, piano, music system, television, refrigerator and tea/coffee making facilities. The house is air-conditioned. Guest accommodation comprises three bedrooms in the house and the garden cottage. Breakfast is served in the breakfast room which overlooks the pool and orange grove and is supervised by Angus, the resident cat. Non-smoking establishment, not suitable for children.

Alice Springs
Nthaba Cottage B&B *B&B*

Anne & Will Cormack & Pets
83 Cromwell Drive
Alice Springs
NT 0870
2.5 km N of Town Centre

Tel (08) 8952 9003
or 0407 721 048
Fax (08) 8953 3295
nthaba@nthabacottage.com.au
www.nthabacottage.com.au

Double $125-$155 Single $100-$125
Includes full breakfast
Visa MC accepted
1 King/Twin 1 Double (2 bdrm)
Bathrooms: 1 Ensuite 1 Private

S urrounded by the spectacular MacDonnell Ranges, Nthaba features a quality cottage separate from the main house plus a private suite under the main roof. The cottage has one kingsize or two single beds and the cosy sitting-room with T.V. has Edwardian chairs and other favourite pieces. The suite has a double bed, ensuite bathroom and private entrance. Both open onto a lovely private garden. Nthaba is convenient to the new convention centre, casino and golf course. Your host, Will, is keen to share his local bird knowledge with you. Resident friendly cat and dog.

Alice Springs

Kathy's Place Bed & Breakfast *B&B Homestay*
Kathy & Karl Fritz
4 Cassia Court
Alice Springs
NT 0870
3 km E of Alice Springs

Tel (08) 8952 9791
or 0407 529 791
Fax (08) 8952 0052
kathy@kathysplace.com.au
www.kathysplace.com.au

Double $135 **Single** $75
Child $ 20 per child
Includes full breakfast
$30 3rd person in same room
Visa MC BC accepted
2 Queen 1 Single (2 bdrm)
Bathrooms: 1 Guest share

Friendly Australian home, courtesy arrival transfers, tours arranged and help provided so you can enjoy the treasures the "Alice" has to offer, taking at least two days to enjoy. Air conditioning, swimming pool and garden outdoor area with native birds. Combustion heating in the cooler months providing a cosy atmosphere to chat, read, watch T.V. or play snooker. You will be welcomed by Neischka our ever friendly Hushy.

Alice Springs

The Hideaway *B&B Apartment with Kitchen*
John and Pauline Haden
18 Lewis Street
Alice Springs
NT 0871
500 km NE of Ayers Rock

Tel (08) 8953 1204
or 0428 531 204
Fax (08) 8953 1204
info@hideawayinalice.com
www.hideawayinalice.com

Double $120
Full Breakfast Provisions
Family $180
1 Queen 2 Single (2 bdrm)
Bathrooms: 1 Private

You will be greeted with a welcome "cuppa" to your liking. Bassa the resident cat will be there to add to the welcome. All rooms have fans, electric blankets and the apartment has ducted air-conditioning, a gas heater is available in winter in the separate lounge/dining area. Your hosts John and Pauline have a combined 80 years of personal local experience, we look forward to sharing this knowledge with you. We are within 5 minutes walk from the famous Cultural Precinct and a 5 minute drive from the World acclaimed Desert Park.

Humpty Doo - Darwin
Mango Meadows Homestay *B&B Homestay Cottage with Kitchen*

Nola & Ray Nendick
2759 Bridgemary Crescent
Humpty Doo, NT 0836
38 km SE of Darwin

Tel (08) 8988 4417 or 0409 036 168
Fax (08) 8988 2883
info@mangomeadows.com
www.mangomeadows.com

Double $95-$150 **Single** $85
Continental Breakfast
Dinner $30
2 B/R Apartment $180/nt. Budget
Cottage $80/nt.
Visa MC accepted
1 King/Twin 2 Queen 1 Single (3 bdrm)
Bathrooms: 1 Guest share

S et in a lush tropical garden, alive with native birds and surrounded by 6 acres of Mango and Lime trees. Enjoy a large air conditioned lounge with satellite television, video/DVD and stereo system with a self contained kitchen. Adjoining our games verandah is a large pool and spa. Why not try all the homemade Mango products: mango wine, dried mango, frozen mango, mango jam, mango chutney and fresh mangoes in season. We are centrally located to both Litchfield and Kakadu National Parks and many more tourist attractions. Feed our barramundi in the fish pond. On arrival our dog will make you very welcome.

~

Pine Creek
Bonrook Country Stay *B&B*

Suzy & Sam Forwood
Bonrook Station, c/- Stuart Highway
Pine Creek
NT 0847
10 km S of Pine Creek

Tel (08) 8976 1232
Fax (08) 8976 1469
info@bonrook.com
www.bonrook.com

Double $85-$95 **Single** $50
Child $12
Continental Breakfast
Visa MC BC accepted
5 Queen 6 Double 12 Single (11 bdrm)
Bathrooms: 11 Ensuite

B onrook Station - The only wild horse sanctuary in Australia. Bonrook Country Stay is a simple, charming and beautifully located bed & breakfast guesthouse located on the shady banks of the Bonrook Creek. With no telephones or televisions in the rooms, you canít help but sit back, unwind and enjoy a drink by the pool. We offer BBQ cooking facilities for those that donít wish to dine in Pine Creek. We are situated at the gateway to Kakadu, 90 km north of Katherine. Other nearby attractions include Edith Falls, Umbrawarra Gorge and Douglas Daly Hot Springs.

Queensland

Brisbane

Brisbane's inner city suburbs are packed with culture and curiosities. Take a trip during the day or night, there is always something new to see and experience. Historic Paddington and Rosalie are just a few minutes from the city, cast across the steep hills and terraces that characterise the inner western suburbs. Queenslander cottages of weatherboard and corrugated iron, painted in a mix of heritage shades and vibrant tropical colours. Cottage industries fill the converted cottages along the main street, intermingled with cafes and a large antique market, housed in a former cinema.

Paddington is a shopper heaven.... there are interesting boutiques with a variety of goods seldom seen in the major shopping centres. There are great places to dine and history buffs will enjoy exploring the local heritage trail. No other precinct can match the eclectic diversity offered in this unique district.

Heather Humphrey, Fern Cottage Bed & Breakfast, Brisbane.

Cairns

Warm, sunny tropical days tempered by cooling onshore breezes. The days are warm, the nights balmy and the endless possibilities of things to do make holidaying here an experience of a lifetime. Cairns is the ideal base to explore and experience the many attractions of Tropical North Queensland. Visit the Great Barrier Reef, the largest reef in the world extending over 2300 km along the Australian coast, by fast motor boat or sit back and relax on a small sail boat and really enjoy the journey. Take a guided tour or a self drive trip to our rainforest. Around 17,000 hectares between Daintree River & Cape Tribulation is declared National Park and much of this area is also World Heritage listed to ensure the protection of the rainforest which has been evolving for 120 million years. Take a day trip to the picturesque Cairns Highlands & explore this beautiful area.

Vicky Riddle, Billabong B&B, Cairns.

Daintree

Experience one of Australia's most breathtaking journeys into the heart of Daintree through an ever-changing tropical landscape of white sandy palm-fringed beaches, waving cane-fields and jungle clad misty mountains. See lush rural farmlands bordered by World Heritage listed rainforest and the majestic Daintree river.

Explore the world's oldest living rainforest, picturesque rivers and surrounding mangrove habitats, home to a diverse array of flora and fauna with abundant bird and wildlife, butterflies and the prehistoric crocodile.

River cruises, bird watching, rainforest tours, fishing, health spas, outdoor theatre, horse riding, tropical exotic nurseries, wildlife sanctuaries, aboriginal culture, timber gallery and museum, photographic tours, scenic golf course.

Glimpse into Australia's colourful past at Daintree Village, forged from the spirits of gold rush pioneers, cedar timber getters and farmers. Today, a quaint rural village with a laid back tranquil atmosphere, hosting travellers from Australia and all parts of the world.

Only 60 minutes north of Cairns and 20 minutes north of Port Douglas, the gateway to the Great Barrier Reef.

Gil Talbot, Daintree Mangroves Wildlife Sanctuary and Daintree Village Tourist Association.

Fraser Coast

Just perfect; we thought when we fist arrived at 'The Bay'. And that was just the beginning of a long love affair: Mild weather, endless beaches, a welcoming ocean, charming hinterland and extremely friendly people. What else do we need? Ok, Fraser Island and being the Whale Watch Capital might be the draw card for many, but move away from the tourist hub and you will find enchanted fishing villages, magic river moorings, hills and mountains and heaps of weathered Queenslander. El Dorado not only for outdoor enthusiasts but for people with lust for the good old times.

Come on, stay with us and enjoy the Fraser Coast.

Sven & Paul, The Doghouse Bed & Breakfast, Hervey Bay.

Gold Coast Hinterland

To escape the hustle and bustle of ultra-touristy Surfers' Paradise, more and more travellers are discovering the quiet, rich beauty of the Gold Coast Hinterland, an easy 30-minute drive of Gold Coast beaches. The Hinterland boasts World Heritage rainforest reserves and historical, charming rural villages and offers a magnificent range of eco-tourism, cultural and heritage attractions plus a variety of outdoor activities. Mt Tamborine is a 'must' where exploration of the many gift shops and art galleries makes for a pleasant day. Some of the most popular

bushwalks are in the Tamborine National Park, which include areas of beautiful pristine forests with rare and exquisite native wildlife. At Thunderbird Park you can view the world's largest 'thunder egg' deposit.

Lamington National Park is a popular bushwalking area with circuit walks ranging from 1km to 20 km and includes a series of densely forested valleys and ranges with the most extensive areas of subtropical rainforest in the world.

Caroline Marchesi, Riviera B&B, Gilston.

Hervey Bay

Hervey Bay is one of the most sought after holiday destinations a scenic three and a half hours drive north of Brisbane and only 45 minutes by air. Hervey Bay's pristine environment and expansive sheltered waters enhance its reputation as the Whale Watch Capital of the world for the Humpback Whales from late July to November. With beautiful Beaches, calm stinger-free waters you can enjoy an experience you will never forget. Visit World Heritage listed Fraser Island, the wonderful Great Sandy Straits. Hervey Bay also offers great access to Lady Elliot Island and the Southern Great Barrier Reef.

Pauline & Max Harriden, Alexander Lakeside B&B,
Kathie Ryan, The Chamomile B&B, Hervey Bay

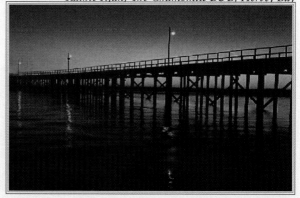

The Granite Belt

The Granite Belt, so called because of its spectacular granite outcrops, is situated just north of the New South Wales border, around the small town of Stanthorpe. Because of its altitude, the area has become well-known during 'Brass Monkey Season' (winter) as the coldest place in Queensland, when locally produced red wines, 'Christmas in July' dinners and cosy log fires attract large numbers of tourists to the area.

The four National Parks in the area, Girraween, Bald Rock, Boonoo Boonoo and Sundown, each with its own individual character, offer plenty of opportunity for walking, climbing, photography and bird-watching..

Weekly craft and produce markets are held in Stanthorpe, and the area features a wide variety of dining experiences from up-market restaurants to casual lunches at cellar door cafes.

Margaret Taylor, Jireh B&B, Severnlea.

The Whitsundays

Seventy-Four Islands and the Great Barrier Reef set in the pristine Coral Sea. 70% protected by National Park and Marine Park a unique destination. We had a lovely English couple stay with us; their travel agent had them booked to fly Brisbane to Cairns. Then the kids came home for Christmas and said "But Mum & Dad the best bit is in the middle" They stayed a week and did not want to leave. The colours are phenomenal bright blues, crystal greens. Snorkel, dive, sail, see some of the 1500 species of coral fish, 400 types of coral animals turtles and whales in season one of the definite " must do's" The Whitsunday's Out of The Blue.

Peter J Brooks, Whitsunday Moorings B&B, Airlie Beach.

Toowoomba New

Queensland's garden city, and come spring, hosts the renowned Carnival of Flowers. Situated just 90 minutes west of Brisbane, Toowoomba's crisp, clear mountain air, awaits the traveller. The city is home to the wonderful art deco Empire Theatre, and to the many art galleries, antique shops and fine eating places, which demand further exploration.

Travel north, and discover nurseries, cafes and galleries. To the west there are first class wineries amongst the rolling plains and fertile farming land. North-west are the Bunya Mountains, with rainforests, waterfalls, and walking tracks. The largest remaining stand of Bunya pine trees can be viewed here, and bird life abounds. To the south, Steele Rudd country awaits those interested in Australian folklore, as the 'selection' and shingle hut where the Rudd family lived, and from where the classic 'Dad and Dave' stories were based, makes interesting viewing.

In all, Toowoomba has something for everyone, with its moderate climate, and distinct four seasons, spectacular valley views, and over 150 public parks and gardens.

Jeanette Wehl , Sugarloaf Mountain Country Retreat, Kingsthorpe.

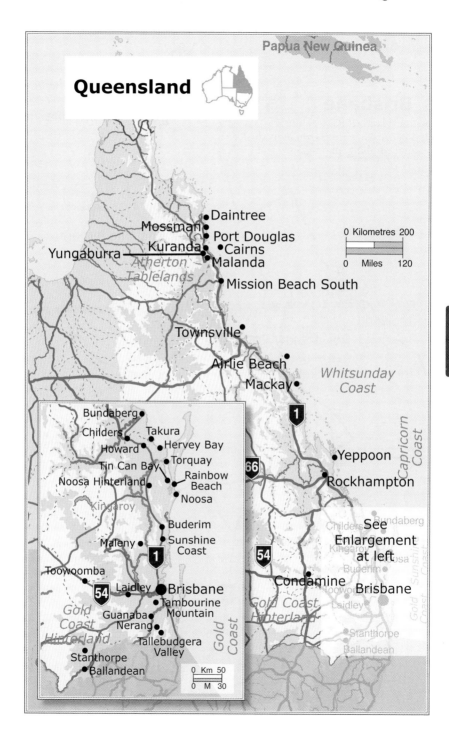

Queensland

Papua New Guinea

Queensland

0 Kilometres 200
0 Miles 120

Daintree
Mossman
Port Douglas
Yungaburra
Kuranda
Cairns
Atherton
Tablelands
Malanda
Mission Beach South

Townsville

Airlie Beach
Mackay
Whitsunday
Coast

Capricorn Coast

Yeppoon
Rockhampton

See
Enlargement
at left

Bundaberg
Childers
Takura
Howard
Hervey Bay
Tin Can Bay
Torquay
Noosa Hinterland
Rainbow
Beach
Noosa
Kingaroy
Buderim
Maleny
Sunshine
Coast
Toowoomba
Gold
Coast
Hinterland
Laidley
Brisbane
Tambourine
Mountain
Guanaba
Nerang
Tallebudgera
Valley
Stanthorpe
Ballandean
Gold
Coast

Condamine
Brisbane

Childers
Bundaberg
Kingaroy
Noosa
Buderim
Gold Coast
Hinterland
Toowoomba
Laidley
Stanthorpe
Ballandean

0 Km 50
0 M 30

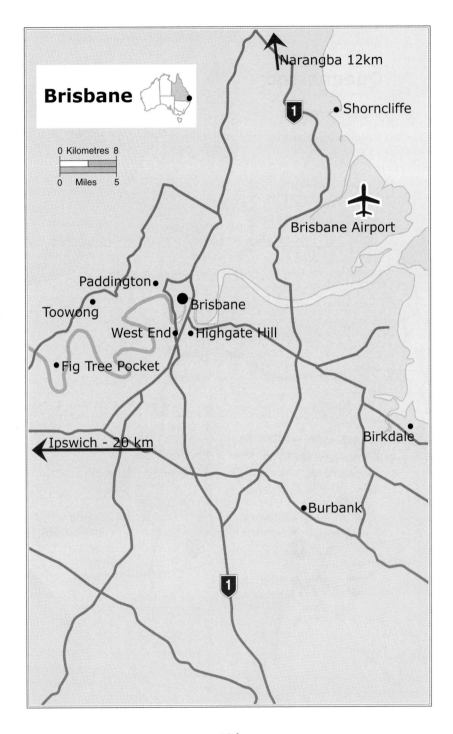

Narangba 12km

Shorncliffe

Brisbane Airport

Paddington

Toowong

Brisbane

West End • Highgate Hill

• Fig Tree Pocket

Ipswich - 20 km

Birkdale

• Burbank

Airlie Beach - Whitsunday

Whitsunday Moorings B&B *B&B*
Peter Brooks
37 Airlie Crescent
Airlie Beach
Qld 4802
0.3 km SW of Airlie Beach

Tel (07) 4946 4692
Fax (07) 4946 4692
info@whitsundaymooringsbb.com.au
www.whitsundaymooringsbb.com.au

Double $165 Single $145
Child $30
Includes full breakfast
Visa MC BC Diners Amex Eftpos accepted
2 Queen (2 bdrm)
Bathrooms: 2 Ensuite

Our studio apartments abut magical gardens, private terrace, poolside, with unbelievable views. Breakfast on fresh juice, tropical seasonal fruit, cereals, choice of cooked Australian homestyle mains, toasts, homemade jams, teas and coffee. Apartment feature crisp starched linen, daily servicing, air-conditioning, ceiling fans, 40ch satellite TV, en suite with shower, hairdryer, 'Gilchrist & Soames' toiletries, kitchen, refrigerator, microwave, equipped for light meals, clock radio, laundry facilities. Relax in the pool with a cool drink and watch the sun setting as boats return to the marina below.

Atherton Tablelands - Yungaburra

Williams Lodge *Luxury B&B*
Peter & Lyn Williams
Cedar Street
Yungaburra
Qld 4884
In Yungaburra

Tel (07) 4095 3449
Fax (07) 4095 3439
stay@williamslodge.com
www.williamslodge.com

Double $130-$215
Continental Breakfast
Visa MC BC Diners Amex Eftpos accepted
5 King (5 bdrm)
Bathrooms: 5 Ensuite

Williams Lodge, where Heritage Luxury is available in the heart of Yungaburra Village. The property is one of 20 heritage listed places in Yungaburra, which has within walking distance restaurants, cafes, galleries and walking tracks for wildlife. The award winning property has 5 Suites with King Bed, Ensuite including spa, Kitchen Lounge and reverse cycle air conditioning. The Guest Lounge features large wood fireplace, pool table, internet, pianola and bar. There is also verandahs with outdoor furniture and a pool with a spa. Operated by a fourth generation Williams.

Ballandean

Ballandean Lodge *B&B Homestay*
Dietmar & Dorothy Gogolka
79 Rees Road
Ballandean - Stanthorpe
Qld 4382
20 km S of Stanthorpe

Tel (07) 4684 1320
Fax (07) 4684 1340
ballandeanlodge@halenet.com.au
www.ballandeanlodge.com.au

Double $115-$140 Single $70-$90
Includes full breakfast
Dinner $30-$40pp
Visa MC BC accepted
2 Queen 2 Single (3 bdrm)
Bathrooms: 3 Ensuite

Ballandean Lodge is a 100 year old Queenslander which nestles between the vineyards and stone fruit orchards of SE Queensland. 4 National Parks close by. Enjoy the privacy of your own comfortable room with ensuite and admire the magnificent views from all the verandahs. After a day in the wineries, sip your wine while watching the glorious sunset, before enjoying a home-cooked dinner in the dining room. Dietmar and Dorothy, together with their three beautiful pets, are waiting to make you welcome to the peace and tranquillity of their home.

Brisbane - Birkdale

Birkdale Bed & Breakfast *B&B*
Geoff & Margaret Finegan
3 Whitehall Avenue
Birkdale, Brisbane
Qld 4159
17 km E of Brisbane CBD

Tel (07) 3207 4442
glentrace@bigpond.com
www.bbbook.com.au/birkdalebb.html

Double $100-$110 Single $70-$80
Child $20
Includes full breakfast
Dinner $15-30
No smoking on property
Visa MC BC Diners Amex accepted
2 Queen 1 Double 2 Single (3 bdrm)
Bathrooms: 2 Ensuite 1 Private

Only 20 minutes from Brisbane CBD and airport, but with a lovely country atmosphere. Set in half an acre of beautifully landscaped gardens, Birkdale B&B is a modern English style country home, with a new luxurious motel style guest wing and separate entrance. All bedrooms have private facilities and reverse cycle air conditioning for your comfort. Minibar. Off street parking. Enjoy feeding the birds, go whale watching in nearby Moreton Bay or meet the local koalas. Qualified Aussie Hosts. Dual Tourism Award Winner. Corporate and weekly rates.

Brisbane - Burbank

Natra Nights Bed & Breakfast *B&B*

Sally Jenyns
101 Jenyns Court
Burbank   Qld 4156
20 km S of Brisbane CBD

Tel (07) 3219 0418
or 0404 883 219
Fax (07) 3219 0267
sally.jenyns@bigpond.com
www.bbbook.com.au/natranights.html

Double $150 Single $100
Includes full breakfast
Dinner B/A
Special prices for overnight mid week stays
1 Queen (1 bdrm)
Bathrooms: 1 Ensuite

Secluded amongst the Eucalypt Forest at Burbank, you will enjoy the privacy and peaceful milieu this homestead offers, only 20 minutes from the city and airport. Your comfortable airconditioned room includes, queen bed, fridge and coffee making facilities. Natra Nights Bed & Breakfast is set on 70 acres of a private conservation property and is adjacent to Brisbane Koala Bushlands (reserve). There are plenty of walking tracks for relaxing and absorbing Brisbane's Koala Coast. Fresh eggs from the chooks included in the breakfast. Use of the pool, outdoor woodfire BBQ and even a horse to pat.

Brisbane - Highgate Hill

Carinya Highgate Hill Bed & Breakfast *Traditional B&B*

Hazel Parkins
117 Dornoch Terrace
Highgate Hill, Brisbane
Qld 410
1 km S of Brisbane CBD

Tel (07) 3844 1228
or 0412 080 409
carinyabandb@optusnet.com.au
www.carinyabandb.com.au

Double $120-$150 Single $90-$130
Includes full breakfast
 includes breakfast
Visa MC BC accepted
 2 King/Twin1 King 3 Single (3 bdrm)
Bathrooms: 1 Ensuite 1 Family share 1 Private

 AAA Tourism
★★★★

Heritage listed, Carinya is a fine example of a Federation Queenslander. It provides old world charm with the best modern facilities such as wireless broadband internet access and air conditioning. Spacious rooms capture cool breezes and feature high pressed metal original ornate ceilings, stylish antique furniture and doors leading to verandahs. Stroll to cosmopolitan West End and Brisbane City or take a short walk and catch the City Cat ferry to explore the Brisbane River. Enjoy friendly service and your host's local knowledge to make your stay in Brisbane memorable. Ample free parking on street directly in front of Carinya.

Brisbane - Narangba

Richards B&B *B&B*
Richard & Naomi Sieverts
341 Boundary Road
Narangba   Qld 4504
4 km E of Narangba

Tel (07) 3888 3743 or 0417 071 188
1800 10 50 99   Fax (07) 3888 3938
RichardsBnB@bigpond.com
www.richardsbandb.com

Double $85 Single $60
Child 1/2 price cond app
Includes full breakfast
Luxury $130, Bridal $180
Visa MC BC accepted
3 Queen (5 Bedrooms, including 1 luxury & bdrm)
Bathrooms: 2 Ensuite 1 Guest share

Richards located 30 km north of Brisbane 2 mins off Bruce Highway, one hour from Noosa, one hour Dreamworld, Gold Coast with all attractions in between. Our B&B is a large family home set in a tranquil 2 1/2 acre setting rich in bird life. We have a games room, formal lounge with fire place, bar etc, guests have full use of all facilities. Also 20 mins to Morton Bay, Redcliff, fishing, whale watching. We serve a full breakfast and dinners by arrangement. Richards also specialises in wedding night packages and is a pewrfect place for that romantic evening. Late check out. Pick up from train 3 1/2 km or airport 25 km can be arranged.

Brisbane - Paddington

Waverley B&B *B&B Self Contained Apartment*
Annette Henry
5 Latrobe Terrace
Paddington
Qld 4064
1.5 km NW of Brisbane Central

Tel (07) 3369 8973
or 0419 741 282
Fax (07) 3876 6655
waverleypaddington@bigpond.com
www.bbbook.com.au/paddingtonbb.html

Double $120 Single $99
Includes full breakfast
Self contained $550 per week
Visa MC BC accepted
2 King 2 Queen 4 Single (4 bdrm)
Bathrooms: 4 Ensuite

AAA Tourism
★★★★

Known locally as "Waverley" this romantic, 1888 Queensland colonial is deceptively spacious inside with polished timber floors and soaring ceilings. Situated in smart, leafy, cosmopolitan, inner-city Paddington, where interesting shops and cafes line the streets, it has the bonus of off-street parking and easy access to the city. There are two air-conditioned guest suites on the street level and two air-conditioned self-contained apartments with private entrances, fans and fully equipped kitchens on the lower level. Mango trees screen the decks on both levels. One resident cat: Felicity.

Brisbane - Paddington - Rosalie

Fern Cottage B&B *B&B*
Heather Humphrey
89 Fernberg Road
Paddington - Rosalie Qld 4064
2 km W of Brisbane

Tel (07) 3511 6685 or 0412 740 394
Fax (07) 3511 6685
heather@ferncottage.net
www.ferncottage.net

Double $125-$135 Single $95-$100
Child under ten $15
Includes special breakfast
Extra person $35. weekly rates $560 to $700.
Visa MC BC Diners accepted
3 Queen 1 Single (3 bdrm)
Bathrooms: 3 Ensuite

Make Yourself At Home! Fern Cottage is a charmingly refurbished 1930s "Queenslander" located in trendy Paddington/Rosalie . . . a village, only 2km west of downtown Brisbane . . . Enjoy modern conveniences and comforts of home in our 3 fabulously decorated, air conditioned ensuited bedrooms. kitchenette, dining and lounge rooms and individual patios assures your privacy. Sidewalk cafes, fine restaurants, boutiques, antique shops and galleries are within walking distance. A generous continental breakfast starts your day . . . in the tropical garden courtyard. One resident Burmese cat, Coco.

Brisbane - Shorncliffe

Naracoopa Bed & Breakfast *B&B Self Contained Studio Apartment*
Grace & David Cross
99 Yundah Street
Shorncliffe
Qld 4017
21 km NE of Brisbane

Tel (07) 3269 2334
or 0412 147 456
narabnb@bigpond.net.au
naracoopabnb.com.au

Double $130-$140 Single $100-$115
Child $35
Includes special breakfast
S/C $160 double with a two night minimum, and $500 weekly.
No smoking on property
Visa MC BC Eftpos accepted
3 Queen 1 Double (3 bdrm)
Bathrooms: 3 Ensuite

The perfect tranquil getaway - Naracoopa offers luxury and privacy in superior 4 star accommodation. Tastefully appointed bedrooms, designer decorated with private ensuites, verandahs, queensize beds, refrigerator, tea & coffee facilities, air conditioning, outdoor hot spa on back deck for guest use. Naracoopa is positioned in the northern suburbs on Moreton Bay and is a short stroll to the bay, cliffs, cafes, pubs, city train, yacht club and pier. Our new contemporary self-contained Studio Apartment will be available from February 2006 catering up to 4 people.

Brisbane - Toowong - St Lucia

Kensington *Luxury B&B*
Michelle Bugler
23 Curlew Street
Toowong
Qld 4066
5 km W of Brisbane

Tel (07) 3371 3272 or 0407 016 669
kensbandb@iprimus.com.au
www.babs.com.au/kensington

Double $130-$150 Single $110
Child $25, 4 to 14 years
Includes full breakfast
1 King/Twin 1 Queen 1 Single (2 bdrm)
Bathrooms: 2 Ensuite

Kensington, a grand Queensland colonial, is nestled in a quiet, leafy street in Toowong, one of Brisbane's most desirable suburbs.

* 2 luxury suites
* ensuites with shower and full size bath
* marble fire places
* polished floors with Belgian rugs
* under cover parking
* excellent public transport
* privacy assured
* traditional furnishing throughout
* breakfast in dining room, verandah, or in your suite

* afternoon tea or drinks with canapes on arrival
* phone and internet connection
* short walk to Toowong Village - major shopping centre
* abundant birdlife
* easy access to city or university of Queensland.

Brisbane - West End

Eskdale Bed & Breakfast *B&B Homestay*
Paul Kennedy
141 Vulture Street
West End
Qld 4101
2 km SW of Brisbane

Tel (07) 3255 2519
eskdale_brisbane@yahoo.com.au
eskdale.homestead.com

Double $110 Single $70
Child 1/2 price
Continental Breakfast
Every 5th night free
No smoking on property
Visa MC accepted
1 King 1 Queen 1 Double 2 Single (4 bdrm)
Bathrooms: 1 Family share 1 Guest share

Eskdale Bed & Breakfast is a typical turn-of-the century Queensland house close to the restaurant district of West End. It's 2km to the city centre across the Victoria Bridge, and just 1km from the Southbank Parklands and the Brisbane Convention and Exhibition Centre, the Queensland Performing Arts Centre, Museum and Art Gallery. You'll be close to all the action and still be able to relax on the back deck and watch the birds feeding on the Australian native plants in the garden.

Brisbane Central

La Torretta Bed & Breakfast *B&B*
Charles and Dorothy Colman
8 Brereton Street
South Brisbane   Qld 4101
1 km S of Brisbane

Tel (07) 3846 0846 or 0414 465 387
Fax (07) 3342 7863
colmanwilliams@bigpond.com
www.latorretta.com.au

Double $95 Single $75
Child from half price
Continental Breakfast   Minimum 2 nights.
Weekly rate: 7th night free.
Extra person $20
No smoking on property   Visa MC BC Eftpos accepted
1 Queen 1 Twin (2 bdrm)
Bathrooms: 2 Private

AAA Tourism ★★★☆

Ten minutes walk to the Convention Centre, Cultural Complex and beautiful Southbank Gardens, La Torretta is an elegant Queenslander with modern, comfortable, ground-floor guest accommodation and off-street parking. Our many return visitors come for the unfussy but meticulous service, homemade bread and jams, freshly ground Italian coffee, large friendly guest-lounge, with internet access, looking onto the leafy garden. The well-equipped kitchenette has coffee, teas and biscuits always available. West End's convivial cafes and new supermarket complex are just around the corner. "A great find - excellent and friendly service!" CT, UK.

Brisbane City

Eton *B&B Cottage with Kitchen*
Matthew & Ying Lo
436 Upper Roma Street
Brisbane Qld 4000
1 km W of Brisbane

Tel (07) 3236 0115
Fax (07) 3102 6120
etonbnb@yahoo.com.au
www.babs.com.au/eton

Double $110-$130 **Single** $95-$110
Children over 4 welcome by arrangement
Continental Breakfast
Self-contained apartment: $560/week
Visa MC BC Eftpos accepted
2 King/Twin 4 Queen (6 bdrm)
Bathrooms: 6 Ensuite

Eton is a restored inner city colonial house offering quality bed and breakfast accommodation in the heart of Brisbane. We are located within walking distance to the Brisbane Exhibition & Convention Centre, Brisbane's city centre, South Bank Parklands, Suncorp Stadium and inner city dining & entertainment. Roma Street station and the Brisbane Transit Centre are a 5-minute walk and connections to the airport, trains and coaches can be made there. All rooms are traditionally furnished with polished floors, ensuite bathrooms and air-conditioning. Breakfast is served in our dining room or in the tropical courtyard garden.

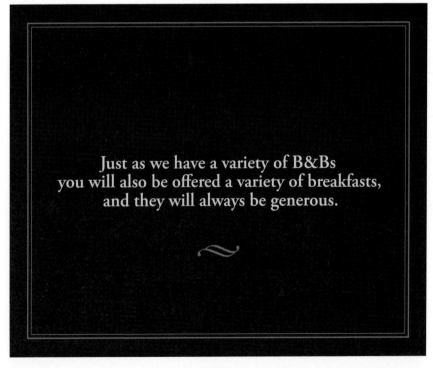

Just as we have a variety of B&Bs
you will also be offered a variety of breakfasts,
and they will always be generous.

Buderim - Sunshine Coast

Aquila Retreat Luxury Accommodation *B&B*

Horst & Ophelia Rechlin
21 Box Street, Buderim, Qld 4556
0.5 km E of Buderim

Tel (07) 5445 3681 or 0417 614 507
Fax (07) 5456 1140
info@aquilaretreat.com.au
www.aquilaretreat.com.au

Double $199-$330 Single $184-$315
Includes full breakfast   Dinner By arrangement
No smoking on property   Visa MC BC accepted
5 Queen (5 bdrm)
Bathrooms: 5 Ensuite

Close to Nature, close to the Beach! Queensland's first green 5 Star Accommodation. Indisputably unique location, magnificent sweeping views, contemporary eco design, linked with comfort, privacy and superior service are the key elements destined to characterize Multi Award Winner Aquila Retreat. Delight in the beautiful scenery and get in touch with your senses, taking in the soothing sounds of the birds and scents amidst the 10 acres of sub-tropical lush gardens below, enjoy the lavish gourmet Breakfast with fresh home grown herbs and edible flowers, served on the sunny deck.

Indulge in the complementary organic Coffee/Tea and delicious European homemade cake. Gaze over the superb, private garden oasis enriched with sophisticated botanical extravagances, into the sweeping Coastal and Mountain views halfway to heaven.

Feel the magic of nature's powerful healing qualities, while you sit out in the evening with a long drink, watching the breathtaking sunsets over the Glass House Mountains, which in the colder months are ablaze with colour, or view the spectacular night sky from the main deck, using the large telescope.

Aquila Retreat is the Sunshine Coast's first eco-accommodation and has been featured on the "Great South East", "The Great Outdoors", "Queensland Escapes" and "Spiegel TV Germany".

Rates include a lavish three-course gourmet breakfast and a delicious afternoon tea ritual with organic espresso style coffee/tea and continental homemade cake is served daily from 3 to 4 pm. Come and do absolutely nothing or absolutely everything - it's up to you!!

Bundaberg

Inglebrae *B&B*
Christina and John McDonald
17 Branyan Street
Bundaberg
Qld 4670
1 km W of Bundaberg

Tel (07) 4154 4003
or 0418 889 971
Fax (07) 4154 2503
inglebrae@interworx.com.au
www.inglebrae.com

Double $95-$130
Includes full breakfast
No smoking on property
Visa MC BC Eftpos accepted
2 Queen 1 Twin (3 bdrm)
Bathrooms: 2 Ensuite 1 Private

Inglebrae is a restored Queenslander circa 1910 with beautifully appointed air-conditioned queen size rooms and ensuites. A leisurely 1 km stroll to the city centre where you will find many fine restaurants in which to dine. Ideally situated close to Bargara Beach, Mon Repos Turtle Sanctuary. Southern tip of the Great Barrier Reef and the departure points for Lady Elliott Island. Enjoy a sumptuously cooked breakfast on the verandah overlooking beautiful gardens. Sorry no facilities for pets - no children - no smoking. A complimentary pick up service is available from airport, rail or bus.

Bundaberg - Bargara Beach

Dunelm House B&B *B&B*
David and Penny Kent
540 Bargara Road
Bargara
Qld 4670
9 km E of Bundaberg

Tel (07) 4159 0909
or 0409 757 165
Fax (07) 4159 0916
dunelm@austarnet.com.au
www.babs.com.au/dunelm

Double $90-$100 Single $70-$80
Includes full breakfast
Visa MC BC accepted
3 Queen 1 Single (3 bdrm)
Bathrooms: 3 Ensuite

AAA Tourism ★★★★☆

Located, 4.5hrs drive North of Brisbane this is an ideal stop for holidaymakers who come to enjoy the Coral Coast. Air-conditioned rooms, comfortable beds, private ensuites and a scrumptious cooked breakfast await the guests. The lounge overlooks the cane fields and has Satellite TV, and video for your use, there is a guestsí barbecue available. Whether short or long stays, golfers, bowlers, divers are catered for due to our location close to Bundaberg, Bargara's beaches, Mon Repos Turtle Sanctuary and cruise departure points.

Cairns - Brinsmead

Jenny's Homestay *B&B Homestay Queen with ensuite*
Jenny & Lex Macfarlane
12 Leon Close
Brinsmead
Qld 4870
10 km W of Cairns

Tel (07) 4055 1639
or 0428 551 639
jennysbb@jennysbandb.com
www.jennysbandb.com

Double $85-$95 Single $70-$80
Includes special breakfast
1 King 2 Queen 1 Twin (4 bdrm)
Bathrooms: 2 Ensuite 1 Guest share 1 Private

Jenny and Lex invite you to our home in Cairns. Wake to the sound of birds and our beautiful rainforest garden. A continental breakfast is served in the sunroom or around the pool. My husband and I are Photographers and enjoy outdoor activities. We are only a short distance from the tropical beaches, great restaurants, golf courses and the famous Kuranda Train and Skyrail. We are booking agents for all tours and rental cars. A complimentary pick up on arrival. "This was our 4th stay at your B&B and we enjoy it more each stay" Gary & Helen Young, Seattle Washington, U.S.A. "Wonderful stay, great hospitality, the best of breakfast. Hope to return in the future" Lee & Monika Parker.

Cairns - Crystal Cascades

Nutmeg Grove - Tropical Rainforest B&B - Cairns *Luxury B&B Homestay*
Ingrid & Terry Douglas
7 Woodridge Close, Crystal Cascades (via Redlynch)
Cairns
Qld 4870
14 km NW of Cairns

Tel +61 7 - 4039 1226
or 0429 391 226
Fax +61 7 - 4039 1226
stay@nutmeggrove.com.au
www.nutmeggrove.com.au

Double $133-$158
Includes full breakfast
Visa MC BC accepted
1 King 1 Queen (2 bdrm)
Bathrooms: 2 Private 1 spa bathroom, 1 ensuite

Stunning 3 acre rainforest property - where you discover peace, privacy and breathtaking beauty of Nutmeg Grove. Elegant luxury living in one of the most awe-inspiring regions of the world. Nestled in the Freshwater Valley, at Crystal Cascades - Cairns, you are surrounded by rainforested mountain ranges with world heritage listed rainforest area, making this an ornithologist and artist's paradise. Private guest wing, a/c, fans, pool with waterfall and spa. Gourmet breakfasts and warm hospitality welcomes you. Central to all tour destinations, Cairns, Beaches, Port Douglas, Great Barrier Reef, Daintree and Cape Tribulation.

Cairns - Holloways Beach

Billabong B&B *B&B*
Vicky & Ted Riddle
30 Caribbean Street
Holloways Beach, Cairns
Qld 4878
10 km N of Cairns

Tel (07) 4037 0162
or 0427 370 044
Fax (07) 4037 0162
info@cairns-bed-breakfast.com
www.cairns-bed-breakfast.com

Double $125-$135 Single $100-$110
Includes full breakfast
Visa MC BC accepted
2 Queen 1 Single (2 bdrm)
Bathrooms: 2 Ensuite

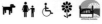

Billabong B&B only 10 minutes from downtown Cairns, 7 minutes from the airport, is a secluded luxury retreat for nature lovers. Set on an island in the heart of a large lily-covered lake teeming with barramundi & surrounded by majestic melaleuca trees, this private home features two guest suites with contemporary decor and large French doors overlooking the billabong. Carefully landscaped to create an outback setting in Cairns. Relax by the billabong with a book or wander over to the nearby coastal beach & local restaurants. Owners Vicky & Ted are friendly & knowledgeable of local tour opportunities. Full Gourmet Breakfast.

Cairns - Stratford

Lilybank *B&B*
Mike & Pat Woolford
75 Kamerunga Road
Stratford Cairns
Qld 4870
8 km N of Cairns

Tel (07) 4055 1123
Fax (07) 4058 1990
lilybank@bigpond.net.au
www.lilybank.com.au

Double $99-$110 Single $77
Includes special breakfast
Extra person in room $33
Visa MC accepted
1 King/Twin 1 King 4 Queen 4 Twin 5 Single (5 bdrm)
Bathrooms: 5 Ensuite

Lilybank - a fine example of traditional "Queenslander" architecture. "Lilybank" owes its success to the happy blend of hospitality and privacy offered to our guests. Bedrooms are air-conditioned, there's a guests' lounge with TV, video, salt-water pool, laundry, BBQ and off-street parking. We'll serve a wonderful breakfast and help you choose and book tours which are right for you. Our excellent local restaurants are within walking distance. Three poodles and a galah live in our part of house. There's a beautiful tropical garden and guests are welcome to pick their own fruit in season.

Cairns - Yorkeys Knob

A Villa Gail *B&B*
Gail Simpson
36 Janett Street
Yorkeys Knob Cairns
Qld 4878
17 km N of Cairns

Tel (07) 4055 8178
or 0417 079 575
Fax (07) 4055 8178
gail@avillagail.com
www.avillagail.com

Double $120-$150 Single $65-$85
Includes special breakfast
Self Contained guest wing $140
1 King 1 Queen 1 Double 1 Twin (3 bdrm)
Bathrooms: 2 Ensuite

Villa Gail on Millionaires Row was designed to make the most of our unique elevated location at Yorkey's Knob. Our cool Mediterranean-style house is set within lush tropical gardens overlooking the beach with breathtaking views across the Coral Sea. From the delightful in-ground swimming pool spacious guest's verandah or your own large room, you can relax and enjoy our tropical lifestyle. Villa Gail is only 15 minutes from Cairns, near to the Skyrail, golf course, tours to the World Heritage Wet Tropics Rainforest, the Outback and the Great Barrier Reef. All pick ups from our door.

Capricorn Coast - Rockhampton

Brae Bothy B&B *B&B*
Judy & Keith Brandt
1184 Yeppoon Road
Iron Pot, Capricorn Coast
Qld 4701
20 km NE of Rockhampton

Tel (07) 4936 4026
or 0427 364 026
Fax (07) 4936 4038
stay@braebothy.com.au
www.braebothy.com.au

Double $90-$130 Single $80-$100
Child $45 or BA
Includes full breakfast
Dinner $25 BA
Visa MC accepted
1 King/Twin 2 Queen (3 bdrm)
Bathrooms: 2 Ensuite 1 Private

 AAA Tourism
★★★★☆

A touch of Scotland in the Central Queensland Bush. Relax in a quaint Scottish bothy nestled in a peaceful tranquil setting with abundant bird and animal life. Cosy guest lounge, tea/coffee facilities. Bedrooms tastefully furnished, air-conditioned, Queen size beds, ensuite and private outdoor garden settings. Guest BBQ facility and swimming pool. Fifteen minutes to Yeppoon's beautiful beaches and ten minutes to Rockhampton shopping centres. The ideal stay over as you drive up the Queensland Coast: 4 hours drive from Hervey Bay and 4 hours drive to or from The Whitsunday area.

Daintree

Daintree Mangroves Wildlife Sanctuary *B&B*
Donna & Gil Talbot
Captain Cook Highway
Daintree   Qld 4873
12 km S of Daintree

Tel (07) 4098 7272
Fax (07) 4098 7200
info@daintreewild.com.au
www.daintreewild.com.au

Double $120 Single $70
Includes special breakfast
Dinner Meals available at restaurant
Additional persons $20
Tarrif includes free entry to park at all times
Visa MC BC Amex Eftpos accepted
4 Queen 2 Twin (4 bdrm)
Bathrooms: 1 Family share 2 Guest share

Find us just north of Port Douglas surrounded by World Heritage Listed National Park and The spectacular Daintree River. Experience the Reef and Mossman Gorge. Walk the beaches from Cow Bay to Cape Tribulation. Browse Daintree, Port Douglas & Cooktown Village. Relax wandering through our tropical gardens, we are a bird lovers paradise with one of the most comprehensive collections of Australian Cockatoos, Parrots, and Finches along with the dozens of migratory species that frequent our sanctuary. Relax in four cool, poolside rooms.

Gold Coast - Hinterland - Tamborine Mountain

Sandiacre House B&B *B&B Homestay*
Margaret & David Carter
45-47 Licuala Drive
North Tamborine
Qld 4272
30 km SW of Oxenford

Tel (07) 5545 3490
or 0407 453 490
Fax (07) 5545 0279
sandiacrebnb@iprimus.com.au
www.babs.com.au/sandiacre

Double $85-$14
Includes full breakfast
Dinner By arrangement
Extra person $50
2 Queen 1 Twin 2 Single (3 bdrm)
Bathrooms: 2 Ensuite 1 Family share

Welcome to Sandiacre House Exquisite Bed & Breakfast on picturesque Tamborine Mountain; with Victorian decor, antique furnishings, log fire for that homely feeling in winter, tranquil gardens, chickens, ducks and bees. Our aim is to make your stay as relaxing and memorable as possible. Centrally located 2-10 minutes drive to all amenities, tourist attractions and craft shops. Weddings, anniversaries, special occasions and gift vouchers are our speciality. Award winning B&B. We have no facilities for children, pets.

Gold Coast Hinterland

Riviera Bed & Breakfast *B&B Retreat & B&B*
Robert and Caroline Marchesi
53 Evanita Drive
Gilston/Nerang   Qld 4211
6 km S of Nerang

Tel (07) 5533 2499 or 0421 853 189
Fax (07) 5533 2500
gilstonretreat@hotkey.net.au
www.babs.com.au/gilston

Double $100-$120 Single $90-$100
Child $15-$30
Includes full breakfast
Dinner $25-$35 B/A
Additional person $40. High Season tariff 20th Dec-3rd Jan $140
Visa MC BC Eftpos accepted
4 Queen 3 Single (4 bdrm)
Bathrooms: 1 Ensuite 1 Family share 1 Private

Unique French Experience on the edge of Gold Coast Hinterland. Peaceful, secluded and exotic location in an Exquisite 100 year old Queenslander on 7 acres of sub-tropical bushland. Close proximity to all Theme Parks and National/Wildlife Parks. Franco-Australian hosts offer sumptuous breakfasts of homemade breads and jams with weekend specialities of French crepes and omelettes. Exotic native birds to handfeed from deck while kangaroos graze nearby. Authentic French Gourmet meals by arrangement. Aussie host offers Therapeutic Massage. Pet friendly.

~

Gold Coast Hinterland - Guanaba

Jiana Park Lodge Bed & Breakfast *B&B Cottage with Kitchen*
Diana & Jim Ingram
685 Guanaba Creek Road
Guanaba
Qld 4210
18 km NW of Nerang

Tel (07) 5533 7887
Fax (07) 5533 7756
info@jianapark.com.au
www.jianapark.com.au

Double $120 Single $90
Child $55
Full Breakfast Provisions
Child under 10 years free
1 Queen 2 Single (2 bdrm)
Bathrooms: 1 Private

An enchanting 13 acres of creek frontage undulating into foothills. Great for walking or resting. We are tucked away in a secluded parkland valley with birdsong, the sound of the creek, wallabies, even fireflies and platypus. Only 15 minutes from Brisbane freeway, Movieworld and Dreamworld. Mt Tamborine restaurants and shops are 15 minutes drive, beaches and shopping 40 minutes. You are absolutely pampered with Champagne or Devonshire Tea on arrival and presented with your Breakfast Basket overflowing with food, then left to the privacy of your own Lodge and courtyard.

Gold Coast Hinterland - Tamborine Mountain

Tamborine Mountain Bed and Breakfast *B&B*

Tony & Pam Lambert
19 - 23 Witherby Crescent
Eagle Heights
Qld 4271
35 km NW of Surfers Paradise

Tel (07) 5545 3595
or 0418 755 517
Fax (07) 5545 3322
info@tmbb.com.au
www.tmbb.com.au

Double $130-$160
Includes full breakfast
1 King/Twin 3 Queen 1 Single (4 bdrm)
Bathrooms: 4 Ensuite

Tony, Pam and their Weimaraner Elle, look forward to sharing their beautiful home with you. Situated approximately 500 metres above sea level on the eastern escarpment of Tamborine Mountain overlooking the Gold Coast. This Bed and Breakfast has simply the best view from Moreton Island to Coolangatta. Ideally situated amongst national parks, arts and craft shops, wineries and restaurants, Tamborine Mountain Bed and Breakfast is the perfect environment to relax and unwind.

Hervey Bay

Tara B&B *B&B*

Kitty & Eddie O'Neill
7 Wright Way
Scarness
Qld 4655
0.5 km S of Post Office

Tel (07) 4124 7072
or 0403 992 423
Fax (07) 4124 7072
tarabb@itfusion.com.au
www.bbbook.com.au/tara.html

Double $90 **Single** $60
Child by age
Includes full breakfast
No smoking on property
1 Queen 3 Double 2 Single (4 bdrm)
Bathrooms: 1 Ensuite 2 Private

Tara Bed and Breakfast can be found in the heart of the city of Hervey Bay, close to all amenities - Post Office, airport, bus terminal, and the magical Fraser Island. We can arrange all bookings - whale watching August to October, Lady Elliott Island, Great Barrier Reef, and Fraser Island. Breakfast can be served in dining room or the privacy of the verandahs. Continental or full breakfast served. Close to all beaches. Air conditioning in all rooms. Access from all rooms to verandahs, pool table, fridge, tea making facilities. Privacy assured.

Hervey Bay

Alexander Lakeside B&B *B&B Separate Suite*
Pauline & Max Harriden
29 Lido Parade
Hervey Bay
Qld 4655
In Hervey Bay

Tel (07) 4128 9448
or 0409 284 122
Fax (07) 4125 5060
alexbnb@bigpond.net.au
www.herveybaybedandbreakfast.com

Double $120-$140 Single $110-$120
Includes full breakfast
S/C suites $140-$150
Visa MC BC accepted
4 Queen (4 bdrm)
Bathrooms: 4 Ensuite

 AAA Tourism ★★★★☆

Luxury accommodation located beside a peaceful wildlife lake. Wake up and enjoy a full tropical breakfast while watching our wildlife - Guest can Participate in turtle feeding Indulge yourself in our heated Lakeside Spa. Fully equipped kitchen and laundry. BBQ facilities. We can organise your tours to view the majestic Humpback Whales (Aug-Nov). Fraser Island and lady Elliott Island the beginning of the Great Barrier Reef. Short stroll to beaches, restaurants and the Urangan Pier. Complimentary pick up from the Transit Centre or the Airport. A warm welcome and a smile awaits you. Your Home Style Resort.

~

Hervey Bay

The Chamomile Bed and Breakfast *B&B*
John and Kathie Ryan
65A Miller Street
Hervey Bay
Qld 4655
0.5 km NW of Hervey Bay Marina

Tel (07) 4125 1602
or 0428 877 709
Fax (07) 4125 6975
info@chamomile.com.au
www.chamomile.com.au

Double $115-$145 Single $95-$100
Includes full breakfast
Visa MC BC accepted
2 Queen 1 Twin (3 bdrm)
Bathrooms: 1 Ensuite 1 Guest share

Relax on our wide verandah as you sip a cappuccino, listen to the calming sound of water spilling over the waterfall and enjoy the peaceful sounds of the birdcalls. Take a stroll down to the Hervey Bay Marina and enjoy the sights and colours of the boats and people. Recharge in the garden spa. Relish the delicious breakfast, morning and afternoon tea. Coeliacs welcome. Courtesy pickup by arrangement. In house massage available. Booking service for Fraser Island, Lady Elliot Island and Whale Watch tours. Chilli our cat likes to greet guests.

Hervey Bay - Howard

Melvos Country House *B&B Country House*
Yvonne & Paul Melverton
20 Pacific Haven Circuit
Howard
Qld 4659
30 km N of Maryborough

Tel (07) 4129 0201
or 0428 290 201
Fax (07) 4129 0201
melvos1@bigpond.com.au
www.bbbook.com.au/melvos.html

Double $90-$110
Includes full breakfast
Dinner B/A
1 Queen 1 Double (2 bdrm)
Bathrooms: 1 Ensuite 2 Guest share 1 Private

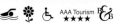

Central located between Maryborough - Hervey Bay - Childers on 44 acres in comfortable and affordable accommodation. Home cooked meals - BBQ facilities BYO alcohol. Tropical gardens - inground pool/spa, TV, DVD, Video. Two saltwater rivers, boat ramp, laundromat, golf course, tennis court nearby. Tours arranged - Fraser & Elliott Islands - whale watching - 4x4 hire, deep-sea fishing, camel rides. Complimentary tea/coffee anytime. Free pickup from Howard Tilt train or bus terminal. Dinner by arrangement. We have small well behaved dogs. Not suitable for children. Smoking outdoors. A warm welcome awaits you.

~

Hervey Bay - Takura

The Doghouse Bed & Breakfast *B&B*
Sven & Paul Reichelt
112 Sanctuary Hills Road
Hervey Bay / Takura
Qld 4655
20 km W of Hervey Bay

Tel (07) 4128 0589
or 0428 482 788
Fax (07) 4128 0715
svenreichelt@dodo.com.au
www.doghouse-oz.com

Double $90-$120 Single $60-$90
Includes special breakfast
Visa MC BC accepted
2 Double (2 bdrm)
Bathrooms: 1 Guest share

Soothing, relaxing, inspiring - best words to describe this tranquil retreat away from home. You will find stylish ambience and mind blowing views, just seven minutes away from private beaches. Bush Walking, Sea Kayaking, Biking, Painting, Pottery are just some of the activities, we can arrange for you. Our friendly dog will show you around. And what about a free welcome treat of either foot massage or Reiki? Enjoy a peaceful time!

Sven & Paul - Don't miss out on our fresh cake, bread and great coffee.

Kuranda - Cairns

Koah Bed & Breakfast *B&B Homestay Farmstay Cottage with Kitchen*
Greg Taylor
Lot 4 Koah Road
MSI 1039 Kuranda
Qld 4881
40 km W of Cairns

Tel (07) 4093 7074
Fax (07) 4093 7074
koah@ozemail.com.au
www.kurandahomestay.com

Double $77 Single $55
Child 50% (under 15)
Continental Breakfast
Visa MC BC accepted
2 Queen 2 Double 4 Twin 2 Single (2 bdrm)
Bathrooms: 1 Ensuite 1 Private

Comfortable country home on 10 acres 10 mins from Kuranda the township in the Rainforest Kuranda and 30 mins from Cairns and Great Barrier Reef. Offering fully self contained cabins for families with balconies overlooking native bushland and large dam. Also homestead accommodation of 2 double bedrooms with double opening doors onto verandah 1 guest bathroom (ensuite) fully insulated and screened with ceiling fans. Each bedroom can be fitted with single folding bed for children, pets also welcomed.

~

Maleny - Montville

Lillypilly's Country Cottages *B&B Cottages with kitchenettes*
Josef & Adele Gruber
584 Maleny-Montville Road
Maleny
Qld 4552
6 km S of Town

Tel (07) 5494 3002
or 0408 943 002
Fax (07) 5494 3499
lillypillys@bigpond.com
www.lillypillys.com.au

Double $187.00-$258 Single $176.00-$247
Includes full breakfast
Dinner $27.50-$30.80 (Main Course)
1/2 to 1 hour massage $36-$66
Visa MC BC Amex Eftpos accepted
5 Queen (5 Cottages bdrm)
Bathrooms: 5 Ensuite 5 Private

 AAA Tourism ★★★★☆

Lillypilly's Cottages for couples overlook picturesque Lake Baroon or are situated in a rainforest garden setting. All cottages are air conditioned and feature log fires, dual-system double spas, separate ensuite, lounge area with television, video, dvd and cd player, kitchenettes, and private verandahs with double hammocks. Gourmet Breakfasts are included in the rate and Candlelit Dinners are available Tues-Sat and served to your individual cottage. An on-site masseur and saltwater pool are also features of Lillypilly's.

Mission Beach South

Leslie Lodge *B&B Apartment with Kitchen*
Don
5 Leslie Lane
Mission Beach South
Qld 4852
120 km S of Cairns

Tel (07) 4068 8618
or 0417 784 965
Fax (07) 4068 9840
leslielodge@dodo.com.au
www.bbbook.com.au/leslielodge.html

Double from $80 Single $60
Child $20 on sofa
Includes full breakfast
S/C Double $70
No smoking on property
1 King/Twin (1 bdrm)
Bathrooms: 1 Private

Secure and private accommodation is offered in delightful property - manicured lawn and garden. 4 mins stroll to delightful sandy beach opposite Dunk Island accessible by water taxi or ferry - rainforest walks and fishing.

Noosa - Cooroy

The Plantation Bed & Breakfast *Luxury B&B*
Robert and Gail Fraser
142 Mary River Road
Cooroy
Qld 4563
1.4 km NW of Cooroy

Tel (07) 5447 7476
or 0416 024 051
Fax (07) 5447 6311
enquiries@theplantation.com.au
www.theplantation.com.au

Double $185 Single $150
Includes full breakfast
Dinner by prior arrangement
Visa MC BC Eftpos accepted
1 King/Twin 2 Queen (3 bdrm)
Bathrooms: 3 Ensuite

AAA Tourism
★★★★☆

Located on 21 acres in the Noosa Hinterland, just 90 minutes north of Brisbane and 20 minutes from Noosa. Luxury accommodation in private wing of stately home. Airconditioned rooms and guest lounge (with DVD/CD/library) open onto wide verandahs and overlook formal gardens, pool and heated spa. Gourmet breakfast and afternoon tea served daily. BBQ facilities available to guests. Close to restaurants, galleries, tennis, golf and local attractions. Gracious hospitality. Total relaxation. Not suitable for children. Family dogs on property.

Noosa - Noosa Valley

Noosa Valley Manor Luxury B&B *B&B*
Kathleen and Murray Maxwell
115 Wust Road   Doonan, Noosa Valley   Qld 4562
10 km SW of Noosa

AAA Tourism ★★★★☆

Tel (07) 5471 0088 or 0400 280 215
Fax (07) 5471 0066
noosa_valley_manor@bigpond.com
www.noosavalleymanor.com.au

Double $165-$195 Single $150-$170
Includes full breakfast   Dinner By arrangement
Standby Rate $175 per night   Visa MC BC accepted
1 King/Twin 3 Queen (4 bdrm)
Bathrooms: 4 Ensuite

Noosa Valley Manor is a modern, custom built Bed & Breakfast that truly reflects its 4.5 star AAA rating. Set in 1.5 acres of award winning tropical gardens in the beautiful Noosa Valley, it assures you of peace and tranquillity yet you are only 10 minutes pleasant drive to the hustle and bustle of Noosa, famous for its beaches, shops and restaurants. It is ideally situated to take advantage of all the attractions that the Sunshine Coast has to offer. For example: Eumundi Market, Fraser Island, Australia Zoo, Ginger Factory, Glasshouse Mountains, Blackall Range, National Parks, swimming, surfing, diving, fishing, golf, tennis, boating etc - all within easy reach.

Our four bedrooms are individually and tastefully decorated. All rooms have ensuites and French doors opening to verandas overlooking the gardens, heated pool and spa. Relax on the magnificent covered terrace taking in the abundant birdlife, stroll through the gardens with many water features, soak in the sunshine round the pool and spa, or enjoy drinks and savouries round the log fire on the cooler evenings. Gourmet fresh food is a feature of your stay with us starting with breakfasts on The Terrace each morning.

Celebrate that special event or anniversary with restaurant quality dinners served by candlelight complete with silver and crystal ware that will make the occasion truly one to remember. Dinners must be arranged in advance. Here is what some guests have said: "Divine food, beautiful house, perfect hosts - we'll be back." "So lovely to be spoilt by wonderful people in a beautiful setting."

Noosa - Peregian

Lake Weyba Cottages *B&B Cottage with Kitchen*
Philip & Samantha Bown
79 Clarendon Road
Peregian Beach
Qld 4573
14 km S of Noosa

Tel (07) 5448 2285 or 0404 863 504
Fax (07) 5448 1714
info@lakeweybacottages.com
www.lakeweybacottages.com

Double $230-$315
Includes full breakfast
Dinner $65
Extra person $65
Visa MC BC Amex Eftpos accepted
2 King/Twin 5 Queen (8 bdrm)
Bathrooms: 7 Ensuite Double spa in each cottage

 AAA Tourism ★★★★☆

Luxury cottages for couples with double spas, a wood fire for winter and air-conditioning for summer. Fabulous views with plenty of peace and privacy. Each morning, a choice of 5 breakfasts is served to your verandah with a newspaper, perfect for relaxing and watching passing kangaroos and the abundant bird life. Only 5 minutes to Peregian Beach and just 15 minutes south of Noosa. Complimentary facilities include canoeing, cycling, swimming, fishing and a video/CD library. Additional services include in-house dinners, massage treatments with aromatherapy and eco tours with your own personal guide.

~

Noosa - Sunshine Coast

Noosa Lakes Bed & Breakfast *B&B*
Sigrid & Otto Simon
384 Lake Cooroibah Road
Tewantin - Noosa
Qld 4565
10 km N of Noosa

Tel (07) 5447 1263
or 0412 714 138
info@noosalakesbb.com
www.noosalakesbb.com

Double upto $115 Single up to $75
Includes full breakfast
Separate Studio $125
1 King 1 Queen 1 Single (3 bdrm)
Bathrooms: 1 Ensuite 1 Private

German-born hosts and world travellers offer you to share their natural, tranquil environment away from it all but only 10 minutes from cosmopolitan Noosa! Walk on our 10-acre "wonderland" to the lake watching the abundant bird and wildlife, go water-sporting, fishing, biking and riding or relax in our rockpool with waterfall. Being Noosa-oldtimers for 20 years, we'll give you insider tips how best to explore the hinterland, Eumundi-market, Fraser-Island or finding the beach just for yourself. Our lovely Labrador welcomes your dog. Broadband web access. We guarantee value for money and a holiday you remember!

Noosa Hinterland - Cooroy

Cudgerie Homestead B&B *B&B*
David & Jenny Mathers
42 Cudgerie Drive
CooroyQld 4563
5 km N of Cooroy

Tel (07) 5442 6681
or 0408 982 461
Fax (07) 5442 6681
cudgerie@hotmail.com
www.cudgerie.com

Double $140-$180 Single $88-$100
Child discount
Includes full breakfast
No smoking on property
Visa MC accepted
2 Queen 1 Double 1 Twin (4 bdrm)
Bathrooms: 3 Ensuite 1 Private

Multi-award winning Cudgerie Homestead is one of the Sunshine Coast's most popular bed and breakfasts, offering you a unique blend of relaxation, ambience and cuisine. Unwind by the sensational swimming pool in summer or around the log fire in winter. A quiet and secluded location with fantastic views across the Noosa Hinterland. Guest Comments: "A place to indulge, superb breakfasts on the verandah. Charming hosts with helpful touring advice." "It doesn't get any better than this, splendid location, warm and friendly hosts and top notch food."

Port Douglas

Coral Sea Retreat Bed and Breakfast *B&B The Tree House - Self Contained*
Marie, Denise, Michael, Michelle
7-11 Bruce Avenue
Oak Beach, Port Douglas
Qld 4877
17 km S of Port Douglas

Tel (07) 4099 3617
info@coralsearetreat.com
www.coralsearetreat.com

Double $99-$160 Single $89-$140
Child Children POA
Includes special breakfast
Dinner Menu available
Extra person POA
Visa MC accepted
2 King/Twin 2 Queen 2 Twin 2 Single (4 bdrm)
Bathrooms: 2 Ensuite 1 Private

Coral Sea Retreat is one of North Queensland's best kept secrets! This delightful, hilltop B&B set amongst lush gardens and orchard, features the choice of tropical style bedrooms with full breakfast or the Tree House - a two bedroom, self-contained unit all with stunning ocean views. Breakfasts are very special here! The Great Barrier Reef, Daintree Rainforest, Cape Tribulation, Tablelands etc. are easily accessible by car. Coral Sea Retreat and the Tree House capture the relaxed lifestyle of the tropics, without the intrusion of a busy resort atmosphere. Treat yourself to a tropical B&B experience!

Stanthorpe

Jireh *Homestay*
Ken & Margaret Taylor
89 Donges Road
Severnlea
Qld 4352
8 km S of Stanthorpe

Tel (07) 4683 5298
ktaylor3@vtown.com.au
www.bbbook.com.au/jireh.html

Double $90-$110 Single $65-$75
Child $25
Includes full breakfast
Dinner $25
3 Double 1 Single (3 bdrm)
Bathrooms: 1 Ensuite 1 Guest share

A cosy farmhouse B&B in a quiet rural setting, close to the wineries and national parks of the Granite Belt. Antiques and country decor reflect family history and memorabilia, and includes many examples of Margaret's embroidery, patchwork, dolls and bears. Hearty home-grown country breakfasts are served and dinner (Traditional or Indian) is by arrangement. The combination of country home, personal attention, household pets, farm animals, and country rambles offers both a unique experience and value for money. " Wonderful friendly atmosphere and simply great food." B&B Book Commended, 2004, 2005.

Sunshine Coast - Ninderry

Ninderry Manor Luxury B&B *B&B*
Aki & Miyuki Kitabatake
12 Karnu Drive
Ninderry, via Yandina, Sunshine Coast
Qld 4561
5 km S of Yandina

Tel (07) 5472 7255 or 0412 417 415
Fax (07) 5446 7089
info@ninderrymanor.com.au
www.ninderrymanor.com.au

Double $160-$180 Single $130
Includes special breakfast
Dinner $40-$50. Snacks available.
In house massage $40 (30min).
No smoking on property
Visa MC BC Diners accepted
1 King/Twin 2 Queen (3 bdrm)
Bathrooms: 3 Ensuite

U nique experiences with taste of Japan, head to the heart of Sunshine Coast. Situated in the Noosa, Eumundi, Coolum Beach Triangle. Relax. Enjoy magnificent views, tranquillity, the Milky Way. Sunset Cocktails. Dine at the Spirit House, Picnics or dine in & enjoy Aki's divine food. We can offer services like Japanese Cooking lesson, calligraphy, tea ceremony and pampering massages/facial. Luxuriously appointed and comfortable ensuited rooms with indulgent extras. "The host's cheerful welcome just about bowled us over, and their attention to detail was exquisite. . . " Alison Cotes, Sunday Mail.

Sunshine Coast - Ninderry - Yandina - Coolum

Ninderry House *B&B*
Mary Lambart
8 Karnu Drive
Ninderry
Qld 4561
5 km E of Yandina

Tel (07) 5446 8556
or 0421 456 804
Fax (07) 5446 8556
enquiries@ninderryhouse.com.au
www.ninderryhouse.com.au

Double $135 Single $80
Includes full breakfast
Dinner $20 - $25
Visa MC BC accepted
1 King/Twin 1 Queen 2 Twin (3 bdrm)
Bathrooms: 3 Ensuite

Central Sunshine Coast location, views overlooking Mt Ninderry and Maroochy Valley to the Ocean. Close to beaches, native plant nurseries, ginger factory, art galleries, craft and produce markets of Eumundi and Yandina. First class restaurants nearby. Three ensuite guestrooms, comfortable sitting room with fire, deck for summer breezes or winter sun. Imaginative meals using fresh local produce. Special diets catered for. Dinner available if requested on booking. Full breakfast included in tariff. Children not catered for. Ph/Fax: 07 5446 8556. Email: enquiries@ninderryhouse.com.au.

Sunshine Coast Hinterland - Goomeri

Boonara Homestead *Luxury B&B Historic*
Ted & Sandra Nesbitt
7191 Burnett Highway
Goomeri
Qld 4601
12 km N of Goomeri

Tel (07) 4168 7298
Fax (07) 4168 7148
boonara@nesbitts-australia.com
www.boonara-homestead.com

Double $147.50-$177.50
Includes full breakfast
Dinner $27.50/pers
Visa MC BC Amex Eftpos accepted
1 King/Twin 1 Queen (2 bdrm)
Bathrooms: 2 Ensuite

Boonara Homestead is a beautifully restored 1862 Grand Colonial home built by David Jones (of department store fame). It is a peaceful oasis that invites relaxation and takes one back to a more gentile time. Boonara offers two guestrooms - The Victorian Room has a four poster canopied bed, polished wood floors, Persian rugs and beautiful linens. The Chinese Room offers an enormous king sized bed, polished wood floors, soft carpets and silk cushions. The hosts share their private accommodation with 3 entertaining dogs.

Sunshine Coast Hinterland - Maleny

Maleny Tropical Retreat *B&B*
Kerry & Ken
540 Maleny-Montville Road
Maleny
Qld 4552
5 km S of Montville

Tel (07) 5435 2113
Fax (07) 5435 2114
unwind@malenytropicalretreat.com
www.malenytropicalretreat.com

Double $160-$195 Single $140-$165
Includes full breakfast
Visa MC BC Diners Amex accepted
3 Queen (3 bdrm)
Bathrooms: 3 Ensuite Include large corner spas with views.

AAA Tourism
★★★★☆

Unique Balinese style B&B with three exquisitely appointed guest rooms. Relax in a warm, bubbling spa. Light the wood fire. Sip your favourite wine. Relax on your private deck listening to the birds. Gaze out on a magnificent vista of rainforest & pastures. Paddle in the private creek with Cassi & Benji as your four-legged bushwalking escorts. Close to galleries, shops, wineries, & local arts, crafts & produce outlets.

Tin Can Bay

Mia Mia B&B *B&B*
Jenny & John Jarvis
13 Bobrei Court
Wallu
Qld 4580
10 km W of Tin Can Bay

Tel (07) 5488 0461
or 0419 300 461
Fax (07) 5488 0574
miamia@spiderweb.com.au
www.miamia.spiderweb.com.au

Double $100-$150 Single $80-$130
Includes full breakfast
Visa MC BC accepted
1 King/Twin 2 Queen (3 bdrm)
Bathrooms: 3 Ensuite

Mia Mia is a contemporary home perched among the trees with views to Fraser Island. Treat yourself to a luxury escape where you can relax on the decks, laze by the pool, unwind in the heated spa or curl up by the fire when the nights are cool. Just a short distance to Tin Can Bay or Rainbow Beach where you can fish, swim or bushwalk, 4WD or visit Fraser Island. Enjoy our hearty breakfast on the deck and, by prior arrangement, our wine, lunch and dinners. "Wow, what a wonderful 'hiatus' in a frantic life."

Toowoomba

Jacaranda Grove B&B *Homestay*
Richard & Jan McIlwraith
92 Tourist Road
Toowoomba
Qld 4350
In Toowoomba

Tel (07) 4635 8394
or 0419 660 544
Fax (07) 4635 8394
jacarandagrove@telstra.com
www.babs.com.au/jacaranda

Double $160-$190 Single $110-$130
Includes special breakfast
Visa MC BC Diners accepted
1 King 1 Queen (2 bdrm)
Bathrooms: 2 Ensuite

AAA Tourism
★★★★☆

Jacaranda Grove. Exclusive romantic Federation multi-award winning Retreat perched atop the Great Divide offering Range views from the delightful deck, legendary stunning breakfasts, splendid art and antiques, fabulous flowers, guests sitting room and entrance, exceptional hospitality and a magical ambience created by your hosts professional interior design skill. R/C air conditioned luxury. Simply Irresistible. Bar fridge, TV, cocktails and canapés Fragrant formal garden. Minutes from CBD, restaurants, antique shops, art galleries, golf courses, wineries and the Empire Theatre. This exquisite 4 star establishment celebrating 10 years of operation. Special weekend and bridal packages.

Toowoomba - Kingsthorpe

Sugarloaf Mountain Country Retreat *Cottage with Kitchen*
Jeanette Wehl
Cutella Road
Kingsthorpe
Qld 4350
20 km W of Toowoomba

Tel (07) 4630 1109
or 0428 963 026
jwehl@icr.com.au
www.sugarloafmountain.com.au

Double $125
Accommodation Only only
$45 per extra person
No smoking on property
2 Queen 1 Single (3 bdrm)
Bathrooms: 1 Private

For a peaceful stay overlooking acclaimed Darling Downs farming land to the ranges beyond, Sugarloaf Mountain Country Retreat is for adults only and is the perfect place to wind down and relax. Sweeping views, roomy lounge, sunroom, bedrooms and decks allow this, plus there is the added bonus of a unique chance to stay in privacy on a 140 acre grazing property. A fully equipped kitchen, laundry facilities, BBQ, reverse cycle air conditioning and additional heating ensures a comfy stay.

Townsville

Canobie House Bed & Breakfast *B&B Homestay*

Philippa Johnson
495 Sturt Street
Townsville
Qld 4810
In Townsville

Tel (07) 4721 2689
or 0417 780 016
Fax (07) 4721 2689
ragj@austarnet.com.au
www.canobiehouse.com.au

Double $115-$135 Single $90-$115
Includes special breakfast
Visa MC BC Eftpos accepted
1 King/Twin 2 Queen 1 Single (4 bdrm)
Bathrooms: 2 Ensuite 1 Guest share

Enjoy a warm welcome to our historic Queenslander, within walking distance of city shops, cinemas and restaurants. You will also enjoy the tranquility of Castle Hill from our rear deck and garden. Only 5 minutes to beaches, airport and ferries. Our interests include music, travel, classic cars, golf and wine. If you wish to explore the goldfields, visit the rainforest or snorkel the Reef we arrange bookings. We have a dog and a cat - your pet is welcome by arrangement.

Yeppoon - Capricorn Coast

While Away B&B *B&B*

Jean and Robin Andrews
44 Todd Avenue
Yeppoon
Qld 4703
2.4 km N of Yeppoon

Tel (07) 4939 5719
or 0400 304 739
Fax (07) 4939 5577
whileaway@bigpond.com
www.whileawaybandb.com.au

Double $95-$125 Single $90-$95
Includes special breakfast
Visa MC BC accepted
1 King 3 Queen 1 Twin (4 bdrm)
Bathrooms: 4 Ensuite

AAA Tourism
★★★★☆

While Away B&B is a purpose built B&B. We offer style, comfort and privacy in a modern home less than 100 m to beach. This property is ideal for couples and unsuitable for children under 10. All rooms have ensuites, television plus air-conditioning. We offer a generous tropical/cooked breakfast - tea/coffee making facilities with cake/biscuits are available at all times. Complimentary pre-dinner drinks and nibbles. We will do our best to ensure you enjoy your stay in this area.

South Australia

Adelaide

Just five minutes drive from Port Adelaide is the coastal village of Semaphore. The foreshore is home to an array of amusements, including an historic carousel, coastal steam train, water slide and ferris wheel. Other features include a wide and sandy beach, safe swimming and a long jetty, perfect for dropping a line. Semaphore also has some excellent cafés, restaurants, hotels and bed and breakfast's. Take a stroll along Semaphore Road, a shopping precinct that offers an interesting array of specialty shops, clothing boutiques and galleries.

Take a leisurely drive along the Coastal Tourist Drive and enjoy the ever changing sea-scape from Semaphore South to the North Haven Marina. Another delightful way to experience the scenery is to walk, roller-blade or cycle along the meandering coastal path.

Port Adelaide VIC.

Clare Valley

Amongst the gentle rolling hills and native grasslands of South Australia's Mid North, just an hour or so from Adelaide, can be found tranquil pastoral countryside: green and lush in winter, dry and golden in summer. The Clare Valley region includes the closest outback scenery to any Australian capital city, the Historic Burra copper mine circa 1845 with its pretty Heritage listed town steeped in history, Martindale Hall of Picnic at Hanging Rock fame, and the beautiful and bountiful Clare Valley with over 40 prestigious wineries. Clare Valley country is a great place to relax and unwind

Maureen Wright, Burra Heritage Cottages, Tivers Row.

Clare Valley,
Sevenhill Cellars,
Clare Valley Secrets,
SATC, SA

Fleurieu Peninsula

Come wander the Fleurieu Peninsula with temperate climate, central highlands and coastal fringe. Experience wine, water and wildlife delights. Over 65 cellar door wine sales and 20 national parks. See kangaroos on hillsides and penguins returning to their nests each evening. Many water recreational activities, long sandy beaches, sheltered coves and rugged cliff scapes. Your family can be part of a living history as you walk the heritage streets, visit museums, galleries and shops.

Spring is wildflower season and winter sees the whales, dolphins, seals arrive. Visit local festivals and markets and taste superb local foods, wines or drive to find another secret of this beautiful peninsula

Romaine Dawson, Trafalgar House Accommodation, Port Elliot.

Murraylands

Murraylands encompasses the lower reaches of the magnificent Murray River from Blanchetown to Wellington on the shore of Lake Alexandrina. From the foot of the Adelaide hills to Pinnaroo, the Mallee town on the edge of the South Australian/Victorian boarder. Ngaut-Ngaut near Nildottie, is dotted with Conservation Parks and historical spots and ancient Aboriginal camps, dating back thousands of years. Mannum was the birthplace of the first paddle-steamer, Mary-Ann, built in 1854. The Shearer Brothers, farm machinery manufacturers, built the first steam car with a differential, in 1897. The PS "Marion" now sailing for over a century, is moored at the Mannum Dock Museum. A variety of vessels offer Murray River experiences embarking from Mannum. Murray Bridge, the largest town, has a "Bunyip" living at Sturt Reserve. A cellar-door winery is just out of town. While there are walking trails and 4 wheel drive tracks. Come and enjoy.

Rae Jarrett, Bonza View B&B, Mannum SA.

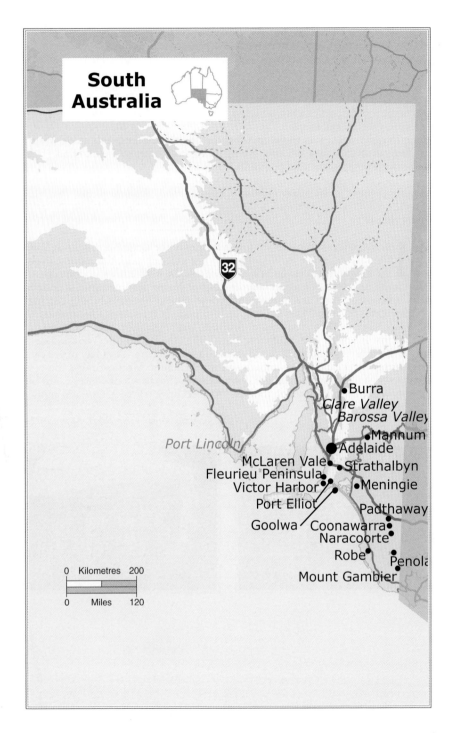

South
Australia

32

Burra
Clare Valley
Barossa Valley
Mannum
Port Lincoln
Adelaide
McLaren Vale
Strathalbyn
Fleurieu Peninsula
Victor Harbor
Meningie
Port Elliot
Padthaway
Goolwa
Coonawarra
Naracoorte
Robe
Penola
Mount Gambier

0   Kilometres 200

0   Miles   120

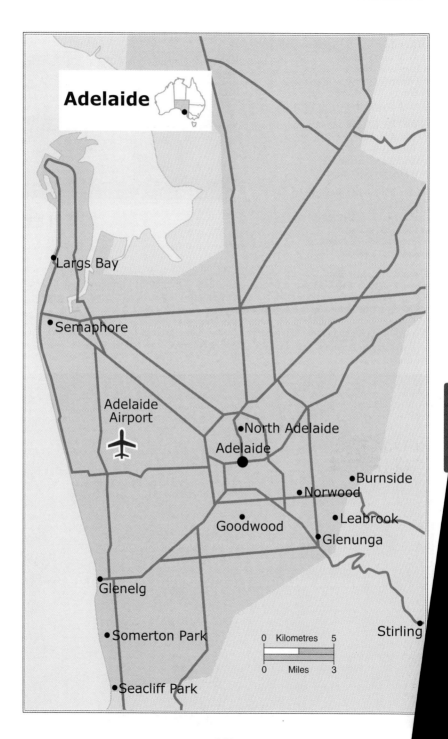

Adelaide - Burnside - St Georges

Kirkendale *B&B Apartment with kitchenette*
Jenny & Steve Studer
16 Inverness Avenue
St. Georges
SA 5064
5 km SE of Adelaide

Tel (08) 8338 2768
or 0413 414 140
Fax (08) 8338 2768
info@kirkendale.com.au
www.kirkendale.com.au

Double $115-$125 Single $105-$115
Child $15-$25
Continental Breakfast provisions
Visa MC BC accepted
1 Queen 2 Twin (2 bdrm)
Bathrooms: 1 Private

I dyllic "Country-style" 3 room suite, nestled in peaceful, leafy garden, sun-dappled patio, French doors, terracotta floors, rose garden. A hint of the Provence. Fresh flowers, fruit basket, generous breakfasts, books, tourist information. Separate entrance, private bathroom, living room, kitchenette, sole occupancy. Quiet location. 5 km city, near restaurants, wineries, wildlife parks. Jenny and Steve are extremely well travelled, this is reflected by their gracious but unobtrusive hosting. Tours arranged. Smoking outdoors. "We loved our accommodation - our best yet in 6 weeks of travel." SS & DC, USA.

Adelaide - Glenelg

"Water Bay Villa" Bed & Breakfast *Luxury B&B - Self Contained*

Kathy & Roger Kuchel
28 Broadway
Glenelg South
SA 5045
11 km SW of Adelaide

Tel 0412 221 724
Fax (08) 8294 8150
glenelg@waterbayvilla-bnb.com.au
www.waterbayvilla-bnb.com.au

Double $225-$260 Single $200
Child $20-$45
Full Breakfast Provisions
Visa MC BC Diners Amex accepted
2 Queen 2 Single (2 bdrm)
Bathrooms: 1 Ensuite

Indulge! Experience the luxury of this 1910 Queen Anne Villa in historic seaside Glenelg. 'The Attic' - your upstairs four room suite with private entry and off street parking. Welcoming bottle of wine, fresh flowers, fruit, chocolates and daily newspaper. Antiques, open fire, claw foot bath and laundry. Kitchenette with cooking facilities. Living area with sofa bed, tourist information, TV, video, CD/Radio. A few minutes stroll through the award winning garden to the nearby beach, Jetty Road, trams, restaurants, cinema, 7-day shopping, summer market and marina. Close to airport and public transport. Come and enjoy! "A little piece of heaven." HF, Canada.

Adelaide - Glenunga

Bayree Homestay *B&B Homestay*
Doris & Cyril Kuehne
5 Rowell Avenue
Glenunga
SA 5064
5 km SE of Adelaide

Tel (08) 8338 3707
or 0417 844 827
Fax (08) 8338 3701
cdkuehne@chariot.net.au
www.chariot.net.au/~cdkuehne

Double $120 Single $100
Includes full breakfast
No smoking on property
1 Queen (1 bdrm)
Bathrooms: 1 Private

Bayree Homestay is an elegant 1930's bungalow, providing luxury accommodation in leafy Glenunga only 5 km from Adelaide Centre. The spacious guest area has olde worlde charm and elegance, highlighted with chocolates, fresh flowers and superb breakfasts. Some of Adelaide's most fashionable shops and restaurants are close at hand. We are a 2 min stroll to public transport, near beaches and wildlife parks. "You are wonderful hosts and we enjoyed every minute of our stay in your lovely home and garden." Doug and Georgia, Wyoming, USA.

Adelaide - Goodwood

Rose Villa *B&B Homestay*
Doreen Petherick
29 Albert Street
Goodwood
SA 5034
2 km S of Adelaide

Tel (08) 8271 2947
Fax (08) 8271 2947
rosevilla@bigpond.com.au
www.picknowl.com.au/homepages/
rosevilla

Double $110-$140 Single $95-$110
Includes full or Continental breakfast
No smoking on property
1 King 1 Queen (2 bdrm)
Bathrooms: 1 Ensuite 1 Private

Treat yourself to a romantic candle lit breakfast in my newly decorated Tea Rose salon. Rose Villa offers an elegant private suite (own entrance) overlooking the garden. Inside is an additional guest room with the use of the exquisite Blue-White-Russian Tea Cup bathroom. Stroll to trendy Hyde Park Road with its delightful cafes and coffee shops, boutiques and flower shops. Close by are buses and trams (to the Bay) and city and The Ghan Terminal. "Rose Villa" is roses, romance and caring hospitality. You are most welcome. 'A romantic and warm place to be. Great hospitality.' Erwin Zwijnenburg, The Hague, Holland.

Adelaide - Largs Bay

Seapod B&B *B&B*
Bernadette McDonnell
146 Esplanade
Largs Bay
SA 5016
18 km NW of Adelaide

Tel (08) 8449 4213
or 0418 851 680
info@seapod.com.au
www.seapod.com.au

Double from $150 Single from $125
Child $40
Includes full breakfast
Visa MC BC Diners accepted
1 Queen (1 bdrm)
Bathrooms: 1 Private

 AAA Tourism ★★★★

Seapod is delightful hosted bed & breakfast accommodation in a superb seaside setting with sublime views and within walking distance of shops, restaurants, cafes, and public transport. Delicious breakfasts are served daily in your suite overlooking the sea. Natural, free range and organic produce with unlimited freshly brewed coffee and tea are standard. You can see dolphins and magnificent sunsets from your table, go for a run on the track across the road, walk along the jetties, swim with the dolphins, or stroll along the beach for miles.

Adelaide - North Adelaide

Cornwall Park Heritage Accommodation *B&B Apartment with Kitchen*

Judy Fitzhardinge
84 Mills Terrace
North Adelaide   SA 5006
1 km N of Adelaide city centre

Tel (08) 8239 0155 or 0411 171 807
cornwall@seekshare.com.au
www.seekshare.com.au

Double $135-$250 Single $120-$165
Child B/A
Includes special breakfast
Visa MC BC Diners Amex Eftpos accepted
1 King/Twin1 King 5 Queen 1 Twin (7 bdrm)
Bathrooms: 5 Ensuite 1 Private 3 with spa suites

Cornwall Park is an 1873 state heritage property, situated around north Adelaide golf course and parklands. Only 1 kilometre from Adelaide city and 500m from some of the best restaurants and cafes in Adelaide. The bluestone residence was sympathetically renovated in 2002-3 to include four lovely spacious bedrooms, two with large spa and two other bedrooms with ensuites in the heritage side. A stunningly modern apartment offers either 1 to 3 bedrooms with 2 bathrooms including one with spa. Open fireplaces and reverse-cycle air-conditioning throughout. A romantic place suitable for people on holiday, weddings as well as the business person. Internet is available for guests. Secure off street parking.

~

Adelaide - North Adelaide

North Adelaide Heritage Group *Luxury B&B Self contained Mansion Apartments, Villas, Houses, Cottages*

Rodney & Regina Twiss
Office Only: 109 Glen Osmond Road
Eastwood   SA 5063
In North Adelaide

Tel (08) 8272 1355 or 0418 289 994
Fax (08) 8272 1355
res@adelaideheritage.com
www.adelaideheritage.com

Double $150-$390   Child $20-$42
Full Breakfast Provisions
Dinner Room Service Available
Visa MC BC Diners Amex accepted
10 King/Twin 10 Queen 10 Double 5 Twin
(A variety of beds in each accomm)
Bathrooms: 10 Ensuite or private bath rooms in all accommodation

Owned and operated by Rodney and Regina Twiss, the North Adelaide Heritage Group features some of Adelaide's best architecture including mews cottages, Buxton Manor mansion, villas, the Friendly Meeting Chapel, the Fire Station Inn and the newest addition, the 5 star Bishops Garden. Built in the 1860's the Fire Station Inn was a working fire station until its recent conversion into luxury accommodation. It comes complete with its own 1942 fire engine. The full range of unique heritage accommodation ranges in style and personal character with each apartment offering true Twiss hospitality and detail! Full Breakfast Provisions, Room service and complementary shuttle bus available 7 days a week.

Adelaide - Norwood
Leabrook Lodge of Norwood *B&B*
Barbara Carter
1/1 Colliver Street
Norwood
SA 5067
2 km E of CBD

Tel (08) 8363 6544
or 0418 831 688
www.bbbook.com.au/leabrooklodge.html

Double $100-$135 Single $95-$120
Includes full breakfast
Visa MC BC accepted
1 Queen (1 bdrm)
Bathrooms: 1 Ensuite Ensuite with spa

A delightful villa in a tree lined street - the pleasures previously enjoyed at Leabrook Lodge is enhanced at our new location. Leabrook Lodge is within walking distance of the Botanical Gardens, National Wine Centre, east parklands and the popular Norwood Parade with its plethora of divine cafes and restaurants. Leabrook Lodge at Norwood is within easy reach of the CBD, Glenelg Tram stop in the city as well as the numerous tourist sites. Off street parking is available.

Adelaide - Seacliff Park - Brighton
Homestay Brighton *B&B Homestay*
Ruth Humphrey & Tim Lorence
PO Box 319
Brighton
SA 5048
2 km S of Brighton

Tel (08) 8298 6671
or 0417 800 755
Fax (08) 8298 6671
timlorence@hotmail.com
www.bbbook.com.au/brighton.html

Double $60-$70 Single $40-$50
Child B/A
Includes full breakfast
1 Double 2 Single (2 bdrm)
Bathrooms: 1 Guest share 1 Private

O ur spacious home and grounds are in a quiet suburb close to Brighton beach, bus and train routes to the city or day trips to the southern Fleurieu Peninsula. Guest rooms are upstairs including a TV-lounge area with heating and cooling. We can discuss your requirements for children, pets or to be met on arrival. Laundry and off-street parking available. Please phone, fax, write or e-mail. 'Home from home' LJ, UK. 'Top class in all respects' KB, Caloundra. 'Like staying with friends' SC, Crookwell. 'Loved staying here, will be back' GB, Melbourne.

Adelaide - Semaphore

Tea Tree Cottage *B&B Cottage with Kitchen*
Gisela Kannis
5 Turton Street
Semaphore
SA 5019
17 km NW of Adelaide CBD

Tel (08) 8449 2543
or 0438 420 004
Fax (08) 8449 2533
info@teatreecottage.com
www.teatreecottage.com

Double $140-$160 Single $130-$150
Child $25
Includes full breakfast
2 Queen 2 Single (3 bdrm)
Bathrooms: 1 Private

Tea Tree Cottage is a delightful seaside setting ideal for families and groups seeking a home away from home. Built in 1910, this charming self-contained holiday home offers three bedrooms, a lounge, a modern kitchen and a bathroom with laundry facilities. The award-winning garden is the perfect place for a BBQ with room for the kids to play, or is simply a tranquil place to relax. The sea, cafes, shops, cinema and transport are all within walking distance. Special rates apply for longer stays.

Adelaide - Somerton Park

Forstens Bed & Breakfast *B&B Homestay*
John & Marilyn Forsten
19 King George Avenue
Somerton Park
SA 5044
2.5 km S of Glenelg

Tel (08) 8298 3393
forstens_bandb@hotmail.com
www.bbbook.com.au/forstensbb.html

Double $70 Single $55
1 King/Twin 2 Single (1 bdrm)
Bathrooms: 1 Ensuite

Located in a residential area 600 metres from beautiful Somerton Beach, 2.5km south of the bustling seaside resort of Glenelg with its miles of shopping and dining along Jetty Road. A city bus passes the house en route to Glenelg and Adelaide. Guests are accommodated in a lovely bedroom with a rear garden view, ensuite bath, TV, private entrance, reverse cycle air conditioning, and off-street parking. Warm fresh bread is included in the cooked breakfast. Laundry facilities available.

Adelaide Hills - Stirling

Berringar Bed & Breakfast *B&B*
Marg & Bruce Trebilcock
Longwood Road
Longwood
SA 5153
5 km SE of Stirling

Tel (08) 8388 5484
or 0414 844 999
Fax (08) 8388 5637
info@berringar.com.au
www.berringar.com.au

Double $160-$175 Single $150-$170
Child $25
Includes full breakfast
Visa MC BC Amex accepted
2 Queen (2 bdrm)
Bathrooms: 2 Ensuite

Marg & Bruce & their dog Lucy invite you to share their special part of Australia. Berringar is a quiet estate only 20 minutes from Adelaide, with a purpose built Bed & Breakfast. We are close to Warrawong sanctuary, Hahndorf & the Adelaide Hills wine region. We are one hour scenic drive to Barossa Valley & McLaren Vale & the southern beaches, so use Berringar as a touring base. Marg specialises in hearty cooked breakfasts, served in the dining room over looking the vineyard. A great start to the day. Let us help you plan your stay so you can experience secrets of the Adelaide Hills.

Burra

Burra Heritage Cottages - Tivers Row *Cottage with Kitchen*
Maureen and Barry Wright
1 Young Street
Burra
SA 5417
1/2 km N of Burra Central

Tel (08) 8892 2461
Fax (08) 8892 2948
wright@burraheritagecottages.com.au
www.burraheritagecottages.com.au

Double $125-$155 Single $105-$135
Child $35
Full Breakfast Provisions
Visa MC BC Diners Amex Eftpos accepted
5 Queen 5 Double 4 Twin (12 bdrm)
Bathrooms: 6 Private

AAA Tourism
★★★☆

Built in 1856 and meticulously restored by Barry and Maureen Wright, Tivers Row cottages provide unique accommodation with heritage listed authenticity. Fully self-contained, each with two bedrooms, the six separate cottages have cosy open fires but include extra comforts grandmother didn't have, like television and underfloor heating in the bathroom. A two day stay is recommended to explore the heritage township of Burra (great for children) and Clare Valley wineries close by. No pets please. Tourism Council of Australia accreditation.

Clare Valley - Sevenhill

Thorn Park Country House *Country House Hotel*
Michael Speers & David Hay
College Road
Sevenhill via Clare SA 5453
6 km S of Clare

Tel (08) 8843 4304 or 0417 822 597
Fax (08) 8843 4296
stay@thornpark.com.au   www.thornpark.com.au

Double $325-$350 Single $225-$250 Child $125
Includes full breakfast
Dinner $75 - $85.00
Visa MC BC Amex Eftpos accepted
3 King/Twin 2 Queen 1 Double (6 bdrm)
Bathrooms: 6 Ensuite

I n the heart of the Clare Valley lies Thorn Park Country
House, a truly magnificent country home of traditional
Australian style. Set in 60 acres of pastoral splendour it
boasts tranquil vistas of undulating farmland studded with
towering gums, grazing cattle and a dam; home to native
ducks and other bird life. The homestead was built in the
1850's from stone quarried on the site and was extensively
restored in recent years to its original magnificence. The
tranquil gardens feature hawthorn, elms and roses; a
surround to the homestead in the traditional manner. The
estate spreads itself to include six bedrooms, each with
its own ensuite, with accommodation for 12 guests. The
reception areas include a spacious drawing room, intimate
library, dining room and an extensive art collection. Thorn
Park Country House is considered one of Australia's
leading Gourmet retreats. David and Michael are devoted
to memorable dining, with food prepared utilising fresh,
local produce. The property also offers a series of Residential
Cooking Schools and there is a large cellar of Clare Valley

wines to complement the cuisine. For enquiries and reservations: Telephone (08) 8843 4304
Fax (08) 8843 4296 South Australian Tourism Award. Winner 1989, 1995, 1996, 1997.
Winner Gourmet Traveller Jaguar Award for Excellence for Gastronomic Travel 2001.

Coonawarra - Naracoorte

Wongary Cottages *B&B Self Contained Cottages*
Diana Hooper
Box 236
Naracoorte
SA 5271
20 km SE of Naracoorte

Tel (08) 8762 3038
or 0418 838 213
Fax (08) 8762 3394
wongary@rbm.com.au
www.wongary.com.au

Double $120-$130 Single $90
Child $20
Continental Breakfast
Visa MC BC accepted
1 King/Twin 3 Queen 1 Double 6 Single (5 bdrm)
Bathrooms: 2 Ensuite 1 Private

Private self-contained multi Award Winning limestone cottages have ambient fires and air conditioning, kitchen, bath and bed linen plus electric blankets, lawn tennis, pond, farm animals, antiques, books, games, TV, magazines and vine-covered BBQ patios. Ralph's Cottage also has a dishwasher, laundry and spa plus free video movies. Surrounded by beautiful farmland and vineyards, Wongary is close to the World Heritage Naracoorte Caves and Coonawarra's winning wineries and restaurants. Pets and children welcome. Also availably are Wongary's self-contained, fully equipped serviced apartments in Adelaide.

Goolwa

Vue de M B&B *B&B*
Pam & Bob Ballard
11 Admiral Terace
Goolwa
SA 5214
In Goolwa

Tel (08) 8555 1487
or 0414 760 232
Fax (08) 8555 1487
vuedemerde@iprimus.com.au
www.vuedemerde.com.au

Double $125 Single $110
Includes full breakfast
No smoking on property
Visa MC BC accepted
2 Queen (2 bdrm)
Bathrooms: 2 Ensuite

Mysterious, Mighty, Murray, Mouth, Muesli, Milo, Milk or Munchies. Call in and ask us about the real name of our 1850's Riverside Cottage. Relax and enjoy the superb river view from the balcony adjoining your room. Two Queen sized bedrooms, each with its own En-suite have been purpose built for your pleasure. Breakfast is served in the Sun Room or, weather permitting, on the Poop deck with magnificent views from the Hindmarsh Island Bridge to the Goolwa Barrage. 'Our most relaxing weekend away in 27 years of marriage. Never stayed in a B&B before, but will definitely again.' Pauline & Gary James, Houghton, SA.

McLaren Vale

Ashcroft Country Accommodation at
McLaren Vale *B&B*

Terry & Julie Jarvis
Johnston Road
McLaren Vale
SA 5171
39 km S of Adelaide

Tel (08) 8323 7700
Fax (08) 8323 7711
welcome@ashcroftbnb.com.au
www.ashcroftbnb.com.au

Double $210 **Single** $210
Child $60
Includes full breakfast
Visa MC BC accepted
4 Queen 1 Twin (5 bdrm)
Bathrooms: 5 Ensuite

Winners of State & Regional awards, 'Ashcroft' is a large country estate with uninterrupted views across vineyards to the magical Willunga Hills. Each of the five guest rooms in our air-conditioned home contains an ensuite bathroom with many extras. Gourmet breakfast, including smoked salmon and kippers. Wheelchair guests, and families with children welcome. French spoken, and one night reservations available at any time. Some guest comments;- 'Beautiful setting' 'Fantastic accommodation' 'Bloody marvellous' 'Brilliant breakfast' 'It was a dream to stay here, thank you.'

McLaren Vale

Bellevue Bed & Breakfast *B&B*
Ciaran Cryan & Jenny McGrath
12 Chalk Hill Road
McLaren Vale
SA 5171
35 km S of Adelaide

Tel (08) 8323 7929
Fax (08) 8323 7914
stay@bellevuebnb.com
www.bellevuebnb.com

Double $170-$190
Includes full breakfast
Visa MC BC Eftpos accepted
2 Queen (2 bdrm)
Bathrooms: 2 Ensuite

Centrally located in the town of McLaren Vale, 35 km south of Adelaide and the city airport. Bellevue is a stylish, modern boutique B&B. Enjoy gourmet three course "table d'hote" menus of cooked or continental breakfasts, served daily. Stroll to award winning restaurants featuring regional produce. Visit any of the 50 cellar doors, all within a 20 minute drive of Bellevue. Enjoy the breathtaking vistas of rolling hills covered with vines, magnificent coastal views and fantastic swimming beaches. Enjoy a wine or two in our courtyard with vineyard views.

Mannum

Bonza View B&B *B&B*
Rae & Bruce Jarrett
31 Esplanade
Mannum
SA 5238
In Mannum

Tel (08) 8569 1111
or 0429 093 269
Fax (08) 8569 8174
jarrett@lm.net.au
www.mannumbonzaview.com.au

Double $119-$149 Single $75-$95
Includes full breakfast
Visa MC BC accepted
2 Queen (2 bdrm)
Bathrooms: 2 Ensuite Riverview ensuite has spa bath

Where tranquillity is the essence. Choose either the Riverview Suite featuring Mediterranean colours and spa bath luxury in the spacious ensuite or the Cherrywood Suite with vibrant oriental decor, private ensuite and the romance of an open fire on cold winter night. Each Suite has reverse cycle air-condition and private courtyard. There is a large bird attracting garden, interspersed with seated alcoves, rose arbour and shade house. Guests can take a photograph, a walk or sit on the verandah watching the river traffic pass-by.

Meningie - Narrung

Poltalloch Station *B&B Cottage with Kitchen*
Beth Cowan
Poltalloch Road
Narrung, near Meningie
SA 5259
30 km N of Meningie

Tel (08) 8574 0043
Fax (08) 8574 0065
info@poltalloch.com
www.poltalloch.com

Double $150-$185 **Single** $135-$170
Child $25 - $45
Full Breakfast Provisions
Visa MC BC accepted
1 King 3 Queen 8 Twin (8 in 3 cottages bdrm)
Bathrooms: 2 Ensuite 2 Family share

Beautiful country estate on the shore of freshwater Lake Alexandrina. Established in 1839, Poltalloch is a sheep and cattle farm with 22 historic buildings, including the jetty house, shearing shed, stables and lighthouse. Our guests stay in private heritage cottages with air-conditioning, sunny verandahs, wood fires in winter and many quality extras. Enjoy swimming, canoeing or sailing, tennis and walking in our extensive pristine bushland. Poltalloch is renowned for seclusion, tranquillity, spectacular sunsets and some of the best bird-watching opportunities in the Coorong and lakes area.

Mount Gambier

Apartments on Tolmie *Apartment with Kitchen*
Sandra Parsons and Martin Svec
27A Tolmie Street
Mount Gambier
SA 5290
1.5 km N of Mount Gambier

Tel (08) 8725 1429
or 0418 816 876
Fax (08) 8725 1852
mail@apartmentsontolmie.com.au
www.apartmentsontolmie.com.au

Double $150 **Single** $140
Child $10
Includes breakfast by arrangement
Extra adult $20.
Visa MC BC Diners Amex Eftpos accepted
1 Queen 1 Double 1 Single (2 bdrm)
Bathrooms: 1 Private

3 x 2 br self contained apartments, each sleeps 7. Full kitchens and spacious living areas. Washing Machine/Dryer. Queen bed, double & single bed & double sofa bed. All linen and towels supplied. Plunger coffee & tea selection. Telephone/Internet access. Gas heating/ducted cooling. Private gardens, Gas BBQ and lock up garages. Pets welcome. No smoking indoors. Cooked breakfast provisions can be supplied on request, $20 per couple, extra Adults $10 & Children $5. Located 1.5km North of the city centre of Mount Gambier.

Naracoorte

Dartmoor Homestead *B&B*
Lorraine and Andrew Oliver
30 McLay Street
Naracoorte
SA 5271
1 km W of Naracoorte

Tel (08) 8762 0487
or 0416 210 645
Fax (08) 8762 0487
dartmoorhomestead@rbm.com.au
www.dartmoorhomestead.com.au

Double $205-$185 **Single** $165-$185
Includes special breakfast
Visa MC BC Diners Amex accepted
1 King 3 Queen (4 bdrm)
Bathrooms: 1 Ensuite 1 Guest share 1 Private

Set in three acres, close to the town centre of Naracoorte this gracious and historical property offers three unique stylishly renovated rooms. Enjoy a personal welcome on arrival, relax in the drawing room, or take a stroll in the grounds. Dartmoor will sweep you away with the friendly atmosphere, attention to detail, and sumptuous breakfast. A perfect base for visiting and enjoying the local attractions including Bool Lagoon Wetlands, local wineries and the World Heritage Listed Naracoorte Caves. Rustic Settlers Cottage also available.

Robe

Criterion Cottages *Cottage with Kitchen*
Sula Harland
c/- 89 Stanley Street
North Adelaide
SA 5276
In Robe Central

Tel (08) 8768 2430
or 0414 841 091
Fax (08) 8768 2180
criterion@seol.net.au
www.bbbook.com.au/criterioncottages.
html

Double $110-$145
Includes full breakfast
Cottage 1: 1 Queen, 2 Twin
Visa MC BC accepted
2 Queen 4 Twin 6 Single (5 bdrm)
Bathrooms: 2 Private

AAA Tourism
★★★☆

Two comfortable old cottages beautifully restored and private, yet in the centre of the old fishing port. Full kitchen facilities with generous supplies for a full cooked breakfast. The two bedroom cottage has a loft bedroom, sitting room with log fire and courtyard/sunroom. The three bedroom cottage has a sitting room with wood stove and an enclosed garden with sunroom. Both with washing machines. Close to beach, restaurants and shops. Wineries, National parks and golf nearby. Children welcome.

Strathalbyn - Fleurieu Peninsula

Watervilla House *B&B*
Helene Brooks
2 Mill Street
Strathalbyn
SA 5255
55 km S of Adelaide

Tel (08) 8536 4099
Fax (08) 8536 4099
www.bbbook.com.au/watervillahouse.html

Double $160 Single $140
Includes full breakfast
Visa MC BC accepted
5 Queen 1 Twin (6 bdrm)
Bathrooms: 1 Ensuite 2 Guest share 1 Private

Watervilla House Bed & Breakfast - This charming 1840's homestead invites you to enjoy a unique and friendly experience, surrounded by 11/2 acres of tranquil gardens. The six bedrooms, guest lounge and dining room feature comfortable, elegant antique decor. Situated in the heart of historic Strathalbyn, centrally located within the Fleurieu Peninsula and close to The Southern Vales and Langhorne Creek wine Regions. One Sunday, 10 years ago Helene came to Strathalbyn for lunch and loved it so much she decided to stay. Watervilla House has been featured on The Great Outdoors and Discovery.

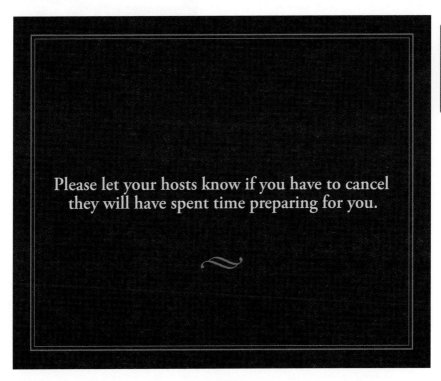

Please let your hosts know if you have to cancel
they will have spent time preparing for you.

Victor Harbor

Encounter Hideaway Cottages *B&B Homestay*
and Parkfield Lodge B&B *Cottage with Kitchen*

Jill Fairchild
66 Rapid Drive
Victor Harbor SA 5211
5 km S of Victor Harbor

Tel (08) 8552 7270 or 0409 527 270
Fax (08) 8552 8386
jill@encounterhideaway.com
www.encounterhideaway.com

Double $110-$150 Single $80
Includes full breakfast   Dinner from $35
$50 per extra adult
3 Queen (3 bdrm)
Bathrooms: 2 Ensuite 1 Private

Encounter Hideaway has two self-contained cottages. Ruby and Bud Cottages are situated just one street back from the sea in the historic part of Encounter Bay, only five minutes drive from the centre of Visitor Harbour. Set in a charming garden, each cottage has a queen-size bed in the main bedroom, second bedroom, sparkling bathroom with a large spa, a well equipped kitchen with generous provisions for a cooked breakfast, a comfortable living room with A/C, TV, VCR, CD player, port and fresh fruit. Encounter Hideaway give you privacy in a delightful setting. A perfect spot to escape from the pressures of everyday life or a great stopover to Kangaroo Island.

Parkfield Lodge is a traditional B&B overlooking the sixth green of the McCracken Golf Course. The three well appointed bedrooms each have a queen-sized bed, two with ensuite and one with a private bathroom. This well-established B&Bs many guests have enjoyed the opportunity to relax and unwind, play a round of golf or just catch up on some reading in the guest lounge room with its panoramic view of the golf course and surrounding hills. A three-course breakfast is prepared daily by the host/chef and silver service dinners are available by arrangement. The city of Victor Harbour and the surrounding areas have so much to offer. Water sports, stunning scenery, nature walks, nearby wineries, galleries, Granite Island with its fairy penguins and famous horse drawn tram, to name a few.

Victor Harbor

Pelican's Rest B&B *B&B*
Sharon and Tony Dobbin
31 Battye Road
Encounter Bay, Victor Harbor SA 5211
85 km S of Adelaide

Tel (08) 8552 5710 or 0404 877 307
Fax (08) 8552 5710
www.pelicansrest.com

Double $125-$140 Single $110-$115
Romance Package $310 Double
Visa MC BC accepted
2 Queen 1 Single (2 bdrm)
Bathrooms: 2 Ensuite

Situated on beautiful Encounter Bay with tranquil sea views and nearby Bluff, only a 5 minute walk to the shoreline to see the pelican's on the bay. A seaside escape close to attractions, Granite Island, the famous horse tram, Fairy penguin's, Cockle train, Seasonal Whale watching. Wildlife park and many other places of interest to visit. You can also Dine out at any of the first class local restaurants and Cafes. Manicured gardens greet you, with colourful kangaroo-paws and roses, relax in our well appointed spacious bedrooms with luxury Queen size beds, each with private ensuite featuring a huge shower, guest lounge/dining room. Tea/coffee making facilities and home made treats, bar fridge, air-conditioning/ heating, TV, DVD and Stereo. In the sun filled dining room, enjoy a Continental Breakfast served with delicious pancakes, home baked bread and fresh fruits. Say hello to Bella (she is a miniature schnauzer) No pet's allowed.

"Beautiful house. Wonderful home cooked food. Thoroughly enjoyed our stay, thankyou for your kindness and hospitality." The Peters Family,

Tasmania

Far South Region

Tasmania's Far South, via the picturesque Huon Valley is a significant part of
the Huon Trail and one of Tassie's best kept secrets. 43 degrees south marks the
southern end of the continent and as far south as one can drive in Australia. Cockle
Creek, located at the beginning of the South West World Heritage Area offers
pristine waterways and wilderness. Numerous bushwalks, recreational fishing,
cruising, kayaking, caving, white water rafting, mountain biking are notable
attractions. On entering the region the Tahune Airwalk on the banks of the Huon
River is a popular destination with wheelchair access. Close by is the most accessible
mountainous region in the state - beautiful Hartz Mountain National Park. The 3hr
return walk to Hartz Peak provides a reward like no other - giving incredible vistas
over Federation Peak, Arthur Range and beyond. Further south Hastings Caves
Reserve, a spectacular dolomite cave system and thermal pool. From time to time
'concerts in the cave' provide a fascinating experience. A strong French connection
can be found. Most notable, Recherche Bay, site of Bruny D'Entrecasteaux's
1792/93 expedition, location of the first European garden in Tasmania and
documented positive interactions with native Australians. Dover, a popular seaside
destination relying on tourism, aquaculture, fishing, orchards and forestry is the
main centre and central to all attractions.

Philip Emery, Riseley Cottage, Dover.

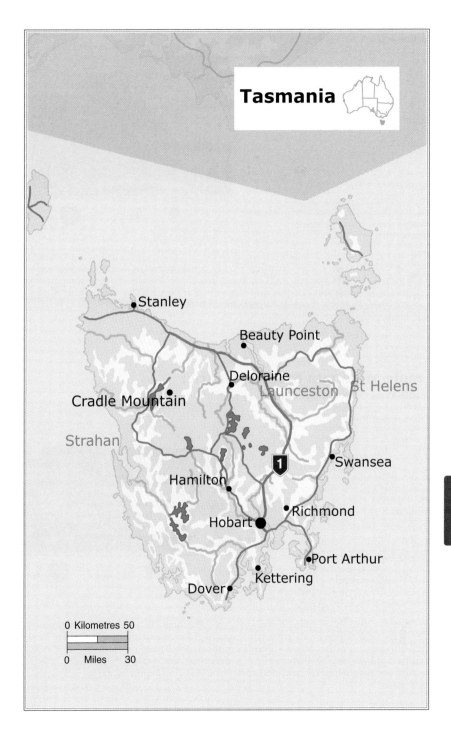

Beauty Point

Pomona Spa Cottages *B&B Cottage with Kitchen*
Paula & Bruce Irvin
77 Flinders Street
Beauty Point
Tas 7270
40 km N of Launceston

Tel (03) 6383 4073
or 0418 143 628
Fax (03) 6383 4074
pomonacottages@bigpond.com
www.pomonaspacottages.com.au

Double $160-$210 Single $190-$190
Full Breakfast Provisions
Visa MC BC Diners Amex Eftpos accepted
4 King/Twin 2 Single (4 bdrm)
Bathrooms: 4 Ensuite

R elax and enjoy a delicious breakfast, or evening drink on the Rotundas, overlooking spectacular views of the Tamar River/valley. Spoil yourself in the new spacious and sunny S/C Spa Cottages. Stroll in the gardens, through grape vines and along river to Restaurants, Seahorses and Platypus House. Explore the Tamar Valley Scenic Wine Route, National Parks, Penguins. Ferry & Airport- within 1 hour. Ideally located between Freycinet and Strahan. B.B.Q.

Cradle Mountain & Lakes District

Cradle Vista *B&B Homestay Apartment with Kitchen*
Janette and Jim Fairley
978 Staverton Road
south of Sheffield
Tas 7306
17 km S of Sheffield

Tel (03) 6491 1129
or 0439 737 661
Fax (03) 6491 1930
yourhosts@cradlevista.com.au
www.cradlevista.com.au

Double $130 Single $100
Includes full breakfast
Dinner $30 by arrangement
Visa MC BC accepted
3 Queen 1 Twin 1 Single (4 bdrm)
Bathrooms: 3 Ensuite 1 Private

O n the scenic route from Sheffield to Cradle Mountain, Cradle Vista provides luxury accommodation on a 50 acre farm property. Nestled under the triple peaks of local mountains with panoramic views from all windows. Imagine the vista from Cradle Mountain to Bass Strait. Explore the farm, admire mountain vistas, go horse riding, enjoy day trips to Cradle Mountain and local attractions. Relax in comfort by the fire talking to other guests.

Cradle Mountain & Lakes District

Glencoe Farm Guest House *Luxury B&B Farmstay*
Marsha Hamill
1468 Sheffield Road
Barrington
Tas 7306
8 km N of Sheffield

Tel (03) 6492 3267
Fax (03) 6492 3229
marsha.hamill@acenet.com.au
www.glencoefarm.com.au

Double $130-$165 Single $100-$120
Child $45
Includes full breakfast
Dinner $35 pp with 48hr notice
No smoking on property
Visa MC BC accepted
1 King 2 Queen 2 Twin 1 Single (3 bdrm)
Bathrooms: 3 Ensuite with shower, basin, toilet & hair dryer.

Glencoe Farm was originally built as a dairy property to federation style in 1909. Now renovated and restored it features 3 ensuite bedrooms, guest living (with entertainment system & library) and dining overlooking the garden. With warm fires in winter and cool high ceiling rooms in summer your comfort is assured. The house, set in gardens on 23 acres used for farming and a few horses, enjoys stunning views of Mt Roland and the fertile Kentish Plains. Easy drive to Cradle Mountain, Sheffield, & Ferry.

≈

Deloraine

Bonney's Inn *B&B*
Trevor & Wendy Doran
19 West Parade
Deloraine
Tas 7304
0.2 km E of Post Office

Tel (03) 6362 2974
Fax (03) 6362 4087
boninn@tassie.net.au
www.bonneys-inn.com

Double $148-$174 Single $110-$130
Child As per adult prices
Includes full breakfast
Dinner Several restaurants in walking distance
Visa MC BC Eftpos accepted
4 Queen 2 Twin 1 Single (5 bdrm)
Bathrooms: 4 Ensuite 1 Private

 AAA Tourism ★★★★

Bonney's Inn is an original 1830's coaching inn, the oldest brick building in Deloraine. We provide English-style B&B accommodation with comfortable beds, modern facilities, generous breakfasts and a homely atmosphere. Relax in the guest lounge in front of the cosy fire, enjoy a free port while reading one of our many books or magazines. Centrally located and opposite the Meander river, Bonney's Inn is ideal for exploring Central North Tasmania, including local caves and attractions, Cradle Mountain, The Great Lakes, Launceston and the Tamar Valley.

Dover

Riseley Cottage *B&B*
Philip Emery & Greg Shelton
170 Narrows Road
Strathblane (Dover)
Tas 7117
7 km S of Dover

Tel (03) 6298 1630
Fax (03) 6298 1630
riseleycottage@hotmail.com
www.riseleycottage.com

Double $105-$140 Single $85-$100
Child $30   Includes full breakfast
Dinner B/A   Visa MC BC accepted
3 Double 1 Twin (3 bdrm)
Bathrooms: 2 Ensuite 1 Guest share

Riseley Cottage's panoramic views to Esperance Bay and Hartz Mountain suggest an ideal location to explore the grandeur and rich natural history of the Far South. The quiet restful charm of cottage gardens (and bushland reserve), quality antiques and period furnishings make for a rewarding experience. Personalised - friendly service, cosy log fires, spacious guest lounge, balcony with a view, comfortable warm beds, delicious home cooked food are but a few of the treats you can expect. Book dinner in advance and enjoy fine regional cuisine served in our elegant dining room, followed by relaxing conversation over a port and chocolate. Wine available. Country hospitality at its very best! Children welcome.

Hobart - Battery Point

Battery Point Manor *B&B Self Contained Cottage*
Roz and John Lambert-Smith
13 - 15 Cromwell Street
Battery Point
Tas 7004
1 km E of Hobart

Tel (03) 6224 0888
Fax (03) 6224 2254
www.batterypointmanor.com.au

Double $95-$190 Single $75-$140
Child $5 - $30
Includes special breakfast
Cottage $75 - $250
3 King/Twin 2 King 2 Queen 1 Double 2 Triples (10 bdrm)
Bathrooms: 10 Ensuite

We offer you fabulous harbour views, big comfortable beds, large comfortable en-suite rooms; spa studio apartment or 2 bedroom cottage, big yummy Tassie buffet breakfasts, fresh air, peaceful and happy surroundings, 5 mins exciting walk to Salamanca, lots to see and do with maps provided, the best café and restaurant info and complimentary refreshments anytime. 'Battery Point Manor', also known as 'Battery Point Harbour View Bed and Breakfast' is a substantial 'Georgian' home restored to our very comfortable 4 * B&B. We hope to meet you soon, with warm regards Roz and John Lambert-Smith.

Hobart - Battery Point

Colville Cottage *B&B Cottage with Kitchen*
Sue and Roger Bastone
32 Mona Street
Battery Point   Tas 7004
1 km S of Hobart Central

Tel (03) 6223 6968
Fax (03) 6224 0500
colvillecottage@bigpond.com
www.colvillecottage.com.au

Double $150-$170 **Single** $136-$140
Child $35
Continental Breakfast
No smoking on property
Visa MC BC Amex Diners Eftpos accepted
6 Double or 4 Twin (6 bdrm)
Bathrooms: 6 Ensuite

AAA Tourism
★★★★☆

E legance and ambience are yours to experience when you stay at Colville Cottage. Antique furniture and rugs, ornate fireplaces, stained glass windows and verandah lacework evoke the gracious living of last century. Modern facilities provide every comfort and convenience, and the warmth of your welcome will enhance your experience. Colville Cottage, built in 1877, is a large mid-Victorian home bordered on all sides by a beautiful cottage garden. Telephones and separate high speed internet connection in each room. We have 2 self-contained cottages especially for families with continental provisions only. No children under 12 in the main cottage.

Hobart - Battery Point - Sandy Bay

Grande Vue and Star Apartments *Guest House Apartments and townhouses*
Annette & Kate McIntosh
8 Mona Street Battery Point
22 Star St Sandy Bay, Tas 7005
1 km S of Hobart Central

Tel (03) 6223 8216 or 0419 104 417
0409 970 411   Fax (03) 6224 8443
starapartments@bigpond.com
www.users.bigpond.com/jarem

Double $150-$220 **Single** $125-$145
Child $20
Continental breakfast provisions
Weekly tariff in apartments on request.
No smoking on property
Visa MC BC Diners Amex Eftpos accepted
2 King/Twin 7 Queen 2 Double (7 bdrm)
Bathrooms: 7 Ensuite 5 spa suites

AAA Tourism
★★★

G rande Vue Private Hotel is located in Hobart's historic Battery Point. (8 Mona Street). This gracious Edwardian mansion c1906 has spectacular views of the Derwent River, Mount Wellington, just 5 minutes walk to the city, restaurants, Salamanca Place and Hobart's waterfront. We also offer studio, water view rooms and spa suites. Star Apartments (22 Star Street Sandy Bay) are modern contemporary design 1 and 2 bedroom stylish apartments and townhouses with kitchens, washer/dryer and central heating. Some have water views, balconies/courtyards, spas and secure undercover car parking. Walking distance to Battery Point, restaurants, Salamanca Place and the city centre.

Hobart - Lindisfarne

Orana House *B&B*
Colin & Leonie Chung
20 Lowelly Road
Lindisfarne
Tas 7015
6 km E of Hobart

Tel (03) 6243 0404
or 0416 250 357
Fax (03) 6243 9017
welcome@oranahouse.com
www.oranahouse.com

Double $120-$160 Single $90-$130
Child $50
Includes full breakfast
Visa MC BC Eftpos accepted
7 Queen 3 Double 4 Single (10 bdrm)
Bathrooms: 10 Ensuite

A large Federation home circa 1909 offering warm hospitality. Orana House is 12 minutes from the airport and six minutes drive to Hobart. Situated one block from the foreshore of picturesque Lindisfarne Bay, it is a convenient base to explore southern Tasmania. Some of our many features include superb breakfasts, great views from the verandah and guest lounge, afternoon tea daily, genuine antiques and open fire. A choice of standard, deluxe or spa rooms, all with ensuites. Pets on property. Superior accommodation and a wealth of local knowledge.

Hobart - Rose Bay

Roseneath Bed and Breakfast *B&B Apartment with Kitchen*
Susan and Alain Pastre
20 Kaoota Road
Rose Bay
Tas 7015
3.5 km NE of Hobart

Tel (03) 6243 6530
or 0418 121 077
Fax (03) 6243 0518
pastre@bigpond.com
www.roseneath.com

Double $110-$160 Single $95-$150
Includes full breakfast
Dinner $28 - $40 BA
Low season/long stay available
Visa MC BC Diners Amex Eftpos accepted
2 King/Twin 1 Queen 2 Double (5 bdrm)
Bathrooms: 5 Ensuite

For true Tasmanian hospitality and warmth with a French accent. Only 5 minutes from CBD/Salamanca and 10 from airport. Spectacular views of Mt Wellington, the Tasman Bridge and Derwent River. An ideal base for exploring southern Tasmania or for business. Choose from a SC studio (kitchenette) or in-house accommodation with ensuites (1 spa). Guest lounge with log fire; conservatory; inground heated (summer) pool; spacious, secluded gardens; BBQ; off street parking. Dinner BA with your French chef host. Pet on property.

Hobart - Rosetta

Undine Colonial Accommodation *B&B*
Patricia & Rocco Di Carlo
6 Dodson Street
Rosetta, Hobart
Tas 7010
10 min km N of Hobart CBD

Tel (03) 6273 3600
or 0409 658 209
Fax (03) 6273 3900
undine@ozemail.com.au
www.ozemail.com.au/~undine

Double $160 Single $160
Child $40
Includes full breakfast
No smoking on property
Visa MC Diners Amex Eftpos accepted
1 King/Twin 4 Queen 6 Single (5 bdrm)
Bathrooms: 5 Ensuite

U ndine - circa 1820, is a splendid Georgian Colonial home set in a large cottage garden with luxurious rooms, complimentary chocolates, fruit and port. Relax and enjoy your stay. Swim in the heated, indoor pool, soak in the private spa, with a coffee and a fresh, home baked treat. Indulge in a country style, cooked breakfast as you plan the day. Undine is located only 10 minutes from Hobart CBD. Children welcome. Sorry no pets.

Port Arthur - Taranna

Norfolk Bay Convict Station *B&B*
Lynton Brown and Lorella Matassini
5862 Arthur Highway
Taranna
Tas 7180
10 km N of Port Arthur

Tel (03) 6250 3487
Fax (03) 6250 3701
norfolkbay@convictstation.com
www.convictstation.com

Double $130-$150 Single $80
Child $50
Includes full breakfast
Visa MC BC Amex Eftpos accepted
2 Queen 2 Double 1 Twin 3 Single (5 bdrm)
Bathrooms: 3 Ensuite 2 Private

N orfolk Bay Convict Station, built in 1838, was once an important part of Port Arthur convict settlement. Ships called here to transfer their passengers to the convict railway and you can still stroll or fish along the jetty in front of the house. We offer warm, comfortable rooms, a sitting room with a log fire and a wonderful breakfast. From here you can visit Port Arthur, drive the Convict Trail, walk in the Tasman National Park or, as we are licensed, relax on the front verandah with a glass of Tasmanian wine.

Tasmania

Swansea

Oyster Bay Guest House *Guest House*
Julie & Mark Elliott
10 Franklin Street
Swansea
Tas 7190
In Swansea

Tel (03) 6257 8110
or 0417 056 876
Fax (03) 6257 8703
oyster.bay@tassie.net.au
www.bbbook.com.au/oysterbay.html

Double $90-$130 Single $70-$90
Child $40
Accommodation Only only
Extra for breakfast
Visa MC BC Eftpos accepted
9 Double (9 bdrm)
Bathrooms: 9 Ensuite

 AAA Tourism ★★★☆

The Oyster Bay Guest House Circa 1840 is in the main street of the historical town of Swansea. Rooms are tastefully decorated all with ensuites, with views over Great Oyster Bay, Freycinet National Park, The Hazard Mountains and Wine Glass Bay. A big balcony with tables and chairs, to sit and watch the sun go down. We have a popular cafe/restaurant and bottle shop in house. A short drive will take you to Kates Berry Farm, Spikey Bridge and the most gorgeous beaches on the coast.

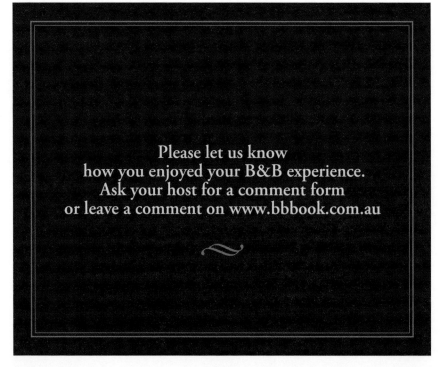

Please let us know
how you enjoyed your B&B experience.
Ask your host for a comment form
or leave a comment on www.bbbook.com.au

Victoria

North East Victoria

North East Victoria is a diverse area comprising mountains forming the Great Dividing Range which encompass the ski fields of Mount Hotham, Falls Creek and Mount Buffalo and relatively flat farming land in the numerous valleys. The Great Alpine Road winds its way through the valleys on its way to the coast. Towns including Bright, Myrtleford, Beechworth and Mount Beauty are synonymous with the northeast and have their own charm and appeal to the visitor. Crystal clear mountain streams with elusive trout, fabulous mountain scenery many wineries with cellar doors, restaurants showcasing locally grown products such as chestnuts, berries and olive oils. The northeast has a rich history of farming, timber, tobacco and hops, high country mountain cattlemen, goldmining and hydro electricity. More recently the area is becoming known for its cool climate wines with many vineyards and cellar doors being established.

Isla MacLeod, Braeview, Mount Beauty.

Central Murray Region

The Historic Port of Echuca on the beautiful Murray River boasts the largest fleet of working paddle steamers in the world. Paddle steamer cruises for one hour, lunch, to a winery or overnight are available.

The authentic red gum port is still fully operational and includes a blacksmith, cooper and wood turner. Included in the historic precinct are many and varied restaurants, cafes, the Beechworth/ Echuca bakery, museums and a surprising number of interesting attractions.

The old iron bridge over The Murray takers you to the town of Moama with its many attractions including the 36-hole rich river golf club.

A tour of the Barmah forest wetlands aboard MV Kingfisher is very special. Echuca is 2 hours north of Melbourne and it offers a mild, sunny climate. It is a wonderful destination for a luxury B&B escape.

Monica Gray, Echuca's River Gallery Inn, Echuca.

Euroa

Euroa, nestled into the Strathbogie Ranges, easily accessible on the Hume Highway, is only one and a half hours from Melbourne and Albury. Once the domain of bushrangers, goldminers and loggers, the Ranges became a major wool-growing region, pioneered by the legendary Eliza Forlonge.

Today the region is recognized for it's renowned horse studs, outstanding wineries and a feast of local restaurants, and an abundance of wildlife (koalas, kangaroos, wombats and echidnas) in their natural habitat.

Euroa's history is preserved with historic buildings, heritage trails, rustic homesteads and outbuildings and in the natural beauty of the land--ancient, mystical and uniquely Australian. Euroa is a four-season town--close to the winter snow, with magnificent autumns, brilliant spring and warm summers.

Jenny Tehan, Forlonge B&B Euroa.

Mansfield

Mansfield is a thriving town a little over a two hour trip from Melbourne. Set in pastoral country studded with beautiful ancient River Red Gums it is located at the southern end of Australia's Great Dividing Range in the North East of Victoria. Drive through Mansfield to Mount Buller - well known as a winter skiing destination

Mansfield is well known as a horse riding centre but you can also take a camel for a short ride, a day trip or even overnight. There are plenty walking trails, streams for fishing as well as kangaroos and koalas in the area.

A trip to Mount Stirling and Craig's hut - where the film " The Man from Snowy River" was made takes you along mountain tracks with wonderful views through beautiful Snow Gums. Most of the year it is possible to visit several old cattlemen's huts, an old gold mining site and old wood milling sites set up in the early settlement days.

There are several wineries close to Mansfield and along the route from Whitfield into Ned Kelly Country. Don't miss Powers Lookout for a great view up the King Valley across to Mount Buffalo.

Mary Luxton, Mary's Place, Mansfield.

Murchison

The township of 'Murchison', established in 1854, grew rapidly after the installation of a punt across Victoria's Goulburn River. Travellers made good use of the punt; from entrepreneurial businessmen in stores and hotels, to labourers seeking work on the large squatter runs, to gold diggers moving between Beechworth, in NE Victoria, and Rushworth, Bendigo and Ballarat to the west. Now surrounded by the waterways of the Goulburn Valley irrigation system, Murchison

is at the heart of Victoria's green agricultural and grape-growing district.Situated on the river bank, with its extensively re-modelled gardens, new bakery and shops, a good pub with excellent meals, a winery with superb wine and cheese, Murchison is still just as popular with travellers who, today, use a unique, and historic, steel span bridge to cross the river.

Andrew Wainwright, Brecon House B&B, Murchison.

East Gippsland

Located on the coastal highway between Melbourne 2 - 3 hours and Sydney 8hrs. East Gippsland has the largest expanse of inland waterways in Australia, a superb climate in both summer and winter, pristine ocean beaches, tall timber forests and mountains with snow in winter. Journey through some of Australia's most unspoilt country - ancient beauty, breathtaking vastness, unique snowy river country, with native flora and fauna. Walk over the dunes and you are on the Ninety Mile Beach! Explore the hinterland along the famous Snowy River, walk in the old growth rain forests of the Errinundra Plateau or view the 600 metre drop of the Little River into the deepest gorge in Victoria. Visit the Buchan Caves and discover beauty underground as well.

Visit the picturesque town of Mallacoota surrounded by the spectacular coastal scenery and walks of the Croajingalong National Park. Lakes Entrance, where the lakes meet the ocean, has many natural attractions as well as many artists, galleries, studios, wineries close by. Through friendly small towns along the old gold routes, to the superbly designed Alpine Village of Dinner Plain and down again through the mountain cattle country.

Kaye Munro, Waterholes Guest House, Bairnsdale and Beverly Gerard Goris, Déjà vu, Lakes Entrance.

Prom County

Almost on Melbourne's doorstep, Prom Country offers visitors an authentic country and coastal experience with unpretentious and friendly hospitality. In just a few hours you can enjoy a variety of spectacular scenery, from rolling green hills and unspoilt beaches to rich grazing land and lush rainforests. Dramatic and beautiful, Wilson's Promontory National Park awaits you, a mecca for visitors from across the globe for its untouched beauty, bushwalking, and abundant wildlife.

Explore our charming villages, enjoy the diversity of local arts and crafts, walk or cycle the area's rail trails, picnic or paddle at beautiful pristine beaches. Renowned for our vibrant produce, be sure to sample local boutique wines, farm fresh produce, freshly caught fish, awarding winning beer or local cheeses. Visit a winery or enjoy a lazy lunch in one of the many cafes across Prom Country. Even visit the wineries and talk to the producer.

Linda Robins, Foster.

The Mornington Peninsula

The Bellarine and Mornington Peninsulas enclose Port Phillip Bay and are synonymous with fun and relaxation. Both feature beguiling beaches, fine food and wine, chic beachfront towns and a variety of family attractions. Sorrento and Portsea on the Mornington Peninsula are home to antique shops, galleries, cafes and numerous walking trails along the ocean-facing coastline. Heading inland, you'll find many boutique wineries and associated vineyard restaurants offering sea views and gourmet dishes to match their individual wines. On the Bellarine Peninsula, the historic town of Queenscliff is dotted with Victorian-era buildings, fisherman's cottages, and fascinating galleries and shops. Both the Bellarine and Mornington Peninsulas offer an assortment of water-based activities. Surfing, sailing, swimming and fishing are widely enjoyed, as is swimming with the resident populations of dolphins and seals. The region is also noted for its markets, artist workshops, gardens, year-round events, championship golf courses and fresh produce – you can pick your own strawberries, cherries and other seasonal fruits or buy a range of food directly from the farm gate.

Inn.House

The Great Ocean Road and the Twelve Apostles

The Great Ocean Road is one of our international visitors must see areas. It begins at Torquay and boarders the edge of the ocean, with many stops at vantage points to enjoy the views. From Apollo Bay the road leaves the coast and enters the Otway Ranges, one of Australia's best examples of Cool Temperate Rainforest. A visit to Cape Otway Light House to learn about the shipwrecks that give the coast its name, and a walk in the treetops at the Otway Fly is a must. On leaving the Otways the road joins the coast again for a different spectacle. The "12 Apostles", these are just one of many seascape attractions to be discovered on this part of the Great Ocean Road.

Lyn Boxshall, Arabella Country House, Princetown.

The Grampians

A spectacular area, and one of the largest National Parks in Victoria, where one can see majestic waterfalls, rugged ranges and placid lakes. The region has a length of about 100km and is about 50km wide and includes about 160km of walking tracks and 600km of roads.

There is a great diversity of vegetation with well in excess of 1000 plant species, a number of which grow nowhere else in the world. This is one of Australia's richest flora areas. The warmer northern and western sides of the Grampians are the best areas to view the wonderful wildflowers in the spring.

There are over 200 species of birds, large mobs of kangaroos as well as many other animals.

The area is also rich in Aboriginal culture with most of Victoria's rock art sites.

Royce & Jeanne Raleigh, Wartook Gardens B&B, Wartook.

Yarra Valley

Nillumbik- Where Melbourne meets the Yarra Valley
Indulge yourself in the Yarra Valley experience of good food, wine, art, heritage, romantic getaways, and all this just 35 minutes from Melbourne and in close proximity to the airport via the Western Ring Road.

12 Award winning boutique wineries are dotted around in this part of the Yarra Valley.

Over 100 years ago our unique beautiful Australian bush attracted artists from the Heidelberg school of Artists, and art became a strong feature of Nillumbik.

The artists formed the artists' colony, Montsalvat, resembling a French provincial village. Artists still live and work there today.

There is plenty to do in Nillumbik, stay in luxury romantic apartments or in quaint mud brick cottages; enjoy indulgent weekends, stroll through markets, play golf, visit artists' studios, go on winery tour or visit beautiful Kinglake National Park.

Diny Van Dyk, Van Dyk's at Tintagel, Yarrambat.

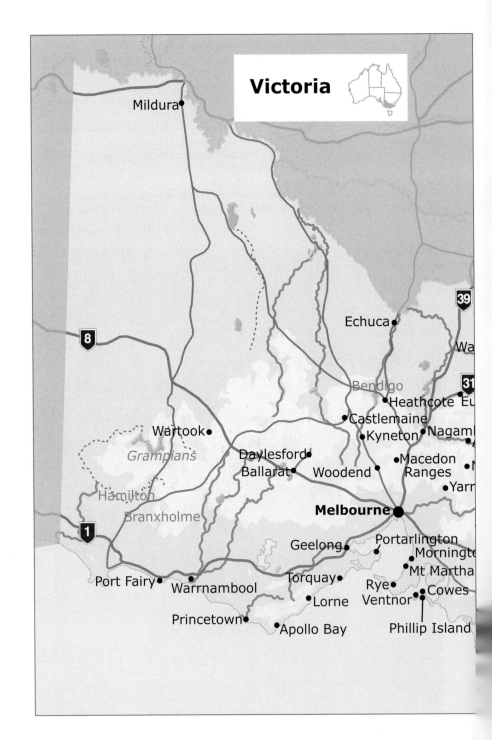

Alexandra

Idlewild Park Farm Accommodation *Farmstay Cottage with Kitchen*

Elizabeth & Don Deelen
RMB 1150
Alexandra
Vic 3714
5 km N of Alexandra

Tel (03) 5772 1178
or 0400 030 677
idlewild@virtual.net.au
www.idlewild.com.au

Double $130-$150 **Single** $80-$100
Child $20
Full Breakfast Provisions
1 King/Twin 1 Queen (2 bdrm)
Bathrooms: 1 Ensuite

Enjoy this 3,000 acre grazing property 128 km NE of Melbourne. The beautiful district offers horse riding, fishing, water and snow sports, bush walking, golf & adventure activities. Stay in a fully equipped two bedroom cottage with a double spa, wood heater, full kitchen air/con. The location is superb with magnificent panoramic views. There is tennis, gas BBQ and a beautiful garden. Property has sheep, cattle, horses and poultry (also native animals and birds). Owners have two friendly Jack Russel dogs.

Apollo Bay

Arcady Homestead *Homestay Farmstay*

Marcia & Ross Dawson
925 Barham River Road
Apollo Bay - Great Ocean Road
Vic 3233
10 km W of Apollo Bay

Tel (03) 5237 6493
or 0408 376 493
Fax (03) 5237 6493
arcady2@bigpond.com.au
www.bbbook.com.au/arcadyhomestead.
thml

Double $110-$120 **Single** $75-$85
Child 50%
Includes full breakfast
Dinner B/A
1 Queen 2 Double 3 Single (4 bdrm)
Bathrooms: 1 Guest share

Set on sixty scenic acres, part farmland and part natural bush. Share breakfast with our Kookaburras, explore the Otway Forest trails, tree-fern and glow worm gullies and waterfalls, see some of the tallest trees in the world or visit Port Campbell National Park, which embraces Australia's most spectacular coastline. The Otway Ranges are a bushwalkers paradise. Bird-watchers? We have identified around thirty species in the garden alone! Many visit our kitchen window! Our home has wood fires & spring water. Our beds are cosy, our meals country-style, and our atmosphere relaxed and friendly.

Apollo Bay

Paradise Gardens *B&B Self Contained*
Jo and Jock Williamson
715 Barham River Road
Apollo Bay
Vic 3233
7.5 km W of Apollo Bay

Tel (03) 5237 6939
or 0417 330 615
Fax (03) 5237 6105
paradisegardens@bigpond.com.au
www.paradisegardens.net.au

Double $120-$220
Continental Breakfast provisions
Visa MC BC Eftpos accepted
1 King/Twin2 King 1 Queen (4 bdrm)
Bathrooms: 4 Ensuite

S ituated on 3 acres of landscaped gardens in a lush rainforest valley, our facility is only 10 minutes from Apollo Bay on a (sealed) scenic road. Our charming new self-contained cottages (one and two bedroom) are built over a lake and feature woodfires, spas, bar-b-cues on the decking and airconditioning. Continental breakfast provided in tariff. Laundry facilities available. Our B&B Unit is cosy and comfortable with double spa and external entrance. Complementary Devonshire tea. Enjoy nearby walks, abundant birdlife and glow-worms at night. Sorry, no pets.

Apollo Bay - Great Ocean Road

Claerwen Retreat *Cottage with Kitchen Guest House*
Cornelia Elbrecht
480 Tuxion Road
Apollo Bay
Vic 3233
6 km N of Apollo Bay

Tel (03) 5237 7064
Fax (03) 5237 7054
cornelia_elbrecht@claerwen.com.au
www.claerwen.com.au

Double $176-$240 Single $154-$220
Child $25
Includes full breakfast
2 King 4 Queen 2 Twin (8 bdrm)
Bathrooms: 8 Ensuite

E xclusively situated on top of the highest hill overlooking the coast with panoramic ocean views from all rooms we offer four spacious suites, two self contained cottages or studios. Set in the peaceful solitude of 130 acres of park, bush and rainforest, it features saltwater swimming pool, hot spa and tennis court. It is close to the famous Great Ocean Road to the Twelve Apostles and the Otway National Park. We offer in-house massages, facials and art classes. In winter every third night is free.

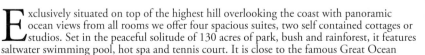

Beechworth

Kinross *B&B*
Terry and Gail Walsh
34 Loch Street
Beechworth
Vic 3747
39 km S of Albury/Wodonga

Tel (03) 5728 2351
Fax (03) 5728 3333
kinross@dragnet.com.au
www.innhouse.com.au/kinross.html

Double $150-$175 **Single** $125-$145
Includes full breakfast
Visa MC BC Eftpos accepted
2 King/Twin 3 Queen (5 bdrm)
Bathrooms: 5 Ensuite

 AAA Tourism ★★★★☆ INN·HOUSE

Terry and Gail invite you to experience their warm hospitality at Kinross which is situated within a four minute walk of historic Beechworth. Kinross c 1858 has five large fully serviced guestrooms furnished with period pieces. In your room, experience the luxury of ensuites, open fireplaces, TV, comfortable chairs, tea and coffee making facilities. Sit with a book and a glass of wine beside an open fire, or on the front verandah enjoying the beauty of the cottage garden. A delicious full breakfast is served.

——————————— ∾ ———————————

Beechworth

Country Charm Swiss Cottages *Cottage with Kitchen*
Judy and Greg Lazarus
22 Malakoff Road
Beechworth
Vic 3747
1.4 km W of Beechworth

Tel (03) 5728 2435
or 0417 376 899
Fax (03) 5728 2436
info@swisscottages.com.au
www.swisscottages.com.au

Double $175-215 per cottage per day
Child No charge under 4
Includes full breakfast
Visa MC BC Amex Eftpos accepted
5 Queen 6 Single (Five 1 or 2 Bedroom S/C Cottages bdrm)
Bathrooms: 5 Ensuite 2 Family share 2 Guest share Double spas

  AAA Tourism ★★★★☆

Delightful, well appointed self-contained cottages set high overlooking the Beechworth Gorge. Our 1 or 2 Bedroom cottages offer tranquillity, privacy and a perfect setting for any occasion. Each cottage has open fires in winter, reverse cycle air conditioning, spa baths, along with TV, CD/DVD players. A guest laundry and outdoor BBQ area are available. Enjoy generous breakfast provisions to be prepared at your leisure. Along with the complimentary treats provided, the ambience of the property and wonderful hosts will ensure a wonderful stay.

Benalla

Rotherlea Lodge *Luxury B&B*
Diana Chomley and Angus Howell
3670 Warrenbayne West Road
Baddaginnie
Vic 3670
20 km S of Benalla

Tel (03) 5763 2262
or 0429 885 676
Fax (03) 5763 2265
ahowell@benalla.net.au
www.bbbook.com.au/rotherlealodge.html

Double $175
Full Breakfast Provisions
Visa MC BC accepted
1 Queen (1 bdrm)
Bathrooms: 1 Private

AAA Tourism
★★★★☆

Rotherlea Lodge is a luxury self-contained Lodge set in a copse of trees on our farm, located 2 hours from Melbourne and 15 mins from Benalla. The Lodge was designed for couples and offers total privacy and seclusion. The mezzanine bedroom has views across the vineyard and a spacious sitting room has television and video. The fully equipped kitchen has full English Breakfast ingredients included in the tariff. Bathroom has a spa and outside floodlights allow you to watch the native wildlife while you soak!

Castlemaine

Clevedon Manor *B&B*
Stuart Ryan & Phil Page
260 Barker Street
Castlemaine
Vic 3450
In Castlemaine

Tel (03) 5472 5212
or 0417 166 769
Fax (03) 5472 5212
clevedon@netcon.net.au
www.bbbook.com.au/clevedonmanor.html

Double $100-$120 Single $80
Includes full breakfast
Dinner $40
No smoking on property
Visa MC BC accepted
5 Queen 1 Double (6 bdrm)
Bathrooms: 3 Ensuite 3 Private

AAA Tourism
★★★★☆

This beautifully restored 19th century home offers elegant living set in 1/2 acre 100 year old gardens. Clevedon offers guests a choice of spa room accommodation, ensuites and private facilities all with queen size beds. Private lounges and dining room with open fire, antique furnishings, central heating. Pool & BBQ. Clevedon is dedicated for guests only and is the perfect choice for either an intimate getaway or for groups wanting the complete package with meals. Clevedon is a 3 minute walk to historical central Castlemaine.

Chiltern

Forest View *B&B Farmstay*
Erika Hansen
Lancashire Gap Road
Chiltern
Vic 3683
3 km E of Chiltern

Tel (03) 5726 1337
or 0411 117 223
www.bbbook.com.au/forestview.html

Double $95 **Single** $85
Includes full breakfast
Dinner $25
1 Queen (1 bdrm)
Bathrooms: 1 Ensuite

Chiltern is very conveniently located between Albury/Wodonga and Wangaratta on the Hume Highway. It is close to Beechworth, Yackandanda and Rutherglen. Forest View is just 2 km from the highway and across the road from an extensive National Park renowned for its wildlife and flowers. A Winery Walkabout in June and a Jazz festival in November are just some of the other attractions in the area. The Murray River, Hume Weir and Snow fields are also within a short distance.

Chiltern

The Mulberry Tree *B&B*
Regina Welsh
28 Conness Street
Chiltern
Vic 3683
20 km S of Albury - Wodonga

Tel (03) 5726 1277
www.tourisminternet.com.au/chmulb.htm

Double $130-$160 **Single** $100-$120
Includes full breakfast
Dinner B/A
No smoking on property
2 Queen (2 bdrm)
Bathrooms: 1 Ensuite 1 Private

AAA Tourism
★★★★

Indulge yourself in the heart of Country Victoria. At The Mulberry Tree you will find a haven to relax and enjoy delightful accommodation with gourmet breakfast. Choose from "The Bank Residence" with it's own lounge with open fire, private bathroom or "The Henry Handel Richardson Suite" with ensuite dining area. This delightful building was built in 1879 as "The Bank of Australasia" and is on the Historic Building Register. Be assured of a warm welcome with special attention to every detail. Situated in the centre of town. Come and see our beautiful cats, 'Paris' and 'Tina'.

Cudgewa - Corryong

Elmstead *B&B Cottage with Kitchen*
Marja & Tony Jarvis
61 Ashstead Park Lane
Cudgewa
Vic 3705
120 km E of Albury - Wodonga

Tel (02) 6077 4324
or 0427 774324
Fax (02) 6077 4324
elmstead@corryongcec.net.au
www.bbbook.com.au/elmstead,html

Double $80 Single $60
Child $8
Continental Breakfast
2 Queen 4 Single (1 in B&B, 2 in cottage)
Bathrooms: 2 Private

This lovely one-room cottage is set amongst magnificent old Elm trees on a working farm with panoramic views. Cudgewa (12 km from Corryong) is nestled in the foothills of the Snowy Mountains close to superb bushland and great fishing streams. Tourist attractions include Burrowa-Pine Mountain National Park, Corryong with its Pioneer Museum and Jack Riley's grave (The Man from Snowy River). Thredbo and Mt Kosciusko are just over an hour away. Secluded 2 bedroom cottage also available. Preferably non-smokers. Children and pets welcome (we have both).

Dandenong Ranges - Olinda

Olinda Country Cottages *2 studio style cottages, 1 family budget S/C Cottage*
Kathy Lucacs & Wally Rotow
1558 Mount Dandenong Tourist Road
Olinda
Vic 3788
0.25 km N of Olinda

Tel (03) 9751 1777
or 0411 969 045
info@olindacountrycottages.com
www.olindacountrycottages.com

Double $140.00-$220.00
Continental Breakfast provisions
Visa MC BC accepted
2 King/Twin 1 Queen 1 Double 1 Single (2 bdrm)
Bathrooms: 1 Private

Modern, lovely, luxurious stand alone private cottages located near the heart of township. King bed, large spa, air conditioned and gas log fires. Located in 100+ year old gardens, Organic produce provisions, organic beauty products, massage, beauty therapy available. Walk to several restaurants, Yarra Valley 30 minutes drive, Melbourne centre 60 minutes drive. Puffing Billy, William Ricketts, Rhododendron gardens, local nurseries in abundance all nearby. Stay midweek and ask about special bonus deals available. Also available 2 BR budget family wing.

257

Daylesford - Hepburn Springs

Pendower House *B&B*
Renee Ludekens and Jacqueline Coates
10 Bridport Street
Daylesford
Vic 3460
0.1 km NW of Daylesford PO

Tel (03) 5348 1535
or 0438 103 460
Fax (03) 5348 1545
pendower@netconnect.com.au
www.pendowerhouse.com.au

Double $150-$380 Single $105-$290
Child B/A
Includes full breakfast
Visa MC BC accepted
3 Queen 1 Twin (4 bdrm)
Bathrooms: 4 Ensuite

AAA Tourism
★★★★☆

Pendower House, a beautifully restored Victorian House, situated in the heart of Australia's Spa Capital - Daylesford. RACV Rated 4.5 Pendower House offers first class amenities: fine linen, antique furnishings, big brass beds, loungeroom /library with open fire. Our luxurious Spa Suite, with corner spa, T.V/DVD & private courtyard is perfect for privacy, peace & pampering. Fantastic country breakfast, Muffins, hollandaise sauce drizzled on Eggs - more like brunch than breakfast! Easy walk to restaurants/galleries. Close to Spa resort. Massages & Spa packages or Gift Vouchers available.

Echuca

Murray House *B&B Cottage with Kitchen*
Peter and Mary Boek
55 Francis Street
Echuca
Vic 3564
In Echuca

Tel (03) 5482 4944
Fax (03) 5480 6432
enquiries@murrayhouse.com.au
www.murrayhouse.com.au

Double $180-$200 Single $140
Includes full breakfast
S/C from $110
Visa MC BC accepted
1 King/Twin 3 Queen (4 bdrm)
Bathrooms: 4 Ensuite

AAA Tourism
★★★★☆

Set in a private garden is this beautifully appointed 1920's home, brought to life with the warmth and hospitality of hosts Mary and Peter. Guests have a choice of four elegant bedrooms and may relax in the sitting room or soak up the ambience of the library where afternoon tea and pre-dinner drinks are served. Breakfast in the sunny dining room is always a delight, a multi course repast that changes daily. For those with children, or wanting privacy, a self-contained cottage is available.

Echuca

Echuca's River Gallery Inn *Separate Suite Boutique Accommodation*
Monica Gray
578 High Street
Echuca
Vic 3564
0.5 km S of Echuca

Tel (03) 5480 6902
or 0427 806 902
Fax (03) 5480 6902
inn@echuca.net.au
www.rivergalleryinn.com

Double $165-$230 Single $130-$180
Continental Breakfast provisions
Visa MC BC Eftpos accepted
8 Queen (8 bdrm)
Bathrooms: 8 Private Spa Baths

Echuca's River Gallery Inn offers eight luxury suites, each a theme of a different country. Private facilities include double spa baths and open fires(May to October) A welcoming lounge, sunny balconies and courtyards are available to guests.In-house massage and beauty therapy available.The award winning River Gallery Inn is located in Echuca's historic Port Precinct. Paddle steamers, wonderful cafes, restaurants, specialty shops and wine tasting are all within a 3 minute walk. Special mid-week packages are available.

Victoria

Inn.House Bed and Breakfast Australia Inc *Luxury B&B*
Inn.House

Tel (03) 5952 3082
president@innhouse.com.au
www.innhouse.com.au

Inn.House Victoria's Best Boutique Accommodation 50 of the best B&Bs in Victoria. Quality assured by the Inn.House Assessment Team Gift Vouchers Available Telephone (03) 5664 3204 or order on line: www.innhouse.com.au/giftvouchers.html

Full details on the Award Winning website www.innhouse.com.au

Echuca

Ayr House B&B *Luxury B&B*
Len Keeper & Doug Hall
62 Hare Street
Echuca   Vic 3564
In Echuca

Tel (03) 5482 1973
Fax (03) 5482 1901
esobab@mcmedia.com.au
www.innhouse.com.au/ayrhouse

Double $150-$200 Single $100-$150
Includes full breakfast
No smoking on property
Visa MC BC accepted
2 Queen (2 bdrm)
Bathrooms: 2 Ensuite

A yr House is new to the Echuca Bed & Breakfast scene, but the proprietors bring with them over 40 years experience and a well deserved reputation for their exceptional hospitality skills. Situated within easy walking distance to restaurants and Echuca's shopping precinct, guests are offered the personal touches one would expect when visiting friends. Ayr House is furnished with wonderful period pieces collected by the owners over the years. The elegant bedrooms each with ensuites exude warmth and comfort, which is mirrored by the sumptuous library lounge and dining rooms. Following a lavish four course breakfast you can set out to explore all that Echuca and the surrounding district has to offer. You might prefer however to sink into a comfy lounge with a good book from the extensive library or enjoy the company of your companions around an open fire. Consult your hosts about your dining whims and they will happily arrange a restaurant to suit your needs. Here's Bed & Breakfast accommodation in the grand style, right in the heart of the historic river port of Echuca. "Come as a guest, leave as a friend . . . a sure recipe to make your visit a memorable one!" If you are contemplating a 'Sea Change' by venturing into the B& B industry, what better training than to sign up for one of Ayr House's three night/two day courses where you will be expertly guided through many of the pitfalls which can catch the unwary.

Euroa

Forlonge B&B *B&B Separate Suite*
Jenny & Michael Tehan
76 Anderson Street
Euroa
Vic 3666
In Euroa

Tel (03) 5795 2460
Fax (03) 5795 1020
forlongebb@eck.net.au
www.innhouse.com.au/forlonge

Double $130-$170 **Single** $90-$150
Includes full breakfast
Dinner From $30
Visa MC BC Diners Amex accepted
1 King/Twin1 King 1 Queen (3 bdrm)
Bathrooms: 1 Ensuite 1 Guest share Ensuite with spa

Forlonge is set in half acre garden with large trees, tennis court, gazebo BBQ - just minutes away from shops, restaurants, hotels and the renowned Sevens Creek Park. Choice of 2 air-conditioned suites. Garden room with ensuite spa, and private terrace. Courtyard suite with 2 bedrooms, sitting room and private facilities. Euroa is a charming country town nestled into the Strathbogie Ranges. It is an ideal environment for relaxation. An easy drive to local wineries, Nagambie Lakes Rowing Course, Winton Raceway, Goulburn Valley and snowfields.

Foster - Wilsons Promontory

Larkrise House Bed & Breakfast *B&B*
Jon and Ros Wathen
395 Fish Creek Road
Foster Vic 3960
2.7 km SW of Foster

Tel (03) 5682 2953
Fax (03) 5682 2951
jonandros@larkrise.com.au
www.larkrise.com.au

Double $150-$190 **Single** $130
Includes full breakfast
Dinner $50
Visa MC BC accepted
2 Queen 1 Twin 1 Single (2 bdrm)
Bathrooms: 2 Ensuite

Larkrise House Bed and Breakfast has sensational views, an extensive garden, and family heirloom furniture for you to enjoy. It is situated on forty acres adjoining the Great Southern Rail Trail, near to Wilsons Promontory National Park. But that's just the beginning! We enjoy growing and preparing food, so get ready to savour a feast of 'home made practically everything'. You'll love our hand-made breads, muesli and preserves, Corner Inlet seafood, local meats and cheeses. Our own garden is a source for many herbs, fruits and vegetables. We turn these freshest and finest ingredients into delicious treats for you, ranging from fine breakfasts and light and tasty seafood dishes to slow-cooked comfort food. Home-made pastas and ice-creams are a specialty. Dinner is served on Wednesdays, Fridays and Saturdays.

Geelong

Baywoodbyne B&B *B&B*
Nola Haines
41 The Esplanade
Drumcondra, Geelong North
Vic 3215
In Geelong

Tel (03) 5278 2658
www.greatoceanroad.org

Double $100-$130 Single $85-$100
Includes full breakfast
No smoking on property
Visa MC BC accepted
2 Double 1 Twin (3 bdrm)
Bathrooms: 1 Ensuite 1 Private

Centrally located accommodation in a lovely 1921 California Bungalow style home. Superb view overlooking Corio Bay; a short stroll to city centre and colourful waterfront precinct. Warmth, comfort, convenience are yours, together with books and music. Offering. Ground floor sitting and breakfast room, open fire, picture window. First floor bedrooms, sitting area and beautiful view. Tea/coffee making facilities. Off-street parking. Easy access to Melbourne, (train or car one hour) and the famous Great Ocean Road. Direct bus service to Geelong from Melbourne (Tullamarine and Avalon) airports.

Gippsland

Broughton Lodge *Luxury B&B Cottage with Kitchen*
Philip Hunter and David Musker
125 Palmer Road
Jindivick Vic 3818
20 km NW of Warragul

Tel (03) 5628 5235
or 0417 056 110
Fax (03) 5628 5235
info@broughtonestate.com.au
www.broughtonestate.com.au

Double $200-$240 Single $110-$180
Includes special breakfast
Dinner $40 - $80
Broughton Hall from $380 per night
Visa MC BC accepted
2 Queen (2 bdrm)
Bathrooms: 2 Ensuite 2 Private

AAA Tourism ★★★★☆ INN·HOUSE

Broughton Lodge offers luxury accommodation for two couples in an idyllic, private rural setting with stunning views over The Taragao Reservoir just over 1 hour from central Melbourne. Broughton Lodge offers 2 fully serviced suites in a 1910 farmhouse with a reading room, lounge and dining room, a modern fully equipped kitchen and boot room. All rooms are luxuriously appointed with quality furnishings and fittings. A gourmet breakfast is provided. We are fully licensed and other meals including hampers are available on request. The acclaimed garden at Broughton Hall is open free of charge to guests at Broughton Lodge anytime during their stay.

Gippsland - Mirboo North

Cullenary Retreat on Grand Ridge *B&B*

Sally and Tom Cullen
9 Balook Street
Mirboo North Vic 3871
1 km W of Post Office

Tel (03) 5668 1430
or 0427 566 025
Fax (03) 5668 1830
cullenfam@bigpond.com
www.cullenaryretreat.com.au

Double $130-$150 Single $90-$100
Child No
Includes full breakfast
Dinner By arrangement
Visa MC BC Diners Amex Eftpos accepted
2 Queen 1 Twin (3 bdrm)
Bathrooms: 1 Ensuite 1 Private

AAA Tourism
★★★★

C ullenary Retreat offers traditional Bed and Breakfast in a gracious Victorian home. Dinner is also available, by prior arrangement, and may be enjoyed with fine Gippsland wines and internationally awarded beer from Mirboo North's Grand Ridge Brewery. Surrounded by bushland, the Retreat is located in picturesque Mirboo North, abutting the spectacular 'Grand Ridge Road' tourist drive. Within Prom Country, it is an ideal base to experience the area's great scenic, historic and cultural attractions, including pristine Wilsons Promontory and the magnificent Strzelecki Ranges.

Gippsland - Neerim South

Janalli *Luxury B&B*

Alan & Phillipa Beeson
285 Wagners Road
Neerim South
Vic 3181
3 km N of Neerim South

Tel (03) 5628 1476
or 0409 217 707
Fax (03) 5628 1158
phillipabeeson@janalli.com
www.janalli.com

Double $170-$190
Includes full breakfast
Visa MC BC Amex accepted
3 Queen (3 bdrm)
Bathrooms: 3 Ensuite Spa in Potager room

AAA Tourism
★★★★☆
INN·HOUSE

J analli provides an idyllic, secluded and restful stay on the shores of Tarago Lake in West Gippsland. Alan and Phillipa Beeson have created a beautiful 10 acre garden nestled in lush, green hills just seventy-five minutes drive from Melbourne. Three suites are available with ensuite bathrooms including Spa in the Potager Room. A Conservatory is available for guests as well as 10 acres landscaped gardens. Janalli is part of the Open Garden Scheme. Cooking classes and Jazz in the gardens are also featured..

Victoria

Gippsland - Nilma North

Springbank B&B *B&B Cottage No Kitchen*
Kaye & Chris Greene
240 Williamsons Road
Nilma North
Vic 3821
8 km W of Warragul

Tel (03) 5627 8060
or 0437 350 243
Fax (03) 5627 8149
bookings@springbankbnb.com.au
www.springbankbnb.com.au

Double from $150-$165
Single from $110-$135
Includes full breakfast
Dinner $100/120 per couple
Visa MC BC Eftpos accepted
2 Queen (2 bdrm)
Bathrooms: 2 Ensuite

The subtle blending of a charming old world home, extensive and delightful cottage gardens, attentive service, homely atmosphere and gentle vistas set on twenty acres of lush cattle and dairy land combining to bring you a relaxing and refreshing experience. Please review our website for more detail.

Grampians - Wartook

Wartook Gardens *B&B Homestay*
Royce & Jeanne Raleigh
Northern Grampians Road
Wartook
Vic 3401
29 km NW of Halls Gap

Tel (03) 5383 6200
Fax (03) 5383 6240
bookings@wartookgardens.com.au
www.wartookgardens.com.au

Double $130-$160 Single $110-$120
Includes full breakfast
Dinner From $35
Visa MC BC accepted
1 King/Twin 2 Queen (3 bdrm)
Bathrooms: 1 Ensuite 2 Private

AAA Tourism
★★★★

Just minutes from the Grampians National Park, and set on 70 acres in the beautiful Wartook Valley famed for its mobs of kangaroos, Wartook Gardens offers elegant country living in a tranquil 5 acre garden of native and exotic plants and 110 bird species. Enjoy our delicious breakfast before visiting waterfalls, walks, wineries, lookouts, wildflower areas. Ceiling fans, air conditioning, saltwater pool, underfloor heating, woodheater, make your stay a very comfortable one - an all seasons destination. Enjoy friendly hospitality. Please phone.

Grampians - Wartook Valley
The Grelco Run *B&B Cottage with Kitchen*
Graeme & Liz McDonald
Schmidt Road
Brimpaen   Vic 3401
15 km W of Wartook

Tel (03) 5383 9221
Fax (03) 5383 9221
grelco@netconnect.com.au
www.grampiansgrelcorun.com

Double $135 **Single** $67.50
Child $27.50
Includes full breakfast
Dinner $60
Homestead $180-$200
Visa MC BC accepted

4 King/Twin 1 King 4 Queen 2 Twin 1 Single (5 bdrm Self contained) 3 bdrm
Bathrooms: 4 Ensuite 2 Guest share

The Grelco Run offers 2 s/c cottages set apart in natural bush, sleeping 6 in each, and a luxuriously appointed homestead with 3 guest bedrooms each with an ensuite. By prior arrangement we serve elegant hosted dinners in a convivial atmosphere. Our son Cameron operates the renowned Grampians Horse Riding Centre with escorted tours from the property. As we are adjacent to the National Park there are superb opportunities for bushwalking, 4WD driving, fishing, viewing abundant wildlife and wild flowers and visiting all major scenic attractions and nearby wineries.

Heathcote - Goldfields
Emeu Inn Restaurant, Bed & Breakfast and Wine Centre *B&B*
Fred & Leslye Thies
187 High Street
Heathcote, VIC 3523
45 km SE of Bendigo

Tel (03) 5433 2668
Fax (03) 5433 4022
bookings@emeuinn.com.au
www.emeuinn.com.au

Double From $180-$250
Single $150-$180
Child $35
Includes full breakfast
Dinner $32 main courses
Visa MC BC Diners Amex Eftpos accepted
6 Queen (6 bdrm)
Bathrooms: 6 Ensuite

Indulge yourself in luxury at the historic Emeu Inn where comfortable suites await you. Dine in The Age Good Food Guide-recommended restaurant where international cuisine and great local wines are standard fare. There's also a wine shop stocked with local wines to take away! This award-winning B&B has six spacious suites with queen-size beds, private ensuites with spas or open fires and all the extras gourmet travellers expect. Enjoy the homemade chocolates and sparkling wine. The lounge is a great gathering place with tea and coffee, nibbles and fresh fruit. Enjoy a game of golf, Lake Eppalock, the forests, the shops or the wine!

Kyneton

Moorville at Kyneton *B&B Country House*
Fran & John Wigley
1 Powlett Street
Kyneton   Vic 3444
84 km NW of Melbourne

Tel (03) 5422 6466
or 0411 208 448
Fax (03) 5422 6460
moorville@bigpond.com
www.moorville.com.au

Double $140-$165 **Single** $100-$120
Child POA
Includes full breakfast
Self Contained $180
Visa MC BC accepted
2 Queen 1 Double 2 Single (4 bdrm)
Bathrooms: 2 Ensuite 1 Guest share

You will find Moorville a relaxing retreat in a quiet picturesque part of historic Kyneton. Experience and enjoy the lifestyle of the Edwardian era, surrounded by the comforts of one of the period's grandest local homes. Special breakfast with a view, featuring local and home made produce, evening meals by arrangement. Spacious living areas, library, veranda, indoor pool, tennis court, petanque. Close to River Walk and Botanic Gardens. Self-contained "cottage style" accommodation available at Pipers Retreat, secreted behind our bookshop. Enjoy Edwardian life style with today's comforts.

Kyneton

The Rectory at Kyneton *B&B*
Lyn Currie & Michael Perri
61 Ebden Street
Kyneton
Vic 3444
84 km NW of Melbourne

Tel (03) 5422 6738
or 0428 312 798
Fax (03) 9824 2788
rectory@bigpond.net.au
www.kyneton.org/user/rectory

Double $150-$175 **Single** $100-$130
Includes full breakfast
2 Queen 1 Double (3 bdrm)
Bathrooms: 1 Guest share

The Rectory is Kyneton's oldest bluestone home built in 1850. National Trust classified, the home is surrounded by mature hedges and boasts 1/2 acre of manicured gardens designed by Paul Bangay. Relax and unwind by the open fire. All rooms have central hydronic heating. Enjoy a fully cooked country breakfast and complimentary wine on arrival. Just one hour from Melbourne and 40 minutes from Melbourne Airport. As featured in Belle Magazine, Herald Sun, RM Williams 2005 Accommodation Guide. "What a find, wonderful atmosphere, great company and wow what a garden."

Lakes Entrance - Bairnsdale - Metung

Waterholes Guest House *B&B Separate Suite Guest House*
Kaye & Bob Munro
540 Archies Road
Waterholes via Bairnsdale   Vic 3875
32 km NE of Bairnsdale

Tel (03) 5157 9330
or 0408 579 330
Fax (03) 5157 9449
inquire@waterholesguesthouse.com.au
www.waterholesguesthouse.com.au

Double $280-$420 Single $160-$210
Includes full breakfast
Dinner $50   Lunch $20
Visa MC BC accepted
3 King/Twin 1 Queen 12 Single (4 bdrm)
Bathrooms: 3 Ensuite 1 Guest share 1 Private

Waterholes enables you to reclaim that mix of freedom and security we experience when our world seems all good! Beautiful light-filled and light-hearted rooms; excellent food served without pretentiousness; superb natural surroundings; interesting history, art-works and nature wildlife. A world apart - just for you. Lots of surprises. "What an amazing place! This fabulously modern imaginatively designed guesthouse 25 km from anywhere! Not just gourmet meals but gourmet lunches delivered to the middle of the bush." Ian Roberts, Sydney. Directions: Follow the signs off southern end of "The Great Alpine Road".

Lorne - Aireys Inlet

Lorneview B&B *B&B Separate Suite*
Nola & Kevin Symes
677 Great Ocean Road
Eastern View
Vic 3231
14 km E of Lorne

Tel (03) 5289 6430
Fax (03) 5289 6735
lorneview@primus.com.au
www.lorneview.com.au

Double $130-$170 Single $120-$160
Continental Breakfast
No smoking on property
Visa MC BC accepted
2 Queen (2 bdrm)
Bathrooms: 2 Ensuite

AAA Tourism
★★★★☆

Lorneview has two spacious guest rooms, separate from main house, one overlooking the ocean and the other overlooking the bush. Each room as QS bed, ensuite, TV, CD player, heating, air conditioning, refrigerator, iron, ironing board, tea and coffee facilities. Delicious breakfast of fresh fruit, homemade muesli, muffins and croissants is served in your room or on balcony overlooking beach. Dinner unavailable, but many excellent restaurants nearby. Barbecue and Games Room provided. Enjoy walks along the beach and go to sleep listening to the waves.

Lorne - Otway Ranges - Birregurra

Elliminook *Luxury B&B Heritage*
Jill & Peter Falkiner
585 Warncoort Road
Birregurra Vic 3242
38 km N of Lorne

Tel (03) 5236 2080 or 0408 107 021
Fax (03) 5236 2423
enquiries@elliminook.com.au
www.elliminook.com.au

Double $150-$230 Single $130-$190
Child not suitable   Includes full breakfast
Visa MC BC Diners Amex accepted
2 Queen 2 Double 2 Single (4 bdrm)
Bathrooms: 3 Ensuite 1 Private Spa Bath in private
Bathroom

Award winning Elliminook c1865 is a beautifully restored and decorated National Trust classified homestead providing a great relaxing getaway. Guests will enjoy the historic garden, croquet, boules, tennis court, open fireplaces, liquor service, sumptuous cooked breakfast, fresh flowers in your room, and welcoming hospitality. From Elliminook you can explore the Great Ocean Road, Twelve Apostles, Shipwreck Coast, Otway Fly Tree Top Walk, including Birregurra's historic walk, waterfalls and rain forest of the scenic Otway Ranges. For a unique accommodation experience be our welcome guest.

"Guests enjoy the serenity of a flourishing garden and the grandeur or a magnificent historic home as seen in Australian House & Garden."

award
winning
gourmet
retreat

Indulge in boutique wines and the finest regional produce in our 'Age Good Food Guide 2004 / 2005' recommended restaurant.

The property hosts two manor and 16 courtyard rooms plus a 2 bedroom cottage set in Edna Walling designed gardens and natural bushland.

CROQUET

Enjoy an extensive range of facilities including tennis, heated pool and spa, golf driving range, petanque, croquet, massages or walks.

Victoria

CAMPASPE HOUSE
A COUNTRY HOUSE HOTEL & RESTAURANT

GOLDIES LANE WOODEND VICTORIA 3442   TELEPHONE 03 5427 2273
www.campaspehouse.com.au

Macedon Ranges - Kyneton
Gainsborough Guesthouse B&B *B&B*
Robert & Leanne Schomacker
60 - 66 Jennings Street
Kyneton
Vic 3444
In Kyneton

Tel (03) 5422 3999
or 0407 823 900
gainsboroughbb@bigpond.com.au
www.babs.com.au/gainsborough

Double $145-$175 **Single** $125-$155
Includes full breakfast
Dinner from $50pp
Visa MC BC Eftpos accepted
1 King/Twin 3 Queen 1 Single (5 bdrm)
Bathrooms: 2 Ensuite 1 Guest share

  AAA Tourism ★★★★

G ainsborough is a circa 1860 National Trust classified home set amongst beautiful gardens near the banks of the Campaspe River. Our guest comments include "Feels like home . . .only better!" and ". . . warm welcome, warm fire, cosy room and rusty autumn leaves . . ." So, whether you're looking to escape for a night or two, a base from which to explore the Macedon Ranges and Goldfields districts or to celebrate a special event, then allow yourself the experience of feeling at home in this small piece of local history.

Macedon Ranges - Kyneton
Wyoming *B&B Separate Suite*
Suzanne Ogden
17 Mollison Street
Kyneton
Vic 3444
Tel (03) 5422 3361
or 0408 013 322
Fax (03) 5422 3361
wyoming@netcon.net.au
users.netconnect.com.au/~wyoming/

Double $155-$175 **Single** $110-$135
Includes full breakfast
2 Queen 1 Double (3 bdrm)
Bathrooms: 2 Ensuite 1 Guest share

T his stately Edwardian home is situated opposite the Botanic Gardens and Campaspe river walk. Wyoming is conveniently located to the local cafes, shops and historic railway station (direct service to central Melbourne). The elegant main en suited bedroom has an antique brass bed, open fire, comfy couch and a baby grand piano. Breakfast is served in your own private garden room. The second large bedroom opens out to the veranda and has a private en suite or shared bathroom with adjoining smaller bedroom ideal for family or friends. Both rooms have queen size beds, television and tea and coffer making facilities. Small pets are welcome by arrangement.

Macedon Ranges - Mount Macedon

Craigielea Mountain Retreat *Luxury B&B Self-Contained*
Simone & Richard Graham
Mountain Road Mount Macedon   Vic 3434
15 km E of Woodend

Tel (03) 5427 0799 or 0411 444 449
Fax (03) 5427 0669
info@craigielea.com.au
www.craigielea.com.au

Double $275-$345
Includes Full Breakfast Provisions
Dinner from $65pp
gourmet, elegant small functions by
arrangement
Visa MC BC Diners Amex Eftpos accepted
3 King (3 bdrm)
Bathrooms: 3 Ensuite Luxury double spa

Only 45 minutes from Melbourne. 5 star self-contained suites, within a stunning, historic 32 acre property which also serves as a private art gallery, small wedding venue and gourmet cooking school. Each suite has a king bed, double spa, wood fire, air conditioner, dvd and sound system, kitchen, original art works and spectacular views of Melbourne and the Bay. Gourmet meals by arrangement. Featured on Great Outdoors, Postcards, Gourmet Traveller, The Age, Sunday Herald Sun, Coxy's Big Break, and many others.

~

Mansfield

Mary's Place - Bed & Breakfast *B&B Cottage with Kitchen*
Mary Luxton
32 Somerset Crescent
Mansfield
Vic 3722
0.8 km N of Mansfield Centre

Tel (03) 5775 1928
Fax (03) 5775 1928
maryluxton@iiNet.com.au
www.bbbook.com.au/marysplacebb.html

Double $120
Child $20
Continental Breakfast
Extra adults $30
1 Queen 2 Single (2 bdrm)
Bathrooms: 1 Private

Mary's Place is a cosy, quiet self contained unit in a beautiful garden with rural view yet close to town centre. Two bedrooms, one with QS bed and 2 singles. Car port, TV, linen, drying room and own bathroom. Provisions for light breakfasts and cooking facilities. With mountains, rivers and lakes there is plenty to see and do. Stay for winter skiing on Mt Buller. There are two welcoming small dogs to either spoil or ignore. Phone for availability. Deposit cheque to Mary Luxton. Children welcome. Cot available.

MELBOURNE'S BEST BED & BREAKFASTS

Melbourne's luxurious and friendly bed and breakfasts offer the personal attention and independence you want in a high quality B&B experience. Enjoy mouth-watering breakfasts, caring, informative hosts and stunning surrounds and all in the heart of the world's most liveable city. So next time you visit wonderful Melbourne, be it for a major event, romantic getaway, shopping and dining soiree or for any other reason, check out the delights of Melbourne's best B&Bs first at www.melbournebest.com.au or call 03 9869 2403.

Melbourne - Blackburn

Treetops Bed & Breakfast *B&B*
Sue & Jim Chambers
16 Linum Street
Blackburn
Vic 3130
18 km E of Melbourne Central

Tel (03) 9877 2737
or 0418 380 633
Fax (03) 9894 3279
treetops@alphalink.com.au
www.innhouse.com.au/treetops.html

Double $121-$155 Single $95
Includes full breakfast
Visa MC BC accepted
3 Queen 2 Double (3 bdrm)
Bathrooms: 3 Ensuite

Treetops B&B is a picturesque homestead with a rustic half acre garden set in a unique National Trust classified area. There are three spacious suites with private entrance, ensuite and their own comfortable lounge area for relaxation or entertainment includes honeymoon suite with spa. A pool and heated spa also available. Each suite has a refrigerator, microwave, TV, Video, CD Player, Queen sized bed, fresh fruit basket and fresh flowers. A light breakfast is provided daily. Suites have airconditioning and heating. It's a short walk to shops, restaurants, train and bus.

Melbourne - Bundoora

Bundoora Homestay *Homestay*
John & Cath Cantrill
6 Amber Court
Bundoora
Vic 3083
12 km NE of Melbourne

Tel (03) 9467 1335
johncan@warrandyte.starway.net.au
www.bbbook.com.au/bundoora.html

Double $60 Single $40
Child 50%
Continental Breakfast
Dinner $15
2 Double 1 Single (3 bdrm)
Bathrooms: 2 Family share 1 Guest share

Bundoora is an attractive suburb situated east of the Melbourne Airport and northeast from the city. Both can be reached by car in 20 minutes. The area is well served by public transport. The tram stop is only a few minutes away and the journey takes about 40-50 minutes. The area is also well served by bus and train. We have a comfortable two-storey dwelling, guests have their own bathroom which includes bath and shower. We are committed to offering warm and friendly hospitality.

Melbourne - Camberwell

Springfields *B&B*
Robyn & Phillip Jordan
4 Springfield Avenue
Camberwell
Vic 3124
9 km E of Melbourne

Tel (03) 9809 1681
Fax (03) 9889 3117
the.jordans@pacific.net.au
www.bbbook.com.au/springfields.html

Double $120 Single $80
Includes full breakfast
No smoking on property
1 King/Twin 1 Twin (2 bdrm)
Bathrooms: 1 Guest share 1 Private

 AAA Tourism ★★★☆

Welcome to "Springfields" - our attractive and spacious family home situated in a quiet avenue in one of Melbourne's finest suburbs. As well as the two guest bedrooms and adjoining bathroom, guests can enjoy the peace and privacy of their own lounge - or join us in our family room. Two city tram routes and a city train (5 minutes) serve popular attractions and the city. "Springfields" is a non-smoking B&B, where children are most welcome. Our home is your home when you next visit Melbourne.

Melbourne - Camberwell

Herb & Lola's B&B *B&B*
Herbert & Lola Suttie
16 Fordham Avenue
Camberwell
Vic 3124
10 km E of CBD

Tel (03) 9836 1618
Fax (03) 9888 6522
herblola@blaze.net.au
www.victourism.com.au

Double $95-$100 Single $75
Child depends on age
Continental Breakfast
No smoking on property
1 Queen 2 Twin (2 bdrm)
Bathrooms: 1 Ensuite 1 Private

Earlston is a 3br solid brick home located on a 1/4 acre block of land in the midst of the tree lined streets of Camberwell. Large back and front garden, the house is warm in winter and cool in summer. Three mins from train and five from tram, our home is 20-25 mins by train from CBD. Melway Ref 60:B2. We serve continental breakfast only and our home is a no smoking home. Queen size room has own ensuite and TV in room, its own bathroom and toilet. We take children 8 years and over.

Melbourne - Eltham

Cantala Bed and Breakfast *B&B*
Bev and Peter Robertson
62 Henry Street
Eltham
Vic 3095
20 km NE of Melbourne

Tel (03) 9431 3374
Fax (03) 9431 3374
cantalabnb@bigpond.com
users.bigpond.com/cantalabnb/

Double $100-$130 Single $85-$100
Includes full breakfast
Visa MC BC accepted
2 Queen (2 bdrm)
Bathrooms: 2 Ensuite

Enjoy superior accommodation at the Melbourne end of the Yarra Valley in a charming period home centrally located in leafy Eltham. Two spacious suites, early Australian furniture, views to tranquil cottage and rose gardens, cosy sitting areas, ensuites, private entrances. Fresh flowers, chocolates, home baked goodies, sumptious breakfasts. Old world ambience, homely comforts, relaxed friendly atmosphere. Whether you venture out to experience sensational food in countless restaurants and cafes nearby, sample wine at local boutique wineries, visit unique Montsalvat and other artist studios or just simply relax on sun dappled verandahs of Cantala, you are sure to go home revitalised.

Melbourne - Hampton

Peggy's Place *B&B Homestay*
Peggy Hayton
19 Orlando Street
Hampton
Vic 3188
16 km S of Melbourne

Tel (03) 9521 9187
cbir8580@bigpond.net.au
www.bbbook.com.au/peggysplace.html

Double $120 Single $90
Continental Breakfast
1 Queen 1 Single (2 bdrm)
Bathrooms: 1 Guest share

My 100 year old cottage with the sweetest garden is by the sea, furnished with antiques and is close to quick public transport, excellent shopping and loads of restaurants. You will share the house with me, Sissie the cat and 2 lovable dogs, Abigail and Sophie. Your breakfast includes home made bread, fresh seasonal fruit, juice, homemade cereal, muesli and jams. Please ring (best time early morning or evening) or leave your name and phone number on my answering machine and I will ring you back as soon as possible.

Melbourne - North Fitzroy

Slattery's North Fitzroy B&B *B&B Apartment with Kitchen*
Jacqui & Ron Slattery
41 Rae Street
North Fitzroy
Vic 3068
2 km N of Melbourne

Tel (03) 9489 1308
www.bbbook.com.au/slatterysnthfitzroybb.html

Double $120 **Single** $95
Continental Breakfast
No smoking on property
Visa MC BC accepted
1 Twin (1 bdrm)
Bathrooms: 1 Private

AAA Tourism
★★★★

Slattery's offers superior self-contained accommodation in Melbourne's first suburb, 2 km from Melbourne's CBD. Air-conditioned, centrally heated accommodation comprises bedroom with twin beds, separate sitting room, bathroom, kitchenette and meals area. Tea & coffee facility, toaster, microwave, fridge, TV, video, hair-dryer, iron and ironing board, electric blankets, garage parking and roof garden with city views. Close to public transport, theatres, Edinburgh Gardens, Royal Exhibition Buildings and Brunswick Street cafes. Breakfast is your choice of juice, cereals, breads, and home-made jams and marmalades. Credit cards.

Melbourne - Preston West

Californian Bungalow Bed & Breakfast *B&B*
Maureen Bailey
24 May Street
Preston West
Vic 3072
9 km N of Melbourne

Tel (03) 9471 2850
www.bbbook.com.au/california.html

Double $95-$110 **Single** $85-$100
Includes full breakfast
No smoking on property
2 Double 2 Twin (2 bdrm)
Bathrooms: 2 Guest share

A classic double fronted renovated Californian home which features a large open plan lounge/living area incorporating a rear entertaining area with a barbecue overlooking a delightful garden. Features include 2 double guest rooms, large open plan kitchen and dining, central bathroom and laundry, polished floors, quality furnishings, ducted heating, open fire places, evaporative cooling. Off street parking. Ideally located in one of West Preston's finest, wide, tree lined streets. Close to transport, Preston Markets, Restaurants. Just 9 km from Melbourne city.

Melbourne - Richmond

Villa Donati *B&B*
Gayle Lamb & Trevor Finlayson
377 Church Street
Richmond Vic 3121
2.5 km E of Melbourne CBD

Tel (03) 9428 8104 or 0412 068 855
Fax (03) 9421 0956
email@villadonati.com
www.villadonati.com

Double $160-$190 Single $130-$150
Includes full breakfast
Visa MC BC Diners Amex Eftpos accepted
1 Queen 2 Double (3 bdrm)
Bathrooms: 3 Ensuite

Cool classic exterior, rich stylish interior- Villa Donati is a chic, inner city bed and breakfast. Previously home to distinguished architects, archbishops and the 'Moulin Rouge' massage parlour, Villa Donati has been restored to capture the essence of the European pensione. Today, this historic and charming property is a stunning mix of contemporary and antique design. Each of the en-suite bedrooms has its own unique style and furnishings - fine bed linen, imported toiletries, antiques and original art works. The guest sitting room offers city views and the café style breakfast room is the perfect place for indulgent breakfasts. Villa Donati is situated in cosmopolitan Richmond, only minutes from the CBD and Melbourne's main shopping, entertainment and sporting precincts.

From the Visitors' Book: Divine - everything!

Victoria

Melbourne - Richmond

Rotherwood *B&B Apartment with Kitchen*
Flossie Sturzaker
13 Rotherwood Street
Richmond, Melbourne
Vic 3121
1.5 km E of Melbourne Central

Tel (03) 9428 6758
Fax (03) 9428 6758
rotherwood@a1.com.au
www.bbbook.com.au/rotherwood.html

Double $145-$180 Single $120-$145
Child Additional
Includes special breakfast
Visa MC BC accepted
1 Queen 1 Single (1 Q in apartment 1 Dble in separ bdrm)
Bathrooms: 1 Private Private bath per apartment

On the Hill in Richmond, "Rotherwood" is at the heart of Melbourne's attractions. Walking distance of the MCG, Royal Botanic Gardens, National Tennis Centre, Royal Tennis Centre, shops and restaurants. Only a 5 minute tram ride to City. Easy access to National Gallery, Concert Hall, Crown Casino, and Southbank. Private entrance to Victorian era apartment. Large sitting room with French doors leading to terrace overlooking garden. Bedroom (Q.S. Bed), private bathroom, and separate dining room with cooking facilities. Special French Breakfast provided. Extra fold-out bed. Airport transport available. Golfing excursions arranged. TV, Video. Suitable for short or long term stay.

Melbourne - St Kilda

Alrae Bed & Breakfast *B&B*
Vivienne Wheeler
7 Hughenden Road
St Kilda East Vic 3183
5 km SE of Melbourne

Tel (03) 9527 2033 or 0409 174 132
Fax (03) 9527 2044
alrae2@bigpond.com
www.bbbook.com.au/alrae.html

Double $145-$185 Single $88-$110
Child $22 - $55
Includes special breakfast Dinner $33 B/A
Spare sofa bed $55-$110
No smoking on property   Visa MC BC accepted
1 Queen 1 Twin 1 Single (3 bdrm)
Bathrooms: 1 Ensuite 1 Guest share

Alrae, a well kept secret, is 5 km. from Melbourne CBD, handy public transport including daytime suburban airport shuttle bus, beach, shops, sports venues, restaurants and theatres. It features a Queen bedroom with ensuite, air-conditioning, fridge, private entrance; Twin and Single bedrooms with guest (share) bathroom/Spa over bathtub; air-conditioned guests dining room cum lounge, specialty breakfasts and dietary variations. All rooms have TV/VCR or TV/DVD, clock radios, books and memorabilia, additional facilities including BBQ, OSP. Corporate, Seniors, Medical profession, Members Motor Organisations, Group rates available. Conditions apply.

Melbourne - St Kilda

Bishopsgate House *B&B Apartment with Kitchen*
Margaret Tudball and Ross Bishop
57 Mary Street
St Kilda West   Vic 3182
5 km S of Melbourne

Tel (03) 9525 4512
or 0402 057 351
Fax (03) 9525 3024
marg@bishopsgate.com.au
www.bishopsgate.com.au

Double $165-$195 Single $145-$175
Includes special breakfast
Dinner B/A   Licensed property
Visa MC BC accepted
1 King/Twin1 King 4 Queen 3 Single (5 bdrm)
Bathrooms: 2 Ensuite 3 Private

As featured on the national travel show 'Getaway' Bishopsgate is a stunningly renovated two storey 1890's terrace home furnished with antiques and original art work. The three individually themed guest rooms and 2 bedroom apartment are luxuriously appointed with quality fittings. Facilities include en-suites, TV, tea and coffee making facilities, and individually controlled heating and cooling. Enjoy using Bishopsgate's own designer toiletries. Bishopsgate is located in a grand, broad, tree-lined street. One block from St Kilda's Fitzroy Street and just two blocks to the beach, rollerblading and bike riding. Bishopsgate is the perfect accommodation for both tourism and business.

Melbourne - St Kilda

Fountain Terrace *B&B*
Heikki and Penny Minkkinen
28 Mary Street
St Kilda West
Vic 3182
5 km S of Melbourne

Tel (03) 9593 8123
or 0412 059 559
Fax (03) 9593 8696
info@fountainterrace.com.au
www.fountainterrace.com.au

Double $165-$245 Single $140-$195
Includes full breakfast
Dinner $30
Visa MC BC Diners Amex Eftpos accepted
 2 King/Twin2 King 3 Queen (7 bdrm)
Bathrooms: 7 Ensuite

Located in a beautiful tree lined avenue. Seven ensuite guest rooms with individual designer decor, lovely dappled light and opening sash windows. Special rates for longer stays and corporates. Relax in comfortable sofas in the guest sitting room or enjoy the sun in the small Tuscan style, North facing courtyard with water feature and tubs of citrus.

Melbourne - Toorak

Toorak Manor *B&B Hotel*
Gail Senior
220 Williams Road
Toorak
Vic 3142
5 km E of CBD

Tel (03) 9827 2689
Fax (03) 9824 2830
toorakmanor@froggy.com.au
www.toorakmanor.net

Double $145-$200 **Single** $145-$200
Continental Breakfast
Full breakfast additional $10
Visa MC BC accepted
18 Queen (18 bdrm)
Bathrooms: 18 Ensuite

Toorak's top hotel in a gracious nineteenth century Victorian mansion. We have 18 individually decorated rooms, drawing room with complimentary port and Foxtel and laundry facilities. We are very close to Toorak road and Chapel Street Melbourne's finest area. Transport very convenient to city and surrounding areas (Casino, Botanical gardens, MCG.) Met and Tram service within a minute walking distance. Breakfast in the tea room and parking is included in your rate.

Melbourne - Williamstown

North Haven By the Sea *B&B*

Marg
Merrett Drive
Williamstown Vic 3016
13 km W of Melbourne

Tel (03) 9399 8399
or 0417 564 676
Fax (03) 9397 8903
info@mw2.com.au
www.mw2.com.au

Double $130-$170 Single $100-$120
Child $50-$75
Includes full breakfast   Dinner $25 pp
Visa MC BC Diners Amex accepted
2 King/Twin2 King 1 Queen (3 bdrm)
Bathrooms: 1 Ensuite 1 Guest share

AAA Tourism
★★★★

A modern home with sea and park views, close to restaurants and public transport. Three guest rooms with ensuite including spa or private bathroom. Private lounge with TV, DVD, VCR and Stereo, tea and coffee making facilities and refrigerator. Ducted heating and airconditioning. Outdoor covered patio, balcony to watch the sun set over the sea, outdoor heated spa and secure offstreet parking. Walking, jogging and cycling track at front door with access to kilometres of trails. Close to JawBone National park. Dinner on request. Multiple night rates available. Children welcome with playground equipment in back yard. Pets welcome. Choice of full a la carte or continental breakfast.

Metung

Clovelly House - Luxury Accommodation *B&B*

Polly and Graham May
5/7 Essington Close
Metung
Vic 3904
0.25 km E of Metung Village

Tel (03) 5156 2428
Fax (03) 5156 2424
clovellybandb@datafast.net.au
www.clovellybedandbreakfast.com

Double $170-$220
Includes special breakfast
Dinner For Groups of Six or Eight Only
No smoking on property
Visa MC BC Amex Eftpos accepted
4 Queen (4 bdrm)
Bathrooms: 4 Ensuite All with Twin Spas

AAA Tourism
★★★★☆

A n award winning B&B of elegance and charm overlooking Bancroft Bay, just 250 metres from the village of Metung. Each queen size room has a large ensuite with twin spa and tropical fern atrium. Wide verandahs in summer and wood fires in winter. Gourmet breakfasts are a feature, served on the sunny verandah or in the cosy dining room. New Clovelly Cottage features sitting room with wood fire, queen sized bedroom, elegant bathroom with double spa and separate shower. No facilities for children or pets.

Mildura

Mildura's Linsley House *B&B Homestay*
Colin & Desley Rankin
PO Box 959
Mildura
Vic 3502
15 km E of Mildura at Trentham Cliffs

Tel (03) 5024 8487
or 0417 593 483
Fax (03) 5024 8914
www.visitvictoria.com/milduraslinsley

Double $110 **Single** $66
Includes full breakfast
No smoking on property
Visa MC BC accepted
2 Queen 2 Single (3 bdrm)
Bathrooms: 2 Ensuite

Linsley House B&B has a magnificent river view. Colin and Desley Rankin take pleasure in welcoming you to their charming and tranquil home which is situated in a quiet rural setting and has panoramic views of the garden and Murray River from the bedrooms. The large lounge/dining area includes: full kitchen facilities, TV, fridge, woodfire, air-conditioning and comfortable antiques. Mildura is renown for its oranges, dried fruits, wineries and Mediterranean weather.

Mornington - Mount Martha

Briarswood Cottage *Luxury B&B Cottage with Kitchen*
Ann and Ian Duncan
559 Esplanade
Mount Martha
Vic 3934
4 km S of Mornington

Tel (03) 5974 2245
or 0403 468 237
Fax (03) 5974 8310
aduncan7@bigpond.com.au
www.briarswood.com.au

Double $165-$190 **Single** $90-$100
Includes full breakfast
Visa MC BC Diners Amex accepted
3 Queen 1 Single (3 in B&B,1 in cottage bdrm)
Bathrooms: 1 Ensuite 2 Private 2 in B&B,1 in cottage

 AAA Tourism
★★★★

Rekindle your dreams in a storybook cottage a haven which inspires reflection, romance and creativity, conversation and evokes fantasies of days of yore. Tastefully decorated in an English Country House style and furnished with antiques. Separate entrance, large sitting room with huge open fireplace and dining alcove. Upstairs 2 queen bedrooms with private bathrooms and one single room. In the garden a self contained cottage just for two with kitchenette and ensuite with breakfast provisions supplied. Situated opposite safe and secluded Craigie Beach.

Mornington

Baystay @ Nazaaray *Farmstay Cottage with Kitchen*
Param & Nirmal
266 Meakins Road Flinders
12 km N of Flinders
2 Gaskin Ave, Hastings
40 Murray Anderson Road, Rosebud

Tel (03) 9585 1138
or 0416 143 439
(03) 5989 0126
Fax (03) 9585 1140
info@nazaaray.com.au
www.nazaaray.com.au

Double $135-$240 Single $100-$200
Child $30
Accommodation Only
Visa MC accepted
1 King/Twin2 King 1 Single (3 bdrm)
Bathrooms: 1 Ensuite 1 Guest share Disability
bathroom/ toilet

Choice of three lovely properties on the Mornington Peninsula - Exclusive use of self contained luxury house or idyllic cottages; romantic getaway or groups; rural views and seclusion or close to marina or swimming beaches. Toasty fires, warm spa, dog friendly, access friendly bathrooms. An easy walk/drive to shops, wineries or golf we have the lot.

Total privacy ensured.

Victoria

Mount Beauty

Braeview *B&B Self Contained Studio & Cottage*
Isla MacLeod
4 Stewarts Road
Mt Beauty   Vic 3699
1.5 km N of Mount Beauty

Tel (03) 5754 4746 (*8.00am-8.00pm*)
or 0418 572 834   Fax (03) 5754 4757
info@braeview.com.au   www.braeview.com.au

Double $120-$290 Single $120-$290
Includes special breakfast   Dinner B/A
Visa MC BC Amex accepted
1 King/Twin 3 Queen 1 Double (5 bdrm)
Bathrooms: 5 Ensuite 4 spa rooms

Multi award winner - *Victoria's Alpine High Country* with a landscape that inspires the imagination. Explore the High Country or simply relax.

How Long Has It Been? - since you *Indulged All* your senses. Imagine the intimacy of a crackling log fire, romantic candlelight dinner wine a spa........ and an early night ....one of life's pleasures!

Indulge yourselves with Ice Cold Champagne, Fabulous Food, Ambience - all of this and more awaits you at *Braeview*.Offering three distinct forms of accommodation - something for everybody
* Reflections Cottage - S/C generous breakfast hamper, spa and wood fire set in its own cottage garden
* Studio Apartment - S/C generous breakfast hamper, spa and open fireplace
* Traditional B&B in the main residence with a-la-carte breakfast, en-suites with corner spas and double showers, wood fire guest lounge room.

In-House guests enjoy a sumptuous cooked breakfast -how does fruit pancake drizzled with maple syrup and topped with yoghurt , or freshly baked muffins hot from the oven with coffee sound ....*hungry?*

Adults retreat where "Inspector Morse" our staffy will greet you at the front gate. Ask about our "Weekend Indulgence Escape" or *"Mid Week Escape" - Book Your Magical Escape Today* or check us out at www.braeview.com.au - Accredited Tourism business.

Nagambie - Murchison

Brecon House *Luxury B&B*
Andrew & Gale Wainwright
55 Stevenson Street
Murchison
Vic 3610
25 km N of Nagambie

Tel (03) 5826 2003
or 0417 560 843
Fax (03) 5826 2036
bookings@bedandbrecon.com
www.bedandbrecon.com

Double $110-$140 Single $90-$110
Includes full breakfast
Visa MC BC Diners accepted
1 King/Twin 1 Queen (2 bdrm)
Bathrooms: 2 Ensuite

 AAA Tourism
★★★★

Brecon House, built circa. 1850, became a residence around 1900 and is now one of Murchison's few remaining original buildings. Andrew and Gale's sympathetic restoration includes complete modernisation, full air conditioning, breakfast room and comfortable guest sitting-room with wood-fired heater. As a guest at 'Brecon House' you can expect a warm welcome while retaining your privacy, a good night's rest and then to be served with a sumptuous breakfast; before being sent on your journey with a friendly wave. Please telephone us for a brochure.

Phillip Island

Abaleigh on Lovers Walk *Apartment with Kitchen*
Jenny & Robert Hudson
6 Roy Court
Phillip Island,
Vic 3922
0.4 km E of Cowes PO

Tel (03) 5952 5649
Fax (03) 5952 2549
abaleigh@nex.net.au
www.abaleigh.com

Double $160-$250 Single $160-$250
Full Breakfast Provisions
Apartment from $190 dble
Visa MC BC accepted
2 King/Twin1 King 2 Queen (5 bdrm)
Bathrooms: 5 Ensuite 5 Private spa

 AAA Tourism
★★★★☆

Abaleigh's FSC absolute beach frontage apartment and studios offer the finest, homely accommodation. Featuring: spas, water views, Jetmaster log fires, double showers, breakfast-stocked kitchens, laundries, courtyards with barbecues for outdoor living, TV, video, stereo and more. Five minutes foreshore stroll to restaurants and central Cowes. Peaceful, private, ideal for couples or small groups of adults. Winner Best New Business, Best Hosted Accommodation Regional Tourism Awards. AAA ****1/2, "Best waterfront situation with privacy & finest homely comforts. M&J Elwood.

Victoria

Phillip Island

Glen Isla House *Luxury B&B Separate Suite Hotel*
Madeleine & Ian Baker
230-232 Church Street
Cowes   Vic 3922
0.15 km W of Cowes

Tel (03) 5952 1882 or 0419 225 618
Fax (03) 5952 5028
infobbb@glenisla.com
www.glenisla.com

Double $235-$350 **Single** $205-$315
Includes special breakfast
Dinner Table d/h dinner B/A
3-Course Dinner $72 per guest
Visa MC BC Amex Eftpos accepted
1 King 5 Queen 1 Twin (7 bdrm)
Bathrooms: 7 Ensuite 7 Private Spa Bath in Anderson Suite

AAA Tourism ★★★★★   INN·HOUSE

Set in the grounds of the historic Glen Isla homestead (circa 1870). Award winning small luxury hotel-style retreat offering elegant surroundings. Absolute privacy in secluded large heritage gardens. 100 meters to the beach. "Arguably the island's best accommodation" - Melbourne Age Featured on TV - Getaway, Coxy's Big Break. Anderson suite cottage offers four-poster king bed, log fire, spa, period furnshings and surround-sound TV/DVD system. Six purpose-architected Glen Isla House rooms with walk-in robe/luggage room, private en-suite, superb garden vistas. Licensed restaurant (guests only - by arrangement), cellar, resident chef. Group gourmet getaway weekends & corporate

≈

Phillip Island - Cowes

Genesta House *B&B Guest House*
Gay Langrish
18 Steele Street
Cowes
Vic 3922
0.3 km E of Cowes PO

Tel (03) 5952 3616
or 0413 013 766
Fax (03) 5952 3616
genesta@nex.net.au
www.genesta.com.au

Double $130-$160
Includes full breakfast
No smoking on property
Visa MC BC accepted
4 Queen (4 bdrm)
Bathrooms: 4 Ensuite

AAA Tourism ★★★★

Genesta is a haven in the heart of Cowes, traditional Victorian with wide verandah, beautiful cottage gardens and gazebo. Only four houses from the beach and Lovers Walk and just 300 metres from Cowes main street full of restaurants and cafes. Genesta has four queen-bed rooms each with own private entrance, en-suite and balcony. There is a guest lounge with books, games and magazines. Outdoors - a saltwater spa, pond, fountain, spacious outdoor seating, BBQ and gazebo. Traditional full English breakfast included. Children not catered for.

Phillip Island - Cowes

Holmwood Guesthouse *B&B Cottage with Kitchen Guest House*
Serena & Eric van Grondelle
37 Chapel Street, (cnr Steele St),
Cowes, Phillip Island   Vic 3922
0.3 km E of Post Office

Tel (03) 5952 3082 or 0421 444 810
Fax (03) 5952 3083
bbbook@holmwoodguesthouse.com.au
www.holmwoodguesthouse.com.au

Double $165-$215 Single $140-$215
Child Under 12 $33
Includes full breakfast
Dinner $ 52.50/3 courses

Visa MC Diners Amex Eftpos accepted
4 King/Twin 5 Queen (3 in B&B, 1 in Cottage, 2 in Tow bdrm)
Bathrooms: 5 Ensuite 2 Guest share Townhouses have one bathroom shared between the 2
bedrooms.

Holmwood Guesthouse provides award winning boutique accommodation within a
cottage garden setting, 300 metres to Cowes' beach and town centre, and a 10 minute
drive to Penguin Parade. Three charming rooms provide traditional style B&B accommodation with ensuites and split system heating/cooling, whereas two self-contained cottages
ensure a more private B&B experience, with ensuites (spa/baths), log fires, A/C, TV, DVD, hifi,
broadband. For families two two-bedroom fully self-contained townhouses, including living,
dining, kitchen and courtyard, offer a more economical alternative just 50m from the beach.

~

Phillip Island - Ventnor

First Class Bed & Breakfast *B&B Farmstay Guest House*
Graeme Wells
648 Ventnor Road
Ventnor, Phillip Island
Vic 3922
6.48 km W of Cowes

Tel (03) 5956 8329
Fax (03) 5956 8373
gwells@waterfront.net.au
www.firstclassbedandbreakfast.com

Double $100-$150 Single $60-$100
Includes full breakfast
Dinner $25-$35.

Visa MC BC Diners Amex Eftpos accepted
7 Queen 2 Single (7 bdrm)
Bathrooms: 7 Ensuite 4 spa

Fine country accommodation with panoramic views of Westernport Bay and the
Mornington Peninsula. A traditional B&B in a tranquil rural setting, a touch of
paradise near to the Penguin Parade, Seal Rocks Sea Life Centre and the Nobbies
boardwalks, the race track. Your friendly host will delight you from our country kitchen.
Luxury Spa Rooms, Log Fire, Pool Table, Horse Riding available.

Victoria

Port Fairy

Boathouse on Moyne *B&B*
Denise & Gordon Harman
19 Gipps Street
Port Fairy
Vic 3284
In Port Fairy Central

Tel (03) 5568 2608
or 0418 577 291
Fax (03) 5568 2740
www.bbbook.com.au/boathouse.html

Double $110-$120 **Single** $80-$90
Includes special breakfast
No smoking on property
Visa MC BC accepted
1 Queen 1 Double 1 Twin 2 Single (2 bdrm)
Bathrooms: 1 Ensuite 1 Private

AAA Tourism ★★★★

The "Boathouse on Moyne" is situated right on the historic Moyne River fishing port. If you wander out the front gate you are right on the jetty where the fishing trawlers bring in their catch. Easy walking distance to shopping centre, main beach and restaurants. Make yourself at home in this spacious bed & breakfast with guests' lounge, TV, kitchen, fridge and tea and coffee-making facilities. We prepare generous breakfasts which include freshly-baked croissants, fresh fruit, fruit juice and locally made jams.

Port Fairy

Cherry Plum Cottages B&B *B&B Cottage with Kitchen*
Anne and John Ardlie
6 Albert Road
Port Fairy
Vic 3284
In Port Fairy Central

Tel (03) 5568 2433
or 0439 682 433
Fax (03) 5568 3006
cherryplum@port-fairy.com
www.port-fairy.com/cherryplum

Double $105-$150 **Single** $100-$150
Child $25
Includes special breakfast
3 Queen 2 Double (5 bdrm)
Bathrooms: 4 Ensuite

AAA Tourism ★★★★

On a quiet country lane in Port Fairy our cottages Cherry Plum and Arrondoon (c1862) are situated on four acres in a leafy garden amongst historic buildings. We deliver breakfast baskets of local produce to your cottage and host served breakfasts for our (c1852) homestead guests. Our accommodation features period furnishings, private entrance, guest sitting rooms, verandahs and off street parking. We are 20 minutes walk to the main street and well located to enjoy the town, restaurants, beaches, golf, or day trips to the 12 Apostles, Grampians and Coonawarra wineries.

Port Fairy

Shearwater House *B&B*
Joy and John Marwood
53 Gipps Street
Port Fairy
Vic 3284
In Central Port Fairy

Tel (03) 5568 1081 or 0438 504 577
Fax (03) 5568 2981
shearwbb@hotkey.net.au
www.shearwaterhouse.com.au

Double $150-$165 Single $140-$155
Child None under 12
Includes full breakfast
Visa MC BC accepted
1 King/Twin 4 Queen (5 bdrm)
Bathrooms: 5 Ensuite

AAA Tourism
★★★★

Shearwater House is an elegant and stylish Bed & Breakfast offering five guest rooms with ensuites. The guest lounge, breakfast area and terrace have magnificent views over the Moyne River only a few metres away. We are situated only one block from the centre of town, seven high quality restaurants,cafes and boutique shops. Shearwater House is also only 5 minutes walk over the adjacent footbridge to the beautiful East Beach. A delicious cooked breakfast is included. On Saturdays in summer, our guests can join in yacht racing on the bay.

Portarlington

Carrick *Cottage with Kitchen*
Kimberlee Darby
30 The Esplanade
Portarlington
Vic 3223
1 km E of Portarlington

Tel (03) 5259 1315
portsale@bigpond.net.au
www.bbbook.com.au/carrick.html

Double $285 per weekend per couple
(minimum 2 night stay)
Full Breakfast Provisions
1 Double 4 Single (2 bdrm)
Bathrooms: 1 Private 1

Carrick is a beautiful 150 year old cottage. It is owned by the family that first acquired it in 1884 and Carrick's colourful history is displayed upon the walls. Comprising cosy living areas open fireplace fully equipped kitchen dining area lounge and set in a large and lovely garden opposite the beach Carrick has 180 degree views of Port Philip Bay the You Yangs and Melbourne can be seen in the distance. Great swimming in summer and beautiful walks and vineyards all year round. B&B guests are welcomed with a free bottle of local wine and breakfast hamper. Just an hour and a quarter from Melbourne. Carrick is utterly romantic.

Victoria

Princetown - Twelve Apostles

Moonlight Retreat *Luxury B&B Self Contained Cottage*
Anthea & Andrew Mitchell
50 Parkers Access
Moonlight Head via Wattle Hill
Vic 3237
15 km E of Princetown

Tel (03) 5237 5277   Fax (03) 5237 5279
B&B@MoonlightRetreat.com
www.MoonlightRetreat.com

Double $185-$295   Child From $35
Includes full breakfast   Dinner From $30/couple
Visa MC BC Diners Amex Eftpos accepted
6 King (6 bdrm)
Bathrooms: 6 Ensuite

Located at the mid-point of the famous Great Ocean Road, Moonlight Retreat is nestled into the ridgeline of beautiful Moonlight Head, capturing views over tranquil bushland to the Great Southern Ocean as it rolls towards the Twelve Apostles. And Moonlight Retreat provides a flexible choice no matter what style of escape you have in mind. If B&B is your preference, there are two gorgeous suites to choose from. Both have a private ensuite and balcony looking over the treetops towards the sea; one also offers a corner spa built for two. Of course, a King-size bed, TV & DVD player, tea and coffee making facilities and reverse cycle air conditioning are there for your comfort while you enjoy a full cooked breakfast, afternoon tea, a complimentary bottle of bubblyí, and the use of a private guests entrance and fireside sitting room.

Perhaps youíd prefer self-contained seclusion? Moonlight Retreat gives you a choice of 1 or 2 bedroom cottages, each providing all of the facilities of the suites, along with a large spa pool, your own crackling log fire, full cooking facilities along with provisions for a continental breakfast on your first morning. Whilst some guests never seem to get much further than the verandah, this very special spot puts you within a short drive of the Great Ocean Roads many attractions Wreck Beach, the 12 Apostles, Loch Ard Gorge, the Otway Fly treetop walk or Cape Otway Lighthouse and that barely scratches the surface. The added bonus? You can even bring your pets along!

Princetown - Twelve Apostles

Arabella Country House *B&B Homestay*
Lynne & Neil Boxshall
7219 Great Ocean Road
Princetown Vic 3269
6 km E of Princetown

Tel (03) 5598 8169
Fax (03) 5598 8186
arabella.ch@bigpond.com
www.innhouse.com.au/arabella.htm

Double $130-$150 Single $80
Child $25
Includes full breakfast
Dinner $15 - $30
No smoking on property
Visa MC BC Eftpos accepted
3 Queen 1 Double 2 Single (4 bdrm)
Bathrooms: 4 Ensuite

Guests from Australia and overseas enjoy Arabella's quality accommodation while exploring 12 Apostles, Port Campbell National Park and Otway National Park. Lynne and Neil's modern Australian colonial design rural homestead has guest wing with private entry, spacious rooms, queen-size beds, TV, ensuite bathrooms, shared lounge, tea and coffee always available. All rooms have panoramic views. Our small dogs and cats will help you to enjoy our cosy fire or sun filled verandah. Complemented by our sumptuous Australia country breakfast.

~

Rutherglen

Holroyd Bed & Breakfast *B&B*
John Stevenson & Charles Dunn
28 Church Street
Rutherglen
Vic 3685
45 km W of Albury/Wodonga

Tel (02) 6032 8218
or 0409 038 472
Fax (02) 6032 8218
holroyd@net.net.au
www.holroydrutherglen.com

Double $145 Single $110
Includes full breakfast
Visa MC BC accepted
1 King 1 Queen (2 bdrm)
Bathrooms: 1 Ensuite 1 Private

Holroyd is a Traditional Bed & Breakfast circa 1928. Nestled in the heart if town amongst quiet, lush, award winning gardens. Relax and unwind with the moggies. Close by are restaurants, shops and wineries. Choose either the Muscat or Tokay Room. Awake to a full country style breakfast with home made jams and home grown poached fruit. Come, smell the roses or sip a superb Rutherglen wine. Let us show you the sights in our 1968 Benz (POA).

Rye

Hilltonia Homestead *B&B Self Contained*
Jo-Anne & Anthony Colles
Lot B1 Browns Road
Rye
Vic 3941
3 km S of Rye

Tel (03) 5985 2654
Fax (03) 5985 2684
sales@hilltonia.com.au
www.hilltonia.com.au

Double $165-$280
Includes full breakfast
Visa MC BC accepted
1 King/Twin1 King 7 Queen (9 bdrm)
Bathrooms: 9 Private

Experience for yourself the pleasures of Hilltonia Homestead. Set amongst 40 picturesque acres on the Mornington Peninsula (1 hour form Melbourne). Select from five uniquely themed and totally private cottages marked around the property. Each with bayviews or dazzling sunset views over rolling sand dunes. Spa's, TV/Video/CD, Kitchen, Gas Log Fires, Balcony with BBQ. Alternatively, select from four traditional B&B suites within the main homestead. Lagoon swimming pool & Tennis court. Minutes to Bay & Ocean beaches, fine wineries and superb golf courses.

Torquay - Surf Coast

Ocean Manor B&B *B&B Separate Suite*
Helen & Bob Bailey
3 Glengarry Drive
Torquay
Vic 3228
17 km S of Geelong

Tel (03) 5261 3441
or 0407 597 100
Fax (03) 5261 9140
oceanmanor@bigpond.com
www.bbbook.com.au/oceanmanorbb.html

Double $110-$150 Single $90-$10
Child $20
Continental Breakfast
Visa MC BC accepted
1 Queen 1 Twin (2 bdrm)
Bathrooms: 1 Ensuite 1 Family share

The 2 bedroom suite is situated upstairs to ensure privacy and take maximum advantage of the ocean view. The master bedroom features a queen sized bed, en suite bathroom and walk in robe. Adjoining is a combined lounge and dining area which leads onto a decked balcony with sweeping ocean views. The air conditioned lounge has Foxtel, TV and video. The mini kitchen with fridge and microwave leads to a second bedroom with separate toilet facilities and 2 single beds. A generous continental breakfast is included.

Victoria

Inn.House Bed and Breakfast Australia Inc
Inn.House

Tel (03) 5952 3082
president@innhouse.com.au
www.innhouse.com.au

Inn.House Victoria's Best Boutique Accommodation 50 of the best B&Bs in Victoria. Quality assured by the Inn.House Assessment Team Gift Vouchers Available Telephone (03) 5664 3204 or order on line: www.innhouse. com.au/giftvouchers.html

Full details on the Award Winning website www.innhouse.com.au

Wangaratta

The Pelican *B&B Farmstay*
Margaret & Bernie Blackshaw
606 Oxley Flats Road
Wangaratta
Vic 3678
6 km E of Wangaratta

Tel (03) 5727 3240
or 0413 082 758
pelicanblackshaw@hotmail.com
www.bbbook.com.au/thpelican.html

Double $120-$150 Single $75
Child $40
Includes full breakfast
Dinner $30 per person by arrangement
$40 extra in dbl room
Visa MC BC accepted
1 Queen 1 Twin 2 Single (3 bdrm)
Bathrooms: 1 Guest share 1 Private

 AAA Tourism
★★★☆

The Pelican is a charming historic homestead set in parklike surroundings. Cattle and horses are raised on the 400 acres and early risers can go "trackside" to watch the harness horses at work. Guest rooms are in an upstairs wing of the home and have lovely country views where peacocks and pelicans are often spotted. The main bedroom has its own private balcony overlooking a lagoon fringed with giant red gums. Hearty breakfasts feature home grown produce and evening meals are available on request. We have pets.

Warrnambool

Merton Manor Exclusive B&B *B&B Homestay*
Pamela & Ivan Beechey
62 Ardlie Street
Warrnambool
Vic 3280
In Warrnambool

Tel (03) 5562 0720
or 0417 314 364
Fax (03) 5561 1220
merton@ansonic.com.au
members.datafast.net.au/merton

Double $150-$170 Single $130
Includes full breakfast
No smoking on property
Visa MC BC accepted
1 King/Twin 5 Queen 2 Single (6 bdrm)
Bathrooms: 6 Ensuite

AAA Tourism

M erton Manor is a traditional B&B with mews style accommodation set within an
historic Victorian villa. It features antiques, open fires, billiard and music rooms
and grand dining room and is located mid way between Adelaide and Melbourne.
All suites feature private entrances, climate control heating and air conditioning, private
lounge rooms and ensuites with double spas. Merton Manor is situated close to the cultural
attractions and restaurants of Warrnambool. The 12 Apostles, whale viewing, Tower Hill
State Game Reserve and the Maritime Museum are all close by..

Warrnambool

Manor Gums *B&B Separate Suite*
Michael & Kittipat Esposito
170 Shadys Lane, Mailors Flat
Warrnambool
Vic 3275
8 km NW of Warrnambool

Tel (03) 5565 4410
Fax (03) 5565 4409
manorgum@hotkey.net.au
www.travel.to/manorgums

Double $135-$165 Single $120-$135
Child $20
Continental Breakfast
Dinner $35+
Visa MC BC Eftpos accepted
3 Queen 1 Double (4 bdrm)
Bathrooms: 4 Ensuite

AAA Tourism

M anor Gums is a quality and unique retreat surrounded by tall majestic gums and
abundant birdlife. The distinctive architectural style and unique features offer
couples luxury in private self contained suites, all designed to be different and
capture the tranquillity of the bushland setting and superb views. Suites have fully equipped
kitchenette, microwave, TV, VCR, CD player, climate control air conditioning. Some have
a woodfire, balconies or large bath. A generous breakfast hamper is provided to enjoy at your
leisure. Spa, sauna, gym and BBQ are available.

Yackandandah

Time After Time *B&B*
Robyn McCulloch & Jen Haberecht
43 Back Creek Road
Yackandandah
Vic 3749
1.2 km SE of Yackandandah

Tel (02) 6027 1786
or 0419 616 119
robynmc@dragnet.com.au
www.tat.dragnet.com.au

Double $110-$120 Single $110
Includes full breakfast
Additional person/child $20
1 Queen (1 bdrm)
Bathrooms: 1 Ensuite 1

She-Oaks cottage is fully self contained, designed for comfort and relaxation, with a view across the valley to the hills beyond. Great sitting room with full kitchen and dining room with a view. There is one queen size bedroom, and up to 2 extra people can be accommodated. TV, DVD, heating, airconditioning, private BBQ and outdoor sitting areas. The verandah on three sides provides a wonderful place to sit, relax and enjoy the view. We provide a great country breakfast, either a hamper full of homemade and local produce, or if you prefer we will cook for you from the daily breakfast menu. Your four legged friend is welcome, just let us know.

Yarra Valley - Dandenong Ranges

Holly Gate House Bed and Breakfast *B&B*
Loraine Potter
1308 Mt Dandenong Tourist Road
Kalorama
Vic 3766
5 km NE of Olinda

Tel (03) 9728 3218
or 0415 192 690
Fax (03) 9728 3218
reception@hollygatehouse.com.au
www.hollygatehouse.com.au

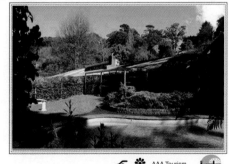

Double $120-$225 Single $110
Includes full breakfast
Dinner Can be arranged on request
Complimentary Transport to and from local Restaurants/Functions
Visa MC BC Diners accepted
3 Queen (3 bdrm)
Bathrooms: 3 Ensuite 2 Rooms with ensuite no Spa, One room with ensuite and spa

AAA Tourism
★★★★

Luxury B&B situated in The romantic Dandenong Ranges, approx 45 km due East of Melbourne. Three Queen size rooms all with private ensuite (one ensuite with Spa). All rooms have TV, Video, CD/Radio. Tariff includes refreshments on arrival, cooked breakfast of your choice served in guest dining room, shared sitting room with log fire. Use of the outside solar heated pool in summer in a pleasant garden setting. BBQ facilities. Complimentary transport to and from any restaurant/function within 10km of Kalorama. Melways Ref: Page52 J9

Victoria

Yarra Valley - Yarra Glen

Valley Guest House *Luxury B&B Separate Suite Cottage No Kitchen*
Ann Flockhart & Ted Secombe
319 Steels Creek Road
Yarra Glen Vic 3775
3 km N of Yarra Glen village

Tel (03) 9730 1822 or 0419 572 882
Fax (03) 9730 2019
enquiries@valleyguesthouse.com.au
www.valleyguesthouse.com.au

Double $160-$240
Child $45
Continental Breakfast
Dinner platter by arrangement $65 per double
massage $130 for 2 x 45 minute or $75 per hour
Visa MC BC Diners Amex Eftpos accepted
1 King/Twin3 King 2 Queen (6 bdrm)
Bathrooms: 6 Ensuite 6 Private

Centrally located in the Yarra Valley - with wineries and restaurants within a short driving distance perfect for wine buffs and food lovers. Once enjoyed, retire to our quiet sanctuary situated in beautiful gardens with rural views. Our accommodation offers first class facilities. 6 suites, 2 Queen, 2 King and 2 King Studio Suites elevated on the hillside. All have fires or air conditioning, double spa baths, heated towel rails, TV/CD, well appointed sitting area. Solar heated pool. Buffet breakfast set in the dining area, Guests can wander in at their leisure and relax with the morning papers.

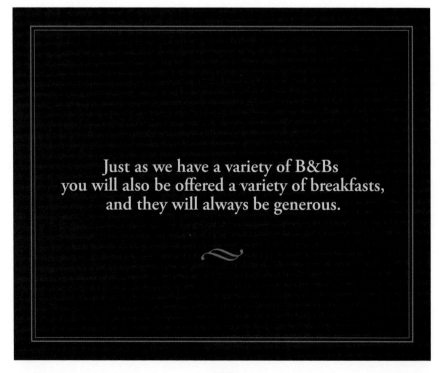

Just as we have a variety of B&Bs
you will also be offered a variety of breakfasts,
and they will always be generous.

Yarra Valley - Yarrambat

Van Dyk's At Tintagel *B&B Apartment with Kitchen*
Hosts
32 Eisemans Road
Yarrambat, Vic 3091
25 km NE of Melbourne

Tel (03) 9436 2212
Fax (03) 9436 2213
enquiries@vandykstintagel.com.au
www.vandykstintagel.com.au

Double $235-$275
Child $40 (over 10 yrs)
Includes special breakfast
Dinner Fully Licensed, $18.50 - $60
2 King 2 Double (2 bdrm)
Bathrooms: 2 Ensuite

AAA Tourism ★★★★☆

2 luxury self contained apartments (sleep 4); King beds plus double sofa beds, bathrooms with double spas, Fully equipped kitchenettes, Rev. cycle A/C, woodfires, TV, HIFI, DVD, VCR. Laundry facilities. Exquisite food, good wine and absolute pampering are part of our mission statement. Our property of 8 acres has stunning 300 degr. views and all that only 35 min from Melbourne or 30 min from the Airport. From your apartment and from your private terrace you can enjoy the truly magnificent scenery spread out before you. Spectacular morning mists drape through the valley at sunrise. The point of difference at Tintagel is not the spectacular views, nor the different species of birds, ducks or kangaroos that mooch around the estate as if they were the paying guests, nor the attention to detail you will find in your apartment. The big drawcard to this piece of paradise is Diny's flair and expertise in the kitchen and her penchant to pamper her guests. For Romantic Weekends For Two-, Anniversary, Honeymoon or Ultimate Indulgence Packages, Diny will lovingly prepare a 3 or 4 course a la carte dinner, using locally sourced and mainly organic produce. Relaxing massages in the privacy of your apartment and door to door winery tours. Close to Yarra Valley wineries, Montsalvat and other artists studios. 5 Min. from Golf course and Driving Range. Enjoy walks and bird viewing in our extensive gardens. For the numerous glowing testimonials please check our website.

Victoria

Western Australia

Albany

Situated on Princess Royal Harbour and King George Sound, Albany is Western Australia's oldest town. Albany's spectacular rugged coastline is unique in its own way, located around Frenchman's Bay is the Natural Bridge and the Gap and Blow Holes which are some of natures wonders. The old Whaling Station, which is now a recognised whaling museum where you can see all the history of a bygone era, explore a whaler the Cheynes IV one of the last whaling ships. There are the spectacular views and sunsets that can be seen from the Wind Farm lookouts.

York Street is the main street of Historical old Albany Town, which has many Heritage listed buildings, like the old Goal and Courthouse, you can sit in one of the many cafe's and restaurants and take in the views of Princess Royal Harbour. Just out of town is Mt Clarence, which features the Old Forts and the Light Horse Memorial to the soldiers and horses, departing for Gallipolli. It's an ideal place to stay whilst visiting the Great Southern area, there are many local wineries, beautiful beaches and the scenic whale walk around King George sound which joins the Bibbulmun Track. There are many seasonal attractions including Whale watching, the wildflowers in spring and the many species of flora and fauna.

Betty Ramsell, Memories of Albany B&B, Albany.

Kojonup

Nestled it the Great Southern region on WA Kojonup is the Gateway to the beautiful South. This bustling rural town still bears all the trademarks of a traditional country settlement with its historic buildings and friendly, safe atmosphere.

Visit the towns Kodja Place Visitor Centre, it is an example of what can be achieve by a very close community. The Kodja place tells the story of the people of the Kojonup area with its interactive displays, photographs and a must to see is the Rose Maze of hundreds of Australian Roses.

Spring is wildflower time. Farrar Reserve and The Myrtle Benn Flora and Fauna Sanctuary The Australian Bush heritage Block are delightful reserves in which to explore the native bush and wildflowers.

Doreen Bignall, Kemminup Farm, Kojonup.

Perth

Perth, the capital of the West, embraced by tree clad hills and golden beaches, opens it's arms to visitors from interstate and overseas. Take a few days to experience the relaxed atmosphere before allowing yourself more time to visit other parts of this vast state. Experience the sight of molten gold at the Mint or a trip to the riverside Casino, explore the Cultural Centre or relax in Kings Park's botanical haven with a birds eye view of the city by day or night. Stroll the elevated walkway and discover why Western Australia looks so different.

Take a ferry down the Swan River to Fremantle, our historic port. Continue to Rottnest Island and enjoy a swim in a magnificent peaceful bay, watch for whales, dolphins or cycle around the island and meet the quokkas. On your return visit the magnificent new Maritime Museum or the Old Fremantle Jail before choosing a restaurant harbour side or in the cappuccino strip.

Visit the Swan Valley vineyards for wines, cheeses and other fresh products or wander into the hills to experience the wildflowers.

Retreat at the end of the day to a welcoming Bed & Breakfast where you can plan the next part of your stay in this enormous state.

Jane Tucker, Caesia House, Nedlands.

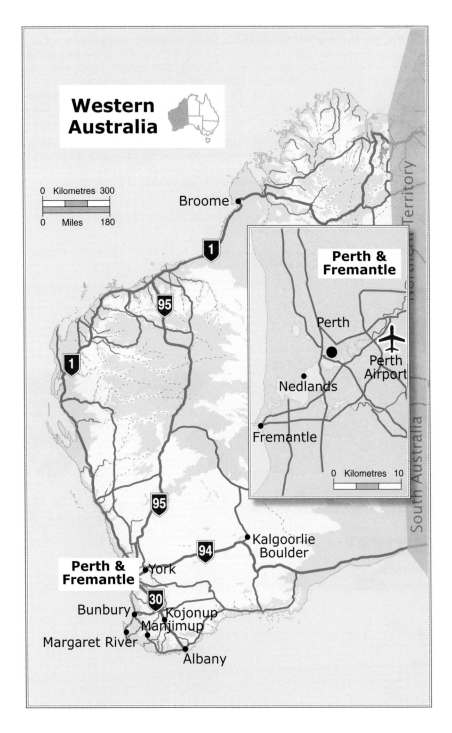

Western
Australia

0   Kilometres 300

0   Miles   180

Broome

1

95

1

Perth &
Fremantle

Perth

Perth
Airport

Nedlands

Fremantle

0   Kilometres   10

95

Kalgoorlie
Boulder

94

Perth &
Fremantle   York

30

Bunbury   Kojonup
Manjimup

Margaret River

Albany

Northern Territory

South Australia

Albany

B&B by the Sea *B&B Homestay*
Sue Buckingham and Les Jones
7 Griffiths Street
Albany
WA 6330
5 km E of Albany

Tel (08) 9844 1135
or 0417 990 673
Fax (08) 9844 1135
holiday@bbythesea.com.au
www.bbythesea.com.au

Double $99-$130 **Single** $90
Child $35
Includes full breakfast
3 Queen (3 bdrm)
Bathrooms: 3 Ensuite

O verlooking stunning coastal scenery on beach frontage in quiet location. B&B By the Sea offers absolute comfort and privacy in ensuite rooms. Relax in our modern and spacious rooms; each with queen bed, TV, fridge, tea/coffee facilities and heating. Enjoy our scrumptious breakfasts, featuring local produce, fruits, muffins, quiche, our famous muesli and a hearty cooked breakfast by Les. Located close to town centre, golf course, and walking trails. Whale watching in season (May to November). Wildflowers in Spring. Swimming in Summer on our secluded beach.

Broome

The Temple Tree B&B *B&B*
Helga & Terry Crisp
31 Anne Street
Broome
WA 6725
1.5 km SW of China Town

Tel (08) 9193 5728
Fax (08) 9193 5121
crisp@tpg.com.au
www.templetreebnb.com.au

Double $135-$145 **Single** $115-$125
Includes special breakfast
Dinner neg
Visa MC BC accepted
2 Double (2 bdrm)
Bathrooms: 2 Ensuite

AAA Tourism
★★★★

T he Temple Tree (a name used in the tropics for the frangipani tree) is located in old Broome within walking distance of Town Beach, shops and restaurants. Accommodation comprises two attractive double rooms each with ensuite and private entrance. Each has remote TV/DVD/CD, fridge, clock radio, air-con/ceiling fans, tea and coffee. Each room has its own outside sitting area. Breakfast and dinner are served on the verandah which is screened from insects. Phone for brochure. Complimentary transfers.

Western Australia

Broome
Waterfront Bed & Breakfast B&B
Gary and Jan-marie Tuck
10 Demco Drive
Broome
WA 6775
3 km N of Town

Tel (08) 9192 6661
or 0400 887 226
Fax (08) 9192 6661
waterfrontbedandbreakfast@westnet.com.au
www.broomebb.com

Double $130-$180 **Single** $130-$180
Includes special breakfast
No smoking on property
Visa MC BC Eftpos accepted
2 King 1 Double (2 bdrm)
Bathrooms: 2 Ensuite 2

We are situated overlooking Roebuck Bay, close to China Town, the airport and easy access to all Broome has to offer. Walk over the bridge of the beautiful 25mtr lap pool to two very spacious rooms, with a broome style outdoor bathroom in the centre. Two poolside rooms, both with king size beds, a/c, fan, t.v. Breakfast includes fresh fruit, cereals, freshly baked bread, tea, plunger coffee and locally made preserves. Adults only, non smokers and no pets please. Check in 2.00 pm. Check out 11.00 pm.

~

Broome
Broometown B&B B&B
Toni & Richard Bourne
15 Stewart Street
Broome
WA 6725
In Broome

Tel (08) 91922006
or 0429 010 161
info@broometown.com.au
www.broometown.com.au

Double $150-$180 **Single** $140-$170
Includes full breakfast
2 Queen 1 Twin (3 bdrm)
Bathrooms: 3 Ensuite

Opening June 2006 - Richard and Toni Bourne welcome you to come and 'relax Broomestyle' at their brand new purpose built Bed & Breakfast. Located in leafy Old Broome and only a 3 minute stroll to Chinatown restaurants, cafes, cinemas and shops. Broometown offers three well-appointed rooms with queens size or twin beds, luxurious ensuites, private entrances, coffee and tea making facelities, TV&DVD, internet, frige, air-conditioning and private outdoor sitting area. In keeping with Broomestyle living guests will enjoy a scrumptious gourmet breakfast served daily in the outdoor living and pool area.
Advanced bookings essential

Bunbury

Colomberie B&B *B&B*

Sandra and Edward Pigott
11 Duffield Place
Sleaford Park, Bunbury
WA 6230
5 km S of Bunbury

Tel (08) 9795 7734
or 0417 913 398
Fax (08) 9795 7735
edp@iinet.net.au

Double $85-$95 **Single** $65-$75
Child On application by age
Continental Breakfast
Dinner By arrangement
No smoking on property
1 Queen 1 Double 1 Single (2 bdrm)
Bathrooms: 2 Ensuite Bath available by arrangement

Colomberie B&B is an ideal location for travellers to and from Perth and the southwest. Two bedrooms, with ensuites, plus a single bed and a cot, provide a variety of accommodation. There is a shared kitchenette, dining and lounge area for guests. Within easy travelling distance are the beaches, golf courses, vineyards, a lavender farm, olive groves, orchards and berry farms of the Capes, Region and the Bunbury amenities. The house, on one acre, is in a quiet cul-de-sac and has a walled garden for the enjoyment of guests.

Just as we have a variety of B&Bs
you will also be offered a variety of breakfasts,
and they will always be generous.

Fremantle

Terrace Central B&B *B&B*
Barry White
83-85 South Terrace
Fremantle
WA 6160
In Fremantle

Tel (08) 9335 6600
or 0428 969 859
Fax (08) 9335 6600
portfremantle@bigpond.com
www.users.bigpond.com/portfremantle

Double $128 Single $118
Child $20
Continental Breakfast
Saturday night only, extra $22
Visa MC BC Diners Amex Eftpos accepted
4 Queen 2 Double 2 Twin 2 Single (8 bdrm)
Bathrooms: 8 Ensuite

Heritage house in the city centre of Fremantle with 8 huge air-conditioned en-suite bedrooms. Close to rail and bus service. 3 minutes walk to Markets, shops. close to all tourist attractions and ferry to Rottnest Island. All rooms air-conditioned, en-suite bathroom, TV & inhouse movies, tea and coffee, fridge, parking.

Kalgoorlie Boulder

Barb's Place *B&B*
Barbara Mattingly
41 Federal Road
Kalgoorlie Boulder
WA 6432
2 km N of PO

Tel (08) 9021 6898
Fax (08) 9021 6893
www.bbbook.com.au/barbsplace.html

Double $100-$120 Single $80-$100
Continental Breakfast
4 Queen 1 Double (5 bdrm)
Bathrooms: 5 Ensuite

AAA Tourism ★★★☆

A rustic old house outside, A modern delight inside. "We had an enjoyable stay at Barb's. Owner so pleasant and helpful, everywhere is so clean with plenty of equipment to use. We highly recommend it for a pleasant stay." Vic & Olive.
Directions: If coming from Perth, turn right at the Wilson Street lights. Wilson Street ends on Federal Road. Turn right onto Federal and I'm in the second building on the left, opposite Mitsubishi motors..

Kojonup

Kemminup Farm B&B *B&B Homestay Farmstay*
Doreen & Trevor Bignell
214 Kemminup Road
Kojonup
WA 6395
12 km NE of Kojonup

Tel (08) 9831 1286 or 0417 311 383
Fax (08) 9831 1907
Kemminupfarm@westnet.com.au
www.westnet.com.au/kemminupfarm

Double $110 Single $92
Child depending on age
Includes full breakfast
Dinner $25.50
No smoking on property
Visa MC BC accepted
2 Queen 1 Twin (3 bdrm)
Bathrooms: 2 Ensuite

AAA Tourism ★★★★

P roviding a world class 'rural experience' working sheep and wool property with the opportunity to interact with farm animals. 3 hours drive from Perth enroute to the Stirling ranges National Park. Step back in time to a bygone era with a collection of old farm machinery, wattle and daub building, distinctive photographic display of native orchids, banksias and wildflowers. Kemminup farm offers exceptional accommodation and 'true blue' country hospitality with guest lounge, wood fire, private entrances to rooms, a full English breakfast and the peace and tranquillity of an overnight stay in the country.

Manjimup

Dingup House *B&B*
Kathy & David Savage
RMB 114 Dingup Road
Manjimup
WA 6258
6 km E of Manjimup

Tel (08) 9772 4206
or 0417 965 923
Fax (08) 9772 4206
dingup@westnet.com.au
www.wn.com.au/dingup

Double $95-$120 **Single** $75-$85
Includes full breakfast
Dinner $30
Visa MC BC Eftpos accepted
1 Queen 5 Double 3 Single (7 bdrm)
Bathrooms: 4 Ensuite 1 Guest share

Just 6 km from Manjimup with state forest as a backdrop is this delightful historic C1870 14 room homestead B&B oozing with romance and charm. 7 heritage bedrooms decorated in period style with ensuite or share facilities. Guests have use of own large lounge and parlour rooms with log fire. Country style cooked breakfasts and superb evening meals are served in our 30 seat dining room with huge log fireplace. All set on 45 acres where you can enjoy the prolific birdlife and peace and tranquillity of country life. Kathy and David invite you to a magical getaway. Friendly Lassie dog on premises.

~

Margaret River

Valley Views B&B *B&B Farmstay*
Jan & Barry Walsh
Lot 2 Tindong-Treeton Road
Margaret River
WA 6285
16 km NE of Margaret River

Tel (08) 9757 4573 or 0429 116 278
Fax (08) 9757 8181
valleyviewsbnb@bigpond.com
members.westnet.com.au/valleyviews

Double $110 **Single** $77
Child 6 to12yrs $25
Includes full breakfast
Dinner $20 - $35
Cot $10
Visa MC BC accepted
2 King/Twin 2 Queen (3 bdrm)
Bathrooms: 1 Guest share bath and shower ,separate toilet

Large homestead on 108 acres of vineyard, olive grove and sheep farm with state forest on two sides. We have fine wool, sheep ,horses, a friendly sheep dog and 4 boys and a girl at home sometimes. We grow wine grapes to sell and produce boutique, extra virgin olive oil. A great place to relax and enjoy country hospitality in a peaceful environment. Guests have large rooms, a comfortable lounge with log fire, library, fridge, tea facilities, microwave, TV, video, stereo and a barbecue outside. A great base to explore the Margaret River Region.

Margaret River

Margaret House *B&B Farmstay Cottage with Kitchen*
Bruce Darby
Cnr Wallcliffe Road and Devon Drive
Margaret River
WA 6285
2.5 km W of Margaret River

Tel (08) 9757 2692
stay@margarethouse.com.au
www.margarethouse.com.au

Double $100-$240 Single $95-$240
Continental Breakfast
Visa MC BC accepted
2 King/Twin4 King (4 bdrm)
Bathrooms: 4 Ensuite

Nestled in fragrant native gardens that attracts an abundance of bird life, our picturesque 7 acre rural property is a charming stopover from which to base your Southwest holiday. Wake up to the sounds of the birds and watch the sheep and kangaroos grazing as you have breakfast on your private sundeck. Good walk trails are nearby with easy access to the golf course, beach, wineries and restaurants. If you would prefer the sound of waves then our Luxury Beach House offers total indulgence with spa ensuites.

Margaret River

Kangaridge *B&B*
Chris and Bob Gregson
cnr Walclffe Road & Devon Drive
Margaret River
WA 6285
2 km W of Margaret River

Tel (08) 9757 3939
or 0417 970 729
Fax (08) 9757 3939
kangaridge@westnet.com.au
www.mronline.com.au/cape/accom/kanga

Double $120-$140 Single $100
Continental Breakfast
$40 extra person
Visa MC BC accepted
2 Queen 2 Twin (4 bdrm)
Bathrooms: 4 Ensuite

Adult Getaway. Unique 4 Star luxury accommodation set on 2.5 acres near Margaret River township, overlooking forest and prolific birdlife. Features indoor heated therapy pool and spa by the log fire. Only four suites so no crowds. All rooms queen sized with own ensuites, private decks, TV, video and tea making. Australian style homestead with rambling decks. Price is all inclusive with buffet continental breakfast (cooked breakfast is available) and mountain bikes. Close to town beaches, wineries, and kangaroo colony. Massages available on request.

Margaret River
The Noble Grape *Luxury B&B Guest House*
Rodney and Donna Carter
Lot 18, Bussell Highway
Cowaramup WA 6284
8 km N of Margaret River

Tel (08) 9755 5538 or 0418 931 721
Fax (08) 9755 5538
stay@noblegrape.com.au
www.noblegrape.com.au

Double $115-$150 Single $95-$115
Child $15 6-12yrs
Includes Continental Breakfast
Dinner B/A
Visa MC BC Diners Amex Eftpos accepted
6 Queen 1 Double 4 Single (6 bdrm)
Bathrooms: 6 Ensuite

The Noble Grape is an intimate guesthouse in the heart of the Margaret River Wine Region. Colonial style charm with quaint antiques nestled in an English cottage garden. Vineyards, beaches, galleries, chocolate and cheese factories are minutes away. Enjoy a leisurely breakfast in our sunny dining room overlooking the rose garden while watching the abundant native birdlife. Spacious country style rooms with ensuite, r.c. air conditioning, TV, refrigerator, tea/coffee facilities, comfortable arm chairs, private courtyard and hairdryer. Guest barbecue available. Catering for families and people with disabilities. Smoking outside only.

~

Perth
Pension of Perth *B&B*
Hoon & Steve Hall
3 Throssell Street
Perth
WA 6000
1 km NE of Perth

Tel (08) 9228 9049
or 0421 739 443
Fax (08) 9228 9290
stay@pensionperth.com.au
www.pensionperth.com.au

Double $135 Single $115
Child $30
Includes full breakfast
Discounts for long stays
1 King 3 Queen (1 Flat - Queen plus Single bdrm)
Bathrooms: 4 Ensuite

The Pension of Perth is the perfect choice for couples looking for a special place to stay or business traveller wanting somewhere value for money sophisticated, homely and private. It has the amenities of a fine hotel. The luxurious refurbishment reflects the elegance and comfort of its origins in 1897. It overlooks Hyde Park. Within walking distance from the centre of Perth. Our A-la-carte breakfast menu will make your stay memorable.

Perth - Airport

Airport Accommodation Perth B&B Self Contained
Wendy & Jamie Brindle
103 - 105 Central Avenue
Redcliffe
WA 6104
8 km E of Perth

Tel (08) 9478 2923
or 1800 447 000
Fax (08) 9478 2770
wendy@accommodation-perthairport.com
www.accommodation-perthairport.com

Double $95 Single $80
Continental Breakfast
Self Contained from $600/wk
Visa MC BC accepted
4 Queen 1 Double 2 Twin (6 bdrm)
Bathrooms: 3 Ensuite 2 Private

irport Accommodation Perth and Airport Bed & Breakfast Perth offers in-house B&B
as well as a self contained two bedroom/one bathroom cottage. Features include *
Airport transfers * 10 minutes drive from central Perth * Five minutes walk to bus stop
* 5 mins drive to Swan Valley and wineries * Easy access to Fremantle with courtesy drop
off at local train station for extended stays. Your hosts have a 'wealth' of knowledge of WA.
Close to the airport without the noise. "Come as guests and leave as friends."

Perth - Airport

Aarn House B&B @ Airport *B&B*
Jim and Hilary Farquhar
101 Fauntleroy Avenue
Ascot
WA 6104
8 km E of Perth

Tel (08) 9479 3556
or 0407 850 583
Fax (08) 9479 3997
bbbook@bedandbreakfast-perth.com
www.bedandbreakfast-perth.com

Double $95-$100 Single $75-$85
Child $30
Continental Breakfast
Dinner $15-25
Visa MC BC Diners Amex Eftpos accepted
1 King/Twin1 King 2 Queen (4 bdrm)
Bathrooms: 4 Ensuite Showers

arn House B&B At Airport offers B&B or self-contained, near Garvey Park on the
Swan River. A perfect haven for overnight accommodation or to use as a base whilst
sight-seeing. Guest lounge, air-con, comfortable seating, radio, magazines, 'swap'
books, and internet connection (printing available). Guest Kitchenette includes a fridge,
microwave, light cooking facility & toaster, wash up facilities and round table with 4 chairs.
12 metre Lap Swimming pool to cool in or exercise. Domestic terminal pick-up.

Western Australia

Perth - Nedlands

Caesia House Nedlands *B&B Homestay*
Jane and David Tucker
32 Thomas Street
Nedlands, Perth
WA 6009
5 km W of Perth Central City

Tel (08) 9389 8174
Fax (08) 9389 8173
tuckers@iinet.net.au
www.caesiahouse.com

Double $95-$120 Single $90-$110
Includes special breakfast
Visa MC BC accepted
1 King/Twin1 King 1 Queen (2 bdrm)
Bathrooms: 2 Ensuite

A quiet serene oasis in the city, only 7 minutes from Perth city centre, and Kings Park, within walking distance of numerous cafes, or wonderful riverside BBQ/picnic spots. Close to UWA, bus to historic Fremantle, and beaches or Perth City centre. Convenient base for day trips to scenic Rottnest Island, the Swan Valley to savour those wines or wildflowers in Perth Hills. Off street parking, ground floor ensuite room in our guest wing. Enjoy a WA breakfast, in our dining room overlooking the sparkling pool!

Perth - Nedlands

Edward House Bed & Breakfast *B&B*
Jenny Holm
26 Edward Street
Nedlands
WA 6009
5 km W of Perth

Tel (08) 9389 8832
or 0418 925 435
jennyholm@it.net.au
www.edwardhouse.com

Double $100-$130 Single $90-$110
Child $30
Includes full breakfast
Reduced weekly rates
Visa MC BC accepted
1 King/Twin1 King 1 Twin (2 bdrm)
Bathrooms: 1 Ensuite 1 Private

L ocated in leafy Nedlands, this gracious character home provides a tranquil, friendly retreat for visitors to this wonderful city. It is within easy walking distance to the University of WA, hospitals, Kings Park, Swan River foreshore, cafes, fine dining and cinema. Edward House is 10 minutes to the City of Perth or the pristine sands of Cottesloe Beach, a few minutes to trendy Subiaco and Claremont and just 20 minutes to City of Fremantle. Two elegant bedrooms and a spacious lounge is provided for your comfort. Spoil yourself with a delicious gourmet breakfast in the garden by the pool in summer, while you enjoy the sounds of our native bird life.

Index By Location

Index By Name of Accommodation

A

Aarn House B&B @ Airport 309
Abaleigh on Lovers Walk 285
Above Wollongong at Pleasant Heights B&B 172
Acacia Grove 130
Accommodation South Coast (NSW) Association (ASCA) 140
Airport Accommodation Perth 309
Alamanda Lodge Sawtell 83
Alexander Lakeside B&B 204
Alrae Bed & Breakfast 278
Annies@Yarralumla 30
Apartments on Tolmie 231
Aquila Retreat Luxury Accommodation 195
Arabella Country House 291
Araluen 63
Arcadia House Bed & Breakfast 144
Arcady Homestead 252
Aronui 147
Arrowee House B&B 94
Ashcroft Country Accommodation at McLaren Vale 229
Auntie Ann's Bed & Breakfast 137
Avoca Valley Bed & Breakfast 73
Ayr House B&B 260
A Villa Gail 199

B

B&B by the Sea 301
Ballandean Lodge 188
Bank Bed & Breakfast 101
Barb's Place 305
Bateau Bay Beachfront Luxury Spa 74
Battery Point Manor 240

Bayree Homestay 221
Baystay 70
Baystay @ Nazaaray 283
Baywoodbyne B&B 262
Beaufort Guesthouse 49
Bed and Breakfast Sydney Central 143
Bed and Views Kiama 114
Beilbys Beach House 122
Bella Vista 117
Bellbird Cottage 60
Bellevue Bed & Breakfast 230
Bellevue Terrace 152
Bellingen Heritage Cottages 58
Benbullen Farmstay 112
Berrima Guest House 61
Berringar Bed & Breakfast 226
Bet's B&B 146
Bethany Manor Bed & Breakfast 65
Billabong B&B 198
Bimbimbi House 59
Binawee Bed & Breakfast 75
Birchfield 23
Birch Corner 24
Birkdale Bed & Breakfast 188
Bishopsgate House 279
Blue Mountains Lakeside 68
Boambee Palms Bed & Breakfas 84
Boathouse on Moyne 288
Bonney's Inn 239
Bonrook Country Stay 180
Bonza View B&B 230
Boonara Homestead 212
Braeside 69
Braeview 284
Brae Bothy B&B 199
Brecon House 285
Briarswood Cottage 282
Bronte Guesthouse 105
Broomelea 64
Broometown B&B 302
Broughton Lodge 262

Brundah B&B 55
Bryn Glas 119
Bumblebrook Farm 73
Bundoora Homestay 273
Burra Heritage Cottages - Tivers Row 226

C

Caesia House Nedlands 310
Californian Bungalow Bed & Breakfast 276
Camerons Farmstay 124
Canobie House Bed & Breakfast 215
Cantala Bed and Breakfast 275
Capers Guesthouse 107
Carinya B&B 171
Carinya Highgate Hill Bed & Breakfast 189
Carrick 289
CasaBelle Country Guest House 59
Catersfield House 105
Cathie Lesslie Bed & Breakfast 153
Cecil Street B&B 160
Cedar Farm Guesthouse 167
Cessnock Heritage Inn 102
Chalet Swisse Spa 56
Cherrywood-by-the-River 56
Cherry Plum Cottages B&B 288
Claerwen Retreat 253
Clevedon Manor 255
Cloudgap 131
Clovelly Bed & Breakfast 148
Clovelly House - Luxury Accommodation 281
Cocora Cottage 90
Colleen & Old Sils Farmhouse 175
Colomberie B&B 303
Colville Cottage 241

Accommodation Welcoming Children

Australian Capital Territory

Canberra
Curtin
   Birch Corner
Hall
   Last Stop Ambledown Brook
   Surveyor's Hill Winery and B&B
   Redbrow Garden B&B
Kambah
   Edwil House Bed & Breakfast
Ngunnawal
   Gungahlin Homestay B&B
Yarralumla
   Annies@Yarralumla
Murrumbateman
   Country Guesthouse Schonegg

New South Wales

Adelong
   Yavendale Garden Cottage
   Beaufort Guesthouse
Albury
   Elizabeth's Manor
Alstonville - Ballina
   Hume's Hovell
Armidale
   Poppys Cottage
   Wattleton
   Glenhope Alpacas - B&B
   Cox's on South Hill
Barrington Tops - Gloucester
   Valley View Homestead B&B
Batemans Bay
   Chalet Swisse Spa

Bathurst
   Cherrywood-by-the-River
   Elm Tree Cottage
Bellingen
   Bellingen Heritage Cottages
Bermagui
   Bimbimbi House
   Bellbird Cottage
Bermagui - Tanja
   Ngairin on Tanja Lagoon

Blue Mountains
Mount Victoria
   The Manor House
Wentworth Falls
   Dove Cottage
Woodford
   Braeside

Byron Bay
   Baystay
Byron Hinterland - Clunes via Byron Bay
   Suzanne's Hideaway
Candelo - Bega Valley
   Bumblebrook Farm
Central Coast - Tuggerah
   Greenacres B&B
Coffs Harbour
   Mount Boambee Retreat
   Coffs Harbour Best B&Bs
Cowra - Mandurama
   Millamolong
Crookwell
   Minnamurra Farmstay
   Markdale Homestead
Dorrigo

Index

Western Australia

Accommodation Welcoming Pets

Australian Capital Territory

New South Wales

322

Contact Us

If you are an existing accommodation operator or opening for the first time, then why not consider including your accommodation in one of our future publications. We have on our team almost 20 years experience in publishing The Bed & Breakfast Book as well as experienced B&B operators. We are committed to supporting and promoting small accommodation operators, particularly Bed & Breakfast and similar styled accommodation. You can write to us or call us and whilst we may not be able to answer all of your questions we will probably know someone who can.

The Bed & Breakfast Book

Website	www.bbbook.com.au
Email	info@bbbook.com.au
Mail	PO Box 8003 Coffs Harbour NSW 2450
Fax	(02) 6658 5701
Telephone	Adelaide (08) 8464 0959
	Coffs Harbour (02) 6658 5701
	Brisbane (07) 3118 5959
	Melbourne (03) 9017 5959
	Perth (08) 6363 5959
	Sydney (02) 8208 5959

Notes

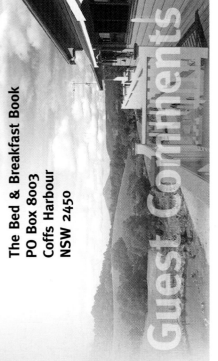

Place stamp here or send forms in one envelope.

The Bed & Breakfast Book

The Bed & Breakfast Book
PO Box 8003
Coffs Harbour
NSW 2450

Australia's leading guide to Accommodation with Character ...

First published in 1989, completely updated each year, **The Bed & Breakfast Book** covers every state and territory from capital cities to isolated farm stations. The Bed & Breakfast Book showcases all styles from the simple to the serene and includs Cottages and Self Contained; Small Hotels and Guest Houses, Boutique Resorts and Deluxe Retreats; Farmstays, Homestays and Traditional B&Bs.

"We received the greatest hospitality, slept in the most wonderful bed and enjoyed the best breakfast in a long, long time. We will return!"
...from one of our guests.

Guest Comments

Bed & Breakfast Book

Tell us about Your Stay

Help us to find great accommodation. Recommend a B&B for **The People's Choice Awards for Great Accommodation.** Tell us about your stay and comment upon the qualities, which made it special for you . . . it could be the warm welcome and outstanding hospitality or special location and great value.

In appreciation, each month we will select one comment and send a small gift to the writer.

Name of B&B _____

Date(s) of your stay _____

Please complete the boxes and rate 1 to 5 with . . .
1 = Fair, 2 = Good, 3 = Very Good, 4 = Excellent, 5 = Perfect

☐ Presentation ☐ Hospitality

☐ Housekeeping ☐ Food ☐ Value

Your Comments

_____

_____

_____

Leave with your host, or return to:
    The Bed & Breakfast Book,
    PO Box 8003 Coffs Harbour NSW 2450
or Save on postage and comment online at, www.bbbook.com.au

May we use your comments to promote this B&B? ☐ Yes ☐ No

Your Name _____

Your Address _____

_____ Post Code _____

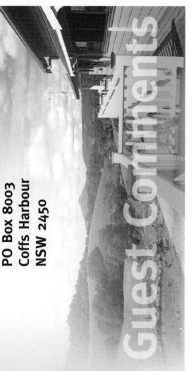

Guest Comments

The
Bed & Breakfast
Book

The Bed & Breakfast Book
PO Box 8003
Coffs Harbour
NSW 2450

Place stamp here or send forms in one envelope.

Australia's leading guide to Accommodation with Character . . .

First published in 1989, completely updated each year, **The Bed & Breakfast Book** covers every state and territory from capital cities to isolated farm stations. The Bed & Breakfast Book showcases all styles from the simple to the serene and includs Cottages and Self Contained; Small Hotels and Guest Houses, Boutique Resorts and Deluxe Retreats; Farmstays, Homestays and Traditional B&Bs.

"We received the greatest hospitality, slept in the most wonderful bed and enjoyed the best breakfast in a long, long time. We will return!"
...from one of our guests.

The Bed & Breakfast Book

Tell us about Your Stay

Help us to find great accommodation. Recommend a B&B for **The People's Choice Awards for Great Accommodation.** Tell us about your stay and comment upon the qualities, which made it special for you . . . it could be the warm welcome and outstanding hospitality or special location and great value.

In appreciation, each month we will select one comment and send a small gift to the writer.

Name of B&B

_____

Date(s) of your stay _____

Please complete the boxes and rate 1 to 5 with . . .
1 = Fair, **2** = Good, **3** = Very Good, **4** = Excellent, **5** = Perfect

☐ Presentation   ☐ Hospitality
☐ Housekeeping   ☐ Food   ☐ Value

Your Comments

_____

_____

Leave with your host, or return to:
   The Bed & Breakfast Book,
   PO Box 8003 Coffs Harbour NSW 2450

or Save on postage and comment online at, www.bbbook.com.au

May we use your comments to promote this B&B?   ☐ Yes   ☐ No

Your Name

_____

Your Address _____

_____ Post Code _____

Guest Comments

TheBed & Breakfast Book

The Bed & Breakfast Book
PO Box 8003
Coffs Harbour
NSW 2450

Australia's leading guide to Accommodation with Character . . .

First published in 1989, completely updated each year, **The Bed & Breakfast Book** covers every state and territory from capital cities to isolated farm stations. The Bed & Breakfast Book showcases all styles from the simple to the serene and includs Cottages and Self Contained; Small Hotels and Guest Houses, Boutique Resorts and Deluxe Retreats; Farmstays, Homestays and Traditional B&Bs.

"We received the greatest hospitality, slept in the most wonderful bed and enjoyed the best breakfast in a long, long time. We will return!"

...from one of our guests.

Guest Comments

The Bed & Breakfast Book

Tell us about Your Stay

Help us to find great accommodation. Recommend a B&B for **The People's Choice Awards for Great Accommodation.** Tell us about your stay and comment upon the qualities, which made it special for you . . . it could be the warm welcome and outstanding hospitality or special location and great value.

In appreciation, each month we will select one comment and send a small gift to the writer.

Name of B&B _____

Date(s) of your stay _____

Please complete the boxes and rate 1 to 5 with . . .
1 = Fair, **2** = Good, **3** = Very Good, **4** = Excellent, **5** = Perfect

☐ Presentation ☐ Hospitality

☐ Housekeeping ☐ Food ☐ Value

Your Comments

_____

_____

Leave with your host, or return to:
The Bed & Breakfast Book,
PO Box 8003 Coffs Harbour NSW 2450
or Save on postage and comment online at, www.bbbook.com.au

May we use your comments to promote this B&B? ☐ Yes ☐ No

Your Name _____

Your Address _____

_____ Post Code _____

Guest Comments

Guest Comments

The
Bed & Breakfast
Book

Place stamp
here or send
forms in one
envelope.

The Bed & Breakfast Book
PO Box 8003
Coffs Harbour
NSW 2450

Australia's leading guide to
Accommodation with Character . . .

First published in 1989, completely updated
each year, **The Bed & Breakfast Book** covers
every state and territory from capital cities to
isolated farm stations. The Bed & Breakfast
Book showcases all styles from the simple to
the serene and includs Cottages and Self Contained; Small
Hotels and Guest Houses, Boutique Resorts and Deluxe
Retreats; Farmstays, Homestays and Traditional B&Bs.

"We received the greatest hospitality,
slept in the most wonderful bed and
enjoyed the best breakfast in a long,
long time. We will return!"
                          ...from one of our guests.

Bed & Breakfast Book — Tell us about Your Stay

Your Comments

_____

_____

_____

Leave with your host, or return to:

The Bed & Breakfast Book,
PO Box 8003 Coffs Harbour NSW 2450

or Save on postage and comment online at, www.bbbook.com.au

May we use your comments to promote this B&B? ☐ Yes ☐ No

Your Name _____

Your Address _____

_____ Post Code _____

Help us to find great accommodation. Recommend a B&B for **The People's Choice Awards for Great Accommodation.** Tell us about your stay and comment upon the qualities, which made it special for you . . . it could be the warm welcome and outstanding hospitality or special location and great value.

In appreciation, each month we will select one comment and send a small gift to the writer.

Name of B&B _____

Date(s) of your stay _____

Please complete the boxes and rate 1 to 5 with . . .
1 = Fair, **2** = Good, **3** = Very Good, **4** = Excellent, **5** = Perfect

☐ Presentation ☐ Hospitality
☐ Housekeeping ☐ Food ☐ Value

australian farm tourism

AFT Bed & Breakfast Reservation Service

AFT B&B provides the ideal way to experience the Australian countryside whilst staying in charming and diverse and cosy Bed and Breakfast establishments. Country Bed and Breakfast properties are located on farms and in small country towns close to some of Australia's best attractions and are renowned for their service, friendliness and quality

AFT B&B offers five standards of Bed and Breakfasts

DELUXE PLUS	Unique properties with the highest level of service and facilities
DELUXE	Deluxe accommodation with additional facilities & services such as gourmet/special breakfasts
SUPERIOR PLUS	Superior accommodation with ensuites and excellent facilities
SUPERIOR	Traditional B&B with private living & dining rooms mostly with private or ensuites bathrooms
STANDARD	Friendly homestay style accommodation with shared or private bathrooms

Properties have been selected to provide quality breakfast and accommodation whilst being located close to country towns to enable selection of restaurants featuring fine country cuisine using the best and freshest local produce and superb Australian wines.

Contact AFT B&B for all Australia wide reservations.
Phone 1300 882 301
Fax (+61) 02 9810 0800
Email res@australianbandb.com.au
Website www.australianbandb.com.au

AFT B&B WOMBAT PASS
New Flexible Australia Wide B&B Accommodation Pass
Travel this vast country staying at quality, traditional and friendly Bed and Breakfasts and homestays.
Information, Purchase pass and booking details at
www.wombatbandb.com.au